Sex and
Generation

Contents

Acknowledgements

I should like above all to acknowledge my debt to my informants for giving me their time and sharing their experiences. It is their skill as raconteurs that gives the account much of its humour. I must also mention my debt to my neighbours for discussing things with me and retailing useful information. I hope that I have represented people's views and actions faithfully, even if they may disagree with my interpretation.

Second, I wish to record my thanks to the many vicars, ministers, and priests who helped me to get in touch with couples in the process of getting married. I am also grateful for the personal pleasantness with which I was received by the Swansea and West Glamorgan Superintendent Registrars and their staff, and Mr Rooke-Matthews at the General Register Office – despite my strictures on GRO secrecy and paternalism.

I am grateful to John Ward and Lesley Button for drawing my attention to the dissertations by students in the education department of the University College of Swansea, which I have used in Chapter 4; to Frances Freedman of the European Market Research Bureau for showing me parts of the Bureau's report on engagement; to Rhona Rapoport for letting me read her socio-psychological study of couples marrying in Boston (Rapoport n.d.; see also 1963, 1964); and to G.C. Jones-Evans of the Home Office (who I met at a wedding reception) for helping me to locate the official statistics on consent to marriage of minors by magistrates courts. (They are to be found, somewhat incongruously, in the annual *Criminal Statistics*, between 'Orders to destroy dogs' and 'Indecent photographs, etc: orders to destroy'.)

I am grateful for domestic help received from, among others, Ann Adams, Marianna Atmatzadou, Ollie Horts, Anna Horwedel, and Eva Soderlind; secretarial help from Rodney Barker, Barbara Cook, Ms E Gratrix, Jenny Flude, and Kyre Wickenham; and general personal and intellectual support, encouragement, criticism, and ideas from the members of the London Women's Anthropology group, The Women's Research and Resources Centre, The Anglo-French study group on Economic Relations in Domestic Groups/Categories de sexe et categories de classe, and Rodney Barker, Gail Chester, Christine Delphy, Leonore Davidoff, Jean L'Esperance, Chris Harris, J.B. Loudon, and John Hood-Williams.

November 1978

The author and publishers wish to thank the following individuals and publications who have given permission to reproduce material in this book: Jo Nesbitt for the cartoon on page 106; *Brides* Magazine for *Figure 2* on page 131, reproduced by the permission of *Brides*, Conde Nast Publications Ltd; Moss Bros for *Figure 3* on page 136; The *Sunday Times* and Mel Calman for the cartoon on page 177; Matchmakers (Book Matches) Ltd for *Figure 9* on page 181; Routledge & Kegan Paul to reproduce part of *Figure 7* on page 253, taken from Table 7.5 in *The Family and Social Change: A Study of Family and Kinship in a South Wales Town* (London, 1965); the Mirror Group Newspapers to reproduce the cartoon on page 268; and the Controller of Her Majesty's Stationery Office to reproduce *Figure 1* on page 278-9.

1 Introduction

'The conventional white wedding obviously doesn't symbolise what we, in the 1970s mean by "mutual society, help and comfort." Few people take what it does symbolise seriously, but if not, why engage in an outdated charade at such a solemn moment in one's life?' (Stott 1971:11)

'Rituals reveal values at their deepest level . . . men express in ritual what moves them most, and since the form of expression is conventionalised and obligatory, it is the values of the group which are revealed. I see in the study of rituals the key to an understanding of the essential constitution of human societies.' (Wilson 1954:240)

Two conflicting views seem to be being put forward in these quotations. In the first, a liberal journalist, Mary Stott, argues that the various elements of a white wedding – the bride being given away by her father in church, her husband putting a ring on her finger, her promising to obey him, and in particular the bride being dressed in a long white dress and veil – are anachronistic. While women used to submit to their husbands, she thinks times have changed. The dual standard of sexual morality and the division of labour and responsibilities in marriage are dead (or dying); what we have now is a partnership of equals.

Maybe 'some are more equal than others'. The *Guardian* Women's Page, which she herself edited for many years, has been credited with 'discovering' the frustrations of the graduate wife in the early 1960s, and it continues to report on women's disadvantaged position in society and the struggles against it. Mary Stott would certainly accept that many women feel constricted by the role of wife and mother they are assigned, but her solution is to continue to reform the division of labour in marriage, to get away from sex role stereotyping, maybe even to open things up a little and (for those who like and can cope with that sort of thing) to move towards 'open marriage' or communal households. But her various writings show that she thinks stable heterosexual relationships and family life with children are essentially Good Things. Marriage, even as it is, gives men, women and children stability, personal support, help with immediate problems and the more general exigencies of life, and much happiness. She believes most people would accept these views, and so is merely left wondering why so many carry on with an elaborate and expensive piece of 'nonsense'.

In the second quotation, a liberal anthropologist, Monica Wilson, reflects on the insights she has gained from observing or studying many different cultures, and she puts forward the argument, which would be generally accepted by her colleagues, that by looking at the rituals of a given society – i.e. at its largely expressive, symbolic, formalized acts[1] – we can get profound insights into its values and institutions. Rituals 'say things which are difficult to think' (Beattie 1966): things the participants may find difficult to express – such as abstract values – or which are embarrassing to say outright.

If we want to explain the continuance of a particular custom – such as the bride wearing a white dress for her wedding – anthropologists would argue that we have to provide a historic account of its development and see what meaning it has for present-day performers (and this account must include looking at this one custom as part of a more general pattern of symbols). They would certainly reject any explanation that suggests that rituals are 'outdated' or 'survivals': meaningless charades continued through force of habit. They would stress that rituals and symbols are not unchanging. They are repeated to reiterate their message, and the rituals associated with the rites of passage from one social status to another are repeated for each individual in the society. Each repetition allows the accommodation of new developments and new interpretations, or builds up pressure for reform if change requires legal enactment. Participants may modify or manipulate or change some parts to express major or minor changes in the message they wish to give; or those involved may try to introduce new customs for extrinsic reasons (e.g., people in trades catering for weddings attempt innovations in order to sell new products). Change therefore not only *occurs* in rituals, it is *endemic* (Cohen 1974). If white weddings are alive and well in the second half of the twentieth century, it is not because they are outdated charades, but rather because they make important statements about, among other things, the nature of marriage and family relations.

I initially became interested in studying weddings from an anthropological concern with describing the scale and assessing the significance of what I knew to be a major ceremonial cycle within my own society[2] – though I had not realised just how complex and important I would find it to be (note the length of chapters 5 and 6). I accepted Monica Wilson's view that looking at the rituals associated with courtship, getting married, and setting up a new household would give me important insights into the nature of relationships between the sexes and generations – that it would be a means of drawing out norms and values that might not be verbally expressed in response to a questionnaire. I also reasoned that for me – as a young, recently married woman – to approach people and ask them to talk about particular semi-public events, such as engagements and weddings, would be more acceptable (i.e., that they would be more willing to cooperate) than if I arrived simply asking them to talk about everyday family matters, which are seen as private and/or uninteresting to an outsider. In addition, weddings would provide occasions for me to participate in family events, which could later be discussed with the participants. I planned, therefore, to use the study of ritual both directly and indirectly as a means of 'opening a window onto opaque urban social processes' (Frankenberg 1966a).

There was little background material on which to draw. There has been scant interest from social scientists in the rites associated with the passage from one social status to another in our culture[3] – except those concerned to argue that the continuing incidence of christenings, marriages, and funerals with religious ceremonies does (or does not) show the continuing salience of religion in a secularizing society (e.g., Wilson 1969, Pickering 1974). Further, there has been no sociological study of courtship in this country – there is virtually nothing on courting behaviour, patterns of mate selection, or the expectations with which people enter marriage – and relatively little beyond the demographic level on age at marriage and household formation[4]. Nor has there been consideration of unmarried adult children's relationships with their parents.

Some studies of adolescents and young adults do contain useful (if dated) descriptive material on their familial, leisure, and sexual lives[5], but unfortunately most work on 'youth' has been social problem and social policy orientated: that is to say, information has been collected with a view to improving the services provided for young people by government or voluntary bodies, or to controlling potential trouble-makers. This has limited the researcher's terms of reference: not only have they viewed 'youth' as a problem without discussing the structure and values of the society within which the young people live, but they have not looked at what happens to young people after they reach the age of eighteen or twenty, for then they pass out of the purview of educational and juvenile agencies. Thus, those who leave youth clubs because they are courting at sixteen (girls) or eighteen (boys) have been viewed as 'sex-mad' and 'letting the side down', without recognition of the importance of courtship, or its various forms. In addition, much more attention has been devoted to those categories perceived as problems – students, commune dwellers, gang members, or those who have left home for the city – than to the great majority: the 'honest, sober, hardworking, credit-worthy young, ready and eager to settle securely down for life', as the Latey Committee[6] characterized them. A final shortcoming of such sociological studies of young people as exist is that almost all show much more concern with boys than with girls, and present the world through male eyes, which was a bias I was anxious to avoid.

At the beginning of this study I was working within a standard British social anthropological structural-functional framework. Unlike the existing (largely American) 'abstracted empiricist' sociological work which I encountered in my chosen area, I was not concerned with establishing who marries whom in terms of the correlation of such variables as social class, age, education, and personality type; nor with measuring the attitudes or role expectations of young people towards 'dating' and marriage; nor with the 'psychological tasks' which need to be accomplished for the satisfactory development of a love relationship and the start of married life. Rather, I sought to produce an ethnographic account along the lines of those in *The Development Cycle in Domestic Groups* (Goody 1966): to see how the personnel of familial institutions were replaced, against the background of the socio-economic structure and values of one town, using the wedding ceremony as my 'window'.

As time went on, however, I became progressively more and more convinced of the need to get right away from any functionalist approach to the family in Western industrial capitalist societies, because, as developed in American and British sociology, such an approach will always tend to make us see 'the family' as a unit, within which there is presumed to be equality and consensus, and will make us presume that there is 'a societal interest' which the family is or is not serving, and 'a family interest' which individual members are or are not supporting – the commentator being presented as able to stand outside marriage and the family (as institutions) as an impartial assessor.

What is needed instead is an approach that recognizes the historicity of the family – its variation with time, locality, and class (particularly as regards what work is done by family members and their isolation or otherwise from other households). But more important still is a move away from seeing the family as a 'unit of consumption' and psychic support, with relationships between 'individuals', to a stress on production and reproduction within the family and the wider society; seeing family relationships as being between those occupying the position of husband, wife, and child.

The decision to stress material relationships within the family – between husband and wife, and parents and children – and the way in which these inter-relate with material relationships in the rest of society, led to the use of a theoretical framework (deriving from Delphy 1970 and 1976) which examines marriage as a particular form of labour relationship between men and women, whereby a woman pledges for life (with limited rights to quit) her labour, sexuality, and reproductive capacity, and receives 'protection', upkeep, and certain rights to children. It also drew on the work of anthropologists who have studied the political economy of lineages and age classes (albeit in agricultural societies – such as Meillassoux 1972 and Terray 1975) to suggest new ways of looking at the cycle of domestic care and economic support of the young and old within the family in this country.

Since neither of these is an obvious approach – indeed the ideology of the society would specifically deny them as heartless and ignoring the 'real' essence of the relationship between kin and affines – they need to be explained a little further, though they cannot be fully explicated here (cf. Delphy and Barker, in progress) and the test of their usefulness and validity must be the insight they give in the account as a whole.

The general public's view has always tended to stress the *social* importance of marriage – as the principal way of validating one's adult status, one's personal and sexual proficiency, and as providing emotional support and stability; and this has been reflected in sociologists' accounts (e.g. Bell 1972, Busfield 1974). But marriage is also an *economic* necessity for most women.

In many societies women are physically forced into marriage, should their socialization to accept it fail; but in Western Europe for the last few hundred years the final constraint has generally been financial. Most women have not inherited land or businesses, etc., and those who work for wages have earned approximately half what men earned in comparable occupations. Consequently, with the exception of a very small number of women with property or well-paid work, they have needed to marry a man from the same background as themselves if they were (or are) to live at the same standard as they enjoyed in their father's house. This applied (and still applies) *a fortiori* if they have a child. Most have, of course, continued to do wage or other work which has provided the cost of their own subsistence when married, while also caring for children, the sick and the elderly, and doing domestic work for their husbands, unpaid. Men could (and can) support themselves reasonably well when single, but have benefitted from women's domestic and sexual servicing, procreative capacity, and child rearing within marriage.

The tasks that women do within marriage have varied with the externally determined needs and the desires of their husbands – how hard a woman has had to work to make a small income stretch to provide food, warmth, and clothing, or whether she has been provided with domestic help to free her for other activities (such as chauffeuring children, acting as a hostess, or for conspicious consumption of leisure) has depended on the class and character of man she has married. For this reason getting married and the choice of a partner has been and still is very important to women: they are not only attaining an important element of female adult status, but also choosing an 'employer' from whom it is very difficult to separate, in a 'job' whose 'organizational embrace' is near total. A man chooses a wife/'worker', and it is important that he gets a devoted, competent, sexually appealing one. But the woman takes her husband's name and is still largely absorbed into his legal persona; she has her standard of living determined by his income, however hard she herself works; her rhythm, pattern, and place of living will be dictated by his; and what is required of her as a wife will be in considerable measure determined by his occupation. As the church service says they become *man* and *wife* (not husband and wife, or man and woman – and certainly not woman and husband).

Parents refer to both the social and the economic aspects of marriage when they talk about being happy to see their children married and 'settled'. But what must constantly be stressed is that what being 'settled' in marriage involves for a man is very different from what it involves for a woman – though this is overlooked when the 'function' of marriage is seen (as in 'commonsense' and most sociology of the family) exclusively in terms of security, companionship, and ego-stabilization for the individual. This is equivalent to talking about the interpersonal relationship between farmers and farm workers while overlooking the fact that the one employs the other. Obviously the relationship between husband and wife differs from that between master and employee and is *sui generis* in a number of respects. For instance, the wife gets upkeep not a wage, the work she does is less defined, the relationship involves a sexual component and is established in our culture on the basis of love, and the right to quit is much more circumscribed. But the deferential nature of the husband-wife relationship, events in courtship, and the ideological importance of romantic love, cannot be understood without a clear recognition of the sexual division of labour, and the fact that there is a *labour relationship* between husband and wife.

Most people (around 90 per cent) in England and Wales not only marry at least once, they also have children – over 80 per cent of the population have had at least one child (Busfield 1974). Although the political economy of marriage has begun to be discussed thanks to the advent of the Women's Liberation Movement, the political economy of parenthood has barely been considered to date and my analysis here is but preliminary.

The relationship between parents and children is status-based in a society where contractual or quasi-contractual relations are dominant. It seems useful to consider them as a version of the relations of production Meillassoux describes between 'those who come before' and 'those who come after', i.e., between senior members of the group and junior ones.

> 'This is not a system of exchange, properly speaking, since the products are never offered for each other and therefore not subjected to the appraisal of their respective value. It is rather a continuously renewed cycle of *advance* and *restitution* of subsistence.' (Meillassoux 1972:101)

In the lineage-based agricultural society he studied, the concern of the older generations is with the control of the younger generation as 'instruments of labour'. All the younger people work to produce the goods (corn) which are controlled by the elders (older men). Not all young people – not even all young men – get to be elders and to benefit from this 'class' position: the few benefit from appropriating surplus labour from the majority.

In the patriarchal family work-unit of pre-industrial Western Europe, the head of the household benefitted directly from the labour of his wife, children and servants, who worked for him for upkeep, being unpaid (or getting minimal wages), as is still to be found on family farms or in family businesses today. Among middle income groups from the nineteenth century, and the general population (except the aristocracy) from the seventeenth century, sons did not marry until they were able to establish an independent household from their parents. They might have to delay marriage for many years until they inherited land, an artisan's workshop, or a shop, or until their parents and their bride's parents (via her dowry) set them up on their own. This pattern of marriage was associated with a high average age at marriage for women (mid to late twenties), a small age difference between husband and wife (less than five years), and a sizeable proportion of the male and female population never marrying at all (Hajnal 1965; Laslett 1973)[7]. Children were generally sent from their parent's houses to be servants or apprentices in other households from the age of seven onwards, and those men and women who did not marry remained attached to other households, often as servants, most of their lives.

With the development of a predominantly wage-labour system in the late eighteenth and nineteenth centuries, marriage became somewhat emancipated from the general economic system, and earlier marriage and marriage for more of the population became possible from the late eighteenth century onwards. Increased economic activity and the drawing-off of male labour by wars made it easier for women as well as men to find employment, and couples could marry on their joint income, so property and dowries (and hence parental control) were less important.

But while the economic system affected the marriage pattern, the marriage pattern also influenced the economic system. The European marriage pattern meant that, especially before the nineteenth century but continuing into the twentieth century, young men had a period of life when they were physiologically mature but without dependents, and during this time many moved around the country and formed semi-formal peer groups (Gillis 1974). Young women also entered the labour market for a time before they had responsibility for childbearing and rearing and the domestic servicing of a husband, though they were never as emancipated from the domestic environment and control by a house-hold head as men (Davidoff 1974). During this period young people usually gave over almost all their earnings to their parents (even when living away from home; see Tilly, Scott and Cohen 1973), but they might be able to save something and/or create a demand for certain sorts of goods. Thus Hajnal suggests it was the delay and deliberation over marriage that accounted for the better housing, better clothing, greater variety of clothes, more furniture and utensils enjoyed by those areas which had the 'European' system of marriage in the eighteenth century.

But if late marriage produced wealth (and supported the development of capitalism), wealth (i.e., the expectation of high living standards, including the expectation of having one's own household when one was married) encouraged late marriage. Whilst in the towns of nineteenth-century Lancashire the marriage rate increased among the working class with economic opportunity (Anderson 1971), from 1870 to the 1920s and '30s the marriage rate among the middle class and skilled working class decreased at a time of rising living standards, because men postponed marriage until such age as they could be certain of maintaining the standards which they had come to expect and to regard as the minimum acceptable (Banks 1954), living meanwhile as lodgers, or using clubs and housekeepers.

Since the First World War there has been a steady increase in the proportion of the population that gets married and a decrease in the age at marriage in all classes to an average lower than at any period for which there is reliable record in this country (the same is true of many European countries and the USA)[8]. This is generally regarded as due to the fact that, for those *in* work, the average level of real earnings has risen steadily since the interwar period, while the welfare state and the spread of birth control have removed the threat of dire poverty due to large families. Hence it is with the advent of full wage-employment, family planning and social security in only very recent times that the 'penniless, homeless match between young people' which we know today has become 'a widespread phenomenon' in Britain (Eversley 1965). It has also lead to a uniformity in the experiences of members of the society far greater than was present in the nineteenth century (Hareven 1977). Now we virtually all marry, all in our early twenties, all have two or three children, see our parents live to old age, and ourselves live to see our children grow up and marry and have children in their turn.

Industrialization, urbanization, improved transport and housing, and declining family size gradually made it possible for young people to live with their parents, working outside the household, till they married. But from making a substantial contribution to their father's household – in kind or in cash – children have come in the mid twentieth century to be in the general population what they were in the upper classes – persons who derive rather than supply benefits, who are enjoyed (used or 'consumed') as beings in themselves and who produce other desirable goods: alliances with other families and grandchildren/heirs (see chapter 3). They may also provide some return on parental investment by giving care or companionship in the parents' old age.

Marriages and parenthood are nowadays given virtually universal support within the ideology of our society – they are presented as inseparable, inevitable, and highly desirable. Not to get married is not an option that most people see as available, let alone attractive. One does not *choose not* to get married, one *fails* to get married. Marriage is what is 'normal', and

> 'Married people have an accepted right to inquire after the sexual, culinary and moral welfare of single people. They can unload as much advice as they want . . . They are free to make as many facetious comments as they wish to any single person whom they hardly know about any person of the opposite sex they happen to see him or her with . . . It does not work the other way. Cracks by the single person about anyone's marriage (or even marriage in general) are considered in extremely bad taste. Attack marriage in polite company and you are about as popular as Mick McGahey at a CBI dinner. You are "chipping away at the fabric of society as we know it today" . . . Single people . . . when they have reached the age of 30, are supposed to be either very inept at sexual manners, or homosexual. Or possibly they have not yet discovered Right Guard. It simply cannot be the case that they have made a rational choice to stay on their own. (Sedgwick 1975)

A whole 'battery of neglect, suspicion and derision' (Comer 1974:208) is directed at the non-married and the childless, and they are stereotyped as shirking their duty, selfish, immature, lonely, bitter, abnormal and unattractive, or pathetic.

Most people then do not wonder *if* they should marry, but rather *who* they should marry. Nor do they question greatly (and they questioned even less before the ideas of the Women's Movement started to spread in the 1970s) what marriage (and parenthood) should be. These are regulated largely by custom, but behind customary patterns are the formal regulations of Church and State, for these two agencies (separately and together) have for centuries controlled and supported marriage and parenthood. They both have firm (if changing) ideas and rules as to what constitutes 'the Holy estate of Matrimony' and Christian parents, or 'Marriage, according to the laws of this country' – though it would require a separate and substantial piece of work to explicate precisely what these are, how they have changed over time, how they have influenced and been influenced by common practice, and how they relate to socio-economic changes, since they are nowhere spelled out and depend rather on precedent and shared assumptions underlying legislative changes.

The intervention of Church and State in the family is however legitimated in terms of their providing protection for those who are necessarily physically and economically dependent (women, children, and formerly aged or infirm parents and kin), and because of the need to restrain sexuality and establish domestic-unit stability for the psychic good of individuals and the well-being of the polity. However, it could more plausibly be argued that they are providing support for husbandly and parental authority (a point I have put forward elsewhere. See Barker 1978b; also Land 1978). In any event, since a considerable amount of the work of ecclesiastical and secular courts has always been concerned with the establishment of the rights and duties of spouses and children and with enforcing damages for injured parties, if has been necessary to establish unambiguously who was married and which children were legitimate, so as to know what was owed by whom to whom. Hence the Church (gradually from the third or fourth century) and the State (especially from the eighteenth century) were concerned with establishing a public marriage ceremony so that they could recognise and penalize promiscuity and/or the dereliction of marital, parental, or kin duties; and those who marry today have to go through formalities deriving from this.

The form of marriage in the early Christian church was taken over from the *confarreatio* form of Roman civil marriage, whereby the woman was handed over to her husband and his kin in a way analagous to the formal transfer of property. No particular ceremony, nor the attendance of any official, nor any registration was required – merely the giving of consent by the parties involved (though associated ceremonial, much of which was incorporated into the later Christian wedding, was customary – see p. 163ff and Barker 1977 Ch.5, and Appendix 5:1).

The medieval Church tried to encourage a public form of marriage – *in facie ecclesiae* (at the church door), with priest and witnesses and after due time for consideration and for impediments to the marriage to come to light (hence three weeks of calling the banns). But the principal stress was on the couple exchanging words giving consent to marriage, and the Church recognised as binding for life weddings that took place anywhere – in houses, gardens, or at the wayside, with or without a priest. All that was necessary was for the couple – the boy needed only to be fourteen and the girl twelve – to agree to take each other as husband and wife using words in the present tense (*per verba de praesenti*), or in the future tense (*per verba de futuro*) if they subsequently had intercourse (Helmholz 1975).

Such non church weddings were never given as full protection in the ecclesiastical or the civil courts as those at church: it was often hard to prove that they had taken place if there were few witnesses; priests (who came increasingly to be seen as necessary) were liable to be punished for conducting them; the bride's parents need not pay her dowry; and the church might excommunicate the couple. But they nonetheless constituted a continuing problem, especially for wealthy families, since men who seduced heiresses gained full control of their wives' property and control of her children, and because unknown 'heirs' might turn up unexpectedly to claim an inheritance and bastardize a whole erstwhile respectable family by claiming to be the fruit of a previous clandestine union of one of the spouses. (These are familiar themes in Restoration comedies.)

Things came to a head in the early seventeenth century when *centres* for the solemnization of non-church weddings developed, especially in and around the Fleet prison in London. Clergy who lacked parishes or who were in prison for debt conducted weddings in the prison chapel or in the rooms above alehouses and coffee houses in the district around. Some were not averse to a little trickery – marrying a couple where one person was very drunk, forced marriages by parochial officers to get pregnant women 'off the parish', and fabricating entries in registers (pre or post dating). But for many people these weddings were quite straightforwardly what they wanted – cheap, quick, and quiet, and they became 'part of the common consensus of London life' (see Brown 1973).

When the Church failed to take action against the rogue clergy involved, a draconian Act was passed through Parliament (1753) requiring *all* weddings (except those of Jews and Quakers) in England and Wales to take place within buildings belonging to the Church of England, and according to its rites. Unless a special licence was obtained from the bishop of the diocese, banns had to be read in the parish churches of both spouses, and if either party was under twenty-one their parents' consent had to be obtained in writing. Thus we changed from a country where marriage was based on consent (supported by Church and State) to one based on an Established Church-State defined contractual identity.

After some fifty years this Act started to be gradually amended to make it less harsh – e.g., there were less ferocious punishments for altering an entry in a parish register (it had been death); and if parental consent was withheld it could be sought from a county or magistrates court, not just from the High Court.

In 1836 a Marriage Act and an associated Births and Deaths Registration Act brought in a centralized system of registering marriages. It also allowed Roman Catholic and Protestant dissenters to conduct their own weddings – though with less autonomy than the Anglican Church[9] – and, somewhat by accident[10], introduced the possibility (for the first time since the Middle Ages) of contracting a fully valid marriage by civil ceremony. Initially the civil equivalent of reading the banns was a reading of the notice of marriage to three weekly meetings of The Poor Law Board of Guardians (followed by a wedding in a register office which was usually the room in the workhouse used by the Guardian's clerk), but after amending legislation in 1856, civil weddings were removed from the Poor Law machinery (see Anderson 1975). There was then a simple posting up of notices of intended marriages in a Superintendent Registrar's office for twenty-one days, with the ceremony held in his office before two witnesses. In this way civil weddings came to provide a means of getting married which, like the Fleet weddings, was cheap and free from publicity (no one went into the register office except on business).

There have been various minor amendments to the 1836 Act, and the Marriage Act 1949, which consolidated all of these, has itself been subjected to half a dozen minor alterations. But current marriage formalities still derive from the long-standing concern of Church and State to control who is and is not married, and is still based on verbal consent (followed by sexual intercourse, otherwise the marriage is voidable) made in an authorized place (church or register office) in front of an authorized person, and then recorded at the General Register Office.

However, while the concern of the 1753 Act was to prevent secret marriages, today, provided both parties have reached the legal age of majority (now eighteen, before 1970, twenty-one) they can marry within forty-eight hours, with no 'public' notice – i.e., effectively without the knowledge of their parents and friends, relatives or neighbours, and certainly without the knowledge of a wider public. With central registration there is no longer dispute as to whether a particular marriage has occurred or not. Reliance that there is no impediment to the marriage depends now, not on publicity, but upon the requirement that the parties to the marriage give their oath that the information they give is true, and on the heavy penalties attached to perjury and forgery.

Couples who decide that they wish to marry thus have to go through certain formalites; but they have, in theory, the choice of several hundred places in which the ceremony could take place – the register office(s) for their home district(s), their parish church(es), or any of the non Anglican places of worship within their registration district(s). But if they want a church wedding they must have the agreement of a vicar, priest, or minister. Where the couple, or one partner, is a member of a particular church or well known to a particular minister or vicar, there is no problem: they can marry in that church or where he is incumbent. If they feel they want to marry in a particular locality they may approach a minister there or get themselves put on the Anglican church roll[11]. If they have no other affiliation they will usually consider themselves 'C of E' and use an attractive Anglican church in their parish, or they may cast around ('delve into their own past . . . find their roots' as one minister put it): where did they go to Sunday School or youth club; in which nice Nonconformist church do they have kin who would speak to the minister on their behalf?

It is customary for the wedding to take place in a church of the bride's denomination (though in the rare event of the groom being a more active churchgoer they may marry in his church) and in a building near the bride's home (though if they want to marry in a particularly attractive church and the groom is eligible to marry there they will use his links). The only important exception to this rule is where the groom is a Roman Catholic. In such cases, if the couple marry in church it will nearly always be a Roman Catholic one. In the past a Roman Catholic who married in the register office was regarded by the Church as 'unmarried', while one who married in the church of another denomination was regarded as having a null and void marriage and was excommunicated.

Although there are some doctrinal differences between the denominations about marriage[12], these are relatively minor and all (except Christian Scientists) agree that marriages should take place in church. But clergy are anxious that those whom they marry should not 'make a convenience' or 'an excuse' of them, their building, or their ceremonial. The Church should be respected. People should only marry therein 'reverently, discreetly, advisedly, soberly, and in the fear of God; duly considering the causes for which Matrimony was ordained' (*Book of Common Prayer*). The clergyman should not be made to look foolish – as some feel he is if he marries a couple where the girl is pregnant ('who have already sinned' as one conservative put it) and he is not informed of this. They are affronted if their co-operation is required rather than requested.

On the other hand, this is a time when the Church feels itself needed and wanted; when it can reach people who never normally enter a church and who do not 'bother' with religion; when there is a chance of making new converts and/or obliging faithful members by doing something for them or their kin. The clergy of all denominations see the conducting of marriages (and funerals) as a service to the couple and the wider community and this, together with such 'marriage preparation' as they provide[13], is part of their pastoral work as servants of God (see Forder 1959, Moore 1970).

The churches certainly do not use weddings as a means to make money. The amounts charged for performing the service are usually very small – £1 to £1.50 in 1969 and about £5 in 1978 for the vicar or minister (usually waived or returned as a wedding present if the people getting married are active members of the church) and 1-2 guineas each for the organist and caretaker. Some church activists (e.g., Anglican parochial committee members) feel more *should* be charged so as to make a contribution towards the upkeep of the church, and sometimes there is more or less discreet 'plate rattling' (e.g., someone standing by the door with a box labelled 'organ fund' as the congregation troops out after the ceremony).

Denominations do differ, however, in who they will agree to marry in their churches. Jehovah's Witnesses, Christadelphians, some Brethren and Pentecostalists excommunicate any members who 'marry out'; thus the only weddings taking place in their churches will be those where both parties are members. An orthodox Jewish synagogue will only marry Jews, though a Liberal or Reform synagogue will accept a 'mixed marriage'. Roman Catholic priests will only marry couples where one member at least has been baptized as a Catholic. They have a rigorous Pre-Nuptial Enquiry – a form is sent round by the priest of the RC parish in which the couple wish to marry to the priests of all the parishes in which the man and woman have lived to check that there is no impediment to the marriage, and to the priest(s) of the parishes where they were baptized to check their status as Catholics. If one partner is not a Roman Catholic and the couple want to marry in a Catholic church, he or she used to have to go through a long period of instruction (in some dioceses lasting six months – as full a course as if they had wanted to convert to Catholicism) and to give a signed promise to allow any children to be brought up as Catholics. In addition dispensation had to be obtained from the bishop[14], no banns were read, and there could be no nuptial mass or nuptial blessing. Since the Second Vatican Council however, as one priest put it, 'there has been a general easing up[15]. Shall we say, the Church has not encouraged mixed marriages necessarily, but it has made it easier to marry in church. As against that, it has lessened the danger of Catholics going elsewhere to marry'.

The Anglican clergyman, on the other hand, holds himself responsible for all those who live within his parish; and all those who have been baptized (whether in the Anglican church or by another denomination) have certain rights in their parish[16]. Most people know which is 'their parish church', and unless they belong to another denomination they expect 'their vicar' to help them when they need him, however rarely they may darken his door. He probably will. One Anglican vicar said that:

'Certainly only two out of ten people we marry or bury are really connected with the church. I don't mind; I find the contact with them very profitable. Quite a number who come to be married stay as church members; especially where the bride is a church member, the husband often comes along with her after they are married.

When they first come they are frightened. I try to get home to them that we're pleased to help them. I see them at 9.30pm onwards – has to be that time to let them get home and change and eat. I encourage them to come as often as they like and to ask me about mortgages or insurance or more personal things. Some clergy I know think it's an imposition – I think it a wonderful opportunity. Quite a few get confirmed after marriage.'

The Anglican Church does require, however, that at least one of the couple have been baptized, and that one member of the couple must live in the parish or be on the electoral roll of the church in which they marry. This can cause problems, especially as the clergy differ markedly in their interpretation of the rules[17].

Nonconformists (including Unitarians and the Society of Friends) have no requirements about baptism or membership for those they marry: it is a matter for the minister or secretary and his congregation (in the persons of the deacons) to decide. But non-members do not feel they have the right to marry in such churches and they would therefore either be members themselves or use past ties or an intermediary who was a member or a regular attender when asking. How approachable the individual minister is seen to be is therefore important[18].

When a couple approach a Superintendent Registrar, or a vicar, priest, or minister about getting married in his or her register office or church, they will be asked various questions, for the State and the denominations specify that a couple have various 'capacities' to be able to contract a valid marriage. By law:

(a) both parties must be over sixteen. If either is over sixteen but under the age of majority he or she must have his or her parents' consent[19] – unless he or she has already been married, in which case he or she is no longer treated as a minor;
(b) they must not be closely related to each other[20];
(c) neither must be already married;
(d) both must be of sufficiently sound mind to be able to understand the nature of the contract they are entering upon;

(e) they must be acting freely and under no fear or duress; and

(f) they must be of the opposite sex.

In addition:

(g) Roman Catholics have prohibited degrees of kindred and affinity which extend well beyond, and the Anglicans have some which extend slightly beyond, those prohibited by statute[21];

(h) most importantly, the Anglican and Roman Catholic Churches regard marriage as indissoluble and they will not marry divorcees. This produces pastoral problems which have been greatly exercising the Anglican clergy for ten or more years.

Some Nonconformist ministers, however, will marry divorcees, especially the 'innocent party', if they are satisfied after a talk with the couple 'that a Christian wedding would help', and if the deacons are agreeable. However, few people who are not closely connected with the chapels know remarriage therein is possible, and the requirement that the minister knows an individual is the 'innocent party' means that the person must be known or 'spoken for' to him. Thus the numbers concerned are not great.

Despite all these formal regulations and restrictions, in practice it can be remarkably easy to get married in Britain – there are no compulsory medical tests or lengthy waiting periods, and (Catholics apart) no rigorous or testing questions or searches made. It can be all over and done within two days with a five-minute 'ceremony'. Various groups – particularly lawyers – express concern about 'the ease with which parties can rush into marriage without giving due thought to the implications of their act' (Bromley 1966:39) and try to consider how to create 'sufficient solemnity for the occasion to draw the attention of the couple to the seriousness of their step' (Eekelaar 1971:68). At present, however, there is no legal requirement to draw the couple's attention to the type of legal obligations being undertaken, or to the effects on property, or, for example, to the changes in the woman's pension or rights to children, or the three-year moritorium on divorce (i.e., 'that there is no quick and simple return to square one' (Eekelaar 1971:73)). On the other hand, it is still considerably more difficult to get *out* of a marriage (i.e., to get divorced) than to get out of most other contractual obligations.

Little mention has so far been made of betrothal, the agreement preceding marriage. Today we have the anomaly that, while a promise of marriage is seen as making something more than a mere contract (a 'holy estate' in church language or 'a status' in lawyers' terms), engagement – the promise to marry in the future – is given less legal support than other comparable (verbal) contracts.

Before the seventeenth century the promise to marry in the future was exclusively an ecclesiastical matter (though civil courts might adjudicate on rights to property which might have passed between parties who failed to marry). As has been mentioned, it was held that if a promise to marry was made by two parties in words in the future tense (*per verba de futuro*) and they subsequently had intercourse, the marriage had been contracted and was binding. If the words were not said at the church door, the couple would be admonished to come and solemnize the contract in church; but the contract held this notwithstanding. Ecclesiastical courts assessed what damages, if any, were due where there had been promises of future marriage but no consummation.

From the reign of Charles I till 1970, engagements were treated like any other parol (word of honour) contracts and were enforceable in the temporal courts. If one party rescinded, he, or rarely she, could not be forced to go through with the marriage, but if the wounded party brought an action the defendant might have to pay monetary damages. These damages could cover financial loss (e.g., due to expenses of a trousseau or arranging a wedding, or finances foregone by loss of consortium, support, and maintenance in the future), damages for wounded pride (including seduction and the fact that having been engaged and rejected was wounding to self-esteem and chances of future marriage), or that having agreed to wait so long for a particular marriage might mean a person, especially a woman, had foregone chances of other marriages.

Although in law each party was able to sue the other, certainly, by the nineteenth century, courts 'ill received' (Hall 1966) a man suing a woman for breach of promise; the assumptions being that since men were accorded the initiative in proposing the contract, they should exercise this power responsibly and deserved only scorn if they were tricked or succumbed to 'feminine wiles' (see *Vanity Fair*); that women were generally younger (often considerably younger) and less experienced than potential husbands; that women were dependents within marriage and must choose their husbands with care; and that it was a woman's prerogative to change her mind.

Contracts to marry were thus treated by and large like other parol contracts, except that one sex was more favourably received – though that sex also received more odium from the publicity that might be attracted. The defence against an action for breach of promise were the general defences common to actions for breach of contract[22].

In recent years many breach of promise actions were the means to get more money for a pregnant woman than she would have got from an affiliation order alone:

'An English woman shop assistant aged 19 met an Irish farmer's son in her home town in 1966. They became friendly and used to discuss his prospects and spoke of "when we got married what we would do". In the October of that year they started to have intercourse and in April the woman found that she was pregnant. She wrote to the young man, who had returned to Ireland, and got a reply which led her to decide to change her religion. But she heard no more from him till August, when he finally wrote to say he did not intend to marry her. She kept the child and subsequent men friends had not wanted to continue a relationship once they knew of her daughter. She was awarded £1,000 and costs.' (*The Times*, October 21, 1969)

Others related to more recently arrived forms of impasse:

'A 25 year old Sikh man went through a Sikh marriage ceremony with a 20 year old Sikh woman. The marriage was an arranged one and the couple had not seen each other beforehand except in photographs. The young man refused to go through an English civil ceremony. Thus the "bride" was married in the eyes of the Sikh community but not in English law. She was awarded £700 and the "groom" had to return £70 worth of presents.' (*The Times* and *The Guardian*, May 20, 1969)

Trial by jury was common in breach of promise actions up until the 1960s (unfortunately the *Civil Judicial Statistics* do not record the frequency of such cases) and on the whole juries tended to make a high assessment of damages – e.g., in 1951 awarding £20,000 (overturned on appeal) (Bromley 1966:25). One might wonder whether juries were not perhaps more alive to the real situations of men and women than were lawyers. To be jilted may be a less serious occurence for a young woman than in the past, but a woman who has waited many years for a wedding that never takes place may have sacrificed her chances of any marriage; intercourse during engagement is now (and probably has long been) frequent, and the girl is left holding the baby, or is at least no longer a virgin; and marriage remains of great *economic* importance to women – most women's work is still menial and low paid, and this is justified on the basis that most women are married.

However, according to the Law Commission's *Report on Breach of Promise of Marriage* (1969), it was policy not to encourage breach of promise actions as society ought not to countenance any possible threat that might push people (men?) into (a particular) marriage. Legal aid was not available, either party could demand a jury, and except by consent or transfer from the High Court, such cases could not be heard in a County Court – i.e., they were made difficult and potentially costly. By the mid-twentieth century, courts were positively hostile to actions for breach of promise (Hall 1966:11–12), and in 1970 the *Law Reform (Miscellaneous Provisions) Act* disposed of the (largely women's) right to enforce engagements at law.

True to form, this Act is mainly concerned with the property of engaged couples and gifts between them, including engagement rings.

The change in the law notwithstanding, engagement is popularly seen as a firm commitment to marry in England and Wales, and its ending is socially traumatic (see chapter 4). Most members of our society assume the institution of monogamous marriage is obvious, natural, and right, and they accept unquestioningly State and Church control, particularly of the process of getting married. But my findings suggest that they would support treating engagement more seriously than does the State.

Conclusion

This introductory chapter has shown that the pattern of most young people living at home until they get married, and then the great majority getting married and founding a new household in their early twenties, is a relatively recent historical development in Western Europe, associated with industrialization and the separation of much of production from the domestic group, improved transportation, social welfare, and the improvement and spread of birth control. Related to this has been the development of a hegemony presenting the family as set apart from the world, a supposed refuge of caring and community in the dominant aggressive, competitive individualism of industrial capitalism.

This ideology of the family was questioned by stressing that not only are there loving relationships between spouses and between parents and children, but there are also hierarchies within the family – of husband over wife, and mature adults over the young and old. Although in some contexts family members may comprise a unit with common interests, in others they have opposing interests that underlie their relationships with each other and with non familial institutions. Particular attention was given to the labour relationships between husband and wife, in which she owes him such domestic work, sexual services, and child bearing and rearing as he wishes, and he owes her upkeep.

It was suggested that a study of the rituals associated with the process of getting married might show symbolic expression of the opposed situations of the sexes (and to a lesser extent of the generations) – some of the 'ideas [about family life] which are difficult to think' or express, and which have been overlooked by those whose research has concentrated on question and answer surveys of family life. The description and analysis of these rituals will occupy the greater part of this book. The next two chapters, however, deal with the ways in which information was collected and the background of the informants.

Notes

1. In defining 'ritual' I drew on the work of Beattie (1966), seeing it broadly as formalized acts having a mainly or largely expressive, symbolic quality, different from that of technical thought or activity. I use 'ritual' to refer to particular acts of this kind, and 'ceremonial' to refer to a series of related rituals (cf. the definitions of Leach, Goody, Gluckman *et al.*, discussed by Beattie).
2. I have used the first person singular in this report so as to acknowledge my presence as an actor in the field and as an interpreter in the analysis.
3. Cf., however, Loudon's study of funerals (1961), Bell's account of christenings (1968), and Firth, Hubert, and Forge (1970) on all three ceremonials. Bocock (1974, Ch.6.) looks at them from from the point of view of the Church of England.
4. The phase is inadequately covered by retrospective accounts (up to 25 years after the event in some cases) in *Patterns of Marriage* (Slater and Woodside 1951), the few published findings of the Population Investigation Committee's Marriage Survey of 1959-60 (Grebenik and Rowntree 1963; Rowntree 1962; Pierce 1963; Coleman 1973); Gorer's surveys for *The People* (in 1950) and *The Sunday Times* in 1969 (Gorer 1955, 1971), and very short sections, again retrospective, in, e.g., *The Captive Wife* (Gavron 1966). Schofield has provided some useful 'social book-keeping' on the sexual knowledge and behaviour of adolescents and young adults (1965, 1973), but most writing on sexuality has been on homosexuality or sexual deviance and prostitution, not 'normal' heterosexuality and marriage.

   In contrast to the situation in Britain, there is a vast American sociological literature touching on the courtship process. An excellent summary of its findings is presented by Burchinal (1964) – and the title of his article itself admirably exemplifies the language in which such work is expressed: 'The Premarital Dyad and Love Involvement'. Much of this research and reporting has, as its objective, helping to predict 'success' and measure 'satisfaction' in engagement and marriage, to provide material for courses on marriage and family life, and to assist in counselling. There is, therefore, a focus on subjects of interest to students – mate selection, courtship behaviour, 'how to know if it's love', honeymoons, sex adjustment in marriage, control of pregnancy – and strong ethical overtones: is dating a good thing or bad (i.e., is it 'an educational process')? What are the pros and cons of premarital intercourse, etc?

   Most American material is wholeheartedly functionalist and firmly in the grip of what it takes to be the scientific method: there is much talk of 'testing hypotheses' on data obtained from interviewer administered or self-completed questionnaires from large scale random samples (or samples of college students) and of 'presenting the results' obtained by a variety of sophisticated statistical techniques (see articles in the *Journal of Marriage and the Family*). Unfortunately much of the relevant European material is in the same mould – e.g., Henryon and Lambrechts' (1968) study of marriage in Belgium; Girard's (1964) psychosociological study of mate selection in France;

Michel's work on various ethnic groups in Paris and the papers given to the 1963 International Sociological Association's International Seminar on Family Research in Oslo (*Acta Sociologica* 1965) on 'The Decision to Marry'.

The principal concern within this tradition has been with discovering who marries whom, and it has established beyond any doubt (should anyone be inclined to doubt) that people marry people possessing similar social characteristics – race, ethnicity, religion, broad occupational grouping, income, location of residence, age, level of education, intelligence, previous marital status, attractiveness, emotional stability, even height – more often than they marry people with different social characteristics. (The few British studies covering these fields – Berent 1954, Rosser and Harris 1965, Coleman 1973 – have looked mainly at class and geographical homogamy. They concur with American findings.)

5. Jephcott 1942, 1948, 1967; Allcorn 1955; Willmott 1966; Veness 1962; Smith 1966; Emmett 1971; and Leigh 1971.

6. The Select Committee on the Age of Majority under the chairmanship of The Honourable Mr Justice Latey was appointed in July 1965 and published its *Report* (recommending the reduction of the age of majority from 21 to 18) in July 1967. This change was enacted in 1970. Discussion of, *inter alia*, the age when 'children' should be able to marry without parental consent was therefore current in the media during the period of my fieldwork (1968-69).

7. Cf. the marriage pattern of many non industrialized societies today, which have high birth rates, quite high death rates, low age at marriage for women, and almost no unmarried women.

8. There is a marked peak in the current marriage rate, especially for women. Half of all marriages of bachelors and spinsters (in all socio-economic categories) now occur between the ages of 20 and 24. (Registrar General 1971, Volume III; Grebenik and Rowntree 1963).

9. (a) Their Authorised Places of Worship had to be registered for conducting marriages; (b) advance notice of the wedding had to be given to the superintendent registrar of the district and his certificate obtained in lieu of banns; and (c) a registrar had to be present to record the marriage. A later Act (1898) allowed the governing body of a registered building to authorize a person (often the priest or minister) to register the wedding so that the presence of the civil registrar was no longer needed. Denominations vary, however, in how far they choose to exercise this right: Methodists do, RCs by and large do not (see Registrar General for 1972, Appendix D5, p.224).

Whilst it became possible, following the 1836 Act, to register Authorised Places of Worship for weddings, Humanists and Scientologists, for example, continue to be precluded from conducting their own ceremonies because their meeting places are not technically places of 'worship'.

10. 'No one had intended this. The legislation of 1836 was simply yet another bargain between political Nonconformists determined to remove the stigmas associated with marriage in chapel, and anti-erastians anxious to spiritualize the Anglican marriage ceremony, and the law of civil marriage was altered almost incidentally as part of a package deal. Civil marriage

had no pressure groups behind it, and seemed too unpopular to be of any importance' (Anderson 1975:66).

11. To be on the electoral roll of a church an individual must be over 17, have been baptized and habitually attended public worship in the church for 6 months (*Representation of the Laity Measure, 1956*). Banns are then given out in both the parishes where the couple are resident and in the church where one is on the roll and where they wish to marry.

12. See Barker 1977, Appendix 2 : 1 for full details.

    None of the denominations contests the right of the State to regulate the marriage – though RCs tend to dismiss it with a wave of the hand as 'the civil aspects'.

13. See Ch.2., p. 35.

14. There are various set 'canonical' reasons which the parish priest can give when applying for this permission for a 'mixed marriage' (one partner a Roman Catholic, the other a baptized member of another church) or where there is 'disparity of faith' (the other not baptized). One reason is that if permission is not given the marriage will take place elsewhere – and Roman Catholics stress the importance of a Catholic priest given the blessing. Others are: 'super adulta' – the woman is of such an age she is unlikely to get another chance, and 'angusta loci' – there are so few Catholics in the district that the choice is very narrow.

15. Until 1966, Papal decree imposed a strict obligation on both partners to ensure a Catholic upbringing of offspring. The ruling was then modified and in 1970 Pope Paul issued a *Motu Proprio Matrimonia Mixta*, which says essentially that the Catholic partner must strive to have children brought up in the faith, but that the non Catholic need not give any promise or undertaking.

    The period of instruction has been reduced to about half a dozen meetings, and it is possible to have a nuptial mass – though of course the non Catholic partner cannot receive it.

16. In Wales the Anglican Church was disestablished in 1902 but it continues to accept the responsibilities of the Established Church, and in South Wales at least many people continue to think of the Anglican Church as 'the' Church, with the other denominations as dissenters.

17. See Barker 1977; 138–40. One conclusion which can certainly be drawn from the confusion, swapping around and use of convenience addresses so as to marry in a favoured church, is that great care must be exercised in using church registers as evidence of geographical homogamy – certainly nowadays, and possibly also in the past.

18. There may be one rather unconventional minister in a town who is seen as especially approachable. In Swansea such a man had been at one church since the 1930s, and he lived most of the time in rooms at the side of the church, giving special help to tramps and other 'down and outs' in the crypt. In his opinion,

    'A minister should be at least as accessible as the police or a doctor. So he should live on the premises and have a location – people must know where to find him. The Sabbath aspect has gone – the work of the world is continuous, so should the church be. We tread on other clergy's toes and get severely criticized and ostracized . . . This building is Congregational-ist, but I don't bother about denominations. It's Congregationalist because it has no bishops. I don't like middlemen. I like to talk direct to the boss, Hot line . . .

I've been here thirty-five years – got a lot of connections with the local people. I helped the unemployed in the '30s and I ran a wartime children's cinema. And I used to go round the pubs to get money to take them to the Empire pantomime – it was some compensation for the little beggars for the unnatural life they were leading. Every other one who comes here and asks about getting married says "I came to your Sunday School" or "You took us to the pantomime". Wonderful contacts! . . . I talk to them . . . that's the only reward I have for my Ministry – that they *come* – and when they come you know they've got a problem. It's a listening ministry, not a preaching ministry. I let them spit out their problem – they're afraid she's pregnant or she thinks he's left her. People are like cars and the church is their parking place.'

Some thirty couples a year marry in his church – because of these past contacts and because he treats divorce and premarital pregnancy not as 'impediments' to marriage but as 'little problems which need sorting out'.

'I ask God . . . under the inspiration of the Holy Spirit (if I should marry a particular couple). Hypocritically ministers of the Church of England refer people to me. They can't get permission from the bishop. I should hate to have to do that. "Till death us do part" – but death of what? I think the whole service needs rephrasing: "While love still lives." I think the law is going in the direction of sanity.'

19. In most cases this parental permission must be given in writing, on a special form, and the signatures witnessed; the exception being marriages after banns in the Anglican Church, where it is assumed that the parents consent if they do not declare their dissent. Parental permission must be consent at the time the marriage is solemnized. Therefore parents can, and sometimes do, and certainly often *threaten*, to retract the consent they have given during the weeks before the wedding.

Age is without doubt the most significant 'capacity' necessary for marriage. Among those I interviewed in 1968/69, when the age of majority was still 21, a quarter had to have parental permission (39 per cent of women and 13 per cent of men), and half of those who needed it had experienced difficulty in getting it.

Where parental consent is refused the couple can apply to a court for its consent. The court for this purpose can be the High Court, or a county court, or a magistrates court sitting as a domestic court – in practice almost all applications (around 400 per year in England and Wales according to the Home Office's statistics) are made to a magistrates court. Only one couple in my sample had 'taken her parents to court' (see pp. 99–102).

20. The category of people who are not allowed by law to marry each other (*Marriage Act 1949*, First Schedule) is much wider than the category of people between whom sexual relations are incestuous (*Sexual Offences Act 1965*).

    Most people in Britain are aware that marriage is not allowed between close relatives – if only because they have perused the 'Table of Kindred and Affinity' in Anglican prayer books during boring sermons. But unless they share a common surname it is unlikely they would be questioned on this by the vicar or Superintendent Registrar.

21. For Roman Catholic regulations see Joyce (1948), and Anglicans see the list in any parish church porch.

22. This is, that the promise had never been given (therefore there had to be corroboration and witnesses to prove it had); that the contract was made when the defendant was under age and not confirmed when he or she was over 21; that the contract was induced by misrepresentation (though this was not a contract *uberrimae fidei* – there was no duty of disclosure of all material facts: the 'buyer' was expected to beware and check the partner's background and character); that the contract was induced by undue influence, especially of a parent on a child (since the child was presumed to trust the parent, who might have encouraged the match for his or her own ends); or that the contract/engagement had been ended by mutual agreement.

    There were, however, special defences to an action for breach of promise – that is, that *since the contract was made* certain facts had come to light (or come to be) such as to make the partner *unfit for marriage*. These facts were physical or mental infirmity (e.g., advanced tuberculosis or impotence or insanity) or moral infirmity (past unchastity in a woman; financial dishonesty by a man – but not that his income had declined).

2 The location, form, and nature of the study

In setting out to see how extensive and important the ceremonial associated with the process of courtship and marriage in Britain might be, and what messages it might convey, limits were immediately imposed on the project by the fact that it had to be done by one person unaided (on a Social Science Research Council post-graduate grant), and close to the place where I was living, which happened to be Swansea where my husband had a job. I had in mind contacting a haphazardly drawn sample of couples in the process of getting married, seeing them before and after their wedding, where possible also talking to their parents, and attending as many and as much of their wedding rituals as proved possible.

I soon decided to study the ceremonial in Swansea itself: there seemed nothing to be gained by spending time and money travelling to another town. This decision was fully vindicated, since it turned out that almost all interviewing had to be done in the evenings as young adults are at work all day. Evening interviewing was not only very tiring but also, because only one interview (at most) could be done each day and one wedding attended each Saturday, the fieldwork was spread out over a long period (see the Appendix). In any case, Swansea has no obvious drawbacks as a fieldwork area – it has, for example, a socio-economic and demographic structure close to the British average – and the definite advantage of having been previously studied by those interested in social stratification, the family, and religion[1]. It was important that this background description was available since I was concerned that, while concentrating on a particular feature of the society – the domestic group – at a particular phase in its cycle, the context within which these courtships and marriages were set should always be kept in view.

Swansea is a large provincial town with a population of some 170,000 people, spread over a wide area. The town follows the curving sweep of Swansea bay and climbs over the coastal hills and up the river valley. To the north are mountainous regions with sheep farming on the hills and coal mining villages and small towns in the valleys; to the west is the Gower peninsular with mixed farming and (relatively little developed) seaside tourism; and to the east are the massive steel works of Port Talbot and the rural Vale of Glamorgan.

The town grew with the industrial revolution and the development of a metal smelting industry, and grew further in the late nineteenth century with steel manufacturing and tinplating (Rosser and Harris 1965). But there is no longer much heavy industry or mining within the County Borough: the river valley has been deserted and is a derelict wasteland, and the new rolling mills have moved onto larger areas of flat ground outside the town itself. The docks, and an associated oil refinery, are still sizeable, however, and a certain amount of light industry has moved in onto industrial estates – cars, toys, paint, potato crisps, and brush factories. In addition, the town provides the services – the business, marketing, entertainment, and local government – for a large area of South West Wales (Edwards 1961).

The rapid expansion and industrialization of the late eighteenth and nineteenth centuries left a legacy of bad housing and lack of other social amenities, but current low incomes and living standards derive from events of the twentieth century as well. After periods of high unemployment, most men in the town in the late 1960s were in employment – in white collar, skilled, and semi-skilled jobs – but individual incomes were somewhat below the British average. And in addition, because of the numbers of aged and chronic sick, and because a low proportion of married women were economically active[2], many *households* had incomes well below the national average (Hammond 1968, Table 7:1:7).

It had often been remarked that class divisions between those living in Wales are less marked than in parts of England – in terms of the origin of income (most of the owners of land and capital are resident outside Wales), the distribution of income, and the difference of life-style. There is also a stress on locality – where one comes from – which masks status differences between wage workers and the few professional and managerial families in the 'urban villages' (cf. Day and Fitton 1975, Stead 1972). There thus appeared to be few differences by socio-economic category among those I interviewed. Further, Wales is still substantially an ascriptive, familistic society, with kinship providing a significant framework for social relations. Even in towns as big as Swansea, *who* you are (i.e., your place in a kin network) is often as important as *what* you are. In local affairs this leads to (what outsiders regard as) nepotism and a preference for locals – which is reflected in courtship patterns. Thus Myra Secombe says of her first meeting with her comedian husband:

> 'We met at the Mumbles Pier Hotel, Swansea, after the war. Harry was on demob leave and crossed the floor and said "May I have the pleasure of the next dance"? Then he asked me if he could see me Sunday. He said he wanted to be an actor. My grannie told me "Don't go bringing any actors home here", but when I told her that Harry was a Swansea boy, we just sailed on from there.' (Reported in Owen 1968)

Within the local domestic group women have considerable managerial autonomy and responsibility – 'it all centres round the Mam' – though men are unmistakably the heads of the households. Men are perceived as dependent on women because they need them to care for them domestically (being 'incapable' of doing such work themselves) and to keep the family together; i.e., to mediate disputes, control children, and maintain links with kin. Outside the home there is a largely masculine world of work, drinking (in pubs and clubs), sport, and the running of chapels, unions, and politics (cf. Brennan, Cooney, and Pollins 1954). But in this it is no different from most of Britain.

There are, however, one or two further particular features of the locality that are relevant to a study of courtship and marriage. First, in terms of where the wedding is held, it should be noted that a high proportion of the population (as compared with England and Wales as a whole) claim to belong to one or other of the various religious denominations and to go to services on Sundays (see Rosser and Harris 1965:127–28), and there is little variation in this by social class (Harris 1963:91). In addition, the choirs, Sunday schools, youth clubs, and sisterhoods, etc., associated with the churches and chapels are also active. One would therefore expect a good proportion of weddings to be with religious ceremony.

Within the town there are 250 religious buildings where weddings can take place – thirty-one Anglican and 167 others (according to *The Official List*, 1965). This is a rather good provision of Anglican churches and an average provision of Roman Catholic and 'other Christian' churches per head (compared with other towns of similar size)[3], but a very large number of Nonconformist churches (Baptist, Congregational and Independent, and Calvinistic Methodist). It is therefore not surprising that there should be a higher than average proportion of Nonconformist weddings,[4] nor that, as Harris stressed, a Nonconformist ethic should influence local sexual mores.

> 'In spite of their relatively small membership the influence of the chapels in Swansea has been considerable. Their members represent an educated, vocal and passionate interest group whose importance is out of proportion to its size . . . [They] are ready to deplore what they

conceive to be immorality and the decline of moral standards, particularly with reference to Sabbath breaking and the behaviour of the young.' (1963:18)

At the time of the fieldwork (1968-69), when London was 'swinging', no sex education was permitted in schools, there was a lack of family planning facilities in the town, the home for unmarried mothers was run on Spartan lines, and there was a general reticence about sex in polite conversation. Swansea was the last university in England and Wales to give up sex-segregated halls of residence (in 1974/5), and the local watch committee exercised quite strict censorship.

When the film of *Ulysses* was eventually shown in 1970 (in Llanelli, not in Swansea) it was delivered by Securicor van. While I would certainly not want to suggest that there is easy discussion of sexuality in any class or area of Britain, nor that girls' chastity is not valued generally, I think it probable that South Wales is more prudish than some other places. I did not include questions on sexual activity when I talked to people (though occasionally it come up in conversation with a woman after the end of the 'interview') because I knew from living in the town what hostile reactions it could provoke. For example

> My neighbour's daughter's friend who lived nearby had a major row with her parents. She had recently got engaged and her mother, on piecing together tiny pieces of torn paper from the waste-paper basket in her daughter's bedroom, discovered they were the printed instruction sheet from a pack of contraceptive pills. They wouldn't speak to her for a week.

> My neighbour's opinion was that the parents were over-reacting ('being silly') since, while she did not condone the girl's action, she *was engaged*, and her parents ought really to be glad she was 'being careful'. (But this liberalism was not reflected in her relations with her *own* teenagers.)

Although a general Nonconformist ethic is strongly present in the town, denominational affiliation is not a significant social boundary and there is no norm that one should marry people of one's own denomination among the major Protestant groups[5]. There is, however, some antagonism between 'Nonconformists' or 'Protestants' and 'Catholics' which is of long-standing here (as in England and Wales as a whole), associated not only with doctrinal differences but more importantly with ethnic hostility to the Irish and to the Roman Catholic Church's line on contraception (and hence large Catholic families). Non-Catholics are well aware of the frosty reception Catholic clergy give to their marrying their members – the rather dismal ten minute service, the compulsory classes and the promises they have to give, etc. (see chapter 1). But this notwith-standing, two-thirds of weddings in Catholic churches in Swansea are mixed marriages[6].

There is a small (and diminishing) Jewish population in the district – only a couple of hundred families are attached to the one synagogue in the town. There is therefore little chance of intermarriage, and it is anyway resisted by the Jews themselves, for the region is renowned for its orthodoxy : 'Half the Rabbis in London are from Llanelli.' Most Jewish young people in the recent past seem to have met their spouse outside the town and have held their weddings in, for example, London, which was easily reached by both sets of kin and where kosher restaurant facilities were available.

There were very few Negroes or Asians living in the town in the late 1960s and so inter-racial courtship and marriage – one of the chief vari-ables in American work on mate selection – was extremely rare. It was viewed with horror. One of the very few cases I heard of[7] was that of a miner's daughter who had gone to Cardiff to become a nurse and had married an Iraqi doctor. Her mother, it was reported, had refused to go to the wedding or to have anything to do with the young woman or her husband, and had retired to bed for three weeks. Her reaction was held by my informant (the mother of the groom in Case 4) to be understand-able but 'a case of shutting the stable door . . . She'll have to accept it sooner or later'.

Having settled on a study of courtship and weddings in a particular town, I was able to study the process both as a participant observer (I lived there for four years as a married woman with children) and by lengthy contact with more than fifty couples around the time of their marriage.

Over the course of a year, and with considerable difficulty (see the Appendix), I contacted a haphazard sample of couples who married in a five-month period (November 1968–March 1969), getting their names and addresses from vicars, ministers, and priests and the Marriage Regis-ter Books kept by the local registrars. Of these couples, twenty-four married in Anglican churches, three in RC churches, seven in Noncon-formist chapels, and twenty in the register office.

The most obvious biases within the sample were an under-representation of brides who married in church when they were pregnant or otherwise at short notice (I should have had about four, and in fact had only one), and I should have had twice as many Catholic weddings. (The reasons for these biases and my calculations of the short fall are discussed in the Appendix.)

The sampling frame (weddings taking place within the town) itself meant that:

(a) Couples who decided to live together without getting married are not included. Experience as a participant observer suggests, however, that such cases are very rare (or that such couples keep their status closely secret). (Note cases on pp. 49–50 and p. 67 note 9.)

(b) Only those whose weddings took place actually within the County Borough are included. Many of the local upper and upper-middle classes live in the countryside around rather than in the town, and their daughters marry either in local country parish churches, or in fashionable London churches.

(c) Nor does the sample cover the sons and daughters of the 'spiralist' middle classes (Watson 1964, Bell 1968). Among the fathers of the brides sampled, none was in the Registrar General's socio-economic category I, and of those in category II, none had been recently geographically mobile and all their daughters had lived in the town all their lives. The 'big weddings' during the period of fieldwork (none of which fell into the sample, though I did interview one couple afterwards and was told a lot about the others) were all of affluent members of the local (burgess) middle class: a secretary marrying a schoolteacher who was a member of the Welsh rugby team, the daughter of a local hospital consultant marrying a technical college teacher, and the daughter of the owner of a small chain of baker's shops. Spiralists probably hold their weddings wherever most of their relatives and friends live, or in a place which is easier to reach than Swansea, e.g., London.

(d) Finally, although the tradition of marrying in the bride's home district continues, commonsense suggests that when young women leave home (as opposed to 'living away', see chapter 3), and especially when they are on bad terms with their parents or disgraced, they would be unlikely to return 'home' to Swansea to marry. In an account such as the present one, which stresses the support, control, protection, and affection of the family, it is salutory to stress the obverse as well: from Case 40

'When his [bride's sister's husband's] sister had to get married, they turned her out. She'd been living in London and the boy was a Londoner. They told her to go back to London and get married there. They wouldn't have her here.'

In sum, my informants comprised a fairly homogeneous, mostly geographically non mobile, lower-middle and upper-working class group. Almost all were salaried or wage-workers. A few men in the building trade were 'self-employed', but they were not employing anyone to help them. A handful were students or on welfare (single mothers). *Figure 1* shows their socio-economic categories on the Registar General's scale[8]. The chief differences in income among them, however, were not by socio-economic category, but between men and women (see next chapter).

Figure 1 Occupation categories of my informants (percentages)

	Registrar General's Socio-Economic Category								
	I	II	Student	IIINM	IIIM	IV	V	Other*	N
Men	4	9	4	11	43	26	4	—	54
Women	—	11	4	48	6	26	—	6	54

* This includes those who had had no job for several years, i.e., women looking after children. Two others temporarily unemployed at the time of marriage are classed by their last job.

There were more marked differences between my informants' parents' standard of living. Most of their fathers were also salaried or waged, but some were petty bourgeois (shop keepers, wholesalers, small businessmen and builders, and a farmer) or professionals.

Figure 2 Occupation categories of the fathers of my informants (percentages)

	Registrar General's Socio-Economic Category							
	I	II	IIINM	IIIM	IV	V	Other	N
fathers of my informants (inc. deceased)	0	13	7 {46} 39		25	12	4	108
England and Wales, 1961 Census	4	15	49		20	9	5	16,330,780

The wealthiest parents, judged by life-style, were a company director and his (non-employed) wife living in a detached semi-bungalow in a large garden in a secluded area near the sea, and a farmer and his wife (who helped him on the farm) on the Gower Peninsular. The poorest family was that of an unemployed labourer (the stepfather of my informant, who described him as a 'lazy layabout') in a council house on an estate with five small children (my informant's step-sibs).

In quite a few cases my informant's fathers were dead (14 per cent) or retired due to illness, bankruptcy, or old age (10 per cent). In one case the woman informant had no father: she was illegitimate and her mother had never married. (Two others were illegitimate but their mothers had married.) Parental incomes must therefore have varied considerably (from wages or salaries, and from profits, fees, rents, investments, pensions, and benefits), but none was very wealthy.

Half of the mothers of my informants had some paid employment[9]. In the majority of cases when they worked they worked part-time and for very low wages[10]. The few with full-time jobs did more prestigeous and better paid work[11]. Their contribution to the total household income must generally have been small, however, given the wages paid and the number of hours they worked – often a matter of no more than a few pounds a week. Nonetheless it gave the woman some money 'of her own' and 'got her out of the house', but without threatening the man's supremacy as 'breadwinner'. The mothers continued to be financially dependent and in the home (as its affective and service centre) for the greater part of their time.

Whether married women went out to work or not depended on their responsibility for the young and the old. Of those five mothers of my informants who had small children (five and under), none went out to work; among the twenty-six who had school-age children (fifteen and under), two-thirds were not working, and similarly among those five with elderly or infirm relatives living in the same household. Among widows who had not remarried, no more were working than among the rest of the population, and the majority of those who did work, worked part-time.

The great majority of my informants were living with their families of origin at the time they married[12] (see *Figure 3*). Those who were living away from home were often living with relatives or in digs or hostels – very few indeed had households of their own or with peers. Most of their unmarried brothers and sisters were also living at home.

Those who married in Swansea but who had their homes outside the town were all students or in non-manual occupations, and they came from non-manual or skilled manual backgrounds (see chapter 3). Among the couples who left after they were married – nearly a fifth of all couples – in all cases but one the groom was either in the forces or merchant navy or in a non-manual job (see chapter 7).

In talking to these informants I expected, and tried to keep clear, differences of awareness and interpretation of the wedding ceremonial in different social groups. Differences by sex were the most apparent for,

Figure 3 Households in which informants were living at the time of marriage

	1st marriage		2nd marriage	
	women	*men*	*women*	*men*
At home (this includes a few older individuals who continued to live in the same house after the death of their parents or previous spouse)	45	40	4	3
With relatives	1	1	–	1
In college/hospital residence/hostel/army, etc.	1	5	–	–
In own flat	3	3	–	–
No information	—	—	–	1
N	50	49	4	5

indeed, while I found it advantageous in terms of getting to talk to people about the family to say that I was concerned with rituals rather than family patterns, this focus was precisely one of the things which prevented me from getting to talk to the groom, since men are culturally defined as less interested and less knowledgeable about such topics. Certainly many of the finer points of wedding detail are lost on them. As one minister commented, 'After every wedding, my wife says to me "What did she [the bride] wear?" – but, for the life of me, I can never remember. They all look alike!'.

With the exception of a few (middle-class) fathers who have clip-boards and filing systems and organize everybody, most middle-aged men keep out of the organization of a wedding, 'except to foot the bill'. The groom is quite often interested in discussing the details of his own particular wedding and will read the etiquette books and magazines that his fiancée buys, but he leaves the management to her and/or her mother – though he may undertake dealings with officials (e.g., giving notice to the registrar or vicar). Young women are very concerned with the details of their own ceremonial – whether the cake should be square or round, two-, three-, or four-tier, with horseshoes or doves as trimmings – and they have memories of 'having read somewhere about the meaning' of a particular element of the ritual (e.g., confetti, or the bride's veil, or why silver slippers were used as decorations); but it is older women who will occasionally sit back and muse over what has happened at past weddings to try to explain the significance of an action or symbol. Thus if ritual 'says' things, much of what wedding ceremonials say is said to women.

If the bride or her mother works in a shop or office or factory they will probably have several work-mates who have recently organized or who are currently concerned with organizing a wedding. Discussion of such topics forms an important part of women's (but not men's) workplace conversation. Advice and opinion is freely exchanged, and this is probably one element leading to the uniformity of those weddings which are planned well in advance. In addition, the bride (and groom) will have been to several church weddings in the past (my informants have been to 1–6 church weddings as guests or 'spectators') but much less often to civil weddings. Thus they knew what should be done for a white wedding, but were much less certain what is correct for a register office ceremony. The latter therefore are variable, scaled-down variants of 'proper' weddings.

Local tradesmen and shop-keepers – jewellers, stationers, caterers, florists, dress shops, car hire firms, bakers, etc. – present uniform basic products with a variety of 'extras' at additional cost. They put a certain amount of pressure on customers not to omit or scrimp on any items: 'It's only once in a life-time; you want to get it right.' (Among their customers it is the men who are more likely to resent the 'commercialism' of the event – perhaps not surprisingly since they are seen as paying the bill.) Such agents might be seen as one form of what anthropologists call 'ritual experts' since they offer practical advice on the usual correct form – the 'done thing': Case 48 (bride), 'I wanted to have pink icing on my wedding cake, but the baker had a fit!' – but they do not provide any explanation of symbolism, other than sometimes giving out a little printed booklet[13].

One informant, a waitress at one of the large town-centre hotels used for receptions, gave interesting insights into variations by social class as perceived by hoteliers. Case 42:

'At the reception 'the *real* thing to do is to have a line; to shake hands at the door and thank everyone for coming . . . Course *we* didn't have a chance to stand at the door – didn't have a bloody chance. Most [guests] got there before us. I would have liked to – not being a snob, but it's a nicer way of doing things. We're not high class, heaven knows. As it was, some people – all I knew was what people had given me. I identified them as "You're Nina, you gave me a so-and-so!". Those people who are brought up in it. They know all about these things . . . We had a private room for sherry, with a bar. I started one

end and went all down talking to everyone. You know how the two
families sit apart? Our side are real stickers [together]. You find that in
most weddings. Only the very, very high class people get together in
weddings. They've got a lot in common. [what?] Well – they can talk
about their new cars . . . [Were the wedding presents on display?]
I put as many as I could out upstairs [at home], but didn't take them to
The Mitre. High class people do . . . The bride and groom usually take
them down the night before – when they go to check the tables,
place-cards, cake, and so on.'

However, most people are not aware of such variations, and certainly are
not concerned with the sorts of upper-class wedding behaviour which
The Tatler or the local 'county' magazine provide. They wish to follow
what is suitable and proper, and are aware, and concerned to avoid, the
danger of behaving in a manner 'above their station' (see, in regard to
men's costume, chapter 6) – which would make them look foolish.

The range of variation available in commercial products and services –
e.g., in the style of the wedding dress, choice of menu for the reception,
or location for the honeymoon – allows customers to feel that within their
price range they are making their wedding a unique and individual affair
(though the range is markedly less than that described for the USA by
Seligman 1974). This 'personalising' (sic) is certainly a goal which the
bride and groom see themselves as striving for valiantly against mounting
pressures to give greater consideration to the wishes of parents and kin.

More important as ritual experts are the vicars, priests, ministers, and
the local Superintendent Registrar, who all feel a pastoral concern for the
couples they marry and who deliberately try to counteract the commercial
pressures they feel the young people come under: to persuade them to
spend less on the wedding and to save their money instead. All officiants
discuss 'the nature of marriage' with the couple to a certain extent,
formally or informally, and give advice on the conduct of the ceremony
itself. Many of the churches hold a rehearsal and, as they go through the
service, some of the church's symbolic interpretations are explained to
the couple. These men also see themselves – as clergy and as older
experienced people – as being able and suitable persons to give advice on
relations with in-laws, getting a mortgage, the importance of fidelity, and
the importance of family planning, etc. St Mary's, as the 'mother church'
of Swansea, organizes a series of wedding preparation classes each
year, open to any couple in the town, with talks by the Family Planning
Association, a solicitor, the Marriage Guidance Council, a priest (about
the marriage service) and others.

In addition to such local ritual experts, all the twenty or more widely
read national women's magazines offer occasional features on organizing

a wedding, and those with advice services for readers will supply 'leaf-lets' (cyclostyled sheets) on Wedding Etiquette, Marriage Formalities, Speeches for Weddings, Wine for the Wedding, Recipes for a 3-tier Wedding Cake, Wedding Headdresses to Make, a List of Useful Wedding Presents, etc. Sometimes the magazines have special issues or supple-ments on getting married, which draw advertising from the makers of furniture, bedding and bed linen, cutlery, and from building societies, as well as from specialist bridal shops and caterers. (See Henson 1976 for American market research on the high proportion of consumer durable sales accounted for by the 'bridal market'.) The local papers follow this lead, giving a double-page spread of articles and advertisements on weddings once or twice a year (usually in the early spring). There are also a few bi-monthly magazines which address themselves directly to brides. At the time of my fieldwork there was the glossy and expensive *Brides and Setting Up Home*, full of clothes and modern furniture and gourmet cook-ery, and a more homely, cheaper magazine, *Bride and Home*, budded off from the general magazine *Woman*. In addition an annual publication comes out from the British Medical Association on *Getting Married*, which is sold at most newsagents and bookstalls. All were widely read by my informants.

A systematic search around the bookshops in the town located half a dozen wedding etiquette books[14], and once it was known that I owned these books they were borrowed by my neighbours and friends of my neighbours.

Most of the information and advice on the actual organization of wed-dings contained in these magazines and books is straightforward – they agree with each other as to 'what should be done', and this is quite close to what I observed to happen to practice. But their accounts of the 'meanings' of various rituals and symbols are a jumble of misinformation – not lacking in sociological interest. It is always assumed that there is a 'reason' for rituals, albeit forgotten now by most people, and that it is interesting to know that this is – to have, in the words of the Michelin guide, 'un peu d'histoire' – so as to understand and give depth to the present. In the 'reasons' given for the rituals, certain cultural values are very clearly expressed. See, for example, the following accounts of the origins of wearing a bridal veil:

> 'The present bridal veil is a delicate descendant from darker, more violent days. It derives from the improvised protective wrapping with which a bold suitor enveloped his bride, having wrested her by force or subterfuge from her father's house, or a rival's stronghold. Either for protection or disguise, the doughty groom reckoned to "wrap up" his newly acquired goods, with thoroughness and care. With the passing

of time, quieter methods of mating evolved, and resistance gave way to response at the altar. But the veil, now a beautiful and gossamer-like symbol, is merely a romantic reminder of the rough and tumble that used to accompany an excursion into matrimony in years gone by!' (*Woman* 6 January, 1973).

'There are several possible explanations of the bride's veil. Many of the customs connected with weddings were connected with good and evil spirits, or the attracting of luck. It is thought that the wedding veil may originally have been meant to conceal the bride from evil spirits.
Although others think it may be a relic of the custom of Purdah, the idea that the bride should be shielded from the eyes of all men except her husband. Once she is married to him, then he lifts the veil. Later in the Jewish religion a canopy was held over the married pair, and this custom was carried on in Anglo-Saxon times when four men held a cloth over the heads of the bridal pair. Eventually this cloth became the bride's veil.' (Bingham 1969:109-10)

'Another symbol connected with weddings is the veil worn by the bride. If we go back to very ancient times, it will be found that the two parties of the marriage were enshrouded in a canopy of flimsy material, in order that their faces might be screened from the gaze of the curious. Today, the groom has lost his share of the covering, presumably because he can endure the ordeal with equanimity; but the bride wears her portion in the shape of a veil, if she is so minded.' (Woodman n.d:118)

'The restrictions which apply to the dress are even more strongly associated with the veil, which should never be tried on with the wedding dress before the wedding day, although a separate fitting is permissible. An old bridal veil, especially if it is the property of a happily married woman, is very fortunate, and many brides today choose to wear their grandmother's or mother's veil for this reason. If the bride should allow a friend to try on her wedding veil after the wedding, there is a dangerous chance that the wearer may run away with the newly married husband.' (Baker 1974:30)

The messages which come through clearly concern female modesty, chastity, and monogamy; male dominance and initiative and aggressiveness; a concern with luck; the couple 'wrapped up' with each other and away from the rest of the world (and the woman staying 'away from the world' even when the man returned to it); continuity of womanly occupation in the home; and antagonism between women because they pose a threat to each other in terms of stealing each other's men.

Etiquette books are certainly bought, but it is hard to give an estimate of their influence. Women told me they read them 'to get ideas' – which seemed to involve getting an outline of the series of things that needed to be done from the engagement onwards (booking the church, when to send out the invitations, how to choose a best man, etc.) and also an outline of the church ceremony itself, since people are very worried that they will do the wrong thing at the wrong time. These books and magazines may also be used for specific advice for particular situations – e.g., how to issue invitations if the bride's parents are divorced. They also make people aware of variations from the local form: e.g., the bride's bouquet in Swansea is either put on a grave or kept as a memento, but my informants knew that elsewhere there is a custom of the bride throwing her bouquet and whoever catches it being the next to marry. In Swansea this custom was said to be American. With one exception[15] they themselves did not do it.

The differences of knowledge, awareness, and explanation of ritual behaviour (as between men and women, young and old, by social class, between clergy and laity, etc.), while complex to handle, are not matters of dispute or interpretation. It is when one seeks to go beyond, to give an observer's view, that one faces a major problem common to all social scientists. This problem is particularly acute when dealing with a non-verbal system of communication, where the actors can provide little rationale for their behaviour, and where there is a constant awareness of the polyvalence of symbols – what Turner calls the 'fan of referents' : the way in which one ritual or symbol carries memories, overtones, and significance from other rituals.

The solution is, of course, not to ignore ritual, since ceremonials and symbols provide comprehensive signs for more or less abstract cultural values, some of which may contradict the (more accessible) verbally expressed values. One can only ground one's selection and interpretation in one's experience in the field and general analysis. I have not attempted any psychoanalytic explanation, nor to uncover the 'deep structures' running through the whole ceremonial (and other of the myths and rituals of the culture), though the material presented is sufficiently detailed for others to embark on this: but rather to suggest simply what the participants' choice of place and form for their wedding conveys about marriage as an institution.

As has been mentioned, this study was begun in 1967 and fieldwork was carried out from Autumn 1968 to Autumn 1969. Analysis and writing-up has been protracted. Partly this was because I lacked an adequate theoretical framework; partly because it was necessary for me to be moved out of the field in order to distance myself from the material; but it was also because I had to get away from what is conventionally involved in being a wife and mother in our culture to have the time and motivation to finish.

This undoubtedly raises the question of how dated the material may be. I think the short answer is that very little has changed, and, further, that what I have to say about Swansea still applies to many areas of the country and across most of the middle and working classes. The wisdom derived from being somewhat geographically and temporally removed from the field suggests the generality of my findings, rather than their specificity.

Some minor changes are nevertheless worth noting. First, from continuing contact with the area, I think there has been some liberalization regarding pre-marital sexuality in 'committed' relationships – but not all that much[16], and I think Swansea is not very different from other provincial towns in this respect. Contraception and abortion are now formally available to the unmarried; but they are still not easily accessible to the unsophisticated and abortion is still not a real, socially acceptable, alternative to 'having to get married'.

Second, there is statistical evidence of a slight rise in the age at marriage and that couples are having their first baby slightly later within marriage. But this is, I suggest, more the result of financial and housing exigencies than a decline in enthusiasm for marriage and parenthood. Since 'marriage is a calculated act, taking account of present assets and future prospects', even within a welfare state, so men's thoughts turn to marriage (generally speaking) when they have the ability to support a family at the level of existence consonant with the expectations of the social group to which they belong. A less bouyant national economy in the 1970s has meant static real wage levels coupled to expectations of rising living standards. And, in addition, since getting married is linked to setting up a new household, all those things that have made it harder to set up households – in particular the working through of mid-60s changes in legislation which have made it more difficult to get rented properties and the sharp rises in house prices in the early 1970s – could have been expected to discourage or cause delay of marriage and childbearing.

Third, while there has been a much stressed national increase in the employment of married women (see Moss 1976), this has been largely the product of women in their forties returning to the labour market after rearing children, thereby making cash contributions to the household in addition to their unpaid domestic work. Most married women in South Wales still work part-time for very low wages, and in no wise are they, or are younger women, less economically dependent on marriage than they were ten years ago. Women who work even full-time still only earn roughly half of what men earn.

Finally, it is worth pointing out that although the media keep pointing out (each time the Registrar General's quinqennial statistics are published) that the proportion of civil weddings is increasing and that in some areas they now out-number church weddings, this is a much more marked trend in the south-east of England and the conurbations than anywhere else. It shows, I think, a decline in the dichotomy between church and register office ceremonies in these areas, not an overall decline in the importance and ceremonial associated with weddings (see chapter 6). Observations in several parts of London show that there are now full-scale weddings in town halls as well as in churches.

What certainly has not changed is people's general desire to get married[17] and men's dominant position within heterosexual couples. Boys still have the unquestioned prerogative of taking the initiative within courtship and still implicitly accept and operate a sexual double standard. Girls still have their geographical mobility greatly curtailed and still accept greater parental control in more areas of their lives than do boys; though perhaps they *are* starting to protest rather more about these and other aspects of sexual division in society. However, as yet, young men and parents have seen their authority and prestige little threatened and they still accept their dominant position as natural and just.

Notes

1. Brennan, Cooney, and Pollins 1954; Harris 1963 and 1974; Rosser and Harris 1965; Hilton 1967; Bell 1968; and Jones 1970.
2. *Figure 4* Female activity rates by region, 1961, 1966, 1971 (percentages)

		1961	1966	1971
	GB as a whole	37.4	42.2	42.7
Lowest	Wales	27.9	33.4	35.7
Highest	W. Midlands	41.5	45.7	45.4

Source: Dept. of Employment (1974:46)

   According to the 1966 census, only 34% of women (over 15) in Swansea were economically active (against the national average of 42%). Only 23% of mothers of primary school children in Wales went out to work at all, compared with 39% in England, and of the 23% who did work, only 9% worked more than 5 hours a day (Gittins Report 1968:18).
3. I made calculations for Wandsworth LB, Sunderland CB, and Exeter CB from *The Official List*. Swansea is a 'stronghold of Nonconformity' not at the expense of Anglicanism, but in addition to it.
4. See also chapter 6. In England and Wales as a whole Methodists perform more weddings than any other Nonconformist denomination – as they have since separate figures became available (1919); though like all Nonconformists their proportion of all weddings is declining (5% in 1967). They are followed

by the Baptists (2%) and Congregationalists (1%), and the rest (Society of Friends, Presbyterians, Jehovah's Witnesses, etc.) (2%).

In Glamorgan, most Nonconformist weddings are Baptist (6%) or Congregationalist (5%), with (Wesleyan) Methodists and Calvinistic Methodists accounting for a further 2–3% each, and the rest 3% all told. (See p. 222.)

5. Pearl Jephcott reports that her girl informants in the 1940s regarded difficulties due to difference of religion to be on par with difficulties arising from a boy's being unable to dance – in fact of rather less significance (Jephcott 1948).

6. In 'The Parish Statistics for 1965–1966' the *Cardiff Archdiocesan Year Book 1967* gives entries for 'Catholic' and 'Total' marriages. In Swansea as a whole, 65% of marriages were mixed in 1965/6: in Morriston 83%, the town centre 66%, St Thomas 66%, and Mumbles 75%.

7. The other was an informant in the pilot sample who had a brother who lived in London, who 11 years before had married a wife who was an East African Indian. 'It was earth-shaking. My parents just didn't know how to take it. But they liked her very much, so they came round to it.' A white man marrying a non-white woman is of course viewed *relatively* favourably (cf. Firestone 1970, Horton 1970).

8. With the caveat that the RG's classification is not a good guide to the relative status and economic standing of women's occupations; and that the table does not take account of job changing, since jobs were often of different 'status'.

9. *Figure 5* The employment of the mothers of my informants

	No.	%
no job	36	50
part-time job*	27	38
full-time job	9	13
	——	——
	72	101
no information	26	
mother dead	10	
	——	
	108	

* a few hours a week to half-time.

Rosser and Harris (1965) found that of all women aged over 21 in Swansea in 1960, 14% of those who were married worked full-time, and 8% part-time.

10. Their work was mainly 'domestic' – as cook or server-out in a school, hospital or factory canteen, cleaning offices or private houses; or 'service' – serving in shops, as barmaids or in petrol stations. Only one worked part-time as a secretary. None worked part-time in a factory. None did voluntary work to such a degree or in such a way that their child counted it as 'part-time' work,

though one son mentioned in this context that his mother was trying to get elected to the local council. None earned money from taking in boarders, or from homework (that I was aware of).

11. A staff nurse, owner of a pub, manageress of a shop, farmer's wife (unpaid, but the daughter gave this as her mother's job when we went through the schedule). There were two mothers who were full-time factory workers (one a belt-leader in charge of 20 women), one clerk cum comptometer operator, and one waitress. This confirms Viola Klein's findings from national surveys (1965:33–6): full-time women workers are mostly skilled or semi-skilled; part-timers are mostly 'domestic and service' workers. It also helps to explain why, when the wives of s.e.c. II men work in Swansea, they are more likely to work full-time, whereas for all other occupational categories of husband, if they work they usually work part-time (see Barker 1977, Figure 3: 15). The wives of middle-class men cannot justify taking low paid, menial work, for it would lose the family status (Cohen 1973).

12. Living at home at the time of marriage is here defined as having been resident with the parents for the month prior to the wedding. Thus a nurse who returned from her London flat for two weeks to organize wedding arrangements, and a soldier home on one week's leave, are excluded; while two sailors, home for several months, are included. The couple who ran away and lived together for five days (see pp. 49–50), before being marched to the register office, have been counted as living at home.

   For those who had been married before, this arrangement gave the woman – who had care of the children – help and babysitters when she was courting for the second time; and it provided the men with housekeepers. For both sexes it afforded emotional support.

   I had no young widows or widowers in my sample. Marris in his study in East London suggests that they, by contrast, try to remain independent and do not want to go back to (what he suggests is seen as) the status of unmarried persons by living with their parents. Also widows are less likely to be thinking of remarrying, nor do they have the same problems about division of property, etc., which face divorced or separated persons (Marris 1968).

13. For example, when one couple bought their engagement ring they were given a booklet on *Getting Married* by the jeweller. This was mainly about making the necessary arrangements and was heavy with advertisements for local firms, but it also included information on the 'meaning' of birthstones, the 'language' of flowers, etc.

14. Mary Woodman: *Wedding Etiquette*; 'Best Man': *Marriage Etiquette: How to Arrange a Wedding*; Vernon Heaton: *Wedding Etiquette Properly Explained*; Barbara Jeffrey: *Wedding Speeches and Toasts*; Madeleine Bingham: *Your Wedding Guide*; and a section in Carlton Wallace : *The Pocket Book of Etiquette*.

15. Case 27. The groom's only sister was two years older than he (27). She had had a series of long and serious illnesses as a child, spending much time in hospital. She was 'just having her first serious boy-friend' at the time of her brother's wedding. 'She's never mixed easily.'

   The bride's mother suggested that the bride give her bouquet to her new sister-in-law 'so as to make sure she was the next to get married'.

16. A survey in 1976 found that many more women marrying from 1945 to 1951 said that they had not slept with the man who became their husband (78% of those marrying aged 20–24 and 66% of those marrying under 20) than was the case in the 1970s (28% of those married aged 20–24, and 18% under 20). Although the general trend is clear, the difference is possibly overstated because of the reluctance of older women to reveal pre-marital sexual experience, and differences in accuracy of recall (Source: *Demographic Survey*, 1978).

17. Fogelman (1976), in the latest report of the National Child Development Survey, found only 3% of 16 year olds said they did not want to get married, and only 4% did not want children.

3 Young people and their homes : intergenerational relationships, spoiling, and 'keeping close'

Among the many myths surrounding adolescence in Britain is the belief that this is a period invariably marked by rebelliousness and friction with all authorities – be they parents, school, university, or police – as the young people struggle for independence. This 'struggle for independence' is not presented as one between age-classes for power, but rather of individuals for self-determination and expression. It is suggested that among those whom young people find particularly oppressive are their parents and kin.

Freud can certainly be counted among the progenitors, and Talcott Parsons and the 'radical psychologists' (e.g., Laing and Cooper) among the nurturers, of the idea that to become an adult and mature a child (especially a boy) must 'free' himself from claustrophobic, restrictive, incestuous, parental authority. From this basic psychologistic position the argument has been continued along the line that, since in Western urban society there is no institutionalization of the readjustment of power between parent and child (in contrast with societies with initiation ceremonies), and because there is a prolongation of the period of dependency because of longer schooling, the individual boy (or girl) must struggle for freedom for a long time. Because he (or she) can never be sure how far the battle has been won, he (or she) will be in an anomic situation and therefore insecure and unhappy. (The reason for putting females in parenthesis here is that most of the information available focuses on young males rather than young people, explicitly or implicitly.)

In the American literature it has been suggested that it is at this point in the life-cycle that the peer group becomes of great importance, giving the young people recognition, status, and security outside the family, and inculcating universalistic norms to enable adjustment from the family to the outside world (Parsons 1962; Eisenstadt 1956).

But we should treat as an empirical question just how much peer (age) grouping there *is* in different cultures and subcultures (it certainly differs by sex in Swansea, see Ward 1974 and chapter 4), just how stormy and unhappy this period is, against which authorities antagonism is directed, and just what sort of independence is sought and achieved by young adults. We certainly should not assume uncritically that peer groups are (structurally) sources of freedom: they are more often ways of controlling intergenerational relationships and maintaining adult power, even if they can sometimes be used to develop age-class consciousness (cf. S. Allen 1968; Gillis 1974).

In this chapter I shall concentrate on one particular aspect of independence – leaving home and setting up a new household – stressing that in this respect most of those who marry in Swansea remain 'dependent' till they marry, but that this 'dependence' continues their (and their fathers') exploitation of their mothers. To this end, I shall discuss the distribution of income and domestic work within the family, and show the consequences for parent-child relationships before and after the 'child's' marriage.

Personal history of my informants

Since weddings are traditionally held in the brides' home district, it is not surprising to find in a sample of those marrying in Swansea that the majority of women were from this town, nor that they had met and courted and were marrying predominantly local men[1]. Most of those whose homes were in Swansea had lived all or most of their lives in the town, usually in the same house. The qualification 'most of their lives' (taken as since the age of five) is needed because of the extensive wartime and post-war movement experienced by their parents. The average date of birth of my informants was 1946-48 and so some were born while their mothers were evacuated, or living with kin while their fathers were away in the army, or in temporary accommodation after having been bombed out, etc. After the war, when their fathers were demobbed, and as the new council housing estates were built, families often moved house within the town.

I always introduced the topic of their education with the young people I interviewed, but most seemed to feel far removed from their school days and were surprised that I should ask about such an 'irrelevant' period in their lives (with the exception, of course, of students, for whom education was significant and continuing). Those who were in their twenties and who had been at work since they were fifteen or sixteen had long got over any 'floundering period' such as Carter describes (1966), and their status in the family as wage-earners and more or less self-supporting 'adults' was established.

Almost all had been to local schools – state or private (the latter includes a commercial school for girls): the local middle class do not have a tradition of sending children away to boarding school. Most had left school at fifteen or sixteen, about 70 per cent having no paper qualifications.

Swansea parents are as aware as those elsewhere of the possible advantages of education; though there are some sentiments that what is taught in schools is largely a waste of time, schooling and qualifications are generally seen as 'a good thing' of which one should get as much as one can. In general parents say they are happy for their children to stay on after fifteen 'if they want to'. (The only arguments I was told about were accounts of how children persuaded their parents to let them leave 'early' – at fifteen). But parents are equally well aware that once their children start to earn their own living, family finances and also parent-child relations improve: a source of friction is removed, a step towards adult status is taken, and parents feel they and their children get closer because they share experiences (as they do also when the children marry).

Parental permissiveness therefore allows 'children' to leave school when they want to (or rather when the state allows them to – hostility is thus directed at the school as the government's representative rather than at the parents), and in the majority of cases there is only a short period when the 'children' are socially (e.g., in leisure activities and sexuality) pubescent but still not earning their own living.

After leaving school at fifteen or sixteen, roughly half my male informants had started to 'learn a trade' (i.e., were apprenticed in a skilled craft for a period of up to five years), though some gave it up before finishing. Those who completed included plumbers, welders, fitters, butchers, and chefs. Very few girls were apprenticed (4 per cent of my informants, both in hairdressing). Those who did apprenticeships could expect good wages in the future, but were all relatively lowly paid until they were twenty to twenty-one years old.

Informants who stayed on at school till they were eighteen (13 per cent of my informants) formed a somewhat separate group with regard to their adolescent experiences. They were in the anomalous position of being treated as 'non-adults' at home and at school while their age peers were earning. They were largely dependent on their parents, despite the fact that most took Saturday and holiday jobs, at a time when they constituted a very substantial financial burden[2]. Those who went on to higher education had their student grants mean-tested on their parents' incomes, and their parents were expected to make up the difference between what was actually given and the full value of the grant (and not all parents did this). If they were students in their home town or nearby, a still lower grant was paid, since it was expected that students would live at home and have their rent and food subsidized thereby. These informants were therefore not only much poorer than their employed contemporaries, but their parents exercised a much more overt authority in their lives.

In addition, technical college, and even more university students were aware of other, outside, standards against which to compare their family and local community – though the extent to which teachers in Swansea schools and colleges are those born, schooled, and trained in the locality restricted this somewhat. Students at college were in formal peer groups and some had adolescent experiences on the 'American' pattern[3], having experienced a fairly turbulent struggle for independence. But this applied to only *some* informants who had been through higher education. At least an equal number seemed to have been marked by very little friction with or separation from parents.[4] Case 17:

> Malcolm Davis, who married a Clydach girl, came from Cardiff. He had lived at home throughout his three years at Cardiff Teacher Training College. He then got a teaching job in Cardiff and continued living at home until he married and moved a few streets away.

Marriage was generally delayed until after apprenticeships or other training was completed, though this pattern was more pronounced among manual than non-manual workers. Only one skilled manual worker married before completing his apprenticeship, while two couples married while both were full-time students and in a few other cases the husband was still taking exams while working full-time (local government officers, police) or training on the job (graduate management trainee).

No young men were unemployed when interviewed, though a handful had recently changed jobs with a short spell out of work, and one man lost his job (as an electrician) and found another over the period of the wedding (i.e., between my two talks with the couple). (This was a period of low unemployment nationally.) Several young women, however, were not working full-time when interviewed (8 per cent of those marrying for the first time and 50 per cent of those marrying for the second time), mainly because of domestic duties – they were caring for children or elderly relatives – though some showed their lack of commitment to the labour-market and their acceptance of financial dependency by being happily prepared to give up their jobs and to rely on their fathers or fiances when pressed by circumstances[5].

I did not collect information on income, or indeed discuss money directly with my informants (see Appendix), but a small street-interview survey on the earnings and leisure activities of 17–20 year olds in Swansea was conducted in 1967 (May 1968). It found that for those in full-time employment, female earnings averaged £8 a week, and male earnings (which were much more variable) averaged £10.75. Male wages started slightly lower than female's, but rose with age and rapidly overtook them, even for apprentices[6].

Marriage was therefore pretty well unthinkable on economic grounds for most young men until they were in their twenties, particularly those who were apprenticed to skilled manual occupations, or who had other prolonged training; and, when courting, girls were likely to be financially much less well off than their boyfriends (their superiors in both age and sex) and hence they were very willing 'to be paid for' on outings to the cinema or pub[7]. It also meant that, while the young wife's wages were necessary for the establishment of a comfortable home, her potential financial contribution was always much less than her husband's, since her earning power was never likely to be more than half of his.

These differences by sex need to be stressed, as does the fact that lack of money is a major constraint on the leisure activities of teenagers (both boys and girls), since, in addition to the myth that young people are rebellious and insecure, there is also a myth that they (all) have a lot of money. In reality, it is only men in their twenties who earn a living wage. What teenagers and unmarried women in their twenties *do* have is a *relatively* large amount to spend 'on themselves' – on clothes, toilet preparations, drink and cigarettes, sweets, meals out, holidays, motorcycles, cars, and entertainment. This is largely because they live with their parents and pay well below cost for their board and lodgings.

Living away from home

Although, as mentioned in chapter 2 (and Barker 1972b), relatively few of my informants were living away from home when they married (10 per cent of brides and 14 per cent of grooms), rather more had had some experience of living away from home (32 per cent of brides and 46 per cent of grooms). But this was clearly seen as a temporary expedient, often brief, and as not at all the same thing as 'having left' home. 'To leave home' implies a breach with one's parents. If one 'lives away' it is for training or for a job, not for independence, and one is expected to go home regularly for visits (every weekend if doing a sandwich course in engineering in Barry or nursing in Cardiff), and to try to get a job locally as soon as possible if one has to accept a first post elsewhere. Considerable pressure may be put on adolescents to prevent them taking up training or jobs which are likely to take them away from their parents (geographically or socio-culturally). For example, one woman, a teacher, the daughter of a widowed skilled manual worker, who had ended up at the university in Swansea, said that she (Case 16) 'had thought of LSE, but my father went berserk. He would have been very hurt. He thought it very selfish and not good for girls to go away anyway.'

Parents seemed more willing to give their blessing to living away for training or a job if this involved living in a hostel, or digs, or with relatives (rather than if the young people were 'looking after themselves' in flats or bedsitters). The young people themselves also often said they preferred these arrangements, and of those who *had* ever lived away for training or work, only eight (8 per cent of the total sample and 21 per cent of those who had lived away, all of them in middle-class occupations (university students, teachers, a nurse, trainee managers and a policeman) had had flats or bedsitters on their own or shared with peers.

It is probably fair to say that 'a home' is seen essentially as something which is developed by a married couple and their children, and that there is no real notion nor, in terms of the housing market, a real possibility, of an alternative kind of domestic unit. To 'make a home' alone or with peers is a contradiction in folk terms[8] and difficult in practice. The idea and actuality of living away from home is uncomfortable. I came across not a single case of a young person setting up a flat in the same town as their parents – neither among those informants and their sibs who lived in Swansea, nor among those who lived elsewhere. The single, reveal-ing, exception is a couple who were refused consent to marry, and who then 'ran away' and got a flat together. Their menage lasted five days before they were marched to the register office.[9] Case 25:

> The couple had met each other in August when they were both seven-teen (a month after the break-up of her previous engagement). 'We decided to get married the week before Christmas. We were going to get married in June. Both parents wanted us to wait – mine for a white wedding, his because he's so young. His father was being awful funny about the time he was getting in and all.
>
> Just before Christmas I asked [my parents'] permission. We were going to get engaged, but, oh, I wasn't getting on at home . . . and I thought, "Why get engaged and have a long engagement? We may as well get married first as last."
>
> My parents wanted me to wait; but they agreed in the end because I told them I was pregnant. Paid for that since, I have; found out I've got blocked tubes and can't carry. But *his* father wouldn't sign. I told his

parents – I told everybody everything – I told them I was pregnant. But his father wouldn't sign.

He didn't have to, because he's only Huw's step-father; but his mother didn't want the wedding to go ahead unless he was willing because it would cause friction between the two of them . . .

We decided on the spur of the moment. Everything was getting me down. The week after Christmas we decided to run off and get married. We got as far as Newport, and then I said "Bugger the lot of them, I'm going back. Either we get married or we live together. They can't stop us doing that, even if they stop us getting married."

We got a flat, on the Monday, in Elizabeth St. Furnished it was: *terrible* place. That settled it. Both mothers came down on the Thursday. Told us we were getting married on Saturday! They gave us three days' peace. Lovely they were!'

To live away from home in the same town would be seen as a deliberate slight to one's parents: 'They'd have been upset'; 'She'd have minded, but not stopped me'. Case 38 (bride): 'I've always lived at home. My parents have always been very protective and because I care a lot and don't want to hurt them, I didn't leave. They'd take it as a personal insult. They do if I disagree!'

Factors likely to cause parents to be upset include worries about criticism from outsiders: 'they'd have been worried that people would think I hadn't got a good home', 'people would think there was something wrong somewhere'; and concern that the young person 'wouldn't take proper care' of him or herself: (groom) 'They frightened me off. They said "Who's going to take care of you if you're ill?".' There is also concern about moral welfare: (bride) 'They said I was too wild. I was then, really cheeky.' But, equally important, some respondents and parents said directly that they valued each other's company: 'It's nice to have someone to talk to when you get home'; or referred to their attachment facetiously: 'I make a lot of noise; they'd miss me!', 'She'd miss her everloving son!' The converse of children not leaving home so as not to slight their parents is that only under major provocation are parents seen to be justified in 'turning them out of the house'.

There is, it is true, a set of values expressed in such set phrases as 'you have to let them go', 'it does them good to stand on their own two feet', and 'you mustn't keep them tied to your apron-strings'. Insofar as I found differences between social classes, this set of values was more common in the middle class[10]; but throughout my sample I felt the balance was towards 'keeping them close', and the clichés were used to justify situations where the parents had failed in this aim, or to cover the parents against a charge of possessiveness. Very little weight was attached to them. For example, in one interview the girl said that her parents' response to her living away would have been 'Murder!'. Her mother added (Case 8): 'That's putting it mildly. We'd have gone off our rocker. [Why?] We've put in so much time over her – childhood and that – we'd worry too much – be afraid that everything not go right. Mind, does them good to get away.'

Few other studies have given adequate information on where young adults live before they marry, but Morton's work on census data (1976) shows that out of the eleven million single adults (eight million never married) in England and Wales, only three million have a place of their own (18 per cent of the total adult population) and 700,000 share. The rest live in other people's households, as children, kin, and 'others'. Most of those who do have their own household are widowed or divorced and/or over retirement age. Of those under thirty, only 8 per cent achieve 'independence' and half of these share.

> 'Only about 40,000 of the 3.7 million adults living independently are under 20, and most of these are students, in digs . . . Only about 360,000 are even aged 20–30, although there are 2.6 million single people in this age group – and five million married people with houses of their own.' (Morton 1976:664)

As she stresses, the single seeking a home of their own get virtually no help from anybody – councils, building societies, landlords or builders[11]. For most people, especially in the working class, 'the only road to independence in housing is through marriage'.

After marriage it is expected that a new couple will establish an independent household, separate from both sets of parents: to live with parents is an emergency or short-term contingency solution (see chapter 7). Even so, emotional emancipation from the family of origin is a gradual and drawn-out process, particularly for girls. Many young women described themselves as being 'homesick' after their marriage – even when living in the same town as their parents. And for years afterwards 'I'm going home' can refer to going to the family group, or to the place of origin, as much as to returning to the household shared with spouse and children.

This evident affection between parents and children should not, however, be allowed to obscure the fact that while 'children' remain with their parents and/or unmarried, parents exercise some control over their behaviour – expecting deference and obedience, particularly from daughters. This is illustrated by Case 21, where the bride's mother claimed to have given her daughter (who was twenty-three years old, divorced, and the mother of two children) 'a good thumping' for coming home late in the evening. Rather, young adults live at home because of the values attached to it and because with longer schooling, earlier marriage, and the lack of accommodation for the unmarried, it does not seem worth moving out, especially when the material situation when living at home is so advantageous.

Financial arrangements with parents

Young children (5–7 years old onwards) are often given pocket money to spend, and in Swansea there was a range of attitudes from apparent permissiveness (which was in fact parental control) to apparent strictness (which gave greater autonomy to the child): from Case 23 (bride's mother), and from pilot sample (bride's mother):

> 'I give them money when they ask for something and I never comes back from the shops without something for them – sweets and that. They moan sometimes that they don't get pocket money like other children, but I tell them "Look how much more in fact you get than the other kids".'

> 'I think it's very important in bringing up children to be strict on routine. I always gave them pocket money every Friday – I wasn't allowed to forget it – they bought whatever they wanted with it.'

The emphasis on routine is slightly more marked among s.e.c. II (who amongst other things can be sure of having spare money each week); but the most general attitude in Swansea is expressed by Case 6 (bride's mother): 'Her father gave her some every week [a few shillings] and if she wanted more, she came and asked me. Spoilt she was!' There was never a suggestion that children should earn their pocket money by doing odd jobs for their parents, though they earned money outside the home, e.g., working in a shop on Saturdays or delivering papers.

When my informants had started in a full-time job, most had reached an agreement with their parents – or rather with their mother – as to how much they should give her for their keep. Some, however, had handed over their whole pay packet (roughly one in five boys and one in sixteen girls) for anything from one to six years (i.e., until they were twenty-one).

Sociologists of the family have until recently ignored the distribution of income within the family (see chapter 7), along with calculative relations between family members generally, and one of the few accounts of young adults' handling of money at home comes from an industrial sociologist's attempt to explain why young women did or did not respond to bonus and other incentive schemes at work (Millward 1968). Those who were 'giving in' at home (handing over their pay packet to their mothers and getting a fixed amount of pocket money in return) were not interested in incentive payment schemes since these involved them in working harder for the same pocket money – unless the extra was given in a separate pay packet. Those who were 'on board' (paying their mother a fixed amount and keeping the rest) did 'respond'.

Millward also found that in the north of England girls usually started by 'paying in', which was justified by their parents in terms of the girls' unfamiliarity with handling large (sic) sums of money (though he suggests that it could be seen as reciprocity for the parents' past expense and a temporary arrangement in the readjustment of social relations – showing the 'child' was not trying to break away from the 'dependent' relationship with the parent). 'The occasion on which [she] changed from one arrangement to another is a significant event in the development of the family and the girl's search for independence.' In the past, he reported, it had been associated with some other event – e.g. one of the girl's birthdays (commonly eighteen), or engagement, or starting to save to get married, or on the birthday or engagement of an older sib. If the girl had replaced the father as the principal breadwinner the change would occur later; if both parents were working, earlier; among higher economic status families, later.

Millward found, however, that girls tended to renegotiate at home when their rates of pay were such that they saw they would be better off 'on board' – thus those with middle-class backgrounds got more pocket money and were better off 'giving in' for longer – and certainly part of the reason for the change-over being on a birthday was related to the wage increment received then. When the change took place other than at a recognised time (e.g., eighteenth birthday), there tended to be family arguments. He points out that since the period between leaving school and getting married is now very much shorter than in the past, and since juvenile pay rates and teenage expenditure aspirations are higher than in the past, 'adjustments in the social relationships between daughter and parents have to be made in a shorter time than before and may therefore be more stressful'.

In Swansea there was little uniformity about the terms used to describe financial arrangements[12] – which suggests a less formalized situation. Very rarely, however, did the housewife/mother get a substantial contribution from a 'child', though cf. Case 49:

When I asked the groom if he had ever thought of leaving home before he got married, he said that he had, because he didn't get on with his step-father, who he claimed was always out of work and 'a lazy sod'. He hadn't gone because 'My mother would have minded. She'd have had no money. [He had 5 young step-sibs, aged 4–14.] She depends on my money.' The bride laughed and said 'She'll have to manage without it soon', and the groom agreed. After the wedding I found out that his mother was now going out to work part-time.

Most who handed over their pay packets had done so when they were apprenticed, or just starting earning and getting low wages. Some held it to be 'old fashioned' or 'very Welsh'. The same pattern as Millward describes – of parents accepting a changeover which they decide on, but contesting one pushed through by the young person – was seen. Case outside sample; bride (wealthy, chapel going, Welsh-speaking family):

> 'I gave my mother my pay packet until about 2–3 years ago [i.e., until 21/22]. My mother suggested we change. She used to just give me what I wanted . . . some pocket money and some I had to put away. She bought me other things. She still buys me tights and underwear even now.'

Case 24 (bride):

> 'When I started work six years ago, I handed over my pay packet to my mother and she gave me pocket money. After a twelve month she gave it all back and took what she needed; that's £2, but £1 since we got engaged, and nothing for the last three months.'

Case 52 (groom):

> 'I stopped giving her lodge money when we got engaged. I told her I was saving to get married. She didn't like that. We had a row alright! I was quite prepared to walk out though.'

Case 5 (bride):

> 'She had £4.10s. out of me for keep when I was only earning £6, and £3.10s. when I was getting £4 dole. She's that mean, that tight!'

While all the informants who had started by giving over the whole pay packet and getting back pocket money had changed to handing over a sum each week before they got married, as the above quotations show, some were living at home gratis in the period shortly before their marriage. Those who were making some contribution to the housekeeping were often very careful not to reveal how much they paid their parents, but it was almost certainly about £2–£4 a week. This was quite a considerable addition to the mother's housekeeping money (which was about £9–£10 a week), especially since she no longer had to pay for their clothes, pocket money, and entertainment, but, of course, it was far less than the young people would have had to pay in rent, heat, light, and food if they were sharing a flat, and it meant that all of them tended to be ignorant of the cost of the living. As one mother said (Case 27):

'Before they got married my daughters wouldn't listen to a word I said about housekeeping. *Now* they do – or at least [the married] one does. They used to think that when I got three pounds a week off them they were being robbed. And when I asked for 2/6d a week rise – I thought the roof would blow off. I got it though! After all, you wouldn't pay less than £4.10s for bed and breakfast in lodgings, would you?'

She and her married daughter were much amused that the elder daughter (my informant) had been shopping for groceries for her new home, and had spent £7. She complained, 'But I got nothing for it – only a few tins, and some coffee – not a real meal amongst it . . .' The mother added, 'And *she* said to *me* "You've no idea how much things cost, mum!". Nor had that one [pointing at married daughter] till *she* got married.'

After her daughter's marriage a mother remains a fount of knowledge and superior skills on the subject of housekeeping and she may help her daughter by 'lending' her a pound (which often becomes a gift) if she runs out of house-keeping money before the end of the week. Then, as during childhood and adolescence, the mother uses her management of money to 'spoil' her children – and she makes them realise she *is* spoiling them. Case 21 (bride):

'I gave my mother board – £5 a week. I had good money and my father wasn't earning much [semi retired]. We all gave some. When my sister started work, she only got £2.15s. She said she'd give 15s! My mother told her to go away and live on her £2.15s. So she went to my aunty's. She [the aunt] said she'd want £2.10s, so my sister came back and gave it all to my mother. She [my sister] knew she'd get it back by the end of the week. As we wanted it, they gave it to us. Very generous parents. If we were asking too much of course, we wouldn't get it.'

Mother's 'help', voluntarily (or, as in case 52 above, involuntarily) by taking little money from those on low wages or doing training of one sort or another, from those on the dole – which may in part explain their disapproval of job changing – and from engaged couples who are saving up for household goods or a deposit on a house[13]. Young people recognise that they are profiting from their parents, and some are slightly embarrassed by their own instrumental attitudes and therefore joke about it. Case 44 (groom): 'I started off by giving in my pay packet till I was seventeen. When I started off I was on very *small* money – so I was better off. Then I changed my job and got big money [£18–20 a week] so knew how I'd be better off! Saw I was onto a good thing!'

Some, however, stress the value of self-reliance. Case 42 (bride):

'My sister used to give all her money over before she was married. My mother clothed her. She done it right up until she married, I think. Think she thought she came out better. She had plenty of clothes and went out a lot. But she didn't have any savings. Right from the start I gave in a certain amount. Bought my own clothes. I don't believe in handing it all over. You learn the value of money better if you organize it.'

In a few cases, the 'child' behaves rather like the head of the household *vis à vis* his or her mother. Case 2 (bride):

'When I first started working, I was only earning £4.10s [as a shop assistant in 1965]. My mother kept me completely free. Then I went to the Dolphin as a waitress and got £7 basic, which made up with tips to £24. I still didn't give her any, but I bought her a dining room suite, two bedroom suites and paid to have the house repapered, and a cocktail cabinet. And if I had any spare, she had it. I've had wonderful parents. They've never made me feel obligated. Never wanted to know how much I was earning or what I spent it on. Even when I was earning more than my father, when he came home [from sea], he'd give me two or three pounds.'

Thus the young wage-earner living at home has an economic relationship with his or her mother which is similar to the one the mother has with her husband: the 'child' hands over an 'allowance' to cover the purchase of food, etc. on the presumption that the mother labours 'for love'. But while the husband provides money for the wife's subsistence as well as his own, and if he is well off and well disposed he may provide her with a good standard of living, most adult children do not make such a contribution to their mother's well being. They strike a very good bargain *for themselves*.

'One of the most startling findings [of a National Opinion Poll survey] was about young earners at home. Single people earned £27 a week on average in June 1975, and of this they only contributed £6.68 to housekeeping money. Their earnings rose more during the year than those of married people. But they had not generally shared their good fortune with their mothers. Their weekly earnings went up by £3.45; of this only £1 went into the housekeeping money. The lions' share they kept for themselves, to spend on the clothes, holidays, records, hairdos, travel, drink and tobacco which constitute so much of the "luxury" spending of today. Mothers at this time of life who have barely enough for necessities could do worse than ask for something more from their unmarried children. The distribution of income between younger and older surely need not be quite so unequal as it apparently is.' (National Consumer Council 1975:6)

Why the parents – and in particular the mother – accept this situation will be discussed shortly.

The division of domestic work between adults in the home

Almost all the daily housework is done by the wife/mother – the cooking, cleaning and tidying, washing and ironing, bedmaking, sewing and shopping. The husband/father in South Wales may make and tend the fire, and he will do occasional work like painting and decorating, some house-hold repairs, and car maintenance. Either husband or wife will look after the garden, though allotments, if taken on, are almost exclusively male preserves. In addition the husband may 'give his wife a hand' with the washing up, and he may drive her to the shops and carry home the purchases on a Saturday, particularly if she has a job. But men almost never take care of (i.e., feed or change) babies or small children within the house, though they may 'keep an eye' on them and take them out for walks.

Among my informants, in families where the mother was dead, her housekeeping role had always been taken over by the eldest daughter living at home.

Case 16:

> One girl who was eighteen when her mother died had kept house while she was at school and later at university. The extent of her management is shown by her comment that 'My father used to give me his pay until two years ago [when he remarried]. He'd take from the bureau drawer what he needed for his spending money.' He had had exactly the same arrangement with her mother.

Case 51:

> Another, when I asked about her experience of domestic work, said: 'I've had years of housekeeping. [I was] only just eighteen when mother died – but I'd done it for a year before as she was in hospital. [Does your father help?] My father?! He can't lift a cup from there to there!' [pointing at two places on the carpet six inches apart]. This young woman had also taken over her mother's role in chivvying her married brothers and their wives and children to come and visit her father.

Where there was no teenage or adult daughter available, a grandmother or parent's sister was called on for help if there were young children, but in households consisting of a widower and a grown son they 'shifted as best [they] could'.

Housework in this culture is not seen as particularly skilled work – 'like all jobs it's a matter of practice', 'a lot of it is commonsense', and 'it just comes' – though certain tasks such as baking cakes or ironing a shirt are seen as more difficult than others. Some men can manage to cook themselves 'a fry up' and make a pot of tea if they come in when their mother/wife is out, or to help her when she is ill, and there is a recognition that young women cannot do housework 'naturally' – they have to learn by trial and error when they get married and have a house to look after.

Young and grown children living at home do very little domestic work. Girls do rather more than boys, but even girls do very little:

'I lay the table and fiddle around in the kitchen.'

'I cook occasionally – when my mother will let me – and I do my own washing.'

'I don't do much. I sometimes cook for Alan [boyfriend] and me, and occasionally I do some shopping or cleaning.'

This light load of domestic help is certainly not a peculiar feature of Swansea. A national survey of young women (aged 16–34) (British Market Research Bureau 1967) found that, among single girls, half hardly ever or never cooked a meal for themselves; a third never made their own beds or washed their own clothes or washed up after they had had a meal, or cleaned or dusted their own room; and a quarter hardly ever or never shopped for themselves. Still less did they do these things for other people. (There was little difference between working class and middle class girls in these respects.)

In Swansea most girls said they only helped when they felt like it or because they enjoyed it, and they did less once they started work than they had done while at school. Even in what might be seen as the critical case (cf. Bossard and Boll 1956) of girls who are the eldest of large families (over six children), only in one case (out of three) was the girl *required* to give regular help (washing up, bedmaking, and cleaning) – and then only at weekends. One informant (the second child in a family of four; the eldest daughter) whose mother had made her give regular help resented it. Case 5 (bride):

'I used to bath my brother and sister on Saturday nights till I was seventeen. And I used to stay in every Tuesday evening to do the ironing, and to do the washing up before going out. My mother was rather ill – she had a big womb op. a few years ago – and she rather played up on it. She's *got* to do (the housework) now and so she *does* it. It was very inconvenient for my mother to let me get married – I did a lot of work.'

But if girls do little, their brothers do less. Case 6:

> (To a couple: 'what do you [groom] do at home?'), (bride) 'Cause
> trouble! Don't listen to what he says [the groom was protesting that he
> helped with the washing up]. He gets the coal in and lights a fire once
> in a blue moon, and that's *all*.'

Case 15:

> 'My brothers do *nothing* – NOT A THING' (the last said very slowly).

Case 9:

> 'I used to ask if she wanted me to help and she said "Help me by
> keeping out of the way!".'

Pilot, groom:

> 'My mother is "a total woman", whether you like that or not. She's
> never asked us to do so much as make our own bed and she never will.'

Many of the young people were waited on by their mothers; their food
was put on the table in front of them, their rooms were cleaned, and their
dirty washing was removed and replaced automatically. Not only did
they do little, they felt they did little, and that their parents expected them
to do little; i.e., they did not feel harassed. Not surprisingly some of them
gave this as a reason for not leaving home – 'I know when I'm well off'.
Both generations justified this solicitude in terms of the long hours the
young people worked and the smaller size of present-day families.

It seemed to be anticipated that times were changing and new relationships would be different (at least initially):

Case 28 (bride):

> 'His breakfast's put on the table and his slippers are put by the fire. He
> won't get that from *me*.'

Case 4, groom's mother:

> 'I don't expect [my daughter-in-law] to slave all her life as I have. They
> don't nowadays. All my life has been giving to people; spoiling the
> menfolk. I love it. But you can't expect the young folk to do what I've
> done. I've carried a heavy burden all my life. Don't expect it now.'

There was also a general feeling that somehow children ought to do more
and that it was 'soft' of the parents/mother not to make sure that they did.
But in only two cases was there any sense of the children having been
trained to do their own domestic work[14]. More generally the sentiment
expressed was along the lines: Case 9 (bride's mother):

'Well, I mean, she hasn't had to do a lot. But I think she's quite capable. Well, I mean, she's working all day so I don't expect it. At weekends she helps dry up, and now – since she's been engaged – she does the odd bit of cooking. I let her get on with it – I don't actively encourage it.'

The lack of demand for help in the house by the mother is certainly not due to her interest in housework, for as housewives gain experience their involvement in housework 'tails off' and they declare themselves increasingly 'unsatisfied' with it later in life (BMRB 1967). One might, therefore, expect them to ask for help to free themselves so that they could go to work, or to bingo, or whatever. But, in fact, although the mothers of half my informants were working, the great majority were working part-time (see p. 32). This was specifically because it enabled them to earn a little extra money 'of their own' to buy luxuries to 'spoil the family', while not preventing them – as full-time work might have done – from doing all the housework and being in the house when the family was at home. This last is important, for while 'anyone can do housework if they try', managing the budgetting and interpersonal affairs of family members, guiding, controlling, and peace-keeping within the group, and 'making a house a home' are seen as needing 'a woman's touch'. Women are not 'by nature' better at housework, but they are supposedly 'naturally' better at keeping the family 'close'. They are held to be more sensitive to the needs and emotions of others, and more interested in maintaining links with kin and neighbours, and it is this ideology that keeps them confined in later life: 'A woman's place is in the home' in Swansea before and after marriage, with or without small children. A married woman should not get a job because she should actually *physically* be in the house as its affective and service centre. Unmarried women are expected to go out to work, but in their free time they should not go out too frequently. Fathers will complain if they see what they feel to be too little of their children – particularly if they see too little of their daughters: 'He likes to have us around the place', not to do housework, but for 'company'.

Finally, while it has been stressed that housework is not seen as difficult, it *is* seen as requiring practice, and there is often 'a knack of doing certain things'. Therefore, in the early days of marriage, young women find they need help and advice and they get this (*inter alia*) from their mothers – even if it is only on how to make non-lumpy gravy or to do household jobs quickly if they are still at work. Their mothers will often also give them physical help if they live sufficiently close, e.g., doing their washing, or popping in during the day and doing some cleaning. This is borne in mind by couples when choosing where to live after marriage.

'Spoiling' and keeping close

The 'myths' of adolescent revolt and rebellion spread by the media, social pathologists, and social scientists are based largely on professional middle-class norms and experience. They suggest that young people should/do want to leave their parents' homes before marriage to achieve (material and psychological) independence. But the material presented in this chapter shows that, with the exception of a small minority (pre-dominantly from middle-class backgrounds and/or in training for profes-sional middle-class jobs), young men and women do not leave home, though between a third and a half live away for a period. Why, one might ask, do they not 'escape' from the settled, domestic, community-regulated everyday world and the patterns of relationships established in their nuclear families of origin?

Some do escape to the big city, though they may try merely to ease but not to break their relationships with their families. Most do not seek even to leave the town, and whether they get on well with their parents (or step-parents) or not, they usually live with them. The reasons why have been partly answered by a consideration of the housing market, the concept of 'home' held by the actors, the social values attached to living at home, and the close, supportive emotional relationships to be found therein. Another part of the answer is that young people *do* escape from their nuclear family of origin: they marry young and form new house-holds. Enormous value is placed on attaining the adult status of being married and having a home of one's own; and the weight of socialization which is directed towards the goal of marriage and getting a home of one's own affects the attitude towards the short period between leaving school and getting married. Thus living away from home for one infor-mant 'never arose; it wouldn't have been worth the bother' (she started courting at sixteen and married at eighteen). The other side of this coin is that, for an older individual, living away from home might be seen as a sign of defeat: as having given up hope of marriage or of finding a marriage partner locally. But a major reason why young people accept the apparent continuation of their childhood situation (including parental interference in their activities before and after marriage) is that it is very much to their material advantage so to do.

The fact that the majority of young people live at home until they marry is of major structural importance. First, because it affects courtship pat-terns: whom one meets, the extent to which one shows commitment, the social (including parental) pressures to continue or discontinue a rela-tionship, and the amount of privacy possible for the development of emotional and sexual intimacy, etc. Secondly, it is important because it encourages marriage: to live alone or with another person one would have to leave the locality – unless, of course, one married the other person – and for the young people concerned, not having any private, comfortable, courting venue makes a home (or even a room) of their own and a marital bed seem delightful. Third, the continuing day-to-day dependence of children on parents means that young people have few goods and chattels or skill in domestic tasks before marriage – and parental help with these during and after the time of the wedding affects relationships in the elementary family.

The problem might perhaps rather be rephrased as, why do parents acquiesce in so unequal an exchange? Why, indeed, do parents have children in the first place, let alone encourage them to live at home when they are teenagers and young adults and cost so much to keep?

The answer lies in the fact that becoming adult, getting married, and having children are so closely related as to be virtually synonymous in our society, and that having children is an important form of conspicuous consumption and vicarious enjoyment of life. Parents certainly do not profit economically from having children nowadays – the young adults studied here do not work for their parents in family enterprises or at home, nor, when they start to earn good wages, do they hand over more than a bare minimum for their keep. Some – those out of work, students, and apprentices and those saving to get married – are a continuing drain on parental resources: they are fed, housed, and serviced for free.

Parents then, provide the home, domestic services, economic and emotional support, while young adults consume and 'reciprocate' by remaining at home and showing affection for their parents. The parents' immediate reward is the appreciation, respect, affection, esteem, and companionship of their children, and the status they gain in the local community from being 'good parents'. (In fact, the children also gain from this, for if the community sees the domestic group as constituting 'a good home' and 'a happy family', they benefit in the marriage market, since it is thought to auger well for the homes they will themselves create and the sort of spouse they will prove to be.) The parents are also – though more problematically – assured of care in old age, and contact with grandchildren.

Disagreement is always likely if equivalence in exchange is not seen as maintained, and since much of the child's response to material gifts is intangible ('affection', 'esteem') or in the future, and since, further, the exchange is informal, rows within the family might seem likely on Blau's analysis (1964). In this respect, the emphasis on *spoiling* seems important. It was mentioned above that adolescence has been described as a time of 'indulgence' in the working class. But the indulgence described for South Wales occurs also in the local middle class and lasts through babyhood, childhood, adolescence, and into adulthood and continues after marriage. It could be claimed that all parents 'spoil' their children – love them, care for them, give they whatever they can – and that this is always a mechanism for keeping the children in contact with their parents and psychologically dependent. As Mauss (1954) says, if people accept your gifts, you own a part of their soul; they return your affection and allow you to have some say (rights) in their lives. But the concept of 'spoiling' stresses that what the parent gives is over and above what a good parent should be expected to give. In part the child thinks that the return for this cannot be expected from him or her, but comes from the parents' own pleasure, self-satisfaction, and status achieved in the community, or security for the future. But the child does also agree that he or she *is* spoilt – 'we really don't thank her enough', 'she really does too much', 'she waits on us hand and foot' – and stays more firmly in the house – 'I know when I'm on to a good thing'. The elements in the exchange which swing the material balance in the child's favour are carefully defined as lying largely outside the sphere of parental obligation, i.e., the grossest exploitation is recognised as spoiling. It is used as the basis for the establishment of an obligation by the child to 'keep close'.

While Swansea society is not itself particularly achievement orientated, it is part of a society whose dominant (bourgeois) ethic is individual achievement. Hence some norms governing parent-child interaction make illegitimate the desire of Swansea parents to keep young adults psychologically, socially, and geographically 'close'. Justification has to be found and this is done by 'spoiling' the child: giving the child benefit over and above what is required by the societal norms governing the parental role is used to place the child under an obligation to exceed the demands made upon them by the norms governing the filial role.

What then becomes problematic is why the universal expectation that parents will go beyond their duty ('spoiling') has not resulted in a redefinition of that duty which fits more closely what they actually do. There is a standard of what should be done, and an expectation that parents will overfill it; why do the normative and the factual expectations not elide? Perhaps it is because parents can 'swing the norms' on their children – can convince their children that what they (the parents) do is *generous* and not just what any good parent would do – if they operate in a homogeneous culture where parental standards are unlikely to be challenged, *and* where the ultimate goals are the same in both generations. Swansea is a closed market where the value of the parents' resources cannot be assessed against outside standards[15]. But, perhaps more important, the grown children do not seek to challenge the evaluations, since they feel they benefit from the arrangement.

Differentiation of power does not necessarily constitute a strain towards change in the structure of social relations. *Mere* power is a hardship from which to escape; but the short and long-term advantages derived may be seen to outweigh the hardships entailed in submission. If those who exercise power are seen as exploitive and oppressive, the reaction is disapproval and antagonism, and if the oppressed communicate their anger and aggression to one another their support reinforces the negative orientation. But, conversely, if the underlings agree that the demands made on them are only fair and just in view of the ample rewards, and if they see their generation as coming to power in its turn, feelings of obligation and loyalty to elders are fostered and legitimating authority is bestowed on them.

So far 'the parents' have been treated as unitary, whereas, of course, the situations of the husband/father/wage earner and the wife/mother/ unwaged (or very low waged) worker are different.

In the world outside the home, which is largely the world of men, exploitation of age-classes is evident, even if hitherto little explored – partly because the boundaries between the 'classes' is vague (Harris 1974). However, the young and old *are* kept 'at arms' length' from full membership of society (see Holt (1974) on children and Townsend (1957) on the old), and in the labour market young and elderly men may form part of the poorly paid, insecure, secondary labour market (along with most working women, the disabled and the blacks – see Baron and Norris 1976) upon which many of the benefits of primary sector workers depend.

In the family, in contrast, although property and financial aid (primarily of significance in the upper and middle classes) pass almost exclusively from older to younger generations and are the means of continuing control of the young, children, and the elderly depend on (i.e., consume) goods purchased with wages, and the domestic labour and nursing of adults: i.e., on the household head and his wife. However, since there is no evidence that the 'wages' for housekeeping passed from the male breadwinner to the female housekeeper in the lower middle and working classes increase proportionately with the number of dependents to be cared for (see Young 1952; Grey 1974; N.C.C. 1975), it can be argued that the dependents, young and old, use (exploit) predominantly the ability of *the housewife* to budget and to supplement deficiencies of cash with her own labour.

The mother's continuing 'spoiling' – gratis provision of her time, labour, skill, and financial aid – after her son or, more particularly, her daughter marries, holds the elementary family together at a time of potential schism. It is thus *her* unpaid work as part of her marriage relationship that gives her (*and her husband*) rights in the lives of their children and grandchildren, and which further increases her (*and her husband's*) basis for a claim to care in old age (a claim which is, in fact, generally fulfilled in Swansea, see Harris 1974). She is assigned responsibility for the young and the old and must labour to care for them and minister to them emotionally. But her husband reaps with her such returns as there may be.

Notes

1. *Figure 1* Place of upbringing of my informants

	1st marriage		2nd marriage	
	women	*men*	*women*	*men*
lived all/most of life in the same house or lived all/most of life in Swansea and district*	45	38	4	3
home in Swansea at time of marriage, but lived most of life elsewhere	3	3	0	0
home not in Swansea: 'outsiders'**	2	8	0	2
N	50	49	4	5

* Immediate district – Gower, Felindre, and Clydach
** All in middle-class occupations or students.

2. Margaret Wynn shows that adolescents cost as much or more to keep than adults, whereas younger children cost less than a half (Wynn 1972).
3. As described, for example, by parents taking part in the Harvard Growth Study (a longitudinal study, 1930–50) (Butler 1956).
4. Of course it is true that one reason why there seemed to be so little conflict between my informants and their parents was because interviewing is not a good way of finding out about domestic conflicts, especially when the interviews take place within the home. I think from participant observation of my neighbours that the period when adult children are living at home clearly *is* marked by certain kinds of conflict – many of which are ritualized. But this is not inconsistent with my central point: that the children do not seek to leave home and that they are made dependent in a variety of (economic, social, and psychological) ways.
5. Of those women marrying for the first time who were not employed,
   – one looked after her widowed father. She had jobs from time to time – what they were varied (telephonist, barmaid, bread van driver) – but she would 'get all behind at home', and would then give it up for a time till she got bored in the house;

- one was living as a wife. She was the mother of the child of the man whom she married (when his first wife divorced him);
- the daughter of a company director, and probably the most well-off family in my sample, had given up work to prepare for the wedding. This had been arranged at short notice, and afterwards she and her husband were going abroad;
- one had left home to live with her boyfriend and gave up her job for the week their menage lasted (see pp. 49–50); and
- two women entering their second marriage were not working because they had small children.

6. *Figure 2* Earnings in Swansea in 1967

(a) *females*	Age	lowest £	highest £	average £	N
	17	6.00	8.50	7.41	8
	18	5.65	8.66	7.28	6
	19	5.80	9.00	7.77	3
	20	7.00	12.47	9.87	3
				8.07	20

(b) *males*	Age	lowest £	highest £	average £	N
	17	5.00	10.50	7.04	11
	18	2.50	20.00	9.25	21
	19	7.50	16.00	11.07	8
	20	12.47	22.00	15.66	3
				10.75	43

Source: May (1968). Figures converted to decimal currency.

The national average wage in 1967 for a full-time male manual worker was £21.38 and a female manual worker £10.56; for male non-manual worker £27.90 and female non-manual worker £14.90 (Dept of Employment 1974:61; Table 36).

7. Abrams survey (1961) showed that among working-class 15–25 year olds, two thirds of all spending is done by males, since they have half as much money again to spend as females. This discrepancy is less marked among the middle class, and least among students, whose grants are not, by and large, sex discriminatory.

8. Home is a place *and* a group of people. It is not only (indeed for young people, not mainly) the place where one lives at present, but also the place (house, town, region, or country) from which one comes – where one was born and

raised – and to which one 'properly belongs' (*Shorter Oxford English Dictionary* 1956) Within this place are presumed to be one's closest kin and family, and particularly one's mother. On this person, this group, and this place much of one's affections centre. In Swansea, to say that someone is a 'proper home bird', or a 'real home pigeon' is to comment favourably on them (and also, of course, on their home). These are values which one would probably find throughout most of Britain – urban or rural – but it is possible that they are particularly marked in Wales, where, as remarked in chapter 2, there is a marked 'locality consciousness'.

9. Three other couples also lived together – longer term – before they were married: one couple in a different town from both sets of parents, the other two under parental roofs.

Case 38:

Two university students had shared a flat for a year. They were, however, rather bashful about this and told me 'We were both in hall in our first year. We met and were going around together for most of that year. But in fact it was purely accidental – we were both just looking for a flat in our second year, and we could neither of us get anyone else to share. But we had trouble avoiding the accommodation office [students of opposite sex were not supposed to live in the same lodgings] and people were talking. So we decided to go straight, and David got a flat round the corner in the third year.' (They were married in the March of that academic year.)

Case 19:

Another couple had lived together for four years – since the woman became pregnant. They married as soon as his first wife divorced him. It had been generally assumed by neighbours and friends and put about by her mother that they were already married.

Case 51:

A woman aged 18 whose parents had refused consent to her marriage returned to Swansea after a short period in London with her fiancé and lived in his parents' house until official consent was obtained from the Magistrates' Court. (For further details see chapter 4 pp. 99–102.)

10. It is therefore worth noting that, in contrast to my findings, Firth, Hubert, and Forge, in their study of affluent middle-class north Londoners, found that the majority of people in their sample of 30 households were migrants to London and in most cases both men and women had been living away from home for some time before they married. (There is no detailed information on men, but two-thirds of the women had lived away from home, all for over a year and the majority for five years or more.) The majority of those interviewed in Highgate had moved to London before they married – for training or jobs; and in two-thirds of the cases the couple had met in London. The siblings of these people had also been geographically mobile, though usually not to London. About a third of the members of the households sampled had lived with kin

after leaving home; frequently this involved young people (particularly young women) staying with a married sister or cousin, or with an aunt or grandmother, while training or starting work (Hubert 1965). In *Middle Class Families and their Relatives* (Firth, Hubert, and Forge 1970) they stress that it was expected that a son or daughter would leave home when adult, and boarding school, university education, and staying with kin were seen as useful intermediaries for training in independence. It was a strongly held norm that grown-up sons and daughters (married or unmarried) should not be dependent for day-to-day service and emotional support on their parents (or vice-versa), though they should be able to call on them in times of crisis.

Bell's study of two middle-class housing estates in Swansea found a rather more mixed situation, with only a quarter of the wives having lived away from home for more than two years before they married (Bell 1968:97). (Note, however, that both these accounts of middle-class life bother to give more information on women living away from home than men living away from home, reflecting the cultural expectation that the former is more of a problem.)

11. Most local housing authorities will not accept applications from any single person under 30, many put the threshold at 40, a few at retirement age. And a place on the council's list is anyway not likely to yield very much, since 'points' go mainly to those who are 'overcrowded', i.e., not the single. House purchase is difficult, especially for single women who have low incomes and are considered poor risks, and joint mortgages with another single person are frowned upon by Building Societies. This leaves only the overcrowded and declining private rented sphere, now effectively the private *furnished* rented sphere (though there was unfurnished accommodation still available, at a price, if one was lucky in Swansea in 1967). As the older bedsitter houses are pulled down or converted into 'family flats', there is no new single person housing being constructed. The needs of the single are generally not considered by national or local government or speculative builders – except when they are a 'threat' or a 'problem', e.g., old people staying on and occupying 'family' housing on their own, and young people squatting or being in 'moral danger' in the big cities.

12. Some informants spoke of 'handing over' or 'giving in my pay packet', or 'giving all my money over', as against 'giving lodge money', 'keeping myself', 'giving an allowance', or, most commonly, 'giving my mother so much every week'.

13. Firth, Hubert, and Forge (1970) also report that among their middle-class families there were instances of sons and daughters staying at home and getting lodgings below the market rate while making a small contribution to family finances. They cite one case where the mother kept all the money her son gave her and handed it back to him when he married.

14. Case 23:

One English father, who had come to Swansea as a floorman (senior foreman) with a newly established branch factory of a light engineering factory centred on the midlands, said of his children:

'We brought both the boys up to be very well domesticated – they can iron or cook or change a nappy. They are both living away now, which is good for them; it makes them stand on their own feet. But they're that independent now it hurts. But it's a good thing. Brings out a streak that they know as much about life as you. You have to wait for them to tell you what they've been doing, rather than feeling able to ask questions. Nor do they seek advice – nor should they. I didn't either. You want other people's views than your parents'. They know where they're going, and they're determined. They can get by on their own.

Many people round here can't understand it. But the world's too tied up with people who try to look after other people. It's catastrophic, this running home – for the relation of husband and wife, I mean. Again, I have no brothers and sisters so I can't discuss my problems. I've got no-one to help me get around my problems, so I solve them instead. If you've got all those [people] backing you up, you lean on them for dependence.'

This is an interesting case, for it represents the antithesis of the aims of Swansea parents.

15. Various reasons for this homogenity have been suggested in the chapter:
    – children go to local schools and often to local colleges and are less aware of alternative norms and values;
    – self-recruitment of teaching staff in the schools;
    – lack of formal peer groups (and thus of a strong alternative youth culture) because of short period of schooling;
    – little class differentiation: little variation in life-styles visible;
    – those who do not accept the values have left the town.

4 Courtship, leisure, and friendship

'I would that there were no age between ten and three-and-twenty, or that youth would sleep out the rest; for there is nothing in between but getting wenches with child, wronging the ancientry, stealing and fighting.' (Shakespeare, *A Winter's Tale*, III·iii·62).

From the writings of family sociologists one might be forgiven for thinking that there *is* 'no age between ten and three-and-twenty', and from the writings on adolescence that today there is no activity of young people beyond work and school, delinquency, and youth clubs. I shall try to remedy some of these deficiences by focusing on the social aspects of the heterosexual activity of young people, using my own material and other sources[1] to sketch a general picture of the leisure and courtship[2] of unmarried people in Swansea. I shall then outline the changes in their leisure activities and friendship patterns with age, and the effects of these of the development of stable heterosexual relationships.

Two caveats must be entered about the material I am using. First, there is a lack of agreed terminology for the early stages of courtship which makes it difficult to establish the history of the individual, or of the particular couple's relationship. My informants were always uncertain as to how to describe the less committed forms of interaction: one could 'have a date', or 'go out' with someone, but there is no noun corresponding to these phrases. There is certainly no formalized, named, stage corresponding to American 'dating'[3]. Note, for example, Case 10:

(How long did you know each other before you started going out together?)
(Groom) 'About the first week in February [i.e. after 4 months].
(To his wife) You know these dates better than I do.' (She confirmed what he had said.)
(What did you call it? dating? courting? going out?)
(Groom) 'I tried never to call it anything!'

Some informants used 'courting' to refer to relationships involving a considerable commitment to a partner, but many regarded this as an old-fashioned term, and they would use 'going out with, you know, seriously', or 'going with', or 'going steady', often specifically bemoaning the lack of the right word. Sometimes they resorted to sketching the shared activities, their frequency, and their commitment: 'We'd meet occasionally at a dance and he'd see me home, but nothing serious.'

'Engaged' and 'engagement' (and of course 'married' and 'marriage') were the only terms of whose usage and meaning my informants were certain, and where there was agreement between the members of a couple and in the sample as a whole. (This is, however, partly a feature of my sample, which contained only couples very shortly before their wedding. Some 'engaged couples' may be in discord as to whether or not they *are* 'engaged'[4].) Engagement for my informants meant a firm commitment to marry in the future, to start saving and making plans for the future household, and, above all, to stop going out with any other member of the opposite sex. The agreement was usually marked by the outward and visible sign of a special type of ring.

The absence of terms referring to less committed relationships is partly a reflection of the attitude of the culture towards sexuality (see pp. 28 and 287). The full expression of sexuality is permissible (indeed, enjoined) within marriage and it is therefore possible to talk about formal and informal commitment to marry. But unformalized interaction between the sexes, where sexuality is part of the purpose of the interaction, is regarded with embarrassment and anxiety. Hesitancy is also evinced because of the extensive games-playing and competiveness of courtship: each partner may have a 'line', and each try to persuade the other of his or her involvement while resisting being emotionally overcome – so as to retain power and control.

Second, even had there not been vagueness among informants due to the lack of clear terminology, such information as recalled age of first going out with a member of the opposite sex is likely to be faulty, since the reputation of the informant is seen to be involved. And, since events throw their shadows backwards as well as forwards, particular points are likely to be seen as crucial when the relationship is to be consummated in marriage, which would have been forgotten if the relationship had ended. Like all oral history, one must accept that these are reconstructions of the past from the point of view of the present.

The courtship career

In our culture, adolescence is seen as essentially a phase of development (a point which will be developed in chapter 8), and this is particularly true of adolescent sexuality and courtship. Each individual is thought to pass through a courtship career as he or she matures physiologically, psychologically, and socially – moving from tentative experimentation with relationships with the opposite sex (and occasional homosexual 'crushes'), through the establishment of heterosexual courting relationships, to the goal of an exclusive, permanent, coital relationship in marriage. There is a sense that the stages and types of relationship passed through are 'achieved abilities', with each subsequent relationship more 'advanced' than the last. (For the reflection of this in sociological literature, see Schofield's (1968) charts of 'accumulative incidence curves' for kissing, dating, breast stimulation over clothes, etc.) But, of course, in practice the acquisition of an 'ability' (or, rather, having had an experience) does not entail subsequent practice, and individuals may (and often do) 'regress' to activities and relationships characteristic of supposedly earlier 'stages'. Having had a courting relationship, she or he may 'revert' to casual dating; having had intercourse in one relationship, she or he may seek or be content with manual stimulation in the next.

In Swansea the actors share the ideology of moving through courtship towards marriage. Though particular individuals may feel they can 'mess around' until they are eighteen or so, generally each new relationship is seen in terms of its possible future and assessed against what are seen as relevant constraints: when one ought to do things (the right age to marry), and when one can afford to do things. For girls in particular there is little sense of enjoying the time when one is young and free, or enjoying a relationship for what it is at a particular time: there is always concern with where a relationship is leading, and with getting married.

In only a minority of cases did my informants marry the first person with whom they had established a courting relationship, although only a few (6 per cent of those marrying for the first time) had been engaged before. Prior to establishing committed relationships most had had early experience of interaction between groups of boys and groups of girls, and later of occasional, once or twice off, outings with a member of the opposite sex.

In outline, courtship appeared to start between the ages of twelve and fourteen for both sexes (i.e., before leaving school). Girls entered a courting relationship at about sixteen and boys at eighteen, and after 2–4 such relationships, women started a relationship with their eventual husband at eighteen, became engaged at nineteen, and married at twenty-one. Men had 0–2 courting relationships before starting a relationship with their eventual wife at just under twenty, becoming engaged at twenty-one, and marrying at twenty-two[5]. A substantial minority of men (1 in 5 of my informants) married the first girl with whom they had a serious relationship (cf. the remarks on this subgroup by Gorer 1955:85), whereas only 1 in 14 of the women I interviewed married their first steady boyfriend.

I tried to ascertain whether there were stages seen within courtship and how long these lasted. For example, I asked a question as to when it had been established that they were actually going to marry each other: when they had decided that 'this was it'. To this in half of all cases I received an answer referring to when they had fixed the date for the wedding. When I persisted, rephrasing the question, many simply did not get my meaning. Others effectively pointed out the presuppositions within *my* problematic: for them there had never been a time when they had *not* been considering whether they might not marry. The very fact of the continuation of the relationship presupposed that they were thinking of marrying each other. The point of decision was not *whether* they would marry, but *when* they would marry. Those who could pin-point a time when they made a decision had done so on average just over a year after starting courtship, often precipitated by jealousy, or after a period of separation (e.g., one of them going away on holiday).

In all cases when the couple or the bride could actually remember the question 'will you marry me?' or 'shall we get engaged/married?' being asked, it was the man who asked the woman. In only one case was it asked in a direct way in a carefully chosen place. Quite frequently it was asked obliquely ('How would you like to be Helen *Jones*?') and in what were seen as unromantic settings (e.g., sitting in his car after an evening out). In only about a quarter of cases was the woman surprised by the question, and then generally the surprise was that it had been asked so soon.

It is a firmly held norm that boys/men should be 1-3 years, but ideally two years, older than the girls/women they go out with and marry. In adolescence this age disparity is explained in terms of girls maturing earlier and thus needing to associate with older boys if they are to meet those who are interested in the same things (specifically, of course, in courtship); but at the time of marriage it seems to be associated more with the presupposition that the husband will be superior to his wife on a whole range of dimensions – age, height, strength, activeness, aggressiveness, and IQ, *inter alia*. Those who went so far as to contravene this by marrying men younger than themselves[6] were defensive:

Case 4:

> (How old were you when you first met?)
> (Bride) 'I was 26. He was 20.'
> (The next question was put)
> (Bride) 'Aren't you going to comment [on ages]? Most do [rather bitterly].'

Case 37:

> (How old were you when you met?)
> (Bride) 'I was 20 and he was 19! [In fact 6 months age gap. She grinned.] I was a bit self-conscious about it at first. Friends teased and said I was "cradle snatching". But he acts a lot older than me anyway, so it's alright, isn't it?'

Not surprisingly, given the present-day uniformity of age at marriage (see chapter 1) the length of a successful courtship varied inversely with the age at which the relationship was established. Thus I found that girls who at the age of fourteen started to go out regularly with the boy they eventually married, married on average six years later; those who started at the age of seventeen married three years later; and those who commenced the relationship at eighteen married two years later. Thereafter the numbers are too small to make generalizations, except that the period of courtship was about 1-2 years, seldom more and seldom less. While there are strong norms about the right age to marry, there are also strong norms against 'hasty' marriage and as to the minimum length of a respectable courtship[7].

Previous descriptions of courtship have not given very detailed accounts of durations, but they do show the same pattern, as I found – the majority of relationships lasting 1–3 years, with very few marrying after having known each other for less than six months or more than five years[8]. The Population Investigation Committee found a similar pattern in all social classes in their national sample. They also found that courtship had not contracted with the fall in the marriage age (people merely started courting younger), but that it had varied with general conditions (longer during the '30s depression, shorter during the war) (Pierce 1963).

For those who leave school at the minimum leaving age, and specifically for the working class, the time between leaving school and getting married has been described as 'a brief flowering period' (Hoggart 1957) in which youth is indulged and has its 'fling' before 'going steady' and 'settling down'. But it also needs to be stressed that (as shown in the last chapter) for the great majority this 'fling' does not include removal from the parent's house and control; and, further, that its duration is getting shorter and shorter. In 1900 youngsters left school at 12–14 and the average age at marriage was twenty-seven for men and twenty-five for women; but in Swansea in the late 1960s the time between leaving school at fifteen or sixteen and getting married at 21–24 was a median of five years for women and six for men, of which several years might be involved in training for a job, 'serious' courtship, and thinking about a forthcoming marriage[9]. One in five of my female informants started 'going steady' with the man she eventually married when she was sixteen or younger, and almost all had begun the relationship with their future husbands before they were twenty. Thus most girls are involved in serious consideration of marriage to a particular man during most of their teens.

Changes in leisure, peer groupings, and courtship with age.

Much vagueness and confusion has resulted in writing on adolescence – particularly adolescent leisure activities – because all the development and changes associated with an 8–10 year period have either been grouped together (often with no distinction made by sex), or because a particular age span – be it 15–18, or 17–20 – has been abstracted and studied, often for no better reason than convenience or the funders' policy interests. Consequently the period seems to be one of turmoil. I hope to avoid this by showing how leisure activities and peer groupings change, and how they integrate with courtship, as children become adolescents and then adults.

(1) Age related changes in leisure activities and relationships with the family of origin

The change from childhood to adolescence is seen as related to puberty, when an 'irresistible sap' starts to rise in the veins of youth (Hadow Report 1926). Its presence is signalled by the youngster's increased concern with the opinion of age mates, a decline in acceptance of parental and school authority, 'selfishness', and starting to take an interest in the opposite sex. Great importance becomes attached to spending time with peers, which is opposed to spending time with family members, and leads to some degree of conflict between the child and his or her parents. Because of the decline in interest and attention at school, there is often conflict with teachers. The tension at home and school to which the change of life interests gives rise leads the young person to see his or her elders as agents of control. It is not surprising, therefore, that, as Smith points out,

> 'Young people refer much less often than adults to their "leisure time" – they use the term *"free* time" or *"spare* time", and it is this theme of freedom from supervision and control which runs through their choice of leisure time activities. Going out – getting away from adults – may be more important than what they do when they arrive wherever they are going. The paradox of the emphasis on free time is that it is combined very often with the complaint from these youngsters that they have "time on their hands" and "nothing to do". They want to be going somewhere, but they have nowhere to go.' (Smith 1966:15)

This is compounded by the fact that they have little money (usually less than £1 a week in 1968/9) to spend. The small amount of pocket money they get regularly is spent on sweets, cigarettes, and make-up; they have to ask their parents each time they want to pay for entertainment (e.g., to go to a dance hall or the cinema).

Young people of 12–14 or 15 when they go out usually gravitate to places patronized almost solely by their peers: places which are cheap, make no demands on them, have the music that they like, and where they can meet their friends and 'chat up' members of the opposite sex. These meeting places (cafés, ice-cream parlours, recreation grounds, and chip shops) often have a reputation (amongst adults) as the haunts of 'lay-abouts', and in consequence some parents try to stop their children going to them. But parental opposition is an added spice for an age group which is attempting to show its independence of familial authority, and conflict becomes ritualized around the time the young person has to get in at night, and how many nights they go out each week, and the clothes and make-up they wear. Girls have to be in earlier, and even more complaints are made about the frequency of their going out and where they go to, than are made to boys.

The desire for acts of bravado is seen also in the start of smoking and drinking. Two studies of adolescent drinking in Swansea (Cahill 1969; Thomsell 1969) found that the average age for having the first alcoholic drink with friends was thirteen or fourteen for both boys and girls. Characteristically the occasion involved a group of youngsters buying cider from an off-licence and drinking in up a side street. For boys there is often a spell of wild drinking at about the age of 15–16, when they first look old enough to get served in a pub[10]. For many boys this is the first time they have got drunk – a new experience and a pleasurable flouting of the law. Girls are always more restrained in their drinking. In general it is held that there is nothing more despicable than a drunk woman; and more specifically it is suggested that a girl will be 'taken advantage of' while incapacitated and will thus end up pregnant. In any event there is not the same possibility of social drinking, for young women will only go into a pub when accompanied by young men, and they are dependent upon drinks being bought for them.

There is generally a decline in 'going out' between the early and mid-teens, associated with a change in type of leisure activity (Smith 1966). The sixteen and seventeen-year-olds may go out less, but when they do go out, they go *somewhere*. For a year or so after leaving school the money young people earn (especially if they are training or apprenticed) may be too limited to pay for entertainment every night, and so they stay at home. But as they get older, boys in particular go out with greater frequency, and stay out later. This is partly because they rapidly come to earn substantially more than girls; but it is also because there is less parental pressure on them to stay at home; less control over where they go; they have wider interests than girls, and because the male peer group and the pub become increasingly important.

> A study of twenty-four non-apprenticed boys aged 15–17 (i.e., on 'good money' for their age group) employed in a steel works in the Lower Swansea Valley, found that 29 per cent of them went out seven evenings a week, and a further 58 per cent went out four to five evenings a week and on Saturday afternoons and evenings.
>
> On a Saturday evening the majority went to the pictures, the rest went to a dance or a club (many of them drank regularly, though they were all under age). On other evenings they might play soccer, go to a youth club, go fishing, or go to a pub.
>
> On Sundays, they stayed at home during the day, often in bed in the morning, but they went out again in the evening, some to church. They thus spent little time around the house with their family. Their main friendships were with other boys from their home area. Their interaction with girls consisted of an occasional date. (Hopwood 1963)

To say that boys have wider interests than girls should definitely not be taken as meaning that in more than a few cases a youth takes part in a great many different activities; rather, the range of things to do which are thought acceptable is much wider for boys than for girls, and most boys 'keep up' one or two hobbies. In particular, they are catered for by public facilities (in youth and sports clubs). They play football, athletics, squash, and music in bands; they go fishing, mend and drive cars or motor bikes, play cards, darts or snooker, go to cadets, etc. – and to the pub. Teenage girls seem to reject all their earlier activities (horse riding, sport, judo, Girl Guides, playing music, ballet or ballroom dancing) as 'childish' or 'unfeminine'. They give up going to youth clubs because their interests are not catered for, because the activities are sex segregated, because they feel they are under instruction ('and they cannot teach you kissing'), and because the boys who go to youth clubs are either not interested in girls, or not interested in them in the context of the youth club[11] (Hanmer 1964, Atteridge 1965, Parnham 1966).

In their later teens young women spend a lot of time at home and develop companionate relationships with their mothers, while young men tend to work increasingly long, irregular hours and are drawn into the male peer group with its regular pub-going (though some of their pub-going may be 'within the family', i.e., with their father or brother). When they are courting, girls generally entertain their boyfriend in their own homes, rather than the two of them spending time at his house. The concern in the literature with what young people do when they go out should not be allowed to obscure the fact that they spend most of their leisure time at home – watching TV, listening to records, talking to friends, sibs, parents and kin, reading (cf. the high magazine 'penetration' in the 16–19 age group (IPC 1969)), 'moaning', or sleeping. In a study of leisure in Cardiff (Crichton, James and Wakeford 1962) 16 per cent of youths and 5 per cent of girls were found to had been out every night the previous week, but 5 per cent of both sexes had been *in* every night.

Two-thirds of young people leave school at fifteen or sixteen and take jobs. Those who stay at school till eighteen have leisure affected by a heavy load of homework and by having little spending money. They are a considerable financial burden on their parents and some parents certainly put pressure on their children to gain the maximum advantage from their continued schooling by not staying out late and by joining school societies. In some cases parents discourage boy or girlfriends as 'distracting'. The study of leisure in Cardiff just referred to found that grammar-school pupils went out less than secondary modern (or ex-secondary modern) school pupils aged 15–18, but that they took part in a more diverse range of activities – sports, religious and formal organizations, holidays abroad, etc.

My informants and my neighbours' children who were in paid employment in their late teens had a fairly well-established adult role within the home, and parents appeared to enjoy the adult companionship of their children (particularly mothers and daughters). This warmer atmosphere within the home may be one factor encouraging young adults to go out less. The leisure pursuits of those in their late teens (see May 1968) are much the same as those of unmarried people in their twenties. They have sufficient money not to need youth clubs or coffee bars, and they avoid such places because they want to keep separate from those younger than themselves. This is one reason for the popularity of pubs, clubs, and licensed dance halls, where (officially) no one under eighteen may be admitted and/or drink alcohol. It seems surprising, therefore, that so little mention has been made of 'drinking' as a social activity and pubs as meeting places, in previous work on courtship and marriage, or on teenage leisure and spending (though on leisure, see Leigh 1971).

Certainly for many young men in Swansea, pub-going is their major spare time occupation and interest. (When asked their religious denomination, some jokingly affiliated themselves to their local pub: 'I'm a Cape Horner!') 'Drinking' is a social activity: only rarely will a young man go to a pub to drink on his own. Members of the male pub-based peer group not only drink together, they also play football together, and may fight side by side when they decide that other people need 'sorting out'. Indeed 'companionship and drinking are pretty well complimentary for them after 8.00 pm' (Cahill 1969). Male drinking is often competitive and has peer group approval. It also sometimes has importance as an initiation ceremony – a fifteen or sixteen-year-old may be bought his (supposedly) first drink by his workmates when he starts work; or a boy may be introduced by his father and enrolled into the father's social club on his eighteenth birthday. (See also drinking and stag and hen parties – chapter 5.) It certainly consumes a lot of money and, because of this, 'heavy drinking' is given up by some aficionados when they start to save up to get married.

Young women also go to pubs, but they will almost never enter one alone to meet a group inside – rather they will meet a girl-friend (at her home or elsewhere in town) and go in with her, or, more likely, they will go with a boy-friend. When a woman goes to a pub it is not 'to drink' – she may have a couple of drinks (sherry, vodka and orange, lager and lime, or proprietary drinks – Pony, Babycham, Cherry B, etc.), but not the several pints of beer and couple of scotches men consume – and not to get drunk. She goes to meet men, or to be with a man. He goes to drink, to play darts, to tell stories, and to talk with his mates. She talks to his mates' girl-friends. Both join in if there is a 'sing-song'. Local pubs are used more for drinking and by those going steady, and town centre ones for first meetings.

(2) Courtship related changes in peer groupings and leisure activities

The early stages of the courtship career are characterized by the lack of specificity in the interaction between the sexes, and a spirit of adventure. It is quite common to see twelve or thirteen-year-old girls hanging around the corridors of their school (if it is co-educational) or on street corners after school, in the hopes of seeing boys, and then cheeking them and giggling (Aubrey 1968), and two single sex peer groups may coalesce from time to time. One such peer group was studied on a council housing estate in Swansea (Speed 1968)[12].

> The group consisted of a core of five girls, all from the same grammar school, though not in the same class, and all living within easy reach of each other. They all met every night – following a complex ritual of 'calling for each other' to go out. It was important to have a friend in order to get out, and one could sanction a friend by not calling for her because she would not then want/be able to go out on her own.

> On Mondays, Wednesdays, and Thursdays the girls went to one youth club, and on Fridays to another (church) youth club. On Tuesdays they went to a café or to each others' houses, where they played records and gossiped. At the weekends they might go window shopping in twos

and threes, or to watch football, and in the evenings they went to the chip shop or the pictures or the Top Rank (a respectable dance hall in the town centre).

The group was friendly with three different groups of boys of the same age; one which hung around a corner near one of the girl's houses; one they met in town; and a third at the chip shop. Some outings with these boys would end in visits to the cinema, where they would pair off and kiss.

In public the girls created a great deal of noise, clowning, and a certain amount of horseplay. This exhibitionistic behaviour was part of the group goal – drawing the attention of boys. But should one girl start seeing too much of one boy she was drawn back into the group by her friends ridiculing her choice, by their ignoring her (e.g., by not calling for her), or by their whispering about her in front of her. Friends were felt by the girls to be very important 'to go places with, to stick by you in trouble, and share problems (chiefly about parents) with you and to talk to'.

More generally, also, the interests of group members were constrained by the group ideology – one girl who would have liked to go to the Top Rank to dance more often was persuaded against as the others preferred local boys; and one who would have liked to have been a nursery nurse was going to do shorthand typing because her friends were going to do this.

Within the schoolgirl clique most girls have a single 'best friend' with whom they are very intimate and on whom they are very dependent (Ward 1974). Groups of boys seem to be smaller, but their friendships are generally less intimate, less dependent, and less centred on school. The girls' peer groups frequently dissolve once they leave school (Speed 1968 ; Chapman 1968), and for the first few months of work, unless they start in the same firm or live close to their 'best friend', they lack companions with whom to break into new groups. At this point (mid teens) they seem often to transfer their affection to one boy, usually two or three years older than themselves; and they may regard others girls as rivals who desire the prestige that having a steady boy-friend confers. The teasing, etc., which hitherto drew the girl from the boy and back into the girls' group, remains intolerable, but instead of leaving the boy, she leaves the group, explaining the other girls' behaviour as 'jealousy'.

Conversation in the young woman's work-place centres on discussion of boyfriends and husbands in a personalized way, whereas among young men it is more impersonal – concerned less with specific relationships than with 'institutionalized Don Juanism'. Women feel the lack of a male companion, and many teenage girls seek, claim or consider themselves to be courting when the boys concerned would deny commitment. If her boy-friend works in the evenings – is on shift or studying for an exam or going to evening classes – a girl often has no set of friends to fall back on (other friends are usually young couples with whom she and her boy-friend make up a foursome) and she may try to persuade the boy from his studies (unless these are seen as for their mutual advantage in their future life together) or other interests, and to cling onto a relationship and to be anxious to get engaged. When a relationship ends, the event is socially as well as personally traumatic for her.

According to the Cardiff survey, teenage girls go out with members of their family more often than do boys (partly because they go to church more, and they go there with kin). Though for both sexes outings with kin fall off with age, they remain much more common for young women than for young men. As they grow up girls go out less with groups of girls or one girl-friend, whereas boys go out more 'with the boys'. Girls very rarely go out alone: they go out with a boy-friend, or they stay at home.

Although most boys of seventeen will have been out with a girl (86 per cent according to Schofield's book-keeping (1968), and indeed a larger proportion than of girls will have had experience of petting and intercourse (with a small number of 'promiscuous' girls), they have fewer dates or prolonged relationships. Even when he does start going steady, a young man can keep his outings with his girl-friend so scheduled (the asking is up to him) that there is time to meet his mates and to continue with his football, billiards, darts, motor cycling, pigeons, fishing, surfing, horse-riding, or whatever. His peer group during his schooldays was neighbourhood based and it remains so. It grows stronger – around sport, hobbies, and/or the pub – in his mid and late teens.

Of course, there are exceptions – some youths do not go to the pub or play sport and some girls resolutely keep up various interests and may be encouraged in this by their boy-friends. For example, in two cases the young woman informant's sporting progress was followed by the man, who went to watch her play netball matches. But another woman talking about one of these two to me made it clear that she was seen as rather 'funny': 'very "jolly hockey sticks" and thick calves'. Some women interviewed who enjoyed dancing but who were courting men who could not dance had, from time to time, been out with girl-friends to dances when he was working late or having 'a night out with the boys'. But as the relationship became more established the man objected and characterized the dance hall as a 'knocking shop' (cf. the hen party described in chapter 5). In one case (no. 5) the wife insisted on her 'night out with the girls' in the local pub as a conscious *quid pro quo* of her husband. But she added, unprompted, that she was not sure how long this would last. No man expressed doubts about how long his night(s) out would continue.

There is a sudden increase in courting by young men at 18–19. After casual dating for 5–6 years, or 'no particular interest in girls', the nineteen-year-old may meet a woman 2–3 years younger than he, decide on marriage quite rapidly, court for a year, get engaged, and married a year later.

The first arranged meetings (dates) (first both in the courtship career of an individual, and in the course of development of a particular relationship) consist of visits to the cinema or a dance, an evening having a drink – of coffee in a cafe (among the youngsters) or of alcohol in a pub or club – or going for a walk or drive. These also are all activities that groups of boys or groups of girls may do together for their intrinsic pleasure and companionship, or as part of their looking for opportunities to meet members of the opposite sex.

Once a couple are courting and have met each others' parents (see below), they spend more time with their families – usually with the girl's family, unless she does not get on well with her parents or her home is crowded with younger sibs. They will be together almost every evening, sometimes going out for commercial entertainment, or to other friends' houses to talk or listen to records. Most often they will be found sitting in the back room with the rest of the family watching TV and drinking tea or beer, or alone together in the 'front room' (which is only used otherwise for receiving visitors (like sociologists), for highdays and holidays, e.g., Christmas, and at funerals). They 'live in each other's pockets'. (See the account of my Case 6 in chapter 3 of Rapoport and Rapoport 1975.)

Despite, or perhaps because of, the very great disapproval attaching to premarital intercourse and the shame of premarital pregnancy (not to say illegitimacy), young people are given considerable freedom to be alone and are often left together in the house when the parents are out or when the parents have gone to bed. The very real fear of what would happen if she were discovered may keep the girl chaste; but if she refrains from intercourse, it is not always due to lack of opportunity[13].

Once a couple are determined on marriage, and especially when they can fix a date not too far ahead (say 1–2 years), they go out less in order to save money and make other economies: one groom sold his car, another stopped drinking so heavily; many took on a lot of overtime. Those couples who start to 'save seriously' for furniture, the deposit on a house, or because their parents' situation is such that they have to meet the costs of their own wedding, may show a complete change in leisure activities.

Case 42:

When they got engaged – seven months before the wedding, 'We stayed in a terrific amount. We had one night out on my twenty-first [birthday] in December. We both worked very, very hard. We both worked over Christmas. Oh, and we've been out once since, to the pictures. [The interview was in February.] We've got the deposit [on a house] and some left over.'

Generally there is less of a 'crash' savings programme (though cf. the article in *Woman*: 'How We Saved £500 in a Year', Hutchinson 1968): just a cut back on expensive outings:

Case 48:

'We used to go to the Abbey National once a week, so it limited us. We used to go on the Monday, so it was just what we could spend over the weekend.'

Case 18:

(Groom) 'We saw each other every night. Oh, yeah, we had to stay in [to save], but we had the [firm's] car, so went for a run to see people, relatives. Petrol was only 4s. odd then. [It was 6s. at the time of the interview.] Didn't do anything separately [from one another].'

The couple may indeed see *less* of each other if the man works long hours of overtime, though most of such leisure time as they have will be spent together. Women work more regular (not shift) hours in shops and offices, and there is less possibility of overtime. The woman therefore stays at home with her family, or drops round to girl-friends or to see the groom's mother; and for the best part of a year she will be busy discussing and making wedding preparations. The man may continue to go to his local pub or to play sport once or twice a week – taking her with him one night when all 'the lads' bring their girl-friends – but otherwise the couple drop all their previous interests and do only what they can do together. They go out only with other couples – still dancing, drinking, babysitting, for a run in the car (his or his father's), to the pictures, or to the beach in the summer. On these outings the man pays all the major expenses (except where both are students), and the woman's money is generally saved.

Case 25:

(When you went out together, who paid?)
(Bride) 'Huw, oh, no, not me. Always Huw. Well, to tell the truth, when we were first courting, he couldn't drive, because he'd been banned. He was to have sold the car, but it was stripped of lights and tyres and all. So he was broke and we used for a time to go dutch. He didn't like it – to my face. But he was bloody glad behind my back, mind!'

Case 5:

> (Groom) 'I paid. Still do [after married]. I don't believe it's the women's place. Wasn't right. I asked her out. She often offered.'

Their Saturday afternoons are spent together, looking at furniture in shops, or finding somewhere to live, or redecorating their future home.

Case 45:

> (Did your parents' attitude change when you got engaged?)
> (Groom) 'Well, they don't worry about leaving us alone or what time we get in at night now.'
> (Bride) 'Not so much now because we're engaged and because they know where we are – and what we're doing. They know we've got a paintbrush in our hands!'

Case 17:

> (Bride) 'When we got engaged I stopped spending so much money on myself and started buying things for my future home. No other differences – though perhaps I got closer to his family – and his mother didn't burst in when we were in the front room together: she knocked first!'

Case 15:

> (Bride) 'I always had to be in at 10.30, until I was 19. Then 11.0. Now it doesn't matter as long as I let them know. They know I'm safe with him.'

Even if it is granted that marriage has become more 'companionate' (which is not to be confused with saying that there is now equality of power or interchangeability of roles), it is certainly true that it is during courtship that men and women are most friendly and close. It is only at this period in the life-cycle (and for this purpose) that they actually seek to be in each other's company for a large proportion of their time.

The additional time spent at home and the ratification of the relationship by engagement usually results in the increasing acceptance of the fiancé(e) into the family group:

Case 20:

> 'She [his mother] no longer talks *to* me about 'Our Tommy' – she talks *about* me as 'our Eileen'; and she shows me photographs and talks about what he was like when he was little.'

Case 16:

> 'Once we got engaged, they trusted me to look after the shop! And they talked about family matters and business in front of me.'

Case 4:

> 'I've met most of her aunts and uncles now. They drop in on her parents when we're there.'

The steady dropping of other interests, the increase of jointly held friends and property, and the attachment of the members of the couple to each others' parents, sibs, and kin make the tie harder to break.

This interaction with the partner's family of origin not only prepares the future spouses for their roles as children-in-law (and the parents for their role as mother- and father-in-law), it also establishes the pattern of social activity which is followed after marriage. The young man becomes more and more part of his wife's family – though she makes regular visits to his home; while the young women's activities centre more and more on her own domestic group. She has virtually no leisure activities which are not courtship orientated, and as 'going out' with her boy-friend/fiancé declines as he is working longer hours, her activities centre more and more on her relatives. Her friends are usually one or two young women – typically in the same situation as herself of being engaged or just married (they are often girl-friends of her boy-friend's friends) – on whom she drops in to chat, and the couples with whom she and her fiancé go out. The young man, on the other hand, often retains his membership of a male peer group (though not all do – some only renew active participation after their marriage).

In the period after marriage and before children are born, the pattern set during the engagement is maintained. The woman depends on her husband to take her out – her pre-engagement activities are no longer suitable since they involved going out with girl-friends to find men, or at least to places where there are unattached men, for certainly many girls enjoy going dancing for the dancing itself. Only later, when she has stopped work, does the young married woman join the young wives' clubs, or go to bingo with a mother, sister, or friend (Whitehead 1976). The husband, however, has independent male leisure pursuits – hobbies that take him out of the house, or sport, or 'going down to the local', or to his club. Since these activities are by no means exclusively orientated to meeting unattached women, his continued activity or membership is not inconsistent with his being married.

Both spouses have relationships with their own sex which provide them with support; but the wife's relationships are *all* with family or girl-friends in a multi-age female network. The husband's relationships are with a male peer group, centred around work, sport, or other hobby or interest and/or the pub or club, *and* with his kin network. As Whitehead points out (1976), it is not that there is a 'female trade union' of mothers, sisters, and neighbours against the 'male CBI' based on work or the pub. Men have the same contact with kin and neighbours as women. Men's work or leisure-based sex peer group is additional to what the women have, and it is a *group*.

The information built up on Swansea brings into question previous work on peer grouping in industrial society. It also sheds light on the way in which people who marry meet each other in the first place, and on the control which parents exercise over their children's courtship. I shall consider these three areas, together with the effects of premarital pregnancy, before drawing some general conclusions.

Peer groupings

Parsons has argued, abstractly, that in our society the individual is born into and socialized within a small kin group which is structurally isolated from both the economic system to which it contributes, and the wider kinship system of which it forms a part (Parsons 1943; Rodman 1966; Harris 1970). The solidarity of this group, or 'nuclear family', composed of a man, wife, and children, is determined largely by the strength of the marital relationship. Since sexual relationships (apart from between spouses) are forbidden within it, it is essential for the children to transfer their primary emotional attachment from their nuclear family of origin to a marriage partner who is unrelated to the previous family situation.

This transference Parsons sees as facilitated by the existence of groups of age peers ('peer groups') which interlink nuclear families (Parsons 1943, and especially Eisenstadt 1965; though cf. Pitts 1960). Such groups tend to be highly solidary because they are based on ascription and not achievement, and because the members belong to the same generation and occupy the same life-space. Individuals are able to transfer their emotional attachment from their family to their peer group, within which they learn both the roles appropriate to individualistic society (since within the group they are evaluated in terms of their achievements, not their kin status), and to establish relationships with the opposite sex. Having found partners, the peer group (assumed to be heterosexual) then breaks up, its members forming nuclear families of their own, and the cycle begins again.

In Swansea, however, the school and neighbourhood peer groups are single-sex groups, and thus they are incompatible with courtship, particularly with the later stages. (The earliest heterosexual interaction, it will be remembered, occurred with transitory mergers of two single sex groups.) Nor does the model, which sees the movement of young people from the family to the age peer group and on into their families of marriage, enable us to understand why a girl seeks a committed relationship at an earlier stage than a boy.

The present account suggests, rather, that for most girls leaving school and taking an outside job is an important stage in the collapse of the female peer group. The school peer group is geographically scattered *vis à vis* the homes and new places of work of its members, and they lack a meeting place. They do not see each other during the day to plan their 'calling for each other' in the evening, and they are not free to meet outside their homes in the evening. (Women do not go out alone.) The group of women and girls with whom they work is significantly differentiated in terms of age, and many already have boy-friends, fiancés, or husbands. Status within this group depends on age and 'success' (committed relationships) with boys/men. Lacking, therefore, both the status and the support that the school peer group gives, the sixteen-year-old girl seeks a permanent relationship with a member of the opposite sex.

A boy of the same age comes from a less solidary peer group (used for companionship rather than social support) and he enters a work group where prestige is conferred by prowess at sport, drinking, 'pulling birds', and possibly by success at work itself. He does not need to acquire a *steady* girl-friend to enhance his status in his work/pub/other interest groups, nor does he need a companion with whom to go out of the house. If he has a steady girl-friend it may merely be because, to quote an informant, 'It is less effort that way'. He continues other interests alongside his outings with girls.

The girl school-leaver therefore seeks to establish a relationship with an older boy, both because he is her superior (on the dimension of age), and because he is more willing to enter a 'committed' relationship. This change in attitude on the part of the young man in his late teens derives from his position at work and its relationship to his familial position. Once he has established his ability to hold down a job – and found a job he is willing to hold down – and is earning 'men's wages', he will regard himself as fully adult and independent. Yet in his family of origin his position will be to some extent subordinate. It is at this point that he seriously contemplates a committed relationship, with a view to getting himself a wife.

In this he compares with the nineteenth-century factory worker who had: 'a considerable motivation to marry and thus to move to a situation where one was the chief person considered in a family and not a subsidiary . . . part of a larger system whose interests by no means always tallied with one's own' (Anderson 1971:132).

The different requirements of a high-status position within the female and male work and friendship groups reflects, of course, cultural expectations as to the chief component of adulthood for the two sexes: wife or wage earner. So in part the seeking by the young woman for a committed relationship is attributable to the economic importance and 'central life interest' of marriage for her. But, more immediately, it is due to her not being able to participate in many activities without a male escort.

The position of the sexes with regard to their peer groups is therefore very different. Whereas the collapse of the girl's peer group induces her to form a committed relationship with one man; in the young man's case it is the decision to form such a committed relationship that destroys his (total) allegiance to his peer group and disrupts its activities. Both sexes feel constrained – the woman feels under pressure to find herself a husband – 'to get a ring on her finger' – and thus to start courting, to get engaged, and to get married as early as possible: 'If you're not engaged by the time you're eighteen in Swansea they act as if you're on the shelf.' While the man sees a rapid narrowing of the field of eligibles and the need to grab a partner while there is still the chance: 'All the people I was at school with are married. It's depressing.'

Meeting one's spouse

The few studies which have sought information on this subject in this country (notably Slater and Woodside (1951), Gorer (1971), and the PIC study (Rowntree 1962; Pierce 1963)) have classified the contexts in which their married respondents claimed to have met their spouses on the basis of one couple, one meeting place. I found, however, that half of my informants (whose meeting with their spouse was a relatively recent occurrence) said that they had started going out together after several meetings in different places and with the mediation of kin and friends. A quarter of the total sample had known each other for over a year before they started courting.

Case 5:

'I first met him in the market. He was a friend of my brother's best friend, and he [the brother's best friend] rather fancied me. But I didn't like him – to tell the truth I couldn't stand him. He was spotty and . . . We met again in the Embassy [dance hall] twelve months later, and he asked me to dance. He was going to ask me if he could take me home, but by the time he got round to it, I'd gone. So he asked my brother if I was courting and he said yes, I was. But when he got home he told me that he'd asked, and so I packed the other boy in and we met down the Embassy the next week, and he walked me home.'

Case 35:

'We were in school together – senior school that is – so we met eight years ago. But we first spoke to each other three years ago; 27 September, 1966, in a café. I was with my friend. He and his friend came over and joined us. He only lived around the corner, but we never said "Hello" when we passed in the street. Anyway, he asked me out. He had a choice: next day or next week [she went to other things – music, judo, etc. – on the other nights]. So it was the next day and every evening from then on [he met her from music, etc., until she gave them up].'

Case 15:

'He was a friend of my brother Paul. They were in school together – he brought him home. I'd not seen him for years, and then my father [a builder] was doing a job for his mother, and he just 'phoned me up and asked if I'd like to go out.'

Case 48:

(Groom): 'We met across the bench in tech. I'd been there for a year and then she turned up in the October.' (Both were lab technicians on day release at the technical college.)
(Bride): 'I hadn't really noticed him until about Christmas, when we – the girls – were discussing the likely talent and decided that he was the best bet! So then I started making up to him! I said to him that I was going down the Top Rank next evening, and he said he was too because he had to meet a friend there to pick up his wages – it was Friday [i.e., he was not going to be at work that day and his friend was bringing his money from work for him]. So *socially* we met in the Top Rank.'

The most obvious reasons for the discrepancies between my findings and those of other studies would seem to be, first, that asking people 'where did you meet?' as one of a number of specific questions in a highly structured interview is likely to produce simple unambiguous replies, however complex the situation may actually have been; and secondly, that it is not unlikely that over time a romantic myth of the meeting is developed. Note that two of the couples quoted above spontaneously gave the date of their first meeting (in one case some two and a half years before), and they also told me that they celebrated this 'anniversary' each year by going out together for a meal. Other couples who discussed, even disputed, many of the events of their courtship with each other when answering my questions, were agreed on the circumstances of their meeting. There was an impression that each of them was contributing a piece here and there to an oft-told story. Indeed, it probably *was* oft told, since when people discovered the subject of my research they would usually proceed to tell me the 'extraordinary coincidence' by which they had met their own spouse and to enquire how I had met mine. Presumably the tale becomes polished, simplified, and refined in the telling over the years.

Figure 1 Circumstances of meeting future spouse – all circumstances mentioned

place, etc.	no. of times mentioned	among those (N=28) who had known each other some time	among those (N=26) who started court-ship after one or two meetings only
dance	14	7	7
street	9	5	4
pub	9	–	9
work	6	3	3
college (tech and university)	5	2	3
party	4	2	2
home	3	3	–
school	3	3	–
blind date	3	–	3
youth club	2	1	1
cafe	2	2	–
choir	2	1	1
on holiday in Devon	1	–	1
on the beach in Swansea	1	–	1
friend of a friend*	17	5	12
known to kin*	8	5	3
neighbour	7	5	2
total contacts for 54 couples	96		

* Importance is certainly understated since it was the *place* which was emphasized by informants and I did not probe.

In any case it is not surprising that in Swansea eventual spouses should have come into contact several times through the mediation of different links. It is a small city, with only 170,000 inhabitants, subdivided into local areas, themselves further subdivided into status groups. There are there-

fore a number of relatively small 'cells' on which an individual's relationships centre, and each individual is a point on a relatively highly inter-
connected network of relationships joining the individuals in each cell. In
such a situation it may well be that the recurrence of contact with the same
person results in that person's being *seen* as socially acceptable, and the
recognition of acceptability is likely to be an important factor in the
decision to establish a courting relationship.

It therefore seems wrong to assume that in the majority of cases (in this
town) leisure activities provide contexts where complete strangers meet,
are attracted, and start going out with each other. While it is necessary to
find a spouse outside the nuclear family, the spouse need by no means be
'unrelated to the previous family situation'. On the contrary, a partner
whose position can be plotted in relation to the network of relationships
extending out from the nuclear family is possibly more likely to be chosen
as a spouse than one whose position cannot.

If the meetings of my informants are classified in terms of one couple,
one (main) meeting, then my findings agree with previous surveys in that
dances and work are important venues, though in Swansea private
houses are less important, and the pub and the street seem more important, than in other places in the past[14].

The PIC national survey found the place of meeting to be related to
socio-economic class: male manual workers tend to meet their spouses at
dances, on the street, or in a coffee bar or pub, whereas non-manual
workers meet their wives at home or at work (Pierce 1963). They also
found (though they give less information) that the place of meeting is
related to the age at which the relationship commences (Rowntree 1962).
My data confirm both these findings:

> Three-quarters of women with category II occupations had met their
> spouses at college; while dances, the pub, and the street were more
> common for category III; and work for women factory workers. The
> pattern was similar, though less marked, among men (Barker 1977,
> Table 4:21). The most common meeting place for girls in their early
> teens and boys in their mid teens was the street or café; dance halls
> were important for girls in their teens but only later for men; and the
> pubs were of passing importance (in the late teens), whereas dances
> and work were of continuing importance in the twenties. (Barker 1977,
> Table 4:22)

I would suggest that since age at commencing the courtship that leads to
marriage is class related, age is an intervening variable between class and
place of meeting; i.e., that age at commencement is related to class, and
that age is an important determinant of the leisure context in which
courtship commences. This makes good sense in the light of the
development of courtship and leisure activities with age sketched above.

Coleman, in a re-analysis of the PIC data from London (1973), has shown that how far apart people who get married are living is related to the place where they meet. Those who meet in dance halls and at work are likely to live a long way apart and not to have many friends in common at the start; whereas those who meet in private houses, clubs, on the street, or through friends and relatives, are likely to live much closer together. My findings from Swansea confirm Coleman's (not surprising) results. Most marriages are endogamous to Swansea – there are enough facilities within the town for most people to work and play there, except among the middle class who believe in young people going away for education and training. However, as Rosser and Harris point out, different districts of Swansea vary in their degree of locality endogamy (from 48 per cent in Morriston to 17 per cent in West Cross) according to how far afield people go for entertainment. The decrease in locality homogamy over the last fifty years they attribute to the decline of the chapels and the local courting parades (see account in Rosser and Harris 1965:241; and in Preston between the wars, Thompson 1975), the development of better transport[15] and the concentration of entertainment facilities in the town centre. In this town as elsewhere, people nowadays look further afield for their mates than in previous generations.

Even so, most of my respondents lived close to the person they married: 30 per cent within half a mile and 80 per cent within five miles at the time when they met. (Of course, when they were living away from home (predominantly categories I and II), their homes might be much further apart[16].)

A further effect of the change in leisure activities with age is that the centres of entertainment of young teenagers (the street corner, the local café, chip shop, or youth club) are closer to home than the dance halls and town-centre pubs frequented by those in their late teens and early twenties. It is therefore not surprising that there is an increase in locality heterogamy with increasing age at commencement of the courtship (Barker 1977, Table 4:11).

The changing location of leisure activities with age also accounts for the fact that among those whose start courting earlier, there are more overlapping ties – e.g., they are neighbours, knew each other at school, he used to fight her brother, and they 'met' in a coffee bar. The distance of most housing areas (council estates or middle-class suburbs) from the centre's entertainment means that the majority of later 'dates' are with people unknown to parents and the local community, and take place without their knowledge.

Parental influences on courtship

Goode (1959) has argued, very plausibly, that in our society parental involvement in courtship is most marked where the individual marriage is of importance to a kin group or a socio-economic stratum – e.g., among farmers and the upper classes. There is then a small field of eligibles and substantial risks to property and social status from exogamous marriages. In such situations there is generally less freedom for young people to make contact with the (generality of the) opposite sex, more socialization on the need for appropriate marriages, more vetting of friends and deliberate provision of situations for courtship (e.g., sending children to single-sex boarding schools and then holding a Season), and more at stake for the young people to make them obedient. Sussman's research on prosperous middle-class families in New Haven, Connecticut, for instance, shows how active parents may be in providing a proper milieu for dating and courting, and in using persuasion and threats to break off unsuitable liasons[17].

Even among my informants, who were certainly not upper class and had little property, there was some degree of parental supervision of courtship, particularly that of girls. I saw little difference by socio-economic category, though there was a slight tendency for the middle and 'respectable' working class to be more actively interventionist.

In reply to a direct question, no informants reported that their parents had tried to direct them towards forming a relationship with a particular individual (cf. Sussman's informants, who had arranged outings and tennis parties or the like to encourage their children to socialize with approved young people), but quite a number could recall being guided away from – 'warned off' – people.

Case 10:

> (Do you think parents should take an active part in determining who their children marry? Will you with your children?)
> (Bride) 'They said it's my life; I've got to live it – to live with what I do. No, they never interfered. I'll leave him [baby son] to it.'
> (Groom) 'I suppose I'd be inclined to do the same. But what do you do if you see them . . . I know my father took me aside once and told me what might and could happen if I carried on with a particular girl. And I used my head.'

Sometimes the approach is more direct, if less successful. Thus, in Case 46, the bride's mother spoke to the young man and tried to get rid of him. Bride:

> 'She thought he was rough, scruffy. The first time she ever saw him [4 months after they met] he was waiting outside for me. She sent me

on an errand and called him in. Told him to keep off. She told him he was scruffy. It wasn't fair, just because he wasn't dressed up. After all we weren't going anywhere special.'

In another case (no. 7) the woman's mother showed her disapproval by shouting out of an upstairs window: 'Get that scruffy layabout off my doorstep!' when the couple were saying goodnight after he had brought her home. Altogether in fifteen cases, one or both sets of parents seemed to have been opposed to the marriage, and, among these, in five cases they actively sought to prevent it (for the extreme case, no. 51, see pp. 99–102. In three of these five cases the bride was from a higher socio-economic category background than the groom[18].

Initial parental 'vetting' is generally indirect, via peers and neighbourhood informants, or by questioning the son or daughter, and 'placing' the boy- or girl-friend. (This way of getting information can be very efficient.) In thirteen instances (12 per cent) the boy- or girl-friend was known to the parents before the relationship started.

Taking the partner home has an important social significance, whether it is passed off casually as 'dropping in for coffee after seeing her home', or a full-scale invitation to a meal: 'the dreaded "Sunday tea".' Meeting parents leads to expectations on the part of others that the relationship is 'serious', and therefore socially commits the person whose home it is. Nonetheless, 47 per cent of boys/men and 34 per cent of girls/women had met the parents of the person they eventually married by the end of the week in which the relationship began.

Girls/young women are more likely to be encouraged to bring friends home than are boys/young men. Indeed, since young men are less required to give an account of what they do when they go out in the evenings or how they are going to get home, their parents are less likely to know that a girl-friend is in the offing. Also men have more relationships with 'not respectable' members of the opposite sex who would not be shown to their parents. Consequently a young man usually meets his girl-friend's parents some time before she meets his[19]. She is under pressure to let her parents see who she is with, and he is likely to go to her house to pick her up or take her home. This, together with the fact that men have fewer courtships than women, results in them taking home fewer girl-friends.

Case 45:

(Groom) 'No, they didn't meet them all. Some weren't respectable enough. Anyway, it puts a girl off – makes it seem very serious.'

Case 5:

(Groom) 'Well, I've taken a few home, but each time my mother said

"Is this *it*?" and I'd say "yeah"; and then we'd pack it in! And she got attached to them – one still drops in to see her. Awkward!'

Case 28

(Bride) 'It was a joke really. *Everyone* asked me for tea. So they all had to come for tea here. I used to think it was something that happened only with the one you were going to settle down with. He was given the first degree the second he came!'

Case 52

(Bride) 'I saw his whole family, and the cat and the dog, watching us out of the window all the way as we was walking up the road [for tea, to which she had been invited].'

Both women and men have good reason for trying to delay taking their partner home until the relationship is well established. The consequences of mixing up your courtship with your peer group or family in a small town where the resultant relationship – or at least occasional interaction – are likely to be maintained, are clearly recognised. The sight of two young people together leads to chaff and questions as to the state of the girl's bottom drawer and to addressing the girl as 'Mrs plus her boyfriend's surname'. It is not only film-stars who find it necessary continually to issue statements to the effect that they and a member of the opposite sex are 'just good friends'. Such situations are indeed 'awkward', especially if one partner is pressing for commitment and the other is trying to evade it. The segregation of leisure activities and family has the effect of making rather more possible the freedom of individual choice which is culturally stressed; but only in the early stages. Once personal committment is ratified by taking the partner home, a whole set of different social pressures come into operation to continue (or discontinue) the relationship.

Case 16:

This couple had a very long courtship: $6\frac{1}{2}$ years.
(Did you take all your boyfriends home?)
(Bride) 'I only had one very serious romance before, and I had taken him home, of course. I had always been out with boys from chapel before, and I'd taken them home. That sort of family [which she had described to me as 'traditional Welsh'] does have the advantage in that your friends are always welcome.'

(Did Colin take his girl-friends home?)
'*Never* had a girl-friend to take home before – But he's taken them home since! When I was doing exams [her finals at the University] he had a "fling". *Not* serious. But the family were very opposed to it: "Doing the dirty on Hazel!" [said in a broad Welsh accent].'

Parental vetting did not seem to occur by means of the parents of the two partners meeting and appraising each other. In one case the parents had *never* met – the bride's father (a widower) refused to go to the wedding – and it was quite common (one in ten) for parents not to meet till the engagement party. Nearly as many (including several middle-class parents who lived far apart and merely telephoned each other and sent Christmas cards) did not meet until the wedding itself.

On the other hand, in a substantial number of cases the parents, or the father or mother, knew the other parent(s) before the start of the couple's relationship, or could work out who they were:

Case 40:

> 'They all knew each other from the war. They'd worked together then.'

Case 24:

> 'Our mothers knew each other from the children's clinic when they pushed us in our prams together! His grandparents live 2–3 streets from here. His father was at school with my mother. Otherwise they met up again when we got engaged.'

Case 28:

> 'They've met casually in the shop across the road. When I told my mother his mother's name she seemed to know who she was.'

Some first meetings were formally arranged:

Case 45:

> (Did your parents know each other before you started going out together?')
> (Bride) 'No'
> (How did they meet?)
> (Bride) 'We all went out to dinner in the Burlington; Christmas 1967 [i.e., around the time they got engaged; six months after the couple's first meeting; 15 months before the wedding].'
> (Bride's father) 'Good it was, straight out of the barrel!'
> (Bride) 'Yes, we went out there so they could meet – on neutral territory!'
> (How often do they see each other now?)
> (Bride) 'Not very often. [To her father] We've been up [to his parents' house]. Remember . . . when we saw the three-piece suite?'
> (How often?)
> (Groom) 'Say, once in six months.'
> (How do they get on? – misunderstood as 'do you get on?')
> (Bride's father) 'Oh, good gracious yes! . . . just so busy – in the six

months to the wedding. The wife works in the mornings, see, and when she gets home and straightens things out . . . then I'm home . . . and things to do, and by the time supper's over – time for bed. And his father being on shift-work makes it difficult.'

Others introduced their parents by the simple expedient of dropping in at the bride's home when taking his mother out for a drive (by prearrangement), usually after the courtship had been going on for some months and the parents had expressed a desire to meet.

Having met, only a quarter of parents continued to see each other once a month or more. These were usually where couples lived near each other and the parents met doing their shopping or helping the couple decorate their new house. (This also includes, e.g., mothers who worked together, whose working together had helped in bringing the couple together in the first place.) For about a half of the couples, 'good relations' between their two sets of parents seemed to consist in (or be maintained by) seeing each other only two or three times in the year before the wedding. A further quarter met very rarely indeed.

'His mother called on mine once, and she called back. That's all.'

'My mother likes a drink and a cigarette. His are very quiet and hardly ever go out. They get on well when they *do* meet, but they're very different types of people.'

It seems likely that contact increases after marriage, since both sets of parents may drop in or be invited to the young couple's household at the same time.

At various points the greater initiative in courtship of the young man and the dependence of the young woman have been mentioned, and this is clearly shown in the ritual whereby the man asks the woman's father for permission to get engaged or marry her. This formality occurred among three-quarters of my informants marrying for the first time, but among none of those marrying for the second time. Nor was the bride's mother formally asked when the bride's father was dead. In the remainder the bride often told the groom that he should ask, but he was too shy, or the couple thought it was not necessary as the parents 'already knew'. In no case did the bride ask the groom's parents permission to marry *him*; he usually told them himself, with little ceremony. Sometimes, however (see case 10 below), he discussed the matter with his father first.

In general the bride's father is expecting the request-cum-announcement. Sometimes the bride has told her mother, who has told her husband; or the bride has told her father that the groom is going to ask. Case 45: 'I told him that Ken wanted to get engaged. He [her father] said "To whom?!". Ken asked him a week later. I was in the house, but upstairs, not in the room.' The bride's father is, after all, unlikely to have been aware of the interest which leads the young man to spend most of his spare time in their house, and for those over twenty-one (at the time of fieldwork) parental consent was not legally required. Nonetheless, despite the fact that it was a minor ordeal for which the young man often took some 'Dutch courage', and which he might put off from day to day for some weeks, he usually did formally ask.

In some cases it was much more of an ordeal. Case 10:

Two students met at the end of September of their first year at college (1967) and they started going out together about the first week of the following February. By the end of April they were talking of getting married, and planning to get engaged on her birthday in November (1968).
(Who did you tell first that you planned to get married?)
(Bride) 'Richard's parents.'
(Groom) 'Well, I told my father – a long time [a month] before I told Catherine. He said "Just be certain you're sure".'
(Did you ask her father's permission? Can you describe what happened?)
(Groom) 'Well, Catherine was around, but not in the room. I was in with her father and I said we were thinking of getting engaged. He'd not been told before, but I still got the feeling he knew, though. He was willing. No problem.'
(Did you have a rough idea of the date of the wedding when you got engaged?)
(Groom) 'Well, I had previously thought August [1969] or a year August [1970] – depending on our financial situation. It was one date you [the bride] could never trap out of me, wasn't it?'
(Bride) 'I'd have liked to have finished college first' [August 1970].'
(How and when did you get engaged?)
(Groom) 'First thing is, I didn't know Catherine was pregnant. [He insisted elsewhere he wouldn't have got married 'just because of the baby'.] I had a substantial sum of money from a tax rebate at the time [October 1968]. So I bought the ring [i.e., the two of them went out and chose it and he paid] and meant to keep it. But you [bride] knocked it out of me! [To me] I knew she wanted to wear it.'

They phoned her parents the next morning to tell them, and since his parents did not have a phone, Richard and Catherine went up the valley to his parents the following morning to tell them.

A fortnight to three weeks later they knew she was pregnant. They both decided to tell both parents together on the same day. They told his and then hers. Richard's mother was working that particular Saturday, so they told his father and then went to Catherine's grandmother where her parents were visiting (in the next town).

(How did they take it?)

(Groom) 'They were upset. Disappointed in us. Well, in fact, it was a *big* upset.'

Later on, when discussing what he called his parents-in-law, he attributed some of his problems to 'a deeper reason'.

'I think it's the way we were married. At the time I nearly had a punch-up with her father. Once the wedding was over, even before, they've been great. But when I actually told him we had to get married, he exploded. I thought, "What do I do if he hits me?". Do I just lie there or do I get up and punch him one? Being if I do that Catherine'll never forgive me. But if I just lie there he'll think "He's not much of a man!". Then I was *really* scared – not knowing what to do.'

Case 51:

In this case the parents of the bride had consistently refused to give consent to the marriage of their eighteen-year-old daughter and the couple 'took them to court'.

The courtship had begun inauspiciously in February 1968. Jennifer and John had known each other for some time. He used to be a 'bouncer' at a local dance hall and she was friendly with one of his friends. However, they started going out together after a dance at a hotel in Oystermouth at which there 'was a rumpus', according to Jennifer, 'and my brother went to interfere. Just like him! It was only two blokes fighting, but John's friend thought that my brother was going for one of the blokes who was *his* friend, and so he gave my brother a black eye. John said to me, "Who's that silly thing down there walking into trouble?". And I said "It's *my brother!*". John had the fault of it as far as my family were concerned, of course.'

Her parents, she said, tried to put obstacles in the path of their relationship, chiefly in terms of refusing to let her borrow a car to go into Swansea from their village and insisting that John see her home.

'There was murder if I ever wanted to go out somewhere. There was a lane where we lived, from the bus-stop. John was supposed to come with me on the bus, walk me down, and then go home. I mean, we could never do it. By the time I'd get in from work [as a clerk in Swansea], change and go back . . . and we'd never've been able to stay to the end of a film. And the buses are so erratic, he'd have to walk back. They've never said anything *before* when I went out. Nor to my brother and sister . . . '

It was not easy to piece together their story, whose chronology was very confused, but apparently things came to a head in the following August, when John sent a birthday card to Jennifer with 'to my fiancée' on it. Her parents had met him by then, but there had been no talk of engagement, other than between the couple, who had 'sort of decided'.

A couple of weeks later John did go to talk to her father.

> 'We were there for three hours standing in the garden – my mother and father and John and me, arguing like mad.'
> (What was wrong?)
> 'That he worked in [the dance hall]. He should have been somebody that worked in a bank or an office. But he wasn't; he was just ordinary.'

(At which point the groom's mother interjected, addressing the baby, 'Your dad's not got much money and your grandpa's got a lot of money'.)

So the young couple decided to go to London to work. Her parents said she could not go, but John had been to the Citizen's Advice Bureau and found out that her parents could not stop her leaving, so he went to her house and collected her. He went up to London about a fortnight before Jennifer with two friends, with whom he shared a flat, and she stayed with two other friends when she arrived. They came home over Christmas, and their friends in Swansea (including his parents, in whose council house they stayed) persuaded them to stay in Swansea. (The other London-dwellers soon came back too.)

> (Groom's mother) 'She came to live here. Her parents come up on the Boxing Day and we thought everything was alright.'
> (Bride) 'My father said we could get engaged.'
> (Groom's mother) 'In this *very room* it was! Then my daughter and I went down to their house. Wonderful welcome we got.'
> (Bride) 'I was going to go back home after Christmas. But then he said he'd said no such thing – and so . . . By then I'd had enough, so we went to the magistrates court to get permission.'

John was said to have asked her father's permission for them to get married 'half a dozen times', and, apart from the brief period around Christmas, it had been withheld: 'Last time he said "No, not under any cicumstances". We knew about the baby, but even so he said no.' John therefore went back to the Citizen's Advice Bureau, who sent him to a solicitor (whose services cost £10 – the final indictment of Jennifer's father as far as her mother-in-law was concerned). He was told that Jennifer would have to go to the magistrates court and summons her parents. This she did in March, and the hearing of the case was the first week in April.

> (Bride) 'The solicitor had had one case [like theirs] before, but it was the

mother who came to him. [She clearly saw what she was doing as very extreme and unusual.] He said I had to go to the magistrates court – before a magistrate and a clerk – and summons my parents. I was so scared because I had to go in on my own. I was shaking like a leaf. I thought John could come in with me, but he wasn't allowed. It *was* an ordeal. I said why I wanted to, and they talked to each other and said alright. Then we had to go and see a secretary to give me a date when we'd appear in front of a court.'

At first they were given a date five weeks ahead, but in the end they got one in three weeks 'because of the baby'.

The pregnancy was 'not really an accident. [We] knew they wouldn't say yes otherwise.'

'We had to be there at 10.30, but there were about thirty maintenance cases ahead of me, so I was pacing up and down. I was in the witness box for twenty-five minutes; then John, then you [to groom's mother].

(Groom's mother) 'The woman's got more to do with the house. The magistrate wanted to know would we be willing to let them stay for the baby and after the baby.'

(Bride) 'My father's solicitor had to say why he didn't like John and why he was against the marriage.' (Why) 'Oh, that he was in and out of jobs, and he'd not saved much, and that I come from a *good* home . . .

My solicitor said my father objected because John was a labourer. He asked him "Do you have any labourers?" and my father said "Yes, and I thinks the world of them". "Why then do you object to your daughter marrying a labourer?" He couldn't say nothing then. The magistrate asked John – or was it the clerk of the court – said "Even if my Lords don't give their consent, you'll still live together?", and more or less putting words into John's mouth. To say that it would make no difference. Very kind little man he was. My father wanted me to go home and have the baby adopted. The magistrate's face fell at that!
John told them his wages and he said "Good Lord. You can keep a wife and child on that!".
The magistrates went out for a few minutes and came back and said that while they were very sorry for the parents concerned, if they didn't give consent it would mean a complete breakdown between my parents and me. They told me to talk to my parents when we came out, but I couldn't. I was weeping my eyes out. I couldn't face anyone. All I wanted to do was to come home [i.e., to groom's house].'

They went down to the register office that afternoon and got a licence and were married the following weekend.

She had no communication with her parents until, some months later, she ran into her mother in Boots in the town centre. They both started crying. Her mother wanted them to have a cup of tea together, but Jennifer 'couldn't face it'. Since then she has written to her mother a couple of times; but John is adamant that her parents shall not see her son.

She claims that many of her relatives ('the ones I've seen') are very shocked by what her father and mother did.

The effects of premarital pregnancy

These two cases show premarital pregnancy associated with a crisis. In the first the upset was short lasting, though its effects lingered on (Richard finding it peculiarly difficult to know how to address his parents-in-law); in the other pregnancy was a product of, and the baby was being used as a weapon in, a major intergenerational breach (as a means to persuade the court to give consent to the marriage, and to punish Jennifer's parents by not allowing them to see their first grand-child). In addition, in previous chapters I have mentioned the stigma for a woman to be discovered to have had premarital intercourse (e.g., my neighbours' friends' reactions to finding their daughter was 'on the pill') and I shall go on (in chapters 5 and 6) to show the 'second class status' of couples who marry when the bride is pregnant.

It is therefore important to stress that most of the couples interviewed who had had a premarital pregnancy seemed to have accepted it fairly calmly, and none mentioned having considered abortion (which would have been a difficult and dangerous expedient in Swansea in 1968/69). Of course, it must be allowed that they were getting or had got married and were well advanced into the pregnancy or had already had the baby by the time of the interview. (But see also the calmness reported by Anderson, Kenna, and Hamilton (1960) among unmarried *prima gravida* adolescents; and the criticism of other studies of premarital pregnancy as projecting middle-class attitudes onto working class informants in MacIntyre (1976)).

Only the student couple (Case 10) – the only s.e.c. I or II couples to have a premarital pregnancy – appeared to have been badly upset and their plans thrown by the event. In two other cases the couple seem to have been overtaken by an at least partially accidental pregnancy (and then taken over by their mothers!). For example Case 7:

They met 'Down at the bus stop! He just come up and asked if he could walk me home. I said no, but he did just the same!'
He was 'sixteen and a bit', she was fifteen.

(When and how did you first start to think/talk about whether you might marry each other?)

'I thought about it right from the start.'

(Did one of you actually say to the other 'will you marry me?'.)

'Yes, he did. Said "Margaret, will you marry me". Asked about three times, and in the end I said yes. We had a lot of quarrels, but next day he'd come running back.'

(Did it come as a surprise (when he asked you to marry him) ?)

'Yes, because he said it in front of his friend.'

They exchanged friendship rings when they had been courting about seven months. 'We would have got engaged – not waited long before doing it.' Then they had 'an accident'.

'Well, they said we couldn't get married; and we both wanted it really bad. So we thought it was the only thing to do. Bit of both really; accident *and* intended . . . When I was a week over I went down the doctor's for a water test, and he said I was. So I came home and told my mother. But my mother didn't believe it, so she went down the doctor's herself and he told her.

I went up to tell his mother. He wouldn't. His mother was quite pleased, really, but my mother played hell at first. She said, NO, I was too young. So his mother came down to see my mother, and my mother agreed.'

This was the first time the groom had met her parents.

(How much time did you spend in each other's houses before you got married?)

'He *never* came down here. Only when my mother knew we was getting married. He'd meet me at the bus stop and we'd go back to his place. He brought me back late one night (a quarter to midnight) and my mother yelled out "Where the bloody hell have you been" – and he ran! I didn't speak to his parents much either – we'd be in the parlour and they'd be in the kitchen, or out.'

(Did your parents know each other before you started going out together? How did they meet?)

'When I went up and told them I was having a baby. They came down the next night and arranged the wedding. I had no say in it . . .

Very rare they see each other now. When they do, they talk, but my mother's not very keen on my mother-in-law.'

The marriage was at the end of November. 'My mother-in-law chose the date. I wanted to wait and get married near Xmas, but she said, "No, straight away".'

Her grandparents did not come because they disapproved. They thought she was too young to be allowed to marry.

The bride and groom lived with her parents for five months, until after the baby was born, and then they moved to the groom's parents' house.

In two other cases 'fate' was left to take a hand and make the final decision about whether and/or when to get married; for instance, Case 12:

They met in work seven months before they started courting. She was eighteen and he twenty-six and just back from the Merchant Navy. (When did you first start to talk about whether you might marry each other?)

'We never talked about it. Yes, just assumed it. He used to say "I'll buy you a gold ring", but I never used to understand what he meant. Thought he just meant he'd buy me a dress ring.'

(Did one of you actually say to the other 'will you marry me?'.) 'No.'

They were courting a year and five months. Then she found she was pregnant.

'I told Robert. He was there when my sister phoned the doctor – I wouldn't! So she knew first, then Robert. We decided straight away to get married.'

(Did he ask your father's permission?)

'My sister [who ran the household, her mother being dead] told (my father). I didn't care – he couldn't do nothing anyway [NB. she was under age]. Robert wanted to get married anyway. But he was frightened. Thought he couldn't have any children. So he wanted to see before we got married. Didn't have to wait long for him to find out either!'

In the remaining five instances of pregnancy it seemed to have been 'used' because its inexorability meant that obstacles – chiefly parental consent (or agreement, since it is not only those whose parents 'have to sign' who feel braked by opposition), or a first spouse's refusal to divorce, or not having anywhere to live – will *have* to be overcome. For example, the couple who took her parents to court contrived that by the time they arrived in court she was pregnant[20] and a man who could not get a divorce moved in with his girl-friend and her widowed mother once she was pregnant. The mother put it about that they were married: 'When people asked her: "How's Pauline these days?" she said "Oh, didn't you know? She's married now and got a baby.' They married when their daughter was two and a half and his first wife decided she herself wanted to remarry. Another instance is the sister of my informant in Case 27 who got a home together when she had to get married thanks to the whole family's efforts at finding a cottage and renovating and redecorating it and (possibly) her elder sister delaying her own marriage. Pregnancy may even be used by a couple who have no way of paying for a large white wedding to justify marrying in the register office.

In all eight cases where the bride was pregnant at the time of marriage it was the first marriage for both bride and groom (i.e., 8/48, 17 per cent of first marriages). In most of these first marriages the bride and groom were young (the average age of the bride was 19.6 as against the sample average of 21.4; of the groom 21.8 as against 22.7[21]). Most had had rather short courtships and only two were engaged before they knew of the pregnancy[22].

The folk myth asserts that women trap men into marriage by getting pregnant. But since the forms of contraception available to most unmarried people in a town such as Swansea are the condom and withdrawal, at first sight the boot would seem to be on the other foot. However, my informants stressed the mutuality of the decision to start the pregnancy – or their shared shock at discovering one had started. Where the pregnancy and marriage are not sought, and where there was not even an intention to leave it to providence, or where it upset plans, both parties may well feel trapped. But the woman feels trapped *by the pregnancy*: she is in a worse situation (particularly when there is no option of abortion) if the man does not agree to marry her; while the man may feel himself trapped *into marriage*. However, if one considers the nineteen-year-old woman in case 46 who spent the last two months of pregnancy in hospital with toxaemia and whose husband would not allow her to go out after the baby was born except in his company (not even for a drink with his sister), quite who is 'trapped' by what seems a moot point.

This chapter has sought to provide an outline of the changes in the leisure activities, peer groupings, courtship activities, and relationships with their families of origin and with future in-laws of adolescents and young adults in Swansea, contrasting the position of men and women.

Just as those concerned with studying the transition from school to work prefer to speak of 'job entry' rather than 'job choice', since the latter suggests the perception of an alternative and the possession of a rational, fully-informed assessment of one's abilities and opportunities (see Keil, Riddell, and Green 1966) – so it seems better to speak of a 'courtship process' rather than 'mate selection'. For, while falling in love and getting married are indeed the 'central life interests' of many young people – especially girls[23], the whole manoeuvre, while inevitable, is a mystery

to the actors: it is 'just something that happens' (Slater and Woodside 1951).

But this mysterious process causes women more anxiety than men. While it is women who depend on marriage economically and who must make a good bargain, since the work that marriage entails for them – the tasks they have to do and the conditions they have to do them in – and their social standing depend on their husband; the values of romantic love, with which they are more indoctrinated than men, forbid them to see their choice of a husband in this way. And in any case they are not able to employ the same direct approach to getting married as they are to getting a job. (Nor can kin play the same manifest role as helpers.)

'Despite the attention which an attractive young girl gets from all men, it is *men* who grow up with the assumption that the decision to marry rests with them. Women, however personable, can never be sure that they will be asked to marry the man they desire. Women may not take an active part in courting. If they chase men they are ostracised . . . they must use guile and finesse.' (Sirjamaki 1948)

It is completely taken for granted in Swansea that men take the initiative in courtship. While a woman may be very active in manipulating the situation – to be in the right place at the right time, to make a man she fancies notice her – none of this must appear on the surface on pain of the man rejecting her or treating her as of 'easy virtue'. A man who tries to 'chat up' a woman also risks being rejected, of course, but the rejection is less shaming, the woman is not put off him by the very fact of his having asked, and his virtue and masculinity is not put in question. Men have the right and obligation to ask women out, to pay for outings and press for sexual 'favours' in return, and to ask women to marry them. (Note the interesting, muted, ritual of reversal in leap year – Shurmer 1972.)

Women are even further hampered and constrained in finding a husband by the continuing restriction on their social and geographical mobility[24]. The disparity between male and female in this respect becomes even wider in adolescence than it was in childhood. Fewer hobbies or sports are considered suitable for adolescent girls and women than for youths and men, and fewer facilities are provided for them. Young women cannot go to certain places or walk home alone at night – they 'need' moral and physical protection and support. When their peer group breaks up, girls need a courting relationship. Young men, on the other hand, may need to demonstrate their sexual prowess when they start work, but they only need a courting relationship when they start to think about getting themselves a wife. Thus women are likely to cling onto existing relationships – which puts them into a disadvantageous bargaining position – and they are likely to accept a marriage which is offered to them even when they are less enthusiastic about it and even though their choice is going to determine their whole life-situation.

Notes

1. The present study was not designed to observe courtship as a whole, nor to establish statistically the relation between the stages of the courtship career and age – this would need sampling of age cohorts or a longitudinal study. But, given the dearth of existing material, since information was gathered from all informants about the history of the relationship which was resulting in marriage, together with some information on previous heterosexual experience, it seems important to sketch an outline of the average courtship career. This will be supplemented by material drawn from a series of small studies of particular age groups in the town carried out by diploma students

in the university around the time of my fieldwork. (Twenty such studies were consulted.)

2. When it appears in the existing literature, 'courtship' is usually undefined. I shall use it in a wide sense, to refer to any interaction between (unmarried) persons where sexuality is significant and part of the purpose of the actors, and I shall use 'courting' to refer to such relationships when both parties acknowledge some commitment to each other (i.e., I would not confine either term to 'marriage orientated' or heterosexual interaction, though in this particular instance I am not concerned with homosexual activities).

    The notion of commitment is difficult. It is perhaps best defined as an element in a voluntary relationship which precludes its termination without explanation. People recognize, however, that because the termination of courtship can be difficult and fraught, one partner may break off abruptly and refuse to cool out the partner or to give any explanation. But this is to behave badly: the explanation is seen as *due*.

    The question immediately raised is then; to whom is the explanation due?, and here there seem to be two types of commitment:

    > *personal*, where explanation is due to the other party;
    > *social*, where the explanation is due to persons not immediately involved, viz kin and peers.

    Jacobsohn and Matheny (1962) suggest that there are four stages of courtship in the USA – dating, going steady, courting, and engagement. Their distinction between 'going steady' and 'courting' is on the basis of the temporary nature of the commitment in the first, and the goal direction towards marriage in the second. Why I do not think this is a valid distinction for South Wales is made clear in this chapter.

3. Waller describes 'dating' as 'not true courtship, since it is *supposed* not to eventuate in marriage; it is a sort of dalliance relationship . . . largely dominated by the quest of the thrill and . . . regarded as an amusement (Waller 1937:279, my italics).

    Dating is competitive and young people are careful not to allow their affairs to exceed a certain pitch of emotional intensity if they can avoid it. There is a rigid set of conventional rules governing behaviour and very light involvement; each individual being interested in the other but assuming *no* obligations as to the continuation of the affair. This is in contrast to courting, which is a step-by-step process of increasing commitment leading to marriage, with less formalized behaviour or regulation of emotional involvement. Other classic accounts of dating in America are Gorer (1948) and Hollingshead (1949). See also Reiss (1960, 1969).

4. The European Market Research Bureau carried out an international survey on engagement for De Beers in 1969/70. They used additional survey material on the UK collected by their related British Market Research Bureau: 'The Target Group Index published by BMRB shows that 2.6% (560,000) of adult women claimed to be engaged, whereas only 2.4% (470,000) of adult men said they were engaged! Who are the other 90,000 girls planning to marry?' (EMRB 1970a:2)

5. *Figure 2* Summary of ages at various points in the courtship with the person who was eventually married (first marriages)

		women	men
age when relationship started	median	18	19/20
	upper and lower quartiles	17–19	18–21
	range	14–26 (37)*	15–26 (30)*
age when got engaged	median	19/20	20/21
	upper and lower quartiles	18–21	20–23
	range	16–26 (40)*	16–26 (33)*
age at marriage	median	21	22
	upper and lower quartiles	20–22	22–23
	range	16–30 (43)*	17–29 (36)*

* One couple courted when in their thirties. They skew the picture given by 'range', so I have given the limits without them, and put them in brackets.

6. *Figure 3* Differences in age of bride and groom (first marriages)

	bride older than groom	groom older than bride	same age
No.	10	31	7
age difference:			
1 year	6	7	
2 years	2	6	
3 years	—	11	
4 years	—	4	
5 years +	2	3	

7. The average length of courtship was 7 months longer for first than for second marriages, and there was a 10 months' reduction in average length with pregnancy. There was no marked difference by s.e.c. The biggest distinction was between courtships leading up to church and civil weddings; the former were over a year longer than the latter.

Figure 4 Variations in length of courtship by marital status, pegnancy, and type of ceremony.

	average length of courtship
first marriage	2 yr 11 mths
second marriage	
for one or both	2 yr 4 mths
not pregnant	2 yr 11 mths
pregnant	2 yr 1 mth
marriage in church	3 yr 3 mths
marriage in register	
office – all	2 yr 1 mth
– first marriages	2 yr

8. See Rowntree (1962), Gavron (1966:64), Slater and Woodside (1951), and Pierce (1963).

   Gorer (1955) and EMRB (1970b) only give the length of time till engaged and the length of engagement – not of the overall courtship.

   The PIC survey found significantly more teenage brides had short courtships (under 6 months and under 18 months) than those in their early twenties, and more pregnant teenage brides had short courtships (under 6 months) than 'prudent' teenage brides (Rowntree 1962). Also, Nonconformists tended to have known each other longer before they married (fewer under a year, more over 5 years) than other denominations (Pierce 1963).

9. *Figure 5* The length of the period between leaving school, courting, and marriage (first marriage of both partners)

		women	men
length of time between	median	2 yrs	6 yrs
leaving school and	upper and lower		
starting courting the	quartiles	0–4 yrs	1½–6 yrs
person who was			
eventually married	range	–2*–22 yrs	0–15 yrs
length of time between	median	5 yrs	6 yrs
leaving school and	upper and lower		
getting married	quartiles	3½–7 yrs	4½–8½ yrs
	range	1–28 yrs	2–21 yrs

* i.e. started courting future husband two years before leaving school.

10. By law a person under 14 is not allowed in the bar of licensed premises during permitted hours (with certain exceptions); at 18 he or she may consume intoxicating liquor in a bar, *Licensing Act, 1964*, ss.18 and 169.

11. Church youth clubs – and particularly those of Nonconformist groups – retain their members much longer than do the secular, local authority clubs. Many of their members and organisers clearly recognise their role in allowing young people to meet and court. Secular youth club leaders, however, seem to discourage courting, and certainly their sex-segregated activities and the whole ethos of the clubs seem inimical to it (Parnham 1966). Church youth clubs often form natural friendship groups. Members stay primarily because they like the people they meet, but in addition they get enjoyment and support from the 'Christian fellowship'. They are often from similar backgrounds and their families are interlinked through church membership. Members look inwards for partners and stay on when courting. This is by no means a peculiarity of South Wales – similar comments have been made about church youth clubs elsewhere in the country. In Swansea, Mt Pleasant Baptist Church (with its Young People's Fellowship and youth rallies) and Morriston Tabernacl (with its choirs, *eisteddfodau*, Urdd Gobaith Cymru, and Aelwyd) are particularly important in this respect.

12. Speed also studied a similar group in Stepney (London).

13. 'In fact the first experience of sexual intercourse took place in the parental home of one or other of the young people concerned in more than half of all the cases. So parents who worry about their sons and daughters coming home late at night should, perhaps, first start wondering what is happening in their own front room when they go out in the evening!' (Schofield 1968:65)

14. *Figure 6* Circumstances of meeting spouse (percentages)

Slater & Woodside (1951) non-commissioned soliders during 2nd World War. Control group		PIC (Pierce 1963) those married in the 1950s		Gorer (1971) national sample		Swansea sample main place of meeting per couple	
street	24	dance	27	dance	24	dance	22
						pub	17
introduced by friends and relatives	22	private house	18	work	15	street	11
						work	11
work	18	work/forces	15	party, social or outing	12		
dance	12	street/ public transport	10	introduced by friends	12		
party	10	café/ restaurant/ pub	10				
other places each accounting for less than 10%	14		20		37	college	8
						home/ neighbour	7
						party	6
						blind date	6
						café	4
						holiday	2
						youth club	2
						beach	2
						choir	2

15. Cf. Perry on the importance of the bicycle in extending the geographical range of courtship in the late nineteenth century in rural Dorset (Perry 1969).

16. *Figure 7* Distance living apart when couple met

	%	
less than ½ mile	30	} 81
½–2 miles	19	
over 2–5 miles	32	
over 5–10 miles	17	
over 10	2	

Figure 8 Distance apart of the couple's homes

	%	
less than a mile	26	} 70
1–5 miles	44	
over 5–10 miles	17	
over 10 miles	13	

17. In New Haven, in 166/195 cases parents said they had sought to influence the marital choice of their child(ren), by providing a proper milieu for courtship (choosing the neighbourhood in which to live, planning activities for young people such as outings and weekend parties, developing the importance of rituals such as engagement and weddings), or by persuasion (teaching the child to honour family expectations in their choice of a mate, threatening to withdraw economic support if a child married a particular person) (Sussman 1951, 1953 a and b, 1954). Cf also Hollingshead (1950) and Bates (1942).

18. Most informants, in fact, found and married someone with the same socio-economic status as themselves (59%), and half married people with the same s.e. background (49%) (cf. Rosser and Harris 1965:98-9).

Figure 9 Socio-economic category of bride's father by that of groom's father

		RG's s.e.c. of groom's father			
		I & II	*III*	*IV & V*	*other*
RG's s.e.c.	I & II	2	2	3	
of bride's	III	4	14	7	1
father	IV & V	1	7	10	2
	other		1		

Figure 10 Socio-economic category of bride by that of groom

		RG's s.e.c. of groom			
		I & II	*III*	*IV & V*	*other*
RG's s.e.c.	I & II	7	1		
of bride	III	2	18	9	
	IV & V		8	7	
	other		2		

19. In the courtships of my informants, in 75% of cases (where applicable) the man had met the woman's parents before she met his; in 5% they met each others' parents at very nearly the same time; and in 20% of cases she met his first (usually when she was on bad terms with her own parents).

20. I talked to a senior probation officer in the town about magistrates courts giving consent to the marriage of a minor. He said:
    'We get [such couples] referred to us from solicitors, courts, Citizens

Advice Bureau, or the Superintendent Registrar. About one every three months. Usually they either stop before it goes to court, or they stop after the first day [in court], or it's adjourned for a Probation Officer's Report. Usually they're so surprised and shocked to find themselves with the Probation Service that they sort it out between them – we don't see them again. The number which actually go through, with the magistrates actually making a decision . . . I'd say one in five, no, perhaps one in two years.'

'What is the basis of the magistrates' judgement?)

'I think if the boy can show he can provide adequately – support a family . . . Or if they're in the family way – that definitely influences the magistrates to give permission.'

21. Six brides and one groom among my 'pregnant' informants were under 21 (the age of majority at the time). The PIC also found that pregnant brides were usually in their teens and were predominantly marrying semi- or unskilled manual workers (Pierce 1963).

22. Non-marital intercourse is rather more acceptable when the couple are engaged than when they have no formal commitment to each other. Nonetheless, three-quarters of the marriages in my sample which were precipitated by pregnancy were not preceded by engagement. (It is likely, however, on hearsay evidence, that some of the weddings in church arranged at short notice – which I missed – were precipitated by pregnancies started during an engagement.)

23. Those who work with adolescent girls repeatedly comment along the lines that:

'Most of the girls I talked to were only fifteen years old and every minute of their lives was taken up exclusively with thinking about, talking about, or being with one boy . . . The vast majority of girls I talked to in the London area who had discontinued their [youth club] membership mentioned *no other interests* apart from going out with their boyfriends.' (Atteridge 1965, emphasis in original)

24. The constraints on women's physical mobility are only slowly being made obvious by writings from the women's movement (e.g., Poggi and Coonaert 1974; Bengis 1973; Brownmiller 1975).

In this description of Swansea it has been shown that young women are not allowed out as often, have to give an account of where they are going, and have to be in earlier than do young men, and the discrimination in treatment increases during adolescence.

In the home girls are expected to be 'by the fire' in the sitting room, whereas boys are able to, e.g., mend bicycles in the garden or to retire to their bedrooms. Outside the home young women have less money to pay for entertainment and are less likely to have their own means of transport. They are liable to hassling – even attack – in the street, especially after dark, often by groups of young men (Peters 1972; Brownmiller 1975), and they have no peer group meeting place comparable to the pub.

5 The ritual cycle of engagement and wedding I: engagement, wedding preparations, and preliminaries

The next two chapters describe the rituals associated with courtship and the process of getting married – engagement, bottom drawers, stag and hen parties, joking at work, weddings, receptions, honeymoons, parties, etc. – with the aim of showing the complexity of the ceremonial cycle and the time, money, and energy devoted to it. It will also show the current duality within the system between 'proper weddings' and those held in the register office.

As was mentioned in earlier chapters, all that is required for a legally valid marriage in England and Wales is that the couple verbally assent to taking each other as husband and wife before an authorised person in a registered church or register office, and that the marriage be then recorded and filed by the General Register Office. But in Swansea most people want 'the full works' when they go through a life-cycle crisis, and for a wedding the full works – a 'proper wedding' – involves being married in a nice church by a minister of religion, with the bride in a long white dress and veil and the groom in a suit (often a morning suit), with several bridesmaids and ushers and as many in the congregation as possible, followed by a reception for forty or more guests in a club or hotel, with a three-course meal and a multi-tiered wedding cake, and then a honeymoon in London or abroad for one or two weeks.

Such weddings are remarkably uniform. There is firm consensus on what is the correct procedure and great concern to 'get it right'. There may be variation in scale – from an 'average' wedding costing £250-£350 (in 1969) to a 'really big' wedding costing over £750 – and in the form of items – e.g., the style of dress and the decorations on the cake – which make it personal: not just anybody's wedding, but John and Mary's wedding. But big or small, the component parts are all included and to the unsophisticated the range would appear slight.

Register office weddings, on the other hand, are varied, ranging from 'very quiet' ceremonies with only the two participants and two witnesses (no special clothes – just Sunday best, no reception, and no honeymoon) to those that have the same basic structure as a proper wedding but with each item drastically reduced (e.g., the bride in a short white dress with no veil, a buffet reception at home) and some items omitted altogether; the whole being marked by less formality, less publicity and less solemnity.

The full ceremonial cycle of engagement and wedding may be spread over about two and a half years. The actual planning for a proper wedding lasts a *minimum* of three months; nine months to a year would be regarded as more reasonable notice to allow for booking the reception and the church, and for parents to save up to meet the costs[1].

The events of the cycle occur in roughly the following order:

Figure 1 Events of the ceremonial cycle of engagement and wedding

event	*when it takes place*	*constituent rituals*
engagement	average of just under 2 years before the wedding	deciding to get engaged; fixing a date for engagement; asking the girl's father's permission (see ch. 4); announcement: buying and wearing rings, party, notice in paper; giving of engagement presents
	variable	starting a 'bottom drawer'
	variable	finding a place to live when married (see ch. 7)
wedding	12–3 months before	fixing the date and booking reception and church; preparation (choice and booking/buying of: wedding dress, what groom will wear, invitations and hymn sheets, cake, flowers, cars, photographer)
	6 weeks before	sending out invitations

week before	stag and hen parties; joking at work;	} order varies
	giving and display of wedding presents (see ch. 7)	
wedding day	segregation of bride and groom before ceremony and of guests in church; wedding ceremony reception;	
	departure of bride and groom evening party	} order varies
weeks after	honeymoon; distribution of cakes and flowers; return to new home; notice in paper; photograph album and keeping of other souvenirs	

Engagement

Engagement is the clear, public marking of a decision to marry having been reached and it is seen as a definite move towards being married. It generally lasts between six months and three years. Case 18:

> (Bride) 'Well, when you're courting there's no ties – you can finish when you like. When you're engaged you're more or less married – got a ring on – half-way there. You know you're going to get married. You can't go with anyone else. If you're only courting you can't start saving or making plans.'

Getting engaged is important as a way of taking the big status transition of marriage step-by-step. One goes from courting and thinking and then talking about marriage, jokingly or in general, to talking about when *we* are engaged, to telling parents one wants to get engaged, to fixing the date for the 'official' engagement, celebrating the engagement, being engaged, fixing the date for the wedding, and finally getting married. This applies in terms of one's own self-perception, and in the ease of broaching the subject to significant others. Quite a number of men asked their girl-friends 'Shall we get engaged' or, even more indirectly, 'If I bought you a ring, would you wear it?'; and it is certainly easier to to ask one's parents if one may get engaged than it is to ask straight out if one can get married: they cannot legally refuse, and one is showing that one is not moving hastily or rashly, or 'having to get married'.

Case 24:

> (Bride) 'We'd decided before we got engaged when we would marry, but we waited until two months after we were engaged before we told my parents the date.'

> (Groom) 'Susan wanted to get married straight away [once they had decided]. When you're engaged first it's OK. But if you get married quickly, people think "Hullo! How's your father! etc.".'

Parents certainly use engagement as a delaying tactic – when the couple are young and/or they want to discourage the match, or simply to make certain that the 'children' are not being irresponsible.

Case 13 (bride):

> The night after they had decided to get married they told her parents together – September 1966, when the groom was home on leave from the army. 'They said "No, I was too young".'

> The bride 'nagged and nagged and quarrelled and fought' until they agreed that they could at least get engaged (March 1967). They married in December 1968.

Case 18:

> The bride and groom were both sixteen when they got engaged. His father 'wanted us to have a long engagement – to be certain. He wanted us to wait till we were twenty-one so we could take up our own mortgage. But after three years, we thought "That's long enough" . . . We didn't save nothing much until about a year before [the wedding]. Just having a bit of fun. Then we started saving with the Abbey National. See, we were going to have a white wedding [for which they would have had to pay as she had no father]. We saw his father. He said "Where were you thinking of living?". We said "In a flat". At first his parents were a bit funny. See, his first brother had to get married. So in the end they asked us outright, did we have to? And we said *no*. So his father said "Wouldn't it be more sensible to get your own place?". I [bride] said it'd be very *nice*, but I wasn't bothered. We'd got £100 odd saved.'

> The bargain was made that they should have a register office wedding and the groom's parents would provide a buffet reception in their house. The couple could use their money as a deposit on a small terraced house, with the groom's father acting as a guarantor on the mortgage.

> In this case, not only was the groom's father a very forceful character

and a prosperous small businessman, he was also the groom's employer.

Whilst there are certainly elements of 'games playing' in this attribution to parents of responsibility for putting a brake on courtship (the one that Eric Berne identifies as 'If It Weren't For You' (1967:45 ff)), parents do in fact have real power to refuse consent or various forms of aid and support (a fact Berne too often overlooks).

While young men favour engagement because it shows that the relationship is respectable and 'to have a tag on her', for a woman engagement is particularly important in giving her security that he 'won't go galavanting any more'. The search for a husband is so important that she cannot afford to stop going out with other suitors unless a relationship is seen 'to be going somewhere'. The giving of the ring is a tangible sign of the young man's commitment. Case 20:

> He proposed three weeks after they started going out. She 'thought he was kidding'. He moved (because of his job) to London four months later and she 'thought that was the end of it'. Despite his protestations that he was serious, she 'hardened herself to it'. But he wrote and came to see her regularly, and eventually he arrived at Christmas with an engagement ring.
> 'It didn't mean much at the time – just got myself a man and a ring on my finger. I'd not thought seriously about marriage until he committed himself.'

This slower development of attachment to a particular relationship by women is culturally recognised (cf. Gorer 1955; Slater and Woodside 1951), but is attributed to women's desire to have an engagement ring, rather than to the importance of marriage to her, the greater significance of whom she marries, and the fact that she can take no direct initiative within a relationship.

Whilst it is held that most people are serious in their intentions when they get engaged, there are 'some who do it to follow the herd'. 'Some men' do it in the hopes of sexual advantage (one Roman Catholic girl broke off her previous engagement because her (non-Catholic) fiancé assumed she would then 'be naughty'). 'Some women' do it 'for show': they 'don't wear gloves for a month', showing off their having 'caught' a man. (As with most dominated groups (cf. Allport 1955) the criticism of women's behaviour is particularly barbed and vociferous from other women.)

Engagement is exclusively associated with first marriage – none of the six couples among my informants where the man and/or woman had previously been married got engaged before their second (or third) wedding, and 20 per cent of those marrying for the first time also 'didn't bother'. Engagement is much more common among those who have a long courtship and among women who marry late (over twenty-three), and more common among non-manual workers (especially male white-collar workers). It is much less common among those marrying in the register office, among those who marry when the bride is pregnant, and among teenage brides[3].

The stress in engagement is on saving and preparing for married life; Case 15:

> (Bride) 'Oh, I wanted to get engaged to save up and buy the things I wanted. It was impossible to get married very soon. I'm old-fashioned: I believe in getting a home together before you're married. Getting engaged meant we really set our minds on saving for a home together. We pooled our resources and got right down to it.'

But for those 30 per cent who do not get engaged, the argument can be turned the other way. Case 8:

> (Bride) 'We think it's a waste of time. Not much better than courting. Most girls sit like this [with hand ostentatiously and clumsily held out so as to keep the ring visible] – they get engaged for the ring.'
> (Groom) 'You're tied, but only half-way there.' (He had, in fact, wanted to get engaged.)
> (Bride) 'We need the money more than a ring.'

Announcing the engagement: the ring, celebration, and notice in the paper

When my neighbour's daughter announced that she wanted to get married her mother spent the whole of the following morning telling neighbours (including me) and talking to relatives on the 'phone. Most people with whom the bride associates, however, get to know of her intended marriage when she starts to wear a diamond ring on the fourth finger of her left hand.

Rings are very special elements of jewelry in Britain, given between kin and couples. In Swansea a woman may wear

> 'dress rings' – i.e., one bought for oneself for its decorative value alone. Worn on any finger except the fourth left, put on and removed at will;
>
> a 'keeper' – a gold ring, with some sort of clasp (e.g., a buckle, or joined hands). Bought for her by a boy-friend. Worn on either hand, but if on the fourth left finger it indicates a steady committed relationship;
>
> an 'engagement ring' – an expensive ring (£20–£40), with a large

precious stone; quite distinctive. If the stone is not a diamond, the setting will almost certainly contain diamonds. Bought by her fiancé. Often worn all the time; certainly whenever she goes out of the house on social occasions;

a 'wedding ring' – gold (or occasionally platinum or white gold), plain or patterned. Bought by her husband and put on her fourth left finger during the wedding ceremony. Other rings are optional; this one, though not legally required, is worn by all married women. Considerable superstition attaches to never taking it off, and most will be buried with it on[4];

'eternity rings' – silver or gold rings, often with tiny stones (diamonds, rubies, sapphires) set all round. She may have several of these. Given by a husband to a wife as a mark of his continuing valuation of her – on a wedding anniversary or the birth of a child. Same pattern of wearing as an engagement ring.

These last four types of ring are all given by the male member of the couple to the female, and they are all worn on the fourth left finger. (A keeper would be moved to another finger, or given away – for example to a younger sister or mother – when the engagement ring was bought.) The last three are all worn together, so that the first joint of the finger may be covered in jostling rings.

Quite a lot of men – and women – are hostile to the idea of men wearing any sort of ring. It is thought to be 'unmasculine' or 'effeminate', and, further, to be dangerous. I was often told of 'a mate who nearly had a finger off' at work or playing sport because his ring got caught on something. However, the sorts of rings a Swansea man *may* wear are:

a 'keeper' (as for women) – rare;

'signet rings' – heavy plain gold rings with a large face, sometimes with his initials engraved on it, or occasionally with a flat dark stone (onyx, bloodstone, cornelian, lapis lazuli), which may also be carved. Worn on third, fourth, or fifth finger of either hand – though if on fourth left it usually (though not invariably) means he is engaged or married. May be bought for self, by parents, or by girl-friend for a Christmas or birthday present, or when they get engaged or married, or after marriage. The same ring may be transferred from, e.g., fourth right to fourth left when he gets engaged;

a 'wedding ring' – like women's wedding rings, except more solid and heavier. Put on during or around the time of the wedding, on fourth left (and other rings removed from this finger).

Thus, for example;

Case 51:

> The groom used to wear two signet rings, on his little fingers. One he 'got off his parents' and the other he won gambing. 'He'll have a wedding ring because he likes rings. But he won't have a plain gold band [i.e., one which is not very ornamental, but unambiguously a wedding ring]. Now [some months after they got engaged] he's taken one of the signet rings and put it on his wedding finger. I [bride] was going to buy him a ring [when we got engaged], but the one he wanted was a bit expensive. So he's having it for his birthday – a fortnight after the wedding.'

Case 48:

> The bride's parents had given her a signet ring when she was nine or ten, which the groom wore on a chain round his neck when they decided to get married, in exchange for his cricket medal (started courting February 1967, decided in April, engaged in November).
>
> (Did you wear any rings before you got engaged?)
> (Groom) 'No, but Jennifer persuaded me. I'd never thought of wearing a ring before, ever. But engagement rings aren't cheap and she wanted to give me something back. I suggested a watch, but she wanted a ring. It'd have upset her to say no. So we got me a signet with my initials [worn on fourth left finger]. And a wedding ring. That was a bit of persuasion, too. I was quite content with the signet; but she said she'd got to wear one, so why not me?'
> (Bride) 'I think it was decided by Malcolm [a close friend] having one.'
> (Groom) '*And* because you'd have nagged!'
>
> When they went to get the engagement ring, 'his little sister came along too'! She wanted a signet ring for her birthday. 'We checked with his mother first – it's usually parents who buy that sort of thing. Like your first wrist watch.'

Women are more sophisticated as to the significance of rings[5], and they notice what rings people wear more often than do men. The rings they themselves wear are unambiguous, worn on particular fingers, and put on formally at particular times. There is a specific rubric covering this in the Roman Catholic and Anglican services, and the Church blesses the woman's wedding ring[6].

The signet rings men commonly wear are ambiguous, and whether to wear one or not depends on individual taste. Very few men wear wedding rings, though the proportion who do is probably increasing. A few couples – mostly middle class or skilled working class and students –

wanted to *exchange* rings as part of their emphasis on the 'symmetricality' of the relationship: since rings are seen as indicating that a person is 'spoken for' they felt it should apply as much to men as to women. That is to say, both husband and wife should equally 'keep themselves only unto their spouse' after marriage. I did not find that it indicated any alteration of the sexual dual standard before marriage, nor any change in the division of labour between the sexes within marriage.

The average couple in Swansea in 1968 spent about £30 on an engagement ring[7] – most were very careful not to tell me the exact cost (though many young women claimed to be able to 'price' other people's rings). The significance of the expense would seem to be that no young man who was not serious would spend that much, and no woman would accept it if she was not.

Approximately half my informants were adamant that one had to have a ring – 'even it it's only Woolworths' – to be engaged; others accepted that one *could* be engaged without a ring, but that it would be difficult.

Case 16:

> 'My sister got engaged without a ring. But she felt she was missing something – so they got her one later [before the wedding]. It didn't seem official somehow.'

Case 23:

> 'You can't be engaged without a ring. You might feel you could but your parents wouldn't. You'd feel a fool. You might just as well say "I'm getting married" and be done with it. Engagement is, well, a ring.'

The actual buying and putting on of the ring is done by the couple together; it is followed by a celebration for relatives and friends; and there is then an announcement to the world at large in the local paper.

(1) Buying the ring: the couple

In almost every case the couple buy the ring together[8]. The woman generally has a fair idea of what sort of ring she fancies – a cluster, twist, or solitaire, and what sort of stone – and the man generally says 'how much she can go up to'. In a few cases the woman makes a preliminary tour of the shops to look before going with the groom; but in general

> 'We trudged through the rain . . . '
> 'He insisted I look in *every* shop . . . '
> or else 'We bought it together in ten minutes flat . . . '

If the groom is living a long way away from the bride, he may buy a ring and bring it to her.

The ring is then usually put on at once, often with amusement about the lack of formality and the banal surroundings for romance:

'In his car, by the bus station!'
'In the milk bar!'
'Upstairs in the Three Lamps!'

Like the accounts of meeting one's spouse, but unlike the accounts of being asked and deciding to get married, these stories sound well-polished set pieces.

(2) Celebration: relatives and friends

The engagement is usually celebrated by a group of 6–15 (either the couple, their parents, and sibs and sibs' spouses; or the couples and their sibs and sibs' spouses and the couple's close friends) going out for a meal or a drink (34 per cent); or having a party at home (34 per cent). It may be the first occasion on which the two sets of parents meet.

Parties in private houses can obviously only accommodate limited numbers – the maximum estimated to have come was seventy – others suggested eight, fifteen, 'no more than twenty', thirty, and two, forty. Smaller parties may be 'sit down meals' of ham, lettuce, and tomato, bread and butter, cakes and tea, followed by an evening of beer for the men and sherry for the women. At larger parties there will be cold buffets (sausages, crisps, sandwiches, and vol-au-vents), with a record player for dancing. Sometimes the engagement party is combined with a party for another purpose – the groom's twenty-first birthday, a leaving party for a flat-mate, Christmas, the evening party of someone else's wedding – just so long as one has 'a bit of a do' to mark the occasion. Some of these end in shambles, with 'people drunk all over the place, at two o'clock in the morning, and [the groom's friend] being sick in the garden'.

Occasionally there are more formal parties at clubs or hotels. The two most elaborate were foretastes of the wedding:

Case 40:

'At the Rock and Fountain, Skewen – all our relatives and friends – about sixty odd. We had a special room in the evening . . . Had an engagement cake – big square one. [She showed me a photograph, with her and her fiancé cutting it. It was like a one-tier wedding cake.] White with pink icing – "To Kay and Tony. Congratulations on your engagement" – and decorated with roses and ferns. I kept some and pressed them in the album with the photos.'

Case 15:

> 'In the Dolphin All our family, relatives, and friends – about ninety. My father paid. We had a buffet but you were waited on at your table. Cooked meats and so on. It was very nice. We had a toast master who sort of announced the engagement and the putting on of the ring. Bit embarrassing.'

All the formal engagement parties were followed by white weddings.

Of those who did 'nothing' when they got engaged (20 per cent), most were in category I or II occupations. Of those who were not, one said her father gave her cash and presents in lieu of paying for a party, and the other 'couldn't bear the fuss'.

(3) Announcements of engagement in the local paper: telling the world at large

Of those who got engaged, 60 per cent put an announcement in the local daily evening paper, the *Evening Post*. The actual process of insertion is not expensive but it takes time. The paper has a form which has to be filled in and returned, and the paper specifies that it be signed by both the young man and the young woman to guard against practical jokes.

The most common reason for putting the announcement in the paper was that the 'parents wanted it'. Often the groom's mother or his parents were reported as requesting or arranging it – even on occasion without consulting the couple. One woman said 'it came as a bit of a surprise'; another was more forthright. Case 39 (bride):

> 'It was in the paper.'
> (Who put it in?) 'By his mother. I wasn't keen on having it in the paper – and if it was in I'd rather it was my parents who did it. Richard's parents did it secretly – she must have forged both our signatures – and she gave it to me on the day of the party (his twenty-first birthday party, where the engagement was announced), saying more or less "Surprise, surprise!". She tries to help, but really she sticks her nose in. I was furious.'

The next most frequently expressed reasons for insertion were: because it seemed 'the natural thing to do', or 'the done thing'; to 'let everybody know'; for the pleasure of seeing one's name in print; to have as a memento ('He bought the first edition and brought it home', 'It's nice to keep – I've got five copies'); and to make the step taken seem even more definite.

Just who is being told via the paper is vague to the actors, since friends are told directly and relations are contacted by letter or phone. I think it is probably to let friends and neighbours *of relations* know, and casual acquaintances. (One informant whom I saw when I was eight months pregnant said she had looked in the births section for an announcement of my baby at the time when it was due, but it was not there. Her mother had said it would not be because 'she doesn't have any family here'.) Parents are more likely to want the announcement in the paper than younger people because they have more 'acquaintances' whom they wish to inform but with whom they are not in personal, frequent contact, and they are likely to have sibs in the town, each with his or her own network.

Since effort and expense is involved in putting the notice in the paper, those who did not (40 per cent) included a large minority who 'didn't bother – just didn't get around to it'; 'No wish not to and no specific wish to put it in'; as well as others who more firmly 'didn't like the idea at all – for everybody to know about it' and who 'didn't want a fuss' and are embarrassed at being the centre of attention. There were also a few who 'didn't believe in it – waste of money, really. As long as you know you're engaged, no need to tell anyone.' Some felt that friends should be told personally, not have it formally announced, while the wider group of acquaintances 'will find out anyway, bound to, sooner or later'.

Businesses (car hire firms, stationers for invitations, etc., furniture shops, businesses hiring out gowns and suits, etc.) use the announcements of engagements as a source of addresses to circulate with their advertisements. Case 32 (bride): 'I got stuff from florists, bridal shops, a photographer, and someone who hires out buses and taxis; and he got stuff on family planning – Lloyds or something similar (manufacturers of condoms).' This leads the couple, should they need any encouragement, to thoughts of the consumer goods for weddings and setting up home, and sex.

Saving up for marriage – the bottom drawer

In the previous chapter the change in leisure activities in the year or so before the wedding when the couple were saving money together was stressed, and earlier in this chapter it was shown that the commitment and security of engagement was important in letting the couple plan for their future together, moving forward at a respectable pace. Their new status is heralded by the giving of 'domestic' presents to them as a couple by parents, kin, neighbours, and friends. These are generally not very expensive presents – a kettle, a set of mixing bowls, a pair of towels, or kitchen scales – usually costing £2 to £3 (in 1969; £6 to £9 at 1978 prices). People do not ask what is wanted: they simply arrive with a present. There is no particular time when these are handed over. One informant kept a complete list of the presents they/she had been given[9]: Case 35:

groom's mother and father – £20
groom's brother – £5
bride's mother's mother – £5
bride's father's mother – chrome sandwich plate stand
bride's father's sister – towels
bride's father's sister's daughter – pillow cases
bride's mother's friend – towels
bride's mother's friend – pillow cases
groom's mother's sister – table cloth and napkins
groom's mother's friend – pillow cases
groom's father's brother's wife – electric clock
groom's mother's friend – table cloth and napkins
bride and groom's friends (engaged couple) – laundry basket
bride's friend – cruet set
bride's friend – wooden nut barrow
groom's friends – tea spoons
groom's brother's fiancée – fruit spoons
bride's friend – kitchen set
groom's mother's friend (neighbour) – pastry knives
groom's brother's wife's mother – towels
groom's brother's wife's mother's sister
  (lives next door to groom) – towels
bride's friend's mother – breakfast set for two
bride's mother and father – teak ottoman
groom's father's parents – bathroom set and pillow cases

The bride's 'bottom drawer' is often formed around this nucleus of engagement presents, though equally frequently it is started by a female relative (grandmother, aunt, or her mother) when the girl is 12–13, or she may have 'started putting things by which I thought might come in handy when I was married' when in her late teens or early twenties.

Case 24 (bride):

'My great aunt, who's now ninety-two, started me off with a packet of dusters and pillow cases when I was twelve and a half. It was a family joke. White heavy cotton with lace all round. I don't think anyone would ever use them nowadays.'

Case 53 (bride):

'Started by my mother when I was thirteen or fourteen. She's done it all for me. Bedding, linen, dusters, floor cloth, canteen of cutlery . . .'

Case 51 (bride):

> 'I've got about six drawers – all full. I started before I even met him (i.e., before twenty-one). Little things. I didn't need them then but I thought they'd be useful when I got married.'

Case 26 (bride):

> 'About a year after I met him (when she was 15–16), *his mother* started it off for me. Talk about hinting! She gave me a water set, pyrex dishes, and tea towels.'

In some cases when they were courting for a long time the couple started saving up and buying things some time before they got engaged; or the young man may buy such things as presents for the woman – 'It got so he never bought me anything else!'. Sometimes the groom also buys things from time to time – 'a rug, a picture, and a coffee table' – and keeps them in his house.

There is a certain ambiguity as to whether these presents are given to the couple or to the bride. Legally gifts made because of the engagement and marriage are conditional on that marriage and become the joint property of the couple when they marry. (If they do not marry the gifts should be returned to the donor.) However, since most of the presents relate to 'women's work' – toasters, bedding, tea-towels, irons, and ironing boards – they are *seen* as given to the bride rather than to the couple (except by those on the groom's side who do not know her at all). An equal number of presents are given from each side. By and large the gifts are kept in the bride's home. According to the etiquette books it is she who is supposed to write 'thank you letters' to those who give presents. (This applies *a fortiori* to wedding presents, which are sent partly at least in response to wedding invitations sent out by the bride's parents.) Thus who it is that is 'marrying the house' (becoming a house-wife) and taking on a new occupation is made clear. The young man is also interested in building up the contents of their new home and will make considerable financial contributions to this end; but it is seen as the woman's responsibility to look after it and its contents.

As the young couple build up joint property, especially nearer the wedding when they receive much more substantial wedding presents and may start buying a house together, and as the wedding preparations gather momentum, it becomes harder and harder to 'call the whole thing off'. There is also a change in self-perception because one is always being treated as part of a couple – even at the level of ownership of a stainless steel teapot.

One woman I met at a reception who had broken off her engagement a few weeks before the wedding, had been taken right away from the town by her parents for several weeks 'while the whole mess was cleared up': the arrangements cancelled, the house put back on the market, and the presents returned. The sister of an informant was reported to have changed her mind about getting married at the last minute – the very night before the wedding. But she was persuaded to change it back again because, as her father said, gesturing at the preparations, 'what are we going to do with all this beer, then?!'.

Others who did break off earlier in the relationship used disposing of the engagement presents as a means of thumbing their noses at their erstwhile partner. Case 5 (bride):

'We had our engagement party on Valentine's Day . . . By June we'd split up! He had his ring back! . . . All the things he'd bought he took back one Sunday afternoon – blankets, saucepans, crockery . . . He took away a whole load of bedding. All the neighbours were watching as he staggered out! He sold if half price for a night out with the boys – a *good* night out. I knew I was going back [to him], so I didn't dare give any back.'

Preparations for the wedding

Engagements last a median of a little under two years and arrangements for a proper wedding may start a year to eighteen months in advance with the booking of the reception and the church. The more popular places for receptions get booked up well in advance and several informants had been very provoked when they found the place they wanted was not available for the date they had chosen. Clergy told me they had bookings for up to eighteen months ahead for popular Saturdays and Bank Holidays. Case 26:

One couple who had started courting in the summer of 1962 (when she was fourteen and he was fifteen), got engaged in March 1965 and started to make the bookings for the wedding in September 1967.
(Bride) 'February 5th [1969] was the only Saturday we could get between September and April. I wanted it last September [1968], but I wanted The Pines, so we waited. I told my mother we'd booked for February. She thought I meant the *next* February [1968], and she said ''You've not given me much time!''. We didn't rush things at all. I was engaged young.'

Most older couples would have tried for a reception elsewhere; but the desire to get everything perfect – in this case having the reception in the place one has 'set one's heart on' – is typical, as is a feeling of being under pressure (to move fast and make bookings) as soon as the date is decided.

Other preparations get into full swing three to six months before 'the big day'. The brides' magazines present a 'wedding count down' which reads like a military operation (see Figure 2). Particular and sustained attention is directed towards the bride's body and costume.

(1) Costume of the bride, groom, and attendants

It is a cultural imperative that a bride should look beautiful and a great deal of time and energy and money is spent to ensure that as far as possible she conforms to this expectation. Bridal magazines suggest starting anything up to six months before the wedding with diets and exercises to lose weight, firm muscles, and improve the skin and hair. They also supply endless streams of advice on make-up to go with white, styles of dress to suit different figures, head-dresses for different shapes of face, and so on; and such advice is read by a majority of those planning white weddings. (Some obviously read more magazines and take more notice of the advice than do others.) The attention to detail, e.g., to the colour of the nail varnish and to the choice of flowers, would be hard to overstate, and a broken nail or a laddered stocking on the wedding day is very upsetting and is reported to friends, neighbours, workmates – and visiting sociologists – weeks after the event.

The wedding dress itself is often bought six months in advance and then kept in the shop till the week before the wedding – so as to keep it secret, sometimes to enable payment in instalments, and because there is no suitable storage available in most working and middle-class housing. Case 6 (bride):

'Well, I started out wanting something I could wear again. So I had a dress and coat in mind. My mother dragged me into the shop. I'd never looked much. Passing "Dorothy's", we were. I thought it would be [cost] too much. [Mother] went in and asked, and it was £30. They had a book of photos [of other styles], but none I liked as much. But it was only a week after we got engaged, and I didn't like to ask them to keep it six months; but they didn't mind. Anyway, I had no money on me, so I went back in after. They're keeping it for me for eight months.'

The details of the dress are usually kept secret from all but a select few – the bride's mother, the bride's closest friends, and sometimes the groom's mother – and in no case did the groom see the dress, much less the bride wearing the dress, before the day of the wedding. Most said that this was 'supposed to be unlucky'; and it seemed to be associated with making the wedding more of an occasion ('like saving parcels till Christmas'). Case 11:

(bride): 'Surprise is the greatest part of making that proud feeling. I want him to fall in love all over again.'

Few wedding dresses are made at home. Case 28:

'I was going to have it made and looked at patterns, but I work in a shop and in the lunch hour I tried one of ours on. I liked it so much I paid a bit more to be sure . . . Rather than have it made and then decide I didn't like it.'

The wedding dress should 'do something' for the bride-to-be when she tries it on (i.e., make her look beautiful, accentuate her best points) and this perhaps explains the rather surprising finding that (as in Case 6 above) quite a lot of dresses are bought on impulse, when mother and daughter are out shopping together and they 'see something they fancy'.

Figure 2 Wedding countdown from 'Brides' magazine (an insert section included in all issues)

BRIDES AND SETTING UP HOME
WEDDING GUIDE

Diary dates

Once you're engaged, you'll want to tell the world. Use local and/or national press. An average length announcement costs from about 10s. 6d. for the former, the latter about £10. See the appropriate paper for exact cost, wording, etc.

☐ Now decide what sort of wedding you want and discuss it with both sets of parents.

☐ Choose the date, again in consultation with both sets of parents.

☐ Use this diary to tick arrangements as they are made.

As soon as the date is settled

☐ See the vicar or minister. He will advise you on all the arrangements and formalities to do with the ceremony—the banns, for instance. If you are to be married in a register office—or anywhere other than the state church—see the Registrar as soon as possible.

☐ Discuss the number of guests and come to an agreement with both sets of parents.

☐ Decide where the reception is to be held and make the booking.

☐ Contact caterers.

☐ Order the cars from a local firm.

☐ Choose a photographer and book him.

☐ Begin a wedding guest list. Make sure both mothers keep to the agreed numbers.

Three months before

☐ Choose your bridesmaids and ushers.

☐ Start thinking about your dress and discuss with your bridesmaids what they're going to wear. Nowadays most pay for their own dresses, so be kind and pick a style that's wearable afterwards.

☐ Book a dressmaker.

☐ Start your "bottom drawer".

☐ See a stationer and order invitations and boxes for cake.

☐ Work on your wedding guest list (make sure your address book is up to date).

☐ Make an appointment with your doctor for a pre-marital check-up.

Two months before

☐ Start a list of presents you'd like.

☐ Choose basic patterns and colours for your linens and china, etc.

☐ Begin to shop for your trousseau.

☐ Consult and confirm with caterers on food and drink.

☐ Choose and order your cake.

☐ See a florist about flowers for the church and bouquets.

☐ Put passport formalities in hand.

☐ If your wedding ring is being specially made, order it now.

☐ Start thinking about hymns and music for the service.

☐ Send out invitations six weeks before the day.

One month before

☐ Last minute for buying your wedding dress and bridesmaids' dresses. If they're being made, check that everything's up to schedule. At the fitting, check if you need a special bra, slip or girdle.

☐ Buy headdresses, veil, shoes.

☐ Check that honeymoon clothes are complete.

☐ Ask both mothers about their dresses so that colours don't clash.

☐ Choose presents for attendants.

☐ Note acceptances on wedding list.

☐ Send marked copies of BRIDES present list to those who've asked what you'd like. Or tell them at which store you have your list.

☐ Keep up to date with thank you letters, ticking them off as you go.

☐ Order service sheets.

☐ Check with your fiancé that he's remembered his clothes, the ring, honeymoon booking, etc.

One week before

☐ Double check all your wedding clothes.

☐ Take your headdress to your hairdresser to rehearse the hairstyle.

☐ Practise wedding day make-up.

☐ Check there are no snags on cars, flowers, catering, etc.

☐ The day before, have a rehearsal at the church, if possible.

☐ Wear your wedding shoes around the house to break them in.

Sending the invitations

Printed invitations aren't essential—a short, hand-written letter from your mother will do just as well—but for any thing other than a very small wedding, they save a lot of time. You can see specimens of type and wording in any stationer's shop. Normally the invitation will come from the bride's parents and will say "Mr. and Mrs. John Sinclair request the pleasure of your company at the marriage of their daughter, etc." Where the situation isn't quite so straight forward the invitations should be sent in the name of whoever is giving the wedding, changing the wording where necessary...

'As soon as I saw her in it, I knew it was Susan's wedding dress.' Bridal magazines and their advertisers certainly foster these ideas.

Hiring dresses and buying one second-hand does not meet with approval from most people[10]. Some did say that they might have considered it if there had been better facilities in Swansea, but since one would have had to go a larger town at some distance and they could all cite 'horror stories' about friends of friends who had hired dresses which on the day had proved to be too small or mud- or wine-stained, they had decided against. About an equal number said they thought hiring was not in fact any cheaper and many said that, anyway, they wanted a dress of their own to keep. These costumes are indeed often kept after the wedding, sometimes for many years. (One or two informants showed me their *mother's* dress, kept as a memento, for luck, and for lack of any clear idea what else to do with it.) A few proposed to use their wedding dress to make the christening gown for their first child. Only two brides said they wanted to sell their dress afterwards, but they had little success. One put an advertisement in the local paper but had only one telephone call in reply (from a woman who failed to keep the appointment).

A further group of more extreme reactions to the suggestion of hiring a dress is particularly interesting:

'I wouldn't fancy wearing what someone else had got married in.'

'If I was going to sink that low I'd have insisted on the registry office and not got married in white.'

And from one woman who told me she *had* hired a dress came a request that I 'keep it quiet' (Case 49): 'I haven't told people at work because they're a catty lot. They'd think of all the things that they'd said about not wearing someone else's dress . . . about it being dirty . . . '

This last point – the pollution involved in wearing clothes someone else has worn – is significant, since it does not seem to apply to men's clothes. When the groom, best man, and ushers wear morning suits, these, and the shirts and even shoes to go with them, are almost invariably hired. In part it seems that the fear of pollution is due to the more intimate contact of the bride's dress (though rationally the contact of a man's hired shirt is as close). It seems indubitable that the bride is to be 'pure' and 'unsullied' in a way not applicable to the groom. To re-emphasize this point, and to show that it is not a personal idiosyncracy of the particular girl, it should be recorded that one group of stores (Pronuptia) specializing in weddings used as its big selling point at the time that, 'Every bride-to-be who purchases from our stores enjoys the luxury of a brand new wedding gown *never tried on* by anyone before' (my emphasis).

The purity of the bride is also symbolized in the colour of her dress.

While people were generally very vague about the meaning of rituals – confetti was 'for luck', horseshoes were 'for luck', etc. (Barker 1972a) – about the whiteness of the wedding dress there was agreement. Case 16: 'Actually I was quite surprised . . . I was going to get married in a gold dress and coat; but when I thought of it, white definitely meant something . . . virginal . . . purity . . . ' Studies on the sexual behaviour of young adults (Schofield 1973) show that the majority of brides are not sexually inexperienced when they marry – as one groom said, 'Everybody has a bite to eat before breakfast nowadays'. But 'virginity' is not necessarily as absolute nor quite what a literalist might have supposed. One young man put it that (Case 37), 'There's virgins and virgins. There's girls who've lost their virginity to lots of fellows, and others who've lost it only to the one they're marrying.' Thus for the bride to wear 'virginal white' indicates merely that she is sexually virtuous. Her appearance also shows her innocence and modesty, via the veil over her face, the expectation that she will be 'blushing', and in the styling of her dress. Wedding dresses are almost always high-necked, certainly never really low-cut, and long-sleeved, with a skirt full to the ground so that the ankles are covered. Make-up is also subdued: according to a beauty editor in a magazine 'Nothing looks more incongruous under a veil than heavy false eyelashes'. She should look like a young girl, not an experienced woman. If any jewellery is worn – and etiquette books suggest that it is not really fitting that any should be – then it must be 'real' (i.e., gold or silver), not paste and gilt. In all respects the bride should be 'pure': young, fresh, innocent, and lacking in artifice or artificiality.

White as a colour has other meanings besides purity. In our culture it is the opposite of black. And in clothing, whilst 'nothing changes so markedly as the popular taste in colour' (Cunnington 1952), black and white have had invariable connotations for at least the last 200 years. Black – or more specifically lustreless, non-shiny black – is a sign of grief and age, as in black crepe for mourning[11]. White conversely is a sign of innocence and youth, and also of joy[12] and leisure (or, at least, non-manual work). Wedding dresses tend to be not just white but lustrous and shiny. This connection of white and light suggests a radiance and spirituality in the bride, a radiance that comes from her inner happiness, tranquility, and purity of heart. She, as maker and physical symbol of the home, will provide a home which is a refuge and retreat from the depressing, corrupt, and hurried world of work for her husband and children (Davidoff, L'Esperance, and Newby 1976).

The different styles of wedding dress – Edwardian, Victorian, Regency, even Medieval – help to confirm the supposition that white wedding dresses have been worn throughout the ages and that in wearing one a bride is conforming to tradition. Here, as so often elsewhere, ritual (and the female role behaviour it expresses) is partly validated and gains part of its force by its supposed antiquity and inevitability[13].

Many women who are pregnant when they marry choose to have a register office ceremony and will wear rather formal 'ordinary' clothes, probably coloured and not white (see chapter 6), but some couples opt to marry in church, particularly if they are already engaged, and the changes this produces in the bride's costume are illuminating. Case 8:

> The couple had a lavish wedding. Her parents had been saving to have an extension built on their house, but when their only daughter had to get married, they used the money to pay for as big a wedding as possible.

(Bride's mother)

> 'Well, actually, I seen [the wedding dress] in David Evans's window . . . [my daughter] also seen it, and it took her eye. I phoned first to find the price – it was a model sent down from London for three days – it cost 72 guineas*, and with the head dress was a hundred pounds. It's *gold* brocade with mink cuffs.'[14] (my emphasis).

Of another couple who were married at the time of my fieldwork, but whose wedding I missed because it was arranged at short notice, I was told by some of the couple's close friends that the wedding had taken place in February instead of June because the couple had 'slipped up', 'but she had all the trimmings, though she wore cream and she had planned white. But she wore a veil.' One bride (Case 27) told me of the wedding of her pregnant younger sister, who had worn a long white dress, but it was 'only from C&A' (i.e., cheap) and she did not have any bridesmaids. In another case where a sister's wedding was described (Case 40, see p. 105) the bride wore a long cream dress but no 'veil or anything'.

Thus when the bride is pregnant there are refinements to the 'proper' wedding costume, but one has to have a discerning eye and come very close to the bride to notice. From the back of the church or in a photograph it is even more difficult to tell, and there is no consensus as to what difference in dress the fact of pregnancy should make[15]. The alterations have considerable importance to the actors, however, and serve, I suspect, to nail future criticisms on the lines of 'Fancy her putting on all those airs when she was carrying', by allowing the reply 'But she didn't: she didn't have any bridesmaids', or whatever. From a more general point of view, the fact that when the women is pregnant she does not have a full white wedding serves to confirm the respectability and 'virginity' of those who do.

---

* £215 at 1978 prices

Very few of the brides who marry in church are 'old' – only about 5 per cent are over thirty. A mature woman, even if marrying for the first time, would usually not wear a long dress, nor a white dress[16], and would have only one friend as matron of honour, not a lot of bridesmaids. Such things are girlish and inappropriate.

Some of the 'messages' being conveyed by the bride's dress can be brought out still more clearly if the woman's costume is compared with the man's. All the men at a wedding will be dressed formally – in a suit (usually a dark, but not black, suit), shirt, and tie. All the men, or just the main actors (the groom, best man, ushers, and father of the bride) may dramatize the occasion by wearing (a form of) morning dress, but in about half the weddings I studied the groom simply wore a suit – not necessarily even a new one. The only ritualization was then the addition of a flower in the buttonhole, but even this is not exclusive to weddings. Advertisements for buying or hiring men's clothes suggest the groom is but 'one of the bride's most important accessories'; that his looks complement hers (see *Figure 3*).

There is no special symbolism attached to the men's costume; nor is specific interest directed to it; nor is it age specific; nor is it linked to sexual status: there are no connotations as to whether the groom is a virgin or not – the very idea appears ludicrous; nor are any alterations made according to whether or not the husband-to-be is also a father-to-be; nor is the groom singled out from all the other men by this dress (all the principals at least will be wearing the same as he). His clothes are not kept afterwards 'for luck'; they are not sacred in any way. Nor is it considered polluting for him to wear hired clothes. However, status differences between men *are* expressed in the clothes they wear at a wedding[17]. Moss Bros (the clothes hire firm) are quoted as saying that

> 'At "fashionable London or country weddings", many, if not most of the male guests still wear morning dress . . . "but lower down the social scale only the bridegroom, best man, ushers and two fathers dress up and most of the remainder of the male guests wear lounge suits. There is a tendency, of course, that if a man is invited as a guest to a wedding and he has a morning suit in his wardrobe he will wear it." '
> (Monsarrat 1973:206–7)

The full version of morning dress – the tailed coat, pale grey double-breasted waistcoat, grey striped trousers, top hat, and grey gloves – was very rarely to be seen in Swansea. Only the local 'Establishment', the upper middle classes, would feel comfortable in it. Even such men sometimes displayed self-consciousness by joking (e.g., lining up and doing a song and dance act in imitation of Frankie Vaughan). Frequently when it was proposed that the men wear morning dress, one or more of the

Figure 3 Advertisement stressing lesser importance of the groom's costume

For Better...?

Well, you are going to look your most beautiful on your day, but what about your man?

How he looks complements how you look and the highest compliment can only be a Moss Bros Morning Suit available at any of our 42 branches throughout the country. And you can hire your Wedding dress from Moss Bros too, our ladies' department at our London Covent Garden Store has a wide range of beautifully styled Wedding dresses.

Your photographs will always tell you you were right.

Moss Bros

Bedford Street, Covent Garden, London WC2E 8JB
(Near Leicester Square Station)
Lime Street, EC3M 7HN and branches throughout the country

Access. Barclaycard, etc.

principals would refuse; ostensibly on sartorial grounds, but also for fear of ridicule in having ideas above one's station. Case 48 (bride, her father, groom, and his father all in s.e.c.II):

> (Bride) 'It all started off, I wanted top hat and tails and he [groom] wanted lounge suits. Even my father refused as he said he'd look like a ladybird – he's so short and plump. Then I went to a wedding where

the groom wore a short jacket [version]; and then he [groom] was an usher at John's wedding where he had to wear the same thing and everyone said how nice he looked. So I think that made him decide that he'd like it for his.'

Crudely, then, the upper class own their own morning dress (the formal day attire of gentlemen at the turn of the century); the upper middle class hire them; the principals at the wedding in the middle class and the skilled working class hire a morning suit which has a jacket without tails and they do not use top hats; those in the armed forces or merchant navy wear dress uniform; and most of the working class wear suits of varying quality. On the other hand brides – all of whom are becoming married women/housewives and mothers – and thus not differentiated by occupational status, are all dressed very much alike. One can also distinguish married from single women among the guests at a wedding by subtle differences in their clothes and appearance. While there were exceptions, married women at the time of the field work wore longer skirts and stiletto heels, and the unmarried women mini-skirts and 'clumpy-heeled' shoes, while single and married men guests looked much alike.

The change in status from unmarried to married woman is much more marked (in our culture) than that from unmarried to married man; and it is the bride during the wedding who is most in a transitional status[18], marked out by her ritual dress. The bridesmaids are usually unmarried, but if one is married she is distinguished by name (as a 'matron of honour') and function (she will be the 'chief bridesmaid', in charge of the others and responsible for taking the bride's bouquet at the top of the aisle). The ushers and best man are also 'traditionally' unmarried, though this criterion is applied less stringently with them than with bridesmaids, and if they are married it does not alter their title.

The bridesmaids' dresses are plainer than those of the bride – simpler in style and with no embroidery. They are usually all dressed in one colour, sometimes in dark magenta, emerald green, turquoise, blue or scarlet, especially in winter since these are 'warm' colours. If there are flowergirls and bridesmaids – a distinction by age (or rather height) – the little ones may be in white and the bigger ones in colour(s). Occasionally they are all in different colours ('a rainbow wedding'), though the middle class tend to think it 'better to have just one'. Bridesmaids rarely wear a hat or head dress, but efforts may be made to make them look alike to the extent of their all having the same (elaborate) hairstyle. Since their dresses are less elaborate and it is less vital that they be perfect than is the case with the bride, and since it is important that they look alike, their dresses are very often made at home by an aunt, or by a dress-maker. It is usually said that the girl or young woman 'can wear it for parties later', but in practice these dresses also tend to hang in wardrobes and never to be worn again; but they are kept because they are inappropriate for other occasions, rather than for luck.

(2) Choice of attendants

No explanation was forthcoming as to why the bride should be followed up the aisle by 1–6 other girls or young women (with the occasional small pageboy)[19]. Having bridesmaids is chiefly a means of honouring particular kin and friends by involving their family in the wedding. It also serves as a means of socializing little girls to the pleasures of being the centre of attention as a bride, and as an additional pressure on individual women to choose to have a white wedding: 'little Susan has *always* wanted to be a/your bridesmaid.' To the observer it shows very clear segregation between the bride, bridesmaids, and pages (women and small boys), and the bride's father, groom, best man, and ushers (adult men).

When choosing the bridesmaids there is great concern for 'balance' between the bride and groom's 'side'; a theme which recurs in the choice of ushers and who should be invited (see Rosser and Harris 1965:261; Firth, Hubert, and Forge 1970:230; Bell 1968). There is, however, usually a marked tilting towards the bride's side. For example, if there are two little flower girls and two women bridesmaids, at least one will be from the groom's side, but the other three may be chosen (according to height and personal preference) from among the bride's sisters, relatives and friends.

Case 6:

> 'I'm an only child and the girl next door and I have been brought up as sisters. It was always understood we'd do it for each other. Also my cousin Sylvia. It's always been promised by my parents. She's never been asked [to be a bridesmaid] before. His sister Ann. Judith's daughter [a relative with whom they were close friends and who lived nearby]. And the fifth's my friend from work. She's always been a great friend to me, and the first thing she asked when I said I was getting married was "Can I be your bridesmaid?".'

Her five attendants were thus –

her 'auntie's' daughter (next door neighbour – no biological link)
her two 'cousins' (bride's mo. mo. sis. da. da. da.)
              (bride's mo. fa. br. da. da. da.)[20]
the groom's sister and
her friend from work.

Case 35:

> 'Three bridesmaids, all pretty big. My sister and two best friends. I invited his cousin in London, but she couldn't make it. I wanted someone from his side, but there was nobody suitable. *No* flower girls. John's [groom] got two little cousins but they're just guests. They wrecked his brother's wedding.'

Case 26:

> 'Two bridesmaids – my younger sister [the bride's only sib] and John's cousin [mo. sis. da. da.]. I've got so many on my side of that age, so if I had one it wouldn't be fair to the others. She's the only one on his side of that age and I want someone from his side. There's one flower girl – a 3 year old – she lives next door but one to us' [close friend of the family].

Similar principles apply to the choice of groomsmen or ushers – the terms are used synonymously[21] – young men in their late teens to early thirties who are reliable and willing to show people to their places in church (and, when appropriate, who will agree to wear a morning suit). The best man, who supports the groom during the wedding, is a sib or close friend of the groom; one who 'is the sort to be a best man – who's sensible and can make speeches'. In the three cases cited above on the choice of bridesmaids, the ushers and best man were as follows:

Case 6:

> (Bride) 'One usher – his mate. A twit. Dull as hell. Acts the fool . . . The best man is his other mate [the man in the couple with whom they spent much of their spare time].'

Case 35:

> Ushers – groom's br.'s wife's br.
>   bride's fa. sis. da. husband
> best man – groom's brother.

Case 26:

> 'Two ushers – John's mate at work and a couple we go out with on a Saturday – because they're friends and I [the bride] haven't got a brother or brother-in-law [sister's husband]. John's brother [his only sib] is best man.'

Precedence in choosing bridesmaids, ushers, and the best man is given to sibs of the bride and groom, but thereafter there is personal choice among relatives and friends. Many closely related people are passed over in favour of those who are liked as individuals. Justification is sought in terms of balance of the two sides (if one has one, one has to have them all); appropriateness of a person's height and capacity to do the job; promises made in the past; and repayment of services ('I was an usher at *his* wedding').

The bride is always 'given away' in church by her father. It is held to be very important that he should do it if at all possible. At one wedding I attended (outside the sample) the bride's father came out of a mental hospital for the day especially for the wedding and was clearly under enormous strain. When the bride's father is dead his place is taken by her eldest brother, and, if she has no brothers by her sister's husband.

(3) Costs of the wedding

To agree to be a bridesmaid or usher involves one in a certain amount of expense as well as the performance of the service itself, for one is expected to pay at least part of the cost of one's costume. The usher or best man pays for the hire of a morning suit if this is worn, or he may have to buy a new lounge suit (the carnation buttonholes are provided by the groom – see on); and the bridesmaid pays the cost of the material and/or the making up of her dress. (If she is offered no say as to colour or style, the bride or bride's parents usually pay the full cost.) In return they may be given small presents (e.g., lockets for the females, cigarette lighters for the males) by the bride and groom.

The other costs of the wedding are formally borne by the bride's parents and the groom. Reference is often made to etiquette books or magazines as to who should pay for what. These suggest that:

> 'It is usual, but by no means mandatory, for the bride's parents to pay for the reception, the cake and everything concerning the celebration after the service, while the groom meets the costs of the wedding itself and the honeymoon afterwards.' (Heaton 1966:62)

or that:

> the bride's parents pay for her trousseau and bottom drawer, the invitations and other stationery (service sheets, place cards, serviettes, etc.), the cars to and from the church, the photographer, the reception and the newspaper announcements; while the groom pays for the bouquets for the bride and bridesmaids and the buttonholes for important male guests, the licence, church fees and wedding ring, the honeymoon, gifts to bridesmaids, and the couple's new home.' (*Brides and Setting Up Home*, 'Wedding Guide', section included in the centre of each issue)

In practice there is a process of 'you pay for this, I'll pay for that' between the couple (the bride contributing as much as the groom) and her parents, with other relatives also helping (e.g., grandmothers or aunts often buy the cake as a wedding present, and uncles who are good photographers may provide an album of photographs). *Figure 4* shows the division of costs as completed by two brides. In Case 9 the total cost of the wedding was just over £300, and in the case outside the sample, just over £200.

(4) The choice of guests

The final decision as to who is to be invited to the reception is made a few months before the wedding, though a general principle – 'the parents' families (sibs and affines) and the grandparents' families, but not the nephews and nieces (bride's and groom's cousins)'; or 'all the (bride's and groom's) cousins, but none of the cousins' children' – is arrived at almost at once, taking into account the size of the kin groups from which the bride and groom come, and the money which is available or can be saved.

As Firth, Hubert, and Forge found (1970:228–40), kin are the customary guests at weddings and there is a very strong sense of obligations between kin at this time – to invite kin to come to the wedding, to attend the wedding of kin, and to give a present (see chapter 7). There is a strong stress on having equal *numbers* from both 'sides', which should ideally be combined with inviting the same *categories* (e.g., all uncles and aunts) on both sides. Much of the discussion involves arguments that 'if we invite X we must invite Y'. In Swansea, however, in contrast to North London, almost all the guests are kin. At an average white wedding with an outside reception for 60–70 guests, only 10–20 would be friends[22]. As in North London, the parents of the bride and groom invite their relatives and the bride and groom invite their friends (Firth, Hubert, and Forge 1970:237), but since there is room for so few friends (the guillotining of the number of kin in order to allow friends to be included, seen in Highgate, is not acceptable in Swansea), the bride and groom complain that the wedding 'is for everybody except us'. However, all friends invited come, but not all relatives invited will be able to attend (compare Bell's findings on christenings in Swansea, 1968).

The parents and grandparents of the bride and groom will always attend the wedding if they are alive, and sibs of the bride and groom (and their husbands and wives) will travel long distances, or the wedding will be delayed so they can attend (e.g., one ceremony was timed for when a brother was home on leave from Singapore). The bride and groom's parents' sibs are also almost always invited, though here there is more likelihood of particular individuals and households being left out if there is tension[23]. The same applies to grandparents' sibs. Some sort of general policy is adopted on cousins – all or none – though if one side has many parents' sibs and the other few, cousins from the second side may be invited to even out the numbers. A few cousins or more distant relatives (e.g., mother's mother's mother's sister's daughter's daughter's son) are included if they are in close and friendly contact. They are seen as kin, though the borderline between their status and that of the next door neighbour who 'has always been called auntie' is vague.

There is indirect negotiation between the groom's parents and the bride's parents as to how many guests each side can have. (It almost

Figure 4 Lists of who paid for the various wedding expenses, completed by informants.

	Who paid	Cost
Bride's dress	BRIDE	24½ gns
bridesmaid(s) dress(es)	BRIDESMAID	£4
~~flower girl/page boy~~		
~~morning dress for the men~~		
invitations (+postage)	BRIDE	£2 " 15s
paying the Registrar/Vicar		
cost of copy of the Marriage Certificate	GROOM	5 gns
use of Church		
use of organ		
~~use of choir~~		
wedding ring(s)	GROOM	£13 " 10s
flowers - for Church	BRIDE	10/-
flowers - for bride and bridesmaid(s) bouquets	"	£6
flowers - for buttonholes	GROOM + BRIDE	£1 " 14s
Hiring cars	BRIDE	£9
Reception - food		
drink	BRIDE'S	£56
wedding cake	MOTHER	
(+ boxes & postage for sending cake out afterwards)		
announcement in the paper	GROOM	12/- ??
trousseau (including 'going away' clothes)	BRIDE	£30
Honeymoon	BRIDE + GROOM	£45
Groom's gifts to the bridesmaid(s)	GROOM .	15/-
" " " best man	"	15/-
Any other expenses HYMN SHEETS	BRIDE	£4

always ends up slightly weighted to the bride's side.) Cues and messages are relayed via the groom and bride, until finally the groom's parents (in the person of his mother) send over a list of names and addresses of suitable length, and the bride's mother (on behalf of her husband and herself) sends out the printed cards (see, as an example, *Figure 5* six weeks before the wedding date.

People are invited as married couples, or sometimes as domestic groups. The life-cycle passage rites – christenings, weddings, and funerals – are the main occasions when kin meet as a group and may indeed be one of the few occasions when husband and wife participate jointly in social activities (Bott 1957:68). Weddings thus act as a reaffirmation of the

	Who paid	Cost
Bride's dress	Bride's parents	£20 whole outfit
bridesmaid(s) dress(es)	" "	approx. £8
flower girl/page boy	—	—
morning dress for the men	—	—
invitations (+postage)	Bride's parents	£4
paying the Registrar/Vicar	Groom	£5
cost of copy of the Marriage Certificate		
use of Church		
use of organ		
use of choir	N/A	
wedding ring(s)	Groom/Bride	£10 each
flowers - for Church		
flowers - for bride and bridesmaid(s) bouquets	Bride's parents	£7
flowers - for buttonholes	both families	£5 approx
Hiring cars		£12 + £3 for coach
Reception - food		
drink	Bride's parents	£130 +
wedding cake		
(+ boxes & postage for sending cake out afterwards)		
announcement in the paper		
trousseau (including 'going away' clothes)	Bride's parents	£30 approx
Honeymoon	Groom	£55 approx
Groom's gifts to the bridesmaid(s)	Groom	
Photographers	Bride & Groom	not known yet
Order of Services sheets	Bride's parents	£6
Any other expenses Printed serviettes	" "	£3

kinship groupings, and especially the marriage relationships of those who attend as guests. The husband and wife sit together in the service and hear the Church's and State's views on the nature of marriage, and they attend a party of kin and friends as a couple.

Sometimes a particular individual will attend 'to represent a branch of the family', several of whose members were invited; but it is not customary to *invite* people as 'representatives'. The middle class are more likely to send invitations to people they know will be unable to attend (because of distance, old age, illness) than are the working class. The working class are more likely to give and accept 'work' as an excuse for non-attendance (i.e., not being able to afford to take a day off), which is obviously related directly to their socio-economic and job situation.

For outside receptions, especially those following church weddings, printed invitations are ordered from stationers – single stiff cards, edged with silver, and printed in black or silver, or double cards with wedding symbols (silver horse-shoes, champagne bottles and glasses, churches, white heather, silver slippers or boots, etc.) printed or embossed on the front and the invitation printed on the inside. The names of the guests are written in by hand, and the invitations to all the guests are sent by the

Figure 5 Example of a wedding invitation (reduced from 7″ × 5″)

Mrs N S Saunders
requests the pleasure of the company of

Mr + Mrs R. Barker

at the marriage of her daughter

Susan May with Mr John Hood

at the Parish Church of St. Matthias and St George,
Church Road, Astwood Bank, Redditch, Worcs,
on Saturday, October 13th, 1970 at 2 p.m.
Reception afterwards at the Southcrest Hotel, Redditch.

108 Evesham Road,
Astwood Bank,
Redditch,
Worcs

R.S.V.P.

bride's parent(s). In Case 11, where both the bride's parents were dead, the invitations were sent by her married, younger sister (her only sib) and the sister's husband. When there was concern to save money (in some church weddings and most register office weddings), stock invitations cards were bought and the name of the bride's parents and the venue written in. For receptions held at home there were very rarely invitations; people being invited 'by word of mouth', and some even 'inviting themselves' by just turning up. This could not happen at an outside reception where a fixed number of meals are ordered.

Joking at work

As the wedding draws near and the bustle and tension increase, many brides and grooms and their parents suffer from 'nerves' and take time off from work because of colds and other minor ills[24]. Case 37:

> The bride stopped work on the Tuesday, instead of the Thursday before the wedding as she had planned.
> 'I couldn't stick it any longer. It was all building up – the work [the wedding]. So much to do. But I had to go back to get their present [a pouffe]. And, oh God! . . . when I came to go . . . they'd sewn up all the sleeves of my coat and stuck things on it. Messages . . . labels hanging from it. Things like "Hot Copper". [She was marrying a policeman] Daft things like that. Nothing obscene. Just soft things. Mind I was in such a bit of a state I couldn't really remember. My mother's still got them. And there was a big message on the back: 'Getting Married'; and *confetti*! I was plastered in it. And they left me standing in Union Street.'

> Then the informant told me about the giving of a 'very misshapen carrot' in a box with a wedding card to another young woman when the informant had been working in another office, and she discussed with the groom if and when he had seen it.
> 'It's funny, they don't do it to everyone; some couldn't take it. Like when I was standing in Union Street a man stopped and asked me to turn round. I'd have been disappointed, I suppose, if it hadn't happened; but I didn't expect so much.'

I was not aware of this custom of elaborate joking when I started the research[25] and only towards the end did I begin to ask systematically if it had happened. Information came initially in reply to such questions as 'Did anybody play any practical jokes on you?' and 'Did anybody throw confetti?', but since this was asked within the context of the wedding itself and not in relation to the week beforehand, I probably missed hearing of some occasions because I did not probe. Witness one of the last cases. Case 54 (bride and groom):

> (Did anyone play any practical jokes?)
> 'No, I don't think so.'
> (Not even when the bride left work?)
> 'Oh, yes! All toilet rolls in my coat lining. Empty ones. And all confetti in my jumper.'
> (Nothing else?)
> 'No, they'd not thought of it.'

In all I had nine cases of elaborate, planned leaving rituals described to me. In another seven cases it was not possible for it to have happened because of the nature of the woman's work, because she was not at work, or because she was ill the whole week before the wedding. In one other case the bride specifically warned her workmates that she did not want it to take place. In the remaining cases there was usually a giggly sherry party at work when the present was handed over, with some risqué jokes or cards, and confetti. For example:

Case 49:

> 'When I went to get my pay they'd put confetti in my purse and pocket and it showered out whenever I paid for anything, like the flowers for the church. And it stuck to the suede of my coat so everyone could see.'

Case 38:

> 'In work, they sent me order forms for family planning . . . it was a laugh . . . they covered me all day in punch card confetti and put it in my purse. Filled *everything*. Pockets, overall, and bag . . . Oh, I enjoyed it. There's not much you can do . . . Just let them get on with it!'

In very few cases was joking at work or in the pub with the groom mentioned – and then it was only verbal, individual teasing around the time of handing over the present[26]. Case 11: 'They're giving him murder at work. They tease him because he's old – thirty-six – and been there a long time . . . like the foreman shook hands with him and said "Glad you're settling down. Now perhaps you'll work weekends!".' Again, when the groom goes back to work after his honeymoon he is greeted jovially: 'The super clapped me on the back and said "Dropping off, then, is it?".'; but there is no collective, planned event.

The joking among women seems most developed and frequent in work situations such as warehouses where there a lot of young women working together. It is also related to how long the individual has worked in a place, how well liked they are personally, and to the circumstances (there were no cases of elaborate joking where the woman was marrying for the second time, though it seemed equally frequent whether the bride was or was not pregnant). There was no set ritual, but a certain lack of inspiration produced uniformity. There was the same mixture as described recently in *Folklore* (Monger 1971, 1974) for such joking in parts of England: i.e., bridal symbols (e.g., confetti, ribbons, veils, flowers made of paper, decorated cars, etc.) and things to make the woman embarrassed (e.g., lavatory rolls, mildly obscene signs attached to her clothes, being taken home decorated through busy roads, handing over of baby's potties or penis-shaped carrots), together with the use in some way of the products being made or used in the factory, shop or office (e.g., card punchings, spark-plugs, or cotton reels hung on her coat, or wrapping papers used to make a hat or streamers).

Similar joking sometimes occurs at hen parties – indeed the two can be interchanged. The informant whose hen party I shall shortly describe said (Case 35):

> 'Knowing the girls in work – and the boys – I was dreading it. Seen it happen to others. I've not done it – just stood and watched. They gave me that box . . . Mrs Davis and two girls. Oh, that was disgusting! Sausage and two meat balls and hair. It was meant to be on the night of the hen party but it didn't come off. Well, I'd gone out cold!
> Another girl they gave two gob stoppers for the pill, and a dummy.'

Stag and hen parties

'Stag' and 'hen' parties are the riotous single-sex evenings which mark the change of status of the young man and woman within the peer and workgroup. The SOED (1956) gives 'stag party' as American slang of the mid-nineteenth century; the suffix 'stag' being used of any male animal in its sexual prime. 'Hen party' is not in this dictionary, 'hen' in the general sense of 'female' is old English and 'hen pecking' refers to wives domineering over or ruling their husbands. These are not, therefore, 'complementary' terms, for each asserts the superiority of one sex.

The evenings out are held one or two days to ten days before the wedding – the interim being needed to sober up. The group of women at a hen party is usually based on the work-group, with the addition of some neighbours, relations (of the same generation as the bride) and other friends; while the nucleus of a stag party usually derives from the neighbourhood pub or sports team, with the addition of workmates, relatives, and other friends, usually, but not always, of the same generation. Some are organized outings to out-of-town clubs in a minibus, others are more informal: 'down the local' pub. Sometimes a kitty system is operated whereby everyone except the bride or groom puts a couple of pounds on the table and all the drinks are bought out of this, or each person (again excepting the bride or groom) takes turns to buy a round. Between two and forty people take part. One hen party I attended was quite typical (Case 53):

> When I first met the bride and was invited to come to the party, she told me that it was to be on the Thursday of the week before the wedding because she 'gets awful bad' after a lot of drink and needs time to recover. We were to have drinks in The Park ('a real "knocking shop", where all the pop groups and their hangers-on go'), and then go to the Top Rank dance hall – 'though whether we'll be in any condition to dance I can't say!'. Many husbands (including her brother) would not let their wives go 'because they don't approve of the boys down the Top Rank'. (You mean they don't like their wives dancing with them?) 'Yes!' I think I was asked to go because, since of 'responsible' status and evidently pregnant, it could be taken that I would not drink very much, would not dance, and could be relied upon to look after the informant.

> The party started at 7.15–7.30 in the pub. I arrived at 8.10 The bride had already had five double brandies and had three more while I was there. Her friends kept buying for her and saying she must drink what they gave her or they'd never speak to her again. There was a line of glasses, full and empty, on the table in front of her. By this time she was drunk and quite willing to down one glass after another. Just before we left the pub she was bought and drank a 'Black Velvet' (Guinness and cider).

> There were six women there when I arrived – the bride, her cousin, her friend from down the road, and two girls from work (sales assistants). We were joined later by the groom's sister and her friend, who was about 10–15 years older than the other women and clearly embarrassed them by her vulgarity. (Her stream of bad language, very low-cut dress on a woman of forty, hitching up her skirt, etc., were commented on when she left to go to buy drinks.)

> There was much giggling and loud laughter, making us a noticeable group in a room which otherwise contained only couples at tables and four men at the bar. The barman enquired, a little testily, what we were doing when I and another woman bought drinks, but he grinned amiably when told it was a hen party. He told the men at the bar what we were doing and they shouted comments to us.

> The friend-from-down-the-road (married, aged thirty, one child) told a few, very long, obscene, not very funny stories, but in general there was just bantering conversation – hints by the best friend to reveal what the bride had done when they went away on holiday together;

threats about the obscene present they had got for her (which finally was given to her at work, see above); reminiscences of hen parties past where the bride had ended up crying that 'she didn't want to go through with it – "I'm not marrying that swine", and everyone yelling "You must, you must!".'

At 9.30 we left for the Top Rank – one friend on each side of the bride, holding her up. As we passed a policeman she made a special effort not to appear drunk, but he laughed and said she still had time to change her mind. Various men made imitations of chickens clucking.

The two bouncers at the door of the dance hall were not amused and not enthusiastic about letting us in (despite the bride again being coached on disguising her drunkeness). They warned us that if she got any worse she'd be thrown out.

Once inside, two of the women who went to the place regularly (the bride's best friend and one from work) pronounced themselves embarrassed by us and went off to dance and I did not see them again. The bride's cousin, another girl from work, and I got the bride some black coffee, which we had to lift to her lips as she could not see to get hold of it. I was left, since I said I was too pregnant to dance, supporting the bride's head – or rather the whole weight of the bride, who was a buxom young woman – to stop her falling off the chair, while the others danced all together in a circle. Then we had to haul the bride to the cloak-room to be sick, and she was put in a taxi and taken home by the woman-from-down-the-road at 10.30–40 pm.

Those who remained agreed, with some satisfaction, that she 'had been very bad' and 'she'll not be in work tomorrow'. (She was not.) The bride said that in fact she was still drunk two days later – on the Saturday. 'Still, never mind. It's only once in your life.'

Not everyone gets 'plastered' or 'stewed out of their minds'. Some are 'tight but knew what I was doing. You don't enjoy it if you're bad [sick]', or 'Just right. Merry. Singing all the way up the road'; but most are somewhat shame-faced the following day.

Case 41:

'The girls went on a trip – about twenty of us from work, all the gang. In a minibus, to the Baglan. Danced a bit and some played bingo. And just got drunk. I was shocked when they told me what I'd been doing! Grabbing the microphone. One of the girls went up and told the compere to announce it. It was embarrassing – everybody coming up and saying "Congratulations" or that I must be mad. And then the band playing "I'm getting married". That's all I can remember. It was on the Thursday night [two days before the wedding]. I usually drank whisky and Pep(si Cola) and a few of them gave me Tia Marias [a liqueur]. I can remember that. Don't know the names of some of the others. And cider. I was as sick as a dog! I finally came round about 3 o'clock on the Friday. Good job it wasn't *on* the Friday!

The stag was the same night. All the boys from the Red Lion. The same gang meet there every week. No, he didn't tell me anything – but then, I didn't tell him anything about me!'

Case 51:

'My hen party was on the Thursday. Twenty-two came. We had a drink first and then up to the Townsman. Not paralytic but not exactly sober! They all buy you drinks and you can't drink them all – I gave half of them away . . . His stag was also Thursday. According to the boys, he drank a whole bottle of scotch and still went to work [as a driver] at 3 am. the following day. Thirty odd or forty of them went down the West Cross. On the way home he took his trousers off –and they took him into a restaurant – the Anglo-Asian – with no trousers on!'

Case 53:

'His stag party was on the Thursday before the wedding. His local [pub] and the Townsmen. Eighteen of them. He was drinking Bacardi's [white rum] and pints – alternately. They had £36 pooled, besides what the boys were buying on the side. And there was only £2 left at the end. He passed out on the sofa when he got home, but he got himself to bed an hour or so later. And he was alright the following day, because he's used to it. He's been worse than that on a [normal] Friday night.'

I obviously could not attend stag parties, though I occasionally observed them when in pubs on my own account. There was the same general pattern of buying the groom drinks, and desultory conversations with occasional sessions of joke telling and singing as in hen parties, and the same concern to get the principal drunk. Case 45:

'The hen party was the week before on the Friday night. At the Three Lamps. We started off with a meal, thank God, to soak up some of the booze. Mostly the women from my office [she was a shorthand typist for a solicitor], then they departed and the young ones went on to some serious drinking. It started with about seventeen and then it went down to about seven who stayed to drink.' (What did you drink?) 'Sherry and then . . . I don't know the name of it . . . Green . . . can't tell you what we called it! [prompt from groom] . . . Shitty rose! [Chartreuse] Mixed with cherry brandy, vodka, Bacardi; it went down well! I thought it was just cherry brandy! I had about six of those. It came out red. Didn't know what the heck I was drinking. It went on for about three hours. And I robbed a sherry glass and ice tongs as souvenirs. And I did a dance on the table and sang a song.' (What?) 'Don't know what it is in English [Welsh National Anthem] – we learned it at school.

I was the worst [i.e. most drunk] of the lot, and I didn't spend a brass farthing. Still their turn's to come – I'll get nobbled then! Des had his stag party on the same night. So the best man took the car and looked after him and picked me and his girl friend [who was at the hen party] up. Des was . . . what's the adjective I can use for you? – "Not well". We were going to take him home [to his parents], but he was so ill we only got him as far as the settee [in her house]. We had to stop *five* times on the way home for him to be sick! And a policeman was looking at us. And I nearly choked him because I wound the window up, not down, not knowing that he had his head out of it being sick!'

(Groom) 'I started off on pints; five or six. Then vodka and orange, which is my favourite drink. Then someone bought me a schooner of sherry in the middle; down in one that was! I bought the first round as they came in. About fifteen – but a few went early.' She had 'a head' the next day; he was '*ill*'!

(Bride) 'Think of the *money*! Still, if you don't get drunk, it's not a good night. I don't think my mum's got over it yet – seeing him . . . When he gets ill, he goes *green*. She [bride's mother] nearly attacked the best man, shouting at him "You shouldn't have let him get in that state!". Thought he had alcoholic poisoning.'

(Groom) 'Don't think I had one straight one after the first two. They laced [mixed] the lot.'

To go out with a group of the same sex to get drunk is much more typical male than female behaviour. Even to go out for a meal and to dance (with a prior visit to a pub to get 'well tanked up') with other women with a view to talking with the women, as opposed to looking for encounters with men, is extraordinary. Thus it is not surprising that only one woman was dubious as to whether her evening out 'counted' as a hen party (Case 46):

'Well, me and my friend went drinking – and on to the Rank. But [other friends] couldn't afford it; didn't have no money. Only the two of us. I was going to go with all the girls from work [sales assistant in a warehouse] but they couldn't afford it neither. Not a proper hen party.'

Whereas in no fewer than seven cases the groom (or the bride reporting for him) was unclear as to whether a trip out had been a 'stag party' – e.g., where 'just the two of them, him and his best man, went out for a drink' (which one did and one didn't think should count). More often the ambiguity arose because 'they have a "stag party" down there *every* Thursday evening – no, it wasn't anything special'.

Half the women informants had hen parties, as against 85 per cent of men who had stag parties (though the latter reduces to 50 per cent if all those men who had stag parties which might or might not 'count' are excluded). In no case did the woman of a couple have a hen party and the man not have a stag party – though there were at least five cases where he had one (generally in his local pub) and she did not. In two cases hen parties which had been arranged were called off, but the only case where a man 'missed out' was when he was ill.

Hen parties were markedly more common among women who married in church than among those who married in the register office, and among those who were engaged, and among the non-pregnant. Stag parties were slightly more common among men marrying in church, but there was no difference by engagement, and they were more common (100 per cent) among men whose brides were pregnant. They were equally common for those (men and women) entering first or second marriages.

There is stress on the symmetry of the stag and hen party – note how frequently they were held on the same night, sometimes even in different rooms in the same pub or club – but the male party occurs more frequently, and is more a part of normal male behaviour. It stresses his changing status within, but continuing membership of, the male peer group. The hen party involves unmarried women who are allowed to behave like unmarried men on one occasion: going out with their own sex for the pleasure of their company and not to seek out the opposite sex, and getting drunk with one's peer *group*. (I say they 'are allowed to behave' because I know from personal experience that a large number of women in a pub in Britain, even when not at all noisy or drunk, will normally draw individual and collective male hostility and aggression, whereas the barman and his cronies and the policeman mentioned in Case 53 were openly tolerant.) The hen party is thus, according to Gluckman's analysis of rites of reversal (1956:Ch. V), a protest against the established order (of differential behaviour by sex) which, since the order is unquestioned, serves as an affirmation of it. The hen party is a licensed statement of a conflict that exists within the relationship between the sexes – i.e., that women are specifically excluded from behaviour defined as pleasurable (going out to the pub[27], getting drunk, having a peer group, etc.). It is possible to express this conflict since people do not, and cannot, question their sex and sex roles. These are ascribed and prescriptive, not achieved or voluntary, and part of the 'indubitable moral order' of society.

Notes

1. When we were living in the town an insurance salesman tried to sell us policies on our daughters (then aged 4 and 2) to mature after fifteen years to pay for the costs of their weddings. He assured us that these were very popular and that he had found the one he had on his daughter, for £350, had proved invaluable – though it had not been big enough.

   In case 44, the couple broke off their engagement, and when they got together again, they had to wait a year to marry because the bride's father was by then committed to having the bride's younger sister's marriage first.

   Middle-class parents are better able to provide for relatively small church weddings at short notice. They may have savings, or shares they can cash, or it may simply be that their credit is better.

2. Many brides and grooms are extremely nervous during the wedding; for example:

   Case 37:

   > (Bride) 'I felt terrible in the hairdressers in the morning. My stomach was turning over like a big dipper! I was wanting to go to the toilet all the time!
   > (Groom) 'Never again! I was a bag of nerves. I was alright till she came to church . . . but she was shaking and holding on to me as we stood at the altar. And she cried her eyes out in the vestry – we were in there for ages. Everyone thought we'd done a bunk out the back!'

   Case 42:

   > (Bride) 'We enjoyed it very much – but I wouldn't go through it again. Too nerve-racking. I'd have exactly the same reception, but the wedding in the register office, in a nice suit, and just close family . . . I enjoyed it after the service, as we came out of church. But I've forgotten *all* the service, *really*. Standing up there in front of people – I was like jelly. I was lovely, well, a bit nervous, at home and in the car. But once I was in church and I seen all the people; well, that was it. I didn't *hear* no bridal march.'

3. See Barker 1977:359, notes 3–6.
4. A colleague described how his wife's mother – a Swansea woman – would put the tips of her left and right fingers together and slowly move the ring from one hand to the other when having an argument with her husband; threatening but never actually taking the ring off. Several of my informants told me, with gusto, of the engagement quarrels when she had thrown her engagement ring at him – but it seemed uncommon with wedding rings (though perhaps it was simply too early to say!). If a ring gets lost (e.g., on the sand on the beach) it is a major upset.

   Hart discusses the dilemma of her divorced female respondents on whether or not to continue wearing their wedding ring – for respectability when they had children and the prestige of not being a spinster, but a hindrance to finding a new partner (Hart 1976: p. 200).

5. Thus they have names for particular settings – bar, twist, solitaire, cluster – which men do not know, and they know the types of stone and their own birthstone.

6. There is no provision in the *Book of Common Prayer* or the *Experimental Version* in use in the Anglican church, nor in the Roman Catholic *Ordo Administrandi Sacramenta* for the blessing of a man's ring or the putting on of such a ring (see on).

7. The BMRB (1970b) found just over half of their 30 newly married women had spent £24–£48 on their engagement ring (range £24–£300 for new rings and £15–£60 for secondhand rings – the latter based on only four cases).

   Overwhelmingly in Swansea, couples want a new, clearly recognised type of ring for an engagement ring. They give little support to magazines that suggest 'unusual', cheaper, antique rings for engagement; nor do they 'fancy' 'fashion' wedding rings, for the ring has to last a lifetime.

   If a grandmother's engagement ring is passed to her granddaughter it will probably be used as a dress ring, though occasionally the groom will have a family heirloom which he gives to his fiancée for an engagement ring.

   My informants were loath to buy a second-hand ring (particularly a wedding ring, but also an engagement ring). What could have befallen the previous owner that her ring had to be sold? It carried ill luck with it.

   Engagement rings are not sold except *in extremis* (or after a broken engagement). Despite occasional talk of their being 'investments', they are not so used (cf., for example, the gold bracelets of Moroccan women given them by their husbands – Maher 1976). Much of the price paid for a ring in a shop is in any case the retailer's 'mark up' ($^{1}/_{3}$ – $^{2}/_{3}$) and purchase tax or VAT, and for the setting. One would have to pay a minimum of £550 (1975 prices) for a stone of sufficient size and quality to prove a good investment (see *Which* September, 1974 and *Sunday Times* 'Shop!' November 30, 1975).

8. Some jewellers make special provision for couples buying engagement rings, having a special area or cubicle to the side or back of the shop where they have privacy. They are usually served by the manager.

9. This list was on the first two pages of an otherwise empty notebook. On the facing page it said: 'John and I started going together 27 November 1966 and got engaged June 1967.' The presents were listed in the order given and numbered. (People's names, not their relationship to the couple, were given.)

10. I recognise that the number of hired and second-hand dresses must have been considerably under-reported to me. For example, a friend's daughter bought a second-hand dress and swore her mother to secrecy (not very efficiently, since her mother told me; but I did not think that to this day her daugher knows that I know). In any case, it is the dominant values about second-hand dresses and the shame of admitting to having had one which are of interest and concern.

11. Note that mourning crepe – in contrast to modern wedding dresses – was *not* kept in the home after the end of the period of mourning: it was thrown away. Hence it is rare to find examples in museums. Wedding dresses in the late nineteenth and early twentieth century were worn as day dresses after the wedding; they were not the distinctive, once worn costume they are today (Cunnington and Lucas 1972).

12. White is also the colour of rejoicing in the church (though here the colour for mourning is purple). Thus the flowers, vestments, and altar hangings at

weddings are white (if they are changed for the service).

13. In fact white was not an invariable choice even for upper and middle-class weddings until the mid-nineteenth century, and was still not common in the working class until after the First World War. (See Barker and Thompson (1973), Monsarrat (1973), and Cunnington and Lucas (1972).) Wedding veils, though known in the seventeenth century, receive no mention in the eighteenth. From the late eighteenth to the end of the nineteenth century veils were worn with hats and, possibly influenced by the Romantic Movement, some brides started wearing long white lace veils and orange blossom wreaths in the mid nineteenth century.

14. I only learned of the pregnancy when I called back two months after the wedding. It was kept quiet during our initial talk.

15. If there were not this 'essential ambiguity', of course, part of the purpose of having the wedding 'in white' would disappear. Further, some brides choose cream or very pale coffee (ecru) coloured dresses because white 'drains the complexion' if one's skin is 'dark'. This was the case with one informant whom I am certain was a virgin when she married.

16. Though I had one informant (Case 11) aged 43 who did. She had been hesitant as to what people would say if she had a white wedding, but her fiancé reportedly said, 'My dear, if that is what you want, it is your right to have it'. So she wore a long white dress and veil. She commented that buying the dress had been embarrassing as the 'very young assistants . . . in one or two shops . . . weren't at all helpful'. The shop where she finally bought her dress 'had a much more mature manageress'.

17. ' . . . what the bridegroom wore . . . until recently . . . has been the least interesting aspect . . . (we didn't even have a slot for it in the weddings forms I used to send out [to couples getting married in the 1950s when the author worked on a weekly paper in Kent]); but in Britain, at any rate, it . . . can cause more pre-marital uproar than almost anything else . . . The bridegroom's clothes . . . until a few years ago . . . were taken as a measure of the class he was born into, had succeeded to, or was aiming at, and to some extent that remains true. If a man who is still only aiming decides to wear a morning suit, he can walk a stormy path (being ridiculed) . . . At the top of the scale . . . for the first half of the century, a bridegroom who did not wear a morning suit (or a uniform) met with icy politeness, condescending civility, or searching questions as to his antecedents.' (Monsarrat 1973:206).

18. Van Gennep (1909/1960) compares rituals associated with passage from one status to another in many different cultures and suggests that life-cycle passage rites typically involve a symbolic 'death' in the old status, a transitional period 'outside' the society, and a symbolic 'rebirth' in the new status – separation, transition, and reincorporation.
It is interesting in this connection to note that children in our culture are quite often a little alarmed at the sight of a bride, thinking she is a ghost (i.e., someone dead, yet not dead).

19. The average was 3–4 bridesmaids in Anglican and 2 in Nonconformist and R.C. weddings. In the register office there was, at most, one flower girl.

20. This 'telescoping' of relationships – regarding a third cousin as a cousin – is common.

21. 'Groomsmen' seems more Welsh and working-class usage. On average there were 2 ushers/groomsmen (range 1–4).
22. cf. Highgate couples, where the average reception consisted of 35–50 guests, of whom only about 10 would be kin; 10–15% of receptions included no kin at all (Firth, Hubert, and Forge 1970:229).

    In Bethnal Green 'each couple in the marriage sample had an average of twenty-one adult relatives at their wedding' (Young and Willmott 1962:85). At a reception attended by the investigators there were 32 guests, and it seems that most were relatives since it is noted that workmates joined in only later, in the pub (Young and Willmott 1962:62–3).
23. In Highgate 72% of available parents of the bride and groom attended. 44% of available sibs of the bride and groom attended. 20% of available parents' sibs of the bride and groom attended.

    While my genealogical information is not sufficiently complete to make comparable computations for Swansea, in only one case did a parent (a widowed father) not attend the ceremony. Three-quarters of sibs attended and more than half of parents' sibs. On the systematic omission of relatives see Whitehead (1971) and Bell (1968). Bell stresses especially the dropping of geographically distant working-class kin by the upwardly mobile.
24. It may even lead to quite severe illness: One informant had had bouts of chronic diarrhoea throughout her engagement. (An American psychiatrist suggests that 4/5 contract some sort of illness around the time of their wedding (Holmes 1971).)
25. I have subsequently found reference to it in Morgan (1969) (in an electrical component factory in the North of England) and had it described to me from Glasgow (sweet factory) and London (offices). Monger (1971 and 1975) records about 20 cases and tries to trace the history, distribution, and meaning of the symbols of such customs. He stresses that they are mainly women's customs, and that where they are used by men they are borrowed from women, or are 'displaced' apprentices' 'banging out' ceremonies.
26. There will also usually be a whip-round to provide a present from his work-group or pub mates. Possibly men see the present as the most important feature: in a study of social relationships among women at work, one of the few men in the northern factory studied emphasized giving presents and played down the joking (Morgan 1969).
27. Until the early 1960s it was 'not done' for a respectable married woman to be seen in a pub in Swansea (even with her husband). Only since the modern 'coffee bar' type pubs were built have pubs become places of relaxation for the sexes together (see Rosser and Harris 1965:185).

6 The ritual cycle of engagement and wedding II: the wedding, reception, and aftermath

The care taken to balance the numbers of bridesmaids and ushers, and the numbers of guests invited from among the bride's and groom's family and friends, and the fact that all the attendants are then dressed alike (by sex), and all the invitations to the wedding sent out from one source (the bride's parents), were described in the last chapter. The separation and uniting of the two sides around the marriage is emphasized in three other ways: at the couple level, in that the bride and groom must not see each other before the ceremony on the day of the wedding; at the domestic group/family of origin level, in that they must marry from separate houses; and at the level of kin and friends, in that the guests are seated on opposite sides of the church. After the wedding there is great stress on the unity of the couple and the two households and sets of relatives mixing and eating together at the reception. I shall discuss these further in the order in which they occur in the ceremony.

(1) Marrying from separate houses

This is exemplified only in unusual circumstances, for the possibility of the bride and groom living/being in the same house does not often arise.

Case 51:

> In the case of the daughter whose parents refused to let her get engaged to her boy-friend (described at length in chapter 4), on the couple's return to Swansea they lived with his parents whilst taking her parents to court. On the evening before the wedding the bride was sent to stay at the groom's brother's house (married seven years). The

groom's mother told me 'I said "Out of the house before twelve!"' [midnight]'. The groom, his brother, and a friend went out for a drink while the bride left.

Case 33:

The groom's home was in Leicestershire. He stayed at the bride's house in Swansea on the Wednesday and Thursday beforehand, helping with preparations, but on the Friday he went to stay across the road (ostensibly because the bride's aunt and uncle and grandfather were coming to stay in her house over the wedding).

Outside sample:

A young woman came to Swansea from Merthyr when she was nineteen to train as a nurse at Morriston hospital. She met a young man shortly afterwards and they courted for seven years. She was a member of the Church of England but only went occasionally. Her mother was an English Baptist and her fiancé and his family were part of a close chapel group in Morriston. All her friends (after seven years) were in Morriston, and she decided to marry there. Her mother agreed, saying it was 'up to her' (the daughter) to make this decision. The woman then conferred with her future mother-in-law as to where the actual ceremony should take place. Her mother-in-law pointed out to her that 'she often seemed to veer to [their chapel] and came with us on Sundays when she could. And she knew [the Minister] and he knew her, whereas [the vicar] had never spoken to her all the time she was going there. So that, plus her mother's wishes [for a chapel wedding – unspoken but assumed] swayed her . . . Then she said to me, "Ma, can I marry from here [groom's house]?". But I said "No dear, much as I'd like you to", because the bride and groom couldn't marry from the same house. Well, she didn't want to marry from her digs, and the other possibility was my sister's. But she [the bride] didn't like to ask because my sister's husband had been dead less than a year. So I asked, and when it was put to my sister she was quite happy. She'd known May a long time and they were quite close. But then I said May had better make sure her mother didn't mind. "After all", I said, "you're her daughter". But her mother was quite happy, and my sister could put her up too, so it was agreed.'

(2) Not meeting before the ceremony

There is a strong tradition that the bride and groom should not see each other on the day of the wedding until they meet at the chancel steps (or big seat) in church or chapel, or, more prosaically, in the waiting room at the register office; and in 90 per cent of cases they did not. It was recognised that to meet was supposed to be unlucky, and a minority explained their action entirely in terms of 'being superstitious' or 'tradition'; but most supplemented this with rational reasons – they lived too far apart, or they were too busy. Occasionally the groom had to come to the bride's house – e.g., to get his buttonhole if the florist had made just one delivery (to the woman's house) – but he was kept downstairs and the bride upstairs or, 'When he came down to get the flowers, my mother met him at the corner of the street and wouldn't let him in'. The only exceptions were the two student couples, the two couples who were living together, and one instance before a register office wedding where the groom came round 'to see if I was coming!'.

The groom arrives at the church with the best man 15–30 minutes before the ceremony is due to start and after going to the vestry to pay the vicar and to check the details which are to be put on the marriage certificate, he and the best man go back into the church and sit in full view of the congregation, on the front right-hand pew, 5–10 minutes before the time the bride is due to arrive. Tradition is that the bride is a few minutes late – she should be demure and reticent, not thrusting and decisive, slow in coming forward, making the groom wait. Certainly many grooms suffer some anguish that the woman may leave them looking foolish[1] and the time of waiting is slightly tense, especially in Anglican churches where everybody sits quietly waiting, talking in subdued voices. In chapel people seem to relax more, chatting and moving around to talk to friends, and the groom and best man also turn round and chat to friends behind and below them.

(3) Separation of the guests in church

The ushers/groomsmen also arrive half an hour before the start of the wedding and their task is either to recognise people as they arrive, or to enquire of them whether they are 'bride's or groom's', and to direct them to the left- or right-hand set of pews respectively. They also hand out 'service sheets'. These are specially printed double cards with the names of the couple, the date, and the church (and sometimes also the name of the vicar or minister and the organist) on the front, and the hymns which have been chosen for the service inside (see *Figure 1*). At Anglican weddings the ushers also hand out prayer books, or, when there is an experimental service in use, blue pamphlets containing the wedding service (in line with this church's stress on the congregation participating in a set form of service). The books are collected up again at the end of the service; the service sheets are kept by the guests as souvenirs.

It is universally known that the bride and groom's guests should be separated in church, though some people 'would have to look it up' in an etiquette book to know which side is which. Half my informants could give no reason (just 'etiquette', 'old tradition', 'custom', 'just one of those things') for it. Some, although they had 'never thought about it before', suggested 'It must have something to do with there being two separate families'; while others were more specific, if still uncertain:

Case 4: (groom's mother)

> 'I've often wondered. Because, after you're married, the bride's mother comes out with the groom's father, to show you're all friendly like. So I can't understand why they're separated before – unless it's to show that before the marriage they're separated, and afterwards they're interlocked.'

Case 8: (bride)

> 'I haven't really thought about that. Couldn't have everybody mixed up. Suppose his people hadn't met my people. Relations wouldn't like to chat or feel relaxed. Whereas if you're amongst your own kith and kin, it's different.'

Case 8: (groom)

> 'So some sadistic sod can say "She's got more than he has!".'

Probably because of this last reaction, and so as to maintain the conviviality and bonhomie supposed to pertain to weddings, a small minority declared themselves against the separation: 'Never thought about that. Don't think they ought to be. Should be intermingled. Because it's the joining of two families.'

Since there should ideally be an equal number of guests on each side, when people say they are friends of 'both', they are sent by the ushers to whichever side (usually the groom's) looks less full.

On the two sides of the church the guests arrange themselves so that the 'immediate family' (parents, grandparents, and sibs, and their spouses and children) are in the front two rows, with the other close relations and close and elderly friends behind them. Then, more spread out, are those more distant relatives and parents' friends who have been invited to the reception, and the few bride and groom's friends. Towards the back (or in the gallery in a chapel) are women friends, neighbours, and work mates who have come, without official invitation[2], to see the service and the taking of photographs afterwards.

These 'spectators' (as they call themselves) spread out so as 'to get a good view', but if they sit too far back or to the side an usher may come up and persuade them to move to a more central position so as 'to fill the

Figure 1 Example* of service sheet handed out by usher in church

ST. MARY'S CHURCH.
Swansea.

Marriage

of

Susan Mary Owen

and

Thomas Victor Perkins

March 29th, 1969.   Ceremony 10·15 a.m.

Order of Service

❖❖❖

BRIDAL MARCH " Lohengrin "   ...   ...   Wagner

HYMN

Love Divine, all loves excelling,
Joy of Heav'n, to earth come down,
Fix in us Thy humble dwelling,
All Thy faithful mercies crown.

Jesu, Thou art all compassion,
Pure unbounded love Thou art;
Visit us with Thy salvation;
Enter every trembling heart.

Come, Almighty to deliver,
Let us all Thy grace receive;
Suddenly return, and never,
Never more Thy temples leave.

Thee we would be always blessing,
Serve Thee as Thy hosts above;
Pray, and praise Thee, without ceasing,
Glory in Thy perfect love.

Finish then Thy new creation,
Pure and spotless let us be;
Let us see Thy great salvation,
Perfectly restored in Thee.

Changed from glory into glory,
Till in Heav'n we take our place,
Till we cast our crowns before Thee,
Lost in wonder, love, and praise.

HYMN

The Lord's my Shepherd, I'll not want;
He makes me down to lie
In pastures green: He leadeth me
The quiet waters by.

My soul He doth restore again,
And me to walk doth make
Within the paths of righteousness
E'en for His own name's sake.

Yea, though I walk in death's dark vale,
Yet will I fear no ill;
For Thou art with me, and Thy rod
And staff me comfort still.

My table Thou hast furnished
In presence of my foes;
My head Thou dost with oil anoint,
And my cup overflows.

Goodness and mercy all my life
Shall surely follow me,
And in God's house for evermore
My dwelling-place shall be.

WEDDING MARCH   ...   .   Mendelssohn

* This couple were not part of my sample

place up'. To have an empty church, in which the guests 'rattle', loses one status – hence the fondness for small buildings.

Those who have been invited to the reception dress very formally, often in specially bought new clothes, the women wearing hats and gloves and with 'sprays' or flowers pinned to their lapels, and the men in suits, collar and tie, and with flowers in their buttonholes. Those who merely come to watch are easily distinguished by their everyday clothes, large shopping bags and umbrellas. No men who are not invited as guests attend. Some of the bride's workmates wait outside the church to see her arrive, and they clatter into the church just before she does.

Getting to the church

The guests, ushers, groom's parents, groom, and best man make their way to church in their own cars or by taxi, but two or three large, chauffeur-driven limousines are hired to take the bride's mother, the bridesmaids, and finally the bride and her father to the church from their homes. If they live close by, the 'best car', as opposed to the 'bridal limousine', will do the trip twice. The bridal limousine has the back seat covered with a white cloth, and white heather and cardboard silver horseshoes hang in the windows. All the limousines have white satin ribbon 'streamers' from the bonnet to the side windows, which announces their use in a wedding[3]. Even where the church is just a hundred yards down the road from the bride's house she and her father will come by car.

A crowd of neighbours watched the bride leave the house with her father and when she arrives at the church the photographer is usually waiting to take the first photograph (of them going in). Inside the church a procession forms with the bride on her father's right arm, followed by the bridesmaids. The vicar or priest may have walked down to the church door and will walk ahead of the bride and her father down the aisle[4], or he may wait on the chancel steps. The minister waits on the dais in a chapel. The bridegroom and best man move to stand at the top of the aisle. At a signal, the organist stops playing 'background' music and starts the wedding march (from Wagner's Lohengrin). The congregation stands up and half turns to watch the bride come down the aisle – bringing tears to their eyes and lumps in their throats.

At one marriage preparation class I attended the curate said:

'It's a fad of mine; that it's better come in to the first hymn rather than to "Here Comes the Bride", to which we can all put other [lewd] words! It's better, as soon as the bride comes, to start the actual act of worship. It stops everybody looking round and saying "Oh, isn't she pretty", etc. It's what's done at Royal weddings. But it's purely personal. What do you feel?'

His audience were of one accord – the big, formal entrance to 'Here Comes the Bride' was *essential*: 'part of getting married'.

The bride and her father stop alongside the groom and best man, so that the bride is on the groom's left (see *Figure 2*). The bride hands over the bouquet of flowers she carried to her chief bridesmaid, who then steps away to the left side (and keeps quiet any small flower girls or page boys). If the bride entered with her veil over her face, it is generally lifted back at this point, with help from her bridesmaids, and the ceremony begins.

Figure 2 Position of bridal party during the first part of the wedding service

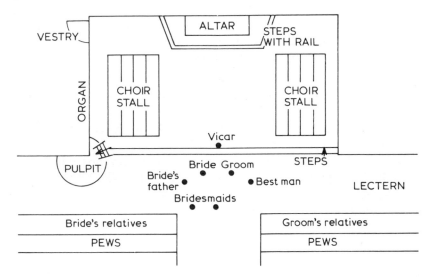

The wedding service

The wedding services of all the main denominations in England (and Europe) have the same structure, which derives from the most solemn form of marriage in Roman law. This had a two-fold ceremony: the espousals (a promise of future marriage) and the actual nuptials. The espousals usually occurred at home, without a priest, and consisted of a verbal contract of future marriage between the bride and groom and an announcement of the exchange of goods that marriage would bring (the bridegroom placed a ring on the bride's finger as a token, and the act of dowry was delivered in writing). The nuptial ceremony was performed in church by a priest and was in three parts: the making of a sacrifice and eating consecrated *panis farreus*, a benediction while the nuptial veil was spread over the bride, and the crowning of the couple with special crowns.

The early Christian Church adopted a modification of this procedure and although the primitive church had only an oral tradition, liturgies were written down by the fourth century (though the oldest extant are from the seventh and eighth century) so that the order of service was soon formalized. There were, however, local variations or 'usages'; the most prominent in Britain at the start of the sixteenth century being that of the diocese of Sarum (Salisbury). It was this usage that formed the basis of the service after the Reformation (1549) and in the 1662 *Book of Common Prayer*. In more than five hundred years the wedding liturgy has therefore remained largely unchanged (that of the Roman Catholic Church has changed even less than the Anglican)[5]. The Nonconformist ministers' manuals, which contain services for weddings and other 'occasional services', also follow the general form of the *BCP*.

In all cases the wedding service today contains:

- an introduction and general statements which establish the Church's support for marriage and say what marriage is and what it is for[6];
- a charge, first to the congregation and the to the couple, that they reveal any impediment to the marriage;
- a declaration by the couple of their desire to marry (possibly deriving from the espousal) followed at once by their plighting their troth (nuptial);
- (blessing and) putting on of the ring:
- a declaration that the couple are married;
- prayers for God's help, and blessing of the couple[7];
- sometimes a sermon or an address; and
- mass or communion (optional) in the Roman Catholic and Anglican churches

Around this basic structure the cultures of the different denominations produce differences of service which make them seem rather 'foreign' to those from other denominations. The Anglican Church, as the Established Church, has hegemony on what a wedding should be, so I will describe its service first and others as variations from it.

(1) The Anglican wedding service

At the time of my fieldwork the Church in Wales was using an Experimental Wedding Service as part of a more general programme of liturgical reform, but its language and structure was still basically that of the familiar *Book of Common Prayer*[8]. However, some vicars were mildly critical of the new form of service and were prepared to amend certain parts (e.g., to bless a ring for the groom as well) instead of following it to the letter.

The vicar or curate directs the service, wearing a cassock and surplice with a stole around his neck[9]. He stands on the chancel steps so that he is slightly higher than the bride and groom and half-reads the service[10], giving the bride and groom directions as to their actions. They, and the congregation, follow him rather gropingly, never quite sure what is going on, and sometimes getting lost and trying to find the place in their booklets.

The service starts with the announcement of the first hymn. In the Anglican buildings, which seem less good accoustically than chapels and have fewer active churchgoers in the congregation, the singing is rather thin. Knowing this, couples try to choose hymns with good tunes 'which everybody knows'. Vicars try to discourage football/rugby favourites such as 'The Lord's My Shepherd', or 'Abide with Me' ('I say to them, "Grand – for a *funeral*"!') or those with *double entendre* – 'Fight the Good Fight', or 'He Who Would True Valour See, Let Him Come Hither'; though 'Lead us Heavenly Father, Lead Us, O'er the World's Tempestuous Sea' gets by. In general, however, it is hymns with 'love' in the title which are favoured (albeit the love referred to is not quite the love the congregation have in mind): e.g. 'Love Divine all Loves Excelling', 'Oh Perfect Love', etc.

Following the hymn the vicar reads the Introduction, which says that they have gathered together 'to join this man and this woman in holy Matrimony'; that the Church sees marriage as having been founded by God and it is to be respected by mankind; and that its purposes are 'the hallowing of the (sexual) union', the procreation and Christian upbringing of children, and 'the mutual society help and comfort' of husband and wife.

He then warns the congregation and the couple that if they know of any reason why they should not marry they should declare it 'or else hereafter forever hold (their) peace'. He asks the groom if he 'wilt have this woman to thy wedded wife', and the groom replies 'I will', and then the question is put to the bride who also answers 'I will'.

The bride is next handed over by her father. (The question used to be asked 'Who giveth this woman to be married to this man?', but this is now left out, though there is a rubric to say that the priest receives the woman at her father or friend's hands.) The groom takes the bride's right hand in his and repeats after the vicar – often looking at the vicar not his bride, and with the sentences so split up as to obscure their meaning –

'I John/ take thee Mary/ to my wedded wife,/ To have and to hold,/ From this day forward,/ For better for worse,/ For richer for poorer,/ In sickness and in health,/ To love, and to cherish,/ Till death us do part,/ According to God's holy ordinance,/ And thereto/ I plight thee my troth.'

Then they loose hands and the bride takes the groom's hand and makes the same promise, except that in addition to promising to love and cherish her husband, she also promises to obey him[11].

The best man puts the ring onto the vicar or curate's prayer book and a blessing is said over it before it is handed to the groom. As the groom puts it onto the fourth finger of the bride's left hand he repeats his promises for the third time: 'With this Ring I thee wed, with my body I thee worship, and with all my worldly gifts I thee endow.' This time the bride does not make a parallel gesture[12].

The bride and groom are then told to kneel (on special white hassocks on the chancel steps) and the instruction is given to the congregation 'Let us pray'. (Some bend forward in Nonconformist or Low Church style, some kneel down.) There is a general prayer of blessing, and the climax of the service is reached when the cleric bends down and joins the right hands of the couple together and wraps one end of his stole round their joined hands[13]. This takes a few moments and the congregation leans forward to see what he is doing. He then announces 'Those whom God hath joined together let no man put asunder'. (The congregation lets out an audible sigh of relaxation of tension.) The priest announces 'that they be man and wife together', and adds a 'dismissal' blessing (laying his hands on them, making the sign of the cross over them, holding his hands above their heads, or holding his right hand up in the air according to his churchmanship).

This concludes the first half of the service and there is usually a second hymn. The second half – the Benediction – varies according to whether or not it is to be followed by communion. (In the vast majority of cases there is no communion, so I shall deal only with this variant here.) One vicar explained the second part of the service by saying to the congregation that the couple 'are now married and the first thing they are going to do together is to pray together to seek God's blessing on their life together'.

The couple walk behind the priest to the altar whilst a psalm is sung. This is the most uncomfortable part of the service since few of the congregation can chant psalms, and it is often a solo by the vicar (or a duo if a deacon or curate is present), with a low mumble, half a phrase behind, from the congregation.

The congregation and the couple are instructed to kneel and they make responses to the vicar's versicles, and join with him in the Lord's prayer.

After this there are three prayers: for God's blessing and protection, for children and their good rearing (omitted if the bride is past child-bearing age), and for strength for the couple in keeping their vows. These prayers are in collect form and archaic language and few in the congregation are likely to know what they are about, or indeed where one ends and another begins, and although the phrases are comfortably familiar, people become a bit restless. There is then a blessing, provision for a sermon (never more than 'a few words' in practice) and a final blessing. (The homily from the scriptures 'touching the duty of husbands towards their wives and wives towards their husbands' was omitted from the Welsh experimental service.)

The vicar motions the bride and groom into the vestry and beckons to the bridesmaids, best man, and bride's father to come in with him. There is usually some uncertainty as to who else is going to go, and some rustling in the front pews as both mothers and the groom's father go forward in a straggling group through the choir stalls to the vestry door.

Vestries are side rooms used by clergy and choir for donning surplices and for storing prayer books and communion wine. They are small (in one case only six foot square) and thus get very crowded. The vicar writes out (or completes writing out) the certificate in his two marriage register books, and he also makes out a copy of the marriage certificate which he gives to the bride. (It is her property.) The couple both sign – the young woman for the last time in her maiden name[14] – the vicar signs and at least two people sign as witnesses (usually the best man and the bride's father). When they are not actually signing, the bride and groom are congratulated and kissed. To complete the confusion, the photographer comes in to take the one picture he is permitted in church (see *Figure 3*).

Meanwhile the organist plays quietly and the friends and relatives wait more or less quietly and patiently. Some of the friends and neighbours sitting at the back and amateur photographers among the guests go out so as to be outside the church to watch the bride emerge.

When all the registration is complete the principals organize themselves into a procession, divided by sex into two sides, but with the families united (see *Figure 4*). A signal is made to the organist who starts to play a march – almost always the Wedding March by Mendelssohn – as they move out and back down the central aisle to the church door. The clergyman usually remains in the vestry (though occasionally he emerges ahead of the procession to request people not to throw confetti and then disappears) and is not seen again. He is not included in any photographs. If he is invited to the reception, and if he accepts (which he will only do with an active church member), he will be asked to say grace. But generally in Anglican weddings he performs the service and takes his departure.

Figure 3 Signing the Marriage Register Book in the church vestry

After the procession has walked slowly back down the aisle with everybody smiling and nodding to their friends and relations on either side (in contrast to the bride's trip up the aisle where she and her father are both very nervous and when it is not correct to try to attract her attention or for him or her to show they recognise anyone), they go out of the church door, and are immediately stopped by the photographer. Thus the congregation, which pours out of its seats behind the procession, gets trapped in a slightly irritable crowd just inside the church. This may be accentuated by the photographer actually shutting the door behind the bridal party so as 'to get a better background'. After a while the crush becomes so great, and people keep opening the door to get out, so the photographer stands aside for a few minutes, before starting work again.

(2) The Roman Catholic wedding service

The interior of a Catholic church in Swansea is not dissimilar to an Anglican church. Both are dominated by the altar with white cloth and coloured frontal, a cross or crucifix, candles, flowers, and reredos. In both, the altar in the sanctuary is separated from the congregation in the nave by the chancel, rail, and steps, and sometimes by the choir stalls as well. The interior is dark because of the stained glass in the windows, and

Figure 4 The wedding procession which returns down the aisle

bride's father	groom's mother
groom's father	bride's mother
best man	chief bridesmaid
younger bridesmaids	
page	
groom	bride

the centre aisle has tiles which ring when one walks. The Catholic church differs, *inter alia*, in having plaster statues of the Madonna and the Sacred Heart, in having the Stations of the Cross round the walls, and in its much greater use of incense and holy water.

The actual wedding ceremony is simpler than the Anglican and closer to the pre-sixteenth centry usage[15]. The priest is assisted by a young boy (who acts as a server in the mass which should follow). The service is short – there is no Introduction, few prayers, and often no hymns – since it is intended simply as the prelude to a nuptial mass. This mass is special for the couple in that they can receive communion 'in both kinds' (wine as well as bread).

No prayer books are given to the guests as they go in, and so many do not know what responses to give (even though this service is now in English, not Latin). If there is a mass the non Catholics get very confused, and rather giggly, about the standing and kneeling in rapid succession, trying unsuccessfully to imitate the Catholics present.

In most Catholic weddings the priest knows at least one member of the couple and he may start the service by addressing a few words to them. In one wedding I attended he spoke of the fact that while the groom was a Catholic the bride was not and how they would have to work to overcome this problem; in another he read rapidly a set piece about the meaning and solemnity of marriage. The priest is more likely than a vicar to be included in one of the photographs and to be invited to the reception.

(3) Chapel weddings (Baptist, Congregational, Calvinistic Methodist)

The minister is likely to know the couple quite well, or at least one of their families of origin, and he builds this knowledge into the actual service – which of course he is free to do since there is no prescribed form (except the legal requirements to take each other *per verba de praesenti*[16]). He performs relatively few weddings and can devote more time and care to each. He is likely to be included in at least one wedding photo, to be invited (with his wife) to the reception, to accept the invitation, and to say grace before the start of the meal.

The first part of the service is very similar to the Anglican one, but shorter, with less archaic language and greater attention to prayers and hymn-singing. (There are usually three hymns (not two), sung with gusto and the whole of the first verse may be read out by the minister in a resounding tone instead of just its number and title being given.) The second part of the service starts with the minister 'reading the scriptures' – usually verses from Corinthians (1 Cor XIII 4–8) on 'Love suffering long and being kind' – after which he gives an address and then a series of long, extempore prayers, ending with the congregation joining him in the Lord's Prayer and a final hymn and blessing. The congregation crouch forwards in their seats rather than kneeling during the prayers, and the minister, while making few gestures (e.g., no signs of the cross), may hold up his arms and screw up his eyes when seeking guidance while praying.

When the minister, couple, bridesmaids, and parents go to one of the offices behind the chapel to sign the register, the atmosphere among the guests is much more relaxed than at the comparable point in the Anglican or Roman Catholic service. People actually move around the building to talk to kin and friends and the conversations are conducted at a normal level, rather than in whispers. (The lesser formality is also seen in the willingness of ministers to allow photographers to take pictures and tape-recordings to be made during the actual service.) When the registration is completed the bridal procession passes along the corridor behind the chapel so as to emerge through the door at the top of the right-hand aisle, down which they then process.

(4) Register Office weddings

When guests arrive at the register office for a wedding they go into the waiting room. In Swansea an elderly man acts (officially or unofficially, I was never quite clear) as an usher – pointing the way, chatting with them, cadging cigarettes off them, telling them why things are running late, how many weddings there have been before that morning, and a bit about what they have to do[17]. It was often commented that the waiting room looked like a doctor's waiting room: a large room divided by a frosted glass partition into the records office and a space with upright chairs; very high ceilinged and semi-basement. Notices of forthcoming marriages are in a glass-fronted cabinet on one wall and the chairs are set in rows down each wall. The tops of tobacco tins act as ashtrays.

The bride may arrive after the other guests but there is little possibility of a formal entry into the already crowded waiting room (there is seating for about a dozen). She and the groom are sat together next to the door. They are fetched first by the deputy registrar to go to the marriage room to check through the particulars on the register.

'If there are any little bits and pieces we can clear up before the friends and relatives are there – e.g., about illegitimacy. And to give them a rough idea what is going to happen and what they're going to declare. Otherwise they can find themselves making an oath and not knowing what they they're going to say.'

The Superintendent Registrar also asks if the parents have come to the wedding.

'What I want to know, Mrs Barker, is where the hell are the mums and dads? As soon as I ask the girl: "Is Dad along this morning?" so that I can sit him beside her, and she says "No", that's upset her. What a send-off for the kids!'

However, the guests are not told why the bride and groom have been taken away and they get worried that they are missing the wedding and try to follow: 'He can't marry them yet; I've got the ring!' The guests get particularly confused because the bride and groom may be taken through the door into the superintendent registrar's office and thence directly to the Marriage Room, while the guests themselves are told to go out through another door and down the corridor. Woman guest (to me), 'I don't know how they work in these bloody places. I've never been to a registry office wedding before.'

The marriage room itself is airy and light, with a carpeted floor and a dozen white leatherette chairs. There are two large vases of flowers on the main table (supplied twice a week by the Parks and Gardens Department); but there is no music[18]. The bride and groom are already in the room when the guests reach it so there is no formal entry, and none of the guests are sure where to sit. Eventually it is sorted out so that the bride and groom's parents (if present) and whoever has the ring are seated at the front, near the couple. The rest range themselves as best they may – the elderly sit, and younger ones stand.

The superintendent registrar is very much in control. For example, he asks that small children be taken out if they disturb the ceremony. (While clergy may try to discourage little ones being used as bridesmaids and pages, they do not ask for them to removed during the service, even when they prove severely distracting.) The registrar stands behind his table and asks the bride and groom to step forward (this is the Swansea Superintendent Registrar's personal practice – he feels it 'draws the attention of all into the ceremony'). He then gives a short prescribed Introduction:

> 'As you know, this room is duly sanctioned as a place where marriages may be performed. I must remind you of the seriousness of the vows you are about to make. Marriage in this country is the union of one man and one woman to the exclusion of all others, voluntarily entered into for life.'

Everyone is then instructed to stand, and the couple repeat after the registrar that there is no lawful impediment to their union. The man then puts the ring on the woman's finger, and they each repeat: 'I call upon these persons here present to witness that I . . . do take thee . . . to my lawful wedded wife/husband (or an exact translation in Welsh).' The registrar declares that they are husband and wife, and the couple kiss each other.

Everyone can then sit down and relax. The deputy registrar has meanwhile completed the register form, and the book with it in is brought round and signed by the couple and witnessed by their parents (if present) and/or others. The couple are given a copy of the certificate, the superintendent registrar shakes hands with them and wishes them success and happiness, and the ceremony is over. Everyone leaves the room, goes down a corridor and then out of the Guildhall.

Taking of photographs

Outside the church or register office guests will mill around talking and many start smoking (so that if they are called by the photographer they stand with one hand behind their backs). The photographic session outside a church can go on for up to half an hour (and may be continued at the reception venue); but it may be very short and informal or may not take place at all, outside the register office.

In Case 6, the following photographs were taken outside the church:

bride, groom, best man and bridesmaids;

bride, groom, best man and bridesmaid + bride's parents;

bride, groom, best man and bridesmaids + groom's mother and brother (his father being dead);

bride, groom, best man and bridesmaids + bride's parents and relatives;

bridesmaids + groom's mother and brother and relatives;

bridesmaids + friends of the bride and groom;

bridesmaids + all friends and relatives;

bride and groom only (several, including one with a small girl giving the bride a wooden spoon);

the bride's entry into the church with her father was restaged since the photographer had not been present at this time;

the groom, best man and ushers;

the bride and bridesmaids.

At the reception more pictures were taken – of the bride and groom 'cutting' the cake (in fact this was staged before the start of the meal while the guests were around the bar drinking, not when the cake was actually cut); and all conceivable combinations of the bride, groom, best man, bridesmaids, and parents. In addition, on request, the bride and groom and others were photographed with particular elderly relatives, notably grandmothers and aunts. In addition friends took snapshots and an uncle took some cine-film.

The bride and groom are carefully posed by the photographer – the bride's long dress and train is arranged spilling out on the ground around her – but in the large groups of relatives there is no formal arrangement. A cry goes up for the 'bride's side to come forward' (and aunts and uncles who hang back are pushed forward) and then the closer relatives stand nearer the centre, and the shorter and younger people are put in front of the taller.

Great importance is attached to the photographic record. The church itself may be chosen because it is 'good for photographs' (a nice background and plenty of grass around it so people can spread out and take their time without being on the pavement or the road), as may the venue for the reception (several of the clubs and restaurants specializing in this sort of trade have special provisions, e.g., a little lake with a small bridge, or 'rustic steps'). Much of the discussion outside the church is in terms of 'how lucky that it's nice and sunny for the photographs', or 'What a pity it wasn't sunny for the photographs. Still, never mind, with these new cameras you don't need much light.' If the weather is really bad the couple may be taken to the photographer's studio on the way to the reception.

The photographer himself is accorded considerable licence to direct everybody to come and go and how to pose, and it is largely due to concern that good photographs be taken that almost everyone who has a 'proper wedding' has a professional photographer (85 per cent)[19] – those who do not, have a very skilful amateur photographer among their relatives or friends. While complaints are made about the length of time the photographer takes outside the church and the extent to which he/she keeps the bride and groom away from their guests at the reception, real bitterness is reserved for incompetents. Case 49:

> 'We had a *terrible* photographer; he couldn't get away fast enough. My dress was blowing between my legs – looked like I was wearing trousers. My mother suggested going inside or round the side of the church. But he was very short with her. My friends were putting pebbles on my train to keep it down! My friend who had recommended him (well, the firm) had the woman – she was at our reception. She was nice. She took us upstairs [in the club] to have more photos taken.' (Groom) 'And when we got down, everybody was drinking like mad things!'

> This couple also had an album of photographs from their honeymoon hotel in Jersey. Jersey advertises itself as specializing in honeymoons and this hotel 'made a big thing of it'. A photographer was employed by the hotel, and one of the photographs in the album showed my informants and all the other couples arranged round the edge of a heart-shaped pool.

Most people choose from among the proof-photographs sufficient for an album. They sometimes also have framed copies to go in their living rooms. The album is then kept carefully, away from everyday life. For example one informant (Case 9) got hers down to show me from its safe place on top of a wardrobe, where its white plastic covers were protected by a cellophane wrapper inside a silver box in a plastic bag. Sometimes the photographs are kept in musical albums which play 'Here comes the Bride' when one opens the front cover. There may also be a little album of photographs for each mother, and cards containing photographs sent out to relatives who could not manage to come. These are not cheap. Case 35:

> 'They took the pictures of him [the groom] and his brother [best man] and the groom's men; and me and my father outside the church going in. And only two of us outside church coming out (one of us by ourselves and one with the little flower girl giving a horseshoe), because there's no porch and it was raining. The photographers

Figure 5 'The bride's side', with 'spectator' in foreground.

Figure 6 Whole congregation watching the taking of photographs outside St James Church

Figure 7 Professional and amateur photographer taking a picture of the groom and best man, flanked by the ushers

Figure 8 Further photographs being taken at the reception

Footnote: From left to right: photographer (in foreground), groom's father, groom's mother, groom's sister, groom, bride, bride's sister, groom's younger sister, bride's mother, bride's father. The child is 'from the groom's side' and was 'in *every* photo'. The bride was angry, but her mother felt they 'couldn't speak out because she was from the other side'.

couldn't take any outside [at the reception] before the meal, so they took some on the stairs. So they [photographer and assistant] sat in on the meal, being as two guests didn't come, and carried on taking photos afterwards.' (Do you have an album?) 'We had one big one with black and white photos and one small one with colour photos which cost £28, and both parents had small albums with colour photos at £12.10s* each.'

Outside the register office there is usually a group of well wishers – neighbours and the bride's work mates among others – who do not attend the wedding ceremony but who come to spectate as the photographs are taken and to throw confetti. About a third of couples who marry in the register office have a professional photographer, sometimes using the one who waits outside the Guildhall for custom on Saturday mornings. Those who use a professional have albums of photographs afterwards, though these are smaller than the albums from church weddings. Others have amateur snapshots – often with disastrous results: rolls of film get lost, or all the photographs are too dark. Sometimes, reportedly, the wedding party goes to have photographs taken in front of the door of a church just down the road[20].

From *Sunday Times, 21 September, 1975.*

Case 46 (bride):

'Yes, we had a photographer. We didn't book – there was somebody out there taking them. Done very nice. Haven't got an album. I just got

* £75 and £37.50 at 1978 prices

all the photographs and bought a book and stuck them in. Not an album. Just like a book, with the engagement and parties you've given. Called a Bride's Book it is.'

Case 10 (groom):

'We had some taken. Only bad thing about the wedding. I wanted to hire a professional photographer, but everyone said "No need – we'll bring all the cameras". And all the photos were very dark (deep sigh). Quite a few outside the registry and they're *hopeless*. We've some big prints, but not worth an album.'

The concern with photographs in our culture (as opposed, for instance, to oral records – less than 5 per cent of weddings are tape recorded) is interesting. They are taken because they are

'compelling and incontrovertible evidence that the events they show actually happened . . . [and they also] constitute a reality, valued in and of itself. Pictures evoke emotions, attitudes and convictions. Photographs, therefore, not only show realities, they create a new plane of reality to which people respond . . . [they are] not only a reflection of . . . reality, but . . . [themselves] become an element in it.' (Milgram 1976:522)

While the taking of photographs outside the church may cause some delay and loss of momentum, this is in fact an advantage – if not carried to excess. It allows the moment to be savoured, for the attention to be focused on the bride and groom: for them publicly to stand together in their new statuses (with the ego support of knowing that the photographer is posing them so that they look at their best), and for the various collectivities ('bridal party', 'groom's side', 'friends of bride and groom', etc.) to come and stand together for a brief time; and for that moment of time, and that statement of group entity, and that visual experience to be 'frozen' and preserved so that it can be shown to others.

While the bride is having her photograph taken, presentations of good luck tokens are made to her: cardboard or plastic replicas of silver horse-shoes (the most common token – one bride was given no fewer than five), silver boots or high-heeled shoes, black cats and chimney sweeps, or actual wooden rolling pins or wooden spoons with a red L on them. These tokens are hung from a loop of white satin ribbon and decorated with plastic silver bells or artificial white heather and lily-of-the-valley. The gifts come from any of those present – guests or 'spectators'; e.g., the bride's mother, a neighbour, the groom's cleaner from college, and the groom's mother's sister. They are carried to the bride by small boys and girls – e.g., the groom's little sister, a neighbour's child – or even by a dog.

After the wedding these tokens are hung up in the couple's new home (e.g., on the chain of the mirror over the fireplace or in china cabinets). If the bride has several, she may give one to her mother, and sometimes also one to the groom's mother.

The horseshoe and the black cat are generally associated with good luck in the culture and it is commonly known that it used to be lucky for a bride to meet a sweep on her wedding day. The silver boot and shoe, though used widely in wedding rituals (as decorations on the wedding cake or on the various types of card – place cards, congratulatory cards, etc.) are less well known or understood. It is thought the boot is 'for the boot they're supposed to tie on the back of your car' as part of the joking when the bride and groom leave on honeymoon; the slipper 'may have something to do with Cinderella', who was found by her Prince Charming because her delicate foot fitted the glass slipper. Both the rolling pin and the wooden spoon represent female 'power' within the home – the rolling pin is for hitting her husband over the head when he comes home late and drunk; and the wooden spoon has to do with her habit of stirring up trouble through gossiping (as in the phrase 'a member of the wooden spoon club'), as well as their obvious connections with her task of cooking. The red L is the same symbol as that used on cars for learner drivers.

After the photographs have been taken the bride and groom are the first to leave. As they cross the church-yard, they are showered with confetti – generally bought by women (of all ages), but thrown by men and women. It is sometimes used rather aggressively – stuffed down the groom's shirt and thrown in the couple's faces – but generally with great good humour.

The bride and groom go from the church to the reception in the bridal limousine and the bridesmaids follow in the 'best car'. Everybody else packs into the other cars, of which there is usually an abundance. (Technically it is the responsibility of the best man to make sure everybody is provided for.) In one parish a coach was often provided to take guests to the reception and back so that they could drink without worrying about driving later, since popular places for receptions were about five miles away from their homes. One in three couples leave the register office in a bridal limousine or large hired car with streamers. Others go to the reception in a taxi or a private car (for preference a white one).

The reception

Most weddings in Swansea take place in the morning and lunch is provided afterwards. In every case except one, those who had church weddings had a reception in a hotel, club, restaurant, or pub (97 per cent) with a median of sixty guests (range 25–116); whereas among those who had register office weddings, only six (30 per cent) had anything similar, and then there were only half as many guests (median thirty-three, range 15–50).

My informants had their receptions in twenty different places – four pubs, three hotels, and a mixed bag of clubs (British Legion, Merchant Navy, Trade Union and drinking clubs) and restaurants. Two were notably popular – The Langland Court, a large mock tudor mansion now surrounded by a rather expensive housing estate near the sea at Mumbles, with a ballroom-cum-banqueting hall in the basement; and The Pines, a collection of one storey new buildings attached to a large house in a district of the town of just south of Morriston. Both had 'lovely grounds for photographs' and 'did a lovely hot meal'. Also popular were two large, newly built hotels in the town centre.

To an extent the number of guests was regulated not only by the price the bride's parents and/or the couple could afford to pay, but also by the exigencies of the accommodation offered. Thus one bride who booked late found that the town centre hotel could offer her 'sixty or 250' (the middle-sized facility being already taken), 'so it had to be the sixty'.

The hotels and restaurants offer variously priced menus and they reinforce the local preference for set meals rather than buffets at receptions by charging more for 'running buffets'. The chief difference between the menus in any one place is according to the amount and type of drink given to the guests (i.e., whether 'table wine' is or is not served during the meal[21] and whether sherry or champagne is provided for the toasts at the end). Hotels are slightly more expensive than restaurants, which are slightly more expensive than clubs (a range of 19s 6d to £1 30s per head in 1969; £2.75 to £4.50 in 1978).

When the guests arrive at the reception from the church they are handed a glass of sweet sherry by a waitress and they may be greeted by the bride's parents (though it is equally possible that the bride, groom, and parents will be somewhere else being photographed). The guests then move into a room with a bar, and after they have finished their sherry they buy themselves (or, if they are women, they are more usually bought) drinks and they talk to such friends and relatives as they know, or they may watch the bride and groom being photographed. After about half an hour they are summoned to eat.

Tables are put together to form a large U or E shape, and set with long white cloths and vases of flowers. There may be specially printed paper serviettes (with the bride and groom's name and the date on one corner) or simply 'wedding serviettes' decorated in silver with bells, horseshoes, hearts, roses, doves, etc. Where people should sit is marked by place cards, either printed or typed or written by a friend with good handwrit-

ing, and with a motif to match the serviettes (see *Figure 9*). The bride and groom, their parents, the best man and the bridesmaids sit along the top table but otherwise seating is relatively flexible. Prestige is attached to sitting near to the bride and groom, and especially close family friends or relatives will be put there. Elsewhere whoever draws up the table-plan (often the bride's father or the bride and groom) will try to put people close to people they know, or to those of similar age and temperament. (Sometimes the early arrivals do some discreet swapping so as to sit near to, or away from, someone.)

The food is served to the guests by waitresses. In the clubs and restaurants the meat is brought already on the plates and dishes of vegetables are put on the tables for guests to help themselves; in the hotels there is 'two handed service' of everything. A typical menu consists of:

Soup

–

Roast turkey with bacon rolls
Roast and mashed potatoes
Peas
Bread sauce

–

Pears and ice cream

–

Coffee

–

Sherry and wedding cake

According to one attempt to provide a structuralist analysis of 'food events' (Douglas and Nicod 1974), the messages which the sharing of such a meal would send to the participants would be that it was a very special meal, being shared by an intimate group of people[22].

Of those informants who did not have an outside reception (all except one of whom married in the register office), one or two went for a small family meal (4–5 people) in a hotel restaurant. The majority, however, had a 'running buffet' reception at either the bride or groom's house, with 10–50 guests invited 'by word of mouth'. These buffet meals are prepared by the mother of the bride or groom and female relatives and friends. Nine were held at the bride's home and three in the groom's when relations with the bride's parents were difficult or the bride's parents' financial circumstances were strained. Tables are set with several kinds of cooked meats and salad, different sorts of sandwiches and vol-au-vents, sausages, cheese on sticks, crisps, nuts and other savouries, and trifles

Figure 10 Plan of a typical reception in a clubhouse

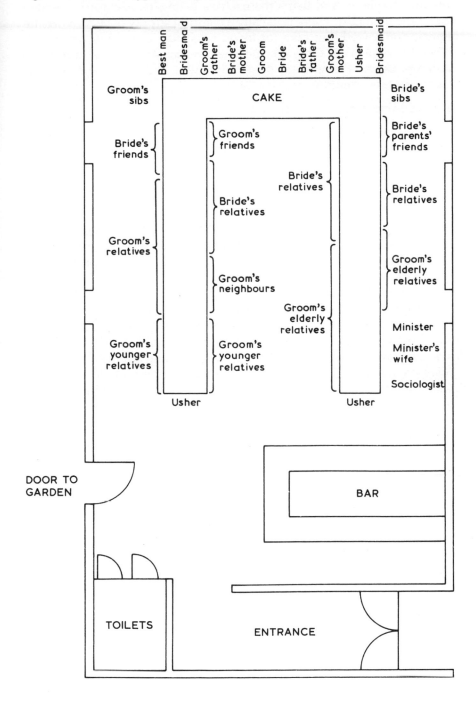

and tinned fruit with cream for dessert. Everyone takes a plate, knife and fork and serviette, and helps themselves, eating standing up or seated round the room[23]. There is usually a plentiful supply of beer, wine and spirits, and a wedding cake (of fewer tiers than in a white wedding). When the cake is cut there are speeches and toasts, but the audience is scattered around the house so many miss them, and those who are in the room pay less attention.

The wedding cards and speeches

When the coffee stage is reached in the meal the best man gets to his feet and calls for order by coughing or banging on the table and announces: 'Ladies and Gentlemen, the Bride and Groom will now cut the cake.' A waitress hands the bride a large knife and, with her husband's hand over hers, she slowly makes a single slice down into the heart of the bottom tier and draws the knife down and out[24]. The guests clap. After this formal cutting, the cake is removed to the kitchen by the caterers, who dismantle it, and a skilled cutter will cut sufficient for the guests who are present, and small pieces are served with sherry or sparkling wine provided for the toasts.

Meanwhile the best man reads out the cards and telegrams of congratulations which have been sent to the couple as 'Mr and Mrs Jones'. Many cards have large and glossy pictures on the front featuring bottles of champagne, wooden spoons, wedding cake, church candles, a bride's veil, silver horseshoes, confetti, wedding rings, and various flowers (red roses – symbolic of love; carnations – as worn in buttonholes; lily of the valley and freesias – as used in bridal bouquets; and white heather – for luck), and 'Best Wishes on Your Wedding Day'. Inside there is a printed doggerel verse and the sender's signature. Others prefer to use a 'notelet' with a picture on the front and plenty of room for their own verse (see *Figure 11*), or they may use a 'standard' verse, commonly:

> 'It has often been said:
> Marriage is like boating.
> If you row together your course
> will be straight and true and the
> going smooth. No storm will be
> too strong for you and you will
> have a happy crew.'

Some of the more risqué ('cheekiest') cards come from workmates. For example, some friends composed the poem shown in *Figure 11* (poem 2) for a couple who both worked in the Addis plastic-ware factory[25]. In other cases the bride's workmates typed out a whole series of couplets, Case 37:

'An apple a day
keeps the doctor away
but what can a pair
Do at night.

Once a Duke
Always a Duke
Once a Lord
Always a Lord
But once a night is quite sufficient.

2 little pillows edged with lace
2 little faces face to face
Everything in its proper place
Goodnight.

Carolyn stood in the garden
With her back against the wall
A figleaf for her trouseau
And that was all.
Edward came into the garden
And he said YUM YUM
There's work to be done
When the leaves start to fall.

God made man, he made him out of string
He had a little over so he made a little thing.
God made woman, he made her out of lace
He didn't have enough, so he left a little space.

Orange blossoms this year,
Orange juice next year.
BUT REMEMBER
A leak tonight
Could mean a pramful tomorrow.

The weather forecast for London
Area for Saturday night,
Very hot and close at night
With a little son later .

With Edward as Captain
And Carolyn first mate
Hoping the crew will follow
At a later date.

Today's the day
Tonight's the night
We've shot the stork
So you're alright.

We wish you luck
We wish you joy
We wish you first a baby boy
And when his hair begins to curl
We wish you then a baby girl.

Signed. The office girls.'

The antithesis between sentimental and sexual messages is clear. The former are sent by members of an older generation (parental – e.g. the customers in a groom's father's pub, or an aunt and uncle – or grand-parental) and the latter by the peers of the bride (and, less often, the groom).

There may be 10–40 cards and half a dozen telegrams, mostly from those who cannot attend but also from some who are at the reception. Although everyone starts by listening attentively and looking expectant, they become rather bored because even close relatives will only know who half the senders are. People looked pleased every time they can identify someone and whispers pass down the table as to who the person is:

'From Auntie May and Trigger'
'That's Jennifer's father's sister. She's not been well and lives in London. And her dog.'

The best man censors some of the jokes so as not to read them out 'in front of grandma and the minister'. At the end everyone agrees with their neighbours at the table that 'it's marvellous the people who remember' (i.e., they assert the strength of the ties the couple have with large numbers of nice people).

There follows a series of formal speeches and toasts:

– a speech by the bride's father welcoming the groom into their family and proposing a toast to the bride and groom (semi-serious in tone);
– by the bridegroom, replying on behalf of 'my wife and myself'; thanking his and her parents for being good parents, and the bride's parents for providing the wedding reception; and proposing a toast to the bridesmaids (fairly serious tone);
– and by the best man, replying on behalf of the bridesmaids (amus-ing).

Figure 11 Example of 'notelets'

POEM FOR TWO
****

I could wish you lots of things;
Seasons of Autumns, Summers and
Springs,
I could wish you wealth untold!
Buckets of silver and bags of gold,
Drinks all round' in the fashion
bars,
Money and mink, and mini'cars,
I could wish you from my den,
The lovliest things from a poets,
pen;
Acres of land, I might bequeath -
Skewen-Llansamlet-and PENTRECHWYTH!
But the greatest wish; and it
should'nt seem odd!
Is that you two people, be blessed
by God!
Because Gods, blessing-truely
unfurled,
Is anyones wish in anyones WORLD.
****

G.J.P.

Mam e Dad Gwynfor

FIRST NIGHT
FROLIC
******

FOR JACKIE' AND GWYNFOR

ON

THE HAPPY OCCAISION OF

THEIR MARRIAGE

****

FROM THE GIRLS, ON THE

PEDAL-BIN LINE
****
****

THIS IS A POEM, FOR JACKIE, AND
GWYN'
HE ON THE "CARTONS" AND SHE ON
THE "BIN"
SO PEDAL-BIN, BREAD-BIN, SQUEEZY-
MOP!
MAY YOUR HAPPINESS, NEVER STOP!
MAY YOU BE BLESSED WITH LOTS OF
TWINS,
FIRST'S AND SECONDS, LIKE PEDAL-
BINS:
SO BREAD-BIN-PEDAL-BIN, BUTTER-
FLY, TOO
MAY ALL YOUR SKIES BE EVER BLUE
AND PRAY THIS NIGHT? BEFORE YOU
SLUMBER,
THE BRIDE AND GROOM, WILL MAKE
THEIR "NUMBER"!
****
****

Particular men will then be called upon by name to speak. Others will simply stand up and speak when the best man asks 'Does anyone else want to say something?'.

> In Case 6 there were 'a few words' from a cousin (groom's fa.mo.sis.son), a workmate of the bride's father ('a big friend'), the bride's mother's brother, a friend of the groom's (recently deceased) father – and a shout from the back from one of the groom's friends to the effect that the groom had better hurry up and get his suit back to Burton's because it was early closing day.

Women very rarely speak: 'they are not really supposed to'. Certainly the bride and her mother and bridesmaids are always spoken *for*. Any woman who speaks would be a very close relative and would speak far down in the order. She would probably be elderly, and probably from the groom's side.

Many of those who make speeches find it a nerve-racking experience and have put time and care into thinking what they are going to say – even to the point of making notes on paper. (The etiquette book of mine which was most frequently borrowed for consultation was *Wedding Speeches and Toasts*[26].) The form and content of the speeches is interesting.

Case 9. The best man called on the father of the bride, who replied:

> 'Thanks for coming to give Mary and Les such a good send-off. We're glad to welcome Les into the family. One only has to look at them to see it will be a happy marriage – they're very much in love. There's no better start to a marriage. Also in their favour is that they're proven stayers. Les is not only a good scholar, but also a good cross-country runner. Mary is also a marathon walker – sixteen miles once. Les came to our house first many years ago – if I'd known then that he was going to take her away, I might have reacted differently. Do you know the story of the two men on the train? The young man asks the older man if he can tell him the time. The older man doesn't reply. At the end he says to the young man, "If I'd told you the time, we might have got into conversation and I might have liked you; I might have invited you home, and you'd have met my daughter, and you might have fallen in love. And I don't want my daughter to marry."
> What else is there to say?
> Well, once Mary knew she was going to get married, she went faithfully to cookery classes – trial and experiment at home. Experiment for Mary and a trial for the wife and me. I'm quite happy, Les, to pass the trial on to you. One last thing: just don't make me a grand dad too soon! Shall we drink a toast to the Bride and Groom?'

We all stood up. My neighbour, a minister, passed me his sherry saying he never drank, and his wife passed her orange juice to a neighbour who also had nothing; and then he and she joined in by raising their coffee cups and we all said 'the bride and groom' and took a sip.

The best man called on the groom to speak:

'I'd like to thank Mary's father for the reception, and for bringing up their daughter so well! Also to thank Jane for being bridesmaid. As you probably know, she herself will soon be wearing white and we wish her the best. We would like to thank her by giving her a small token of our gratitude [handed over a package containing a St Christopher medallion]. I give you a toast then, the bridesmaid! [We all drank to this.] I'd also like to thank the guests and our sociologist for coming.'

The best man thanked the groom on behalf of the bridesmaid; adding

'We'd all agree, she has been a very charming bridesmaid. I'd now like to call on the groom's father to say a few words.'

(Groom's father):

'Very happy to find Mary in the family [next bit was inaudible]. Do hope they'll be very happy.'

Then one of the groom's 'drinking companions' was called on to say a few words. The best man obviously did not know the man concerned – he had a name written on a piece of paper.

The drinking companion climbed rather sheepishly to his feet, protesting and being cheered on by his friends (all of whom sat together on the end of one 'arm' of the table). The man seemed to have been taken unawares – his name having been passed forwards unbeknown to him; but he had obviously been selected for his repartee:

'Well, as you can see, I didn't come prepared to make a speech [promptly pretended to start to look for 'notes' in all his pockets and to wipe the sweat off his brow]. I'd like to say simply that, sorry as his friends are to see Les fall by the wayside, he will make Mary a good husband. Can I propose *another* toast to the Bride and Groom?.' (Yes)

The best man then got up again complaining that it seemed to get around to his turn again very quickly.

'Les asked me to be best man three months ago and I said "I must start to write my speech", but it still isn't finished!' He then mumbled a bit, saying he was sure that the couple would be very happy, before plunging into his story. This was about a man, newly married, who set off on his donkey with his wife walking behind (cries of 'Shame' from

the other guests). 'The donkey won't go, so the man gets off and says
to the donkey, "I've told you once". This happens twice more. The
third time he shoots the donkey. His wife starts to complain, "You
fool, why kill a good donkey?" etc. Her husband says, "I've told you
once . . . "!' (laughter)

The best man then asked if anyone else wanted to say anything, and the
bride's grandfather got up.

'My congratulations to the best man who's doing a good job, and to the
groom, whom I know well as he's been coming down to our house a
long time. Very decent boy. I'd like to thank the bride's parents for a
very beautiful wedding – meeting old friends and making new ones.
Only one other occasion where we do that . . . Well, let's not talk of
that now! I hope Mary and Les make lots of friends in the future. One
can see they've got lots here. Only way to make friends away from
home is by going to church.'

Other guests then called on Uncle Clifford 'to stand up and show how
hard it is to stand up and say something': 'Les's relatives, some here
[gesture around him] and some there and there [pointing], say thank you
and wish the bride and groom all the best.'

There were then further mutterings to try to get someone to say something – clapping the one chosen to try to encourage him to stand up.
Finally the groom's grandmother spoke:

'I'm very pleased to be here today at the wedding of my grandson. I'm
sure they'll be very happy. My first grandson to marry, though several
grand-daughters have. Hope I may live a little longer to see the others
settled.'

Then the bride's brother stood up:

'There's an extra telegram for you, Les. "Very sorry, honeymoon plans
will have to be changed. I need the island myself, Ari".' (Onassis and
Jackie Kennedy had announced their engagement the day before.)

He added that he 'would like to say, now that the last of (his) mother's
children was marrying, (they) would all like to thank her for all she had
done for them. Also did we realise that (his) mother had cooked and
decorated the delicious cake we were eating?' (appreciation expressed
all round.)

These speeches show the same themes of sentimentality, facetious-
ness, and sexual innuendo as are seen in the doggerel in the cards,
though in the speeches there is more putting down of the opposite sex
(women) and they are delivered with greater authority. The actual shape

of each speech is set: it is either short and sentimental, or it may include declarations of affection and welcome *and* jokes – with lurches back and forth between the two. They have many of the characteristics of 'formal speech' outlined by Bloch (1975): fixed intonation of delivery, fixed sequence and type of speech acts, and use of illustrations from relatively limited sources (jokes, proverbs, scriptures). As he argues, formal speech is not saying anything constructive: its function is 'not to report facts but to influence people' and it is typical of systems of traditional authority (in the Weberian sense).

> 'The effect of always comparing particular event to the same general illustrations [here jokes] reduces the specificity of utterances so that all events are made to appear as though they were all alike . . . The individuality and historicity of events [and couples] disappear since irrespective of minor differences (they) are all *like* the scriptural [or joke] examples . . . '

> Further, formalisation of speech 'removes the authority and the event from the speaker himself so that he speaks . . . less and less for himself and more and more for his role . . . '

> The effect of this is 'a comforting sensation of union with a common heritage'. '(T)he most important social effect of this merging of the specific into the eternal and fixed, is that it moves the communication to a level where disagreement is ruled out since one cannot disagree with the right order . . . the order of nature.' (Bloch 1975:15, 16, 17)

The doggerel verses and wedding speeches confirm, amongst other things, the 'axiom of amity' between kin; the pleasures of sexuality – particularly for men; the importance of children to a marriage – though they should not come too soon; the supremacy of the husband within the household; the importance of partnership and love to both spouses' personal and material satisfaction; the thanks owed to parents by children; and the need for luck and God's blessing in an essentially hazardous life.

The departure of the bride and groom

After the speeches the bride and groom go round to say a few words to any guests they have not already spoken to, before going to change out of their wedding clothes into especially smart outfits in which to go away. A changing room is usually provided by the place where the reception is held, and the clothes and suitcases are brought there either the night before or on the morning of the wedding day. Either the bride's mother or the best man is supposed to look after the cases to make sure that they are not tampered with (see on) – the clothes seemingly are immune (cf. coats in joking at work). Occasionally, however, the couple go back to their homes to change – usually in order to show themselves to an elderly or infirm relative who has been unable to go to the wedding. While they are changing, people chat around the table and the men drift back to the bar.

Two-thirds of those who had church weddings left from the reception to go away on honeymoon, as against a quarter of those who had register office weddings and outside receptions (in all, 64 per cent of those who had outside receptions). This departure was the scene of the most rum-bustuous joking associated with weddings. Efforts were made to locate the luggage of the bride and groom and to 'reorganize' its contents – e.g., to take out the groom's pyjama trousers or the bride's nightdress so as to cause the couple the embarrassment of being naked in front of each other; to stuff it with confetti so that this should spill out on their hotel floor, letting the staff know that the couple are newly-weds and likely to be sexually active but novices, etc. If the couple go away by car it will be covered in lipsticked messages and toilet paper, tin cans, or an old boot may be tied onto the back (or traditionally a kipper stuffed in the exhaust pipe), and six or seven young men may lift up the rear wheels so that when the groom tries to move away his wheels will simply spin round. A cautious groom therefore will hide his car and get the best man to drive them to where it is secreted. One of the things looked for in a best man is that he will be on the groom's side and not go over to the 'enemy' at this time.

In the majority of cases, however, the couple left on honeymoon by train. They were driven to the station by the best man, with a noisy escort, and the joking took place around the railway carriage – which it is *not* possible to secrete. Trains to London start from Swansea so the frolickers have plenty of time to do their worst. All the mid-afternoon trains on Saturdays contain some 'happy couples' and more join them at stations down the line. (Even if the couple go home to change, word will be passed on as to the time of the train they are catching and their friends will arrive to wish them good-bye.) This joking becomes aggressive at times, and it is recognised as fair play that the couple try to avoid it as much as possible (more, for example, than the joking at work, where a 'good sport' must stand and take it). Cutting and running is permissible, but if they are caught the joking has renewed force.

Case 45:

> (Bride) 'We went to the station in the best man's car. They'd tied three tins – you know, pint beer cans – on the back. And they wrote in lipstick "An-An and Chi-Chi".'
> (I said that I hoped they'd had more success.
> '*Yes*' they said, 'We've heard that one before'.) 'And a big L sign, and

"Tonight's the night" and "You've never had it so good".'
(Groom) 'The worst thing was that the groomsmen were behind us all
the way – sounding their horn all along the Mumbles Road and up
Wind Street. Everyone was looking and pointing. Then a policeman
stopped us. When he saw what it was, he grinned and stopped all the
traffic to let us into the station.'
(Bride) 'We didn't have much time in the station – Thank God. But they
wrote on the windows: "Santa's Grotto – come in for unlimited pleasure" and twined toilet rolls over the luggage racks and smothered us in
confetti. When we stopped at the stations all the railway workers were
pointing and grinning. We felt as if we were in a zoo.' (Couldn't you
have moved your seat?) 'No, the train was packed – a honeymoon
special – there were seven other couples and a match on.'
(Groom) 'Then when we got off at London the guard said "Yes,
definitely just married".'
(Bride) 'Well, it's good fun, and it's only once in a life-time. But they do
go too far. We were so careful to lock the cases but they prised up the
sides and stuffed in confetti. Ken [the groom] nearly got a black eye
when he tried to grab back the cases.'
(Groom) 'God, they were vicious. It was Jennifer's case – her vanity
case – with perfume. They could have smashed the lot.'

Case outside sample as described by a neighbour:

'At the station they smothered the girl in confetti. And stuck a pair of
frilly panties and a pair of underpants onto the window and wrote
"Going away for a bit – do not disturb!"

The guests couldn't get at the cases – but the bride's mother had the
key, and *she* took out the groom's pyjamas and sewed up the night
dress and filled it with confetti.' (my emphasis)

Attempts will also be made to find out where the couple are going to
spend their honeymoon, with threats to continue to cause acute embarrassment. Actual intrusions into the honeymoon I found to be very rare;
but threats and cautionary tales are common. Case 45:

(Did you have a honeymoon?) 'Yes, six days in London.'
(Did you keep quiet about where you were going?) '*Quiet*, God, we left
a false trail.' (Why?) 'Oh, it would have been murder. They'd have
rung up at two in the morning – "What are you *doing*?". The real
answer was picking confetti off the floor!'
(Did you try not to look newly-wed then?) 'Yes; but we gave it away. I
[the bride] took my hat off so as not to look conspicuous. And we were
walking around as if we'd been doing it for years. I even called out
"Nicer than when we were here last year, darling!". But in the room

the 'phone went. No one knew where we were. We sat on the bed and trembled. It was only the poor old porter ringing to ask if it was my hat. Oh, God, were we scared!'

Guest at Case 8's reception:

'We had a girl at work, and we asked her casually where they were going, and she told us! "So and so hotel in London." So we sent a telegram saying "Come home and get married. All is forgiven." It was given over the phone and written down on the hotel pad and handed to them. Her husband pretty near opened the floor, fell through and pulled it down on top of him!'

The bride and groom are faced outside the church, at the reception, and especially when 'going away' with disruptions of their normal 'presentations of self'. They are at the centre of the stage and are required to perform dramatic parts which emphasize their sexuality to a large audience made up of usually separate groups. These audiences – their parents, relations, and neighbours; workmates and friends; and their new spouse – are just those which, as prudent performers, they would want to keep separate as regards the information relayed about their sexual behaviour.

In part, therefore, the hostility towards the couple which is certainly to be seen in the joking around a wedding may result from what Goffman (1969) describes as the 'aggressive pleasure obtained by discovering (or thinking one is discovering) someone's dark inside, strategic secrets'. But hostility also arises because, at this time, each member of the couple is going over to the enemy, leaving the sex/peer group and the family of origin; and also because there is jealousy at the couple being in love (a highly valued state), at each partner's having found someone willing to marry them, and at their forthcoming sexual pleasure.

The hostility is expressed in actual, if relatively mild, physical attacks: the amount (and the mixtures) which the bride and groom are persuaded to drink at their hen and stag parties must come close to attempted alcoholic poisoning; and the roughhousing with confetti is often a good deal more than 'friendly'. The mockery and embarrassment caused is such that the couple certainly find it hard to pass it off as 'all a joke'. Hostility is also shown in a lack of tact – in a refusal (or threat of refusal) to act in a protective way that will allow the couple to 'present' themselves as they wish. As Anne Allen discovered in the letters written to her, as a Sunday Mirror columnist, about honeymoons, 'Most couples long to be taken as long-married. Most friends seem to be wholly determined that they shall not succeed and that the hotel, or the neighbours, shall be well and truly informed' (Allen 1968:90).

When one talks to people they present this antagonism as simulated and enjoined hostility in which people sometimes get 'carried away' by excitement and drink, but which overlies 'real' amity. And anthropologists have long stressed that joking is characteristic of situations and relationships where there is both conjunction and disjunction, attachment and separation (Radcliffe-Brown 1940, 1949; Sharman 1968). But increasingly it is recognised that joking may be as much privileged aggression as privileged familiarity; that the hostility may be as real as the amity (Douglas 1968; Loudon 1970).

Those couples who did not make an elaborate departure from their reception mostly did not go away on honeymoon at all, but a few (three who had a church wedding, and one who had a register office wedding) left the following day, or after the weekend. Two stayed in a hotel in Swansea overnight so as 'not to miss the fun' in the evening, but so as also to avoid spending the first night 'under their in-laws' roof'. Another couple stayed with parents till they took a flight to Jersey two days later. And one couple were delayed by heavy snow and could not leave by car.

Of those who had outside receptions but did not leave Swansea at all, most explained this by their need to save money and not thinking a holiday in the middle of winter or near Christmas a very sensible idea. Of those (N=8) who had had church weddings, four went directly to their own house or flat, two borrowed a flat or, in one case (students), stayed in a hotel in Swansea. The single case where the couple went directly to live with the bride's parents was also the only case of a bride marrying in church when pregnant.

Among those who had receptions at home (almost exclusively those who had register office weddings), only one couple left on honeymoon at once – by car for two days in a hotel in Cardiff. For the rest (N=13), seven went to their own houses or flats (or sometimes they borrowed one from relatives), and six stayed with one set of parents. Again, those who stayed with parents were pregnant or divorced (N=2); i.e., it seems to be those who are (technically) sexually inexperienced who get out of their parents' house for their wedding night[27].

Those who had 'proper weddings' went to more exotic places for their honeymoons. None of those who had register office weddings went abroad, but seven who had church weddings went to Majorca, Paris, Brussels, or Jersey. London was the most popular place (N=13), being not too expensive and with plenty to do in wintry weather. Others went to Cornwall, Ireland (to relatives), Edinburgh, Bournemouth (with relatives), Brighton, North Wales (with relatives), Bristol, Porthcawl, and Cardiff.

Events following the reception

At the end of the reception those who have not gone to see the couple off, or all the guests when the couple do not leave Swansea, continue at the reception venue till its bar closes, or the drink runs out if it has been held at home. Some then move on to a club which stays open all afternoon, or, more commonly, they go back to various people's homes for tea. Those with young children pick them up from whoever has been minding them, feed them and put them to bed, and then they may go back to join the main group(s) again.

In the evening there may be an organized 'get together' of both sides, either in a hired hall or room, sometimes with a band and 'running buffet' but certainly a bar, or in the groom's or bride's parents' house. Sometimes the two sides remain separate – there is a 'get-together' in the bride's house and in the groom's – and there may be further segregation by age ('all the young ones and some of the older ones went down the Red Cow for a singsong'); or more commonly by sex ('the men went out boozing, the women stayed home – quietly boozing! – and the men came back with a crate [of beer] and joined them'); or else separate small groups or couples and sibs may go to their pub or club or for a meal.

When the couple do not go away on honeymoon they join in these parties or go out for a meal in the evening (typically with the best man). In one case they went to the pantomime. They return from these evenings out to their new homes. By and large they are 'left in peace' – as were those who went away – despite the threats made; but in a few cases further practical jokes were played. For example, the couple in Case 21 (both of them were marrying for the second time) were woken at two in the morning by a group of friends on the pretext of trying to persuade them to get up and go to a party. 'Apple-pie beds' are not uncommon. Case 5 (bride):

> After the wedding in the register office 'there were about 10 of us in the taxi – me, Reg [groom], the best man, his mate, my brother-in-law, my sister, my brother – and the taxi-driver. We had a reception up my mother's house; we laid on a buffet reception for about fifty. The party went on till two am. My sister was all mournful because the car she went down in was caught in the traffic jam and she missed the wedding. Nothing went right that day, did it, Reg? . . .
>
> I changed completely from a white dress to black and we went up the Rum Puncheon [pub] where I tipped a whole glass of cider over my mother-in-law's new coat! Bit tipsy I was by then! Then we came back home. By then it was getting on. Played a couple of records. Had a light tea. And went up to my mother-in-law's for a massive big party.

My brother-in-law came in a borrowed car [to take us] – and it wouldn't go so we had to push it, and I tore my tights! So at my mother-in-law's I asked her if she'd got some I could borrow, but she hadn't. I was nearly in tears! She gave me some black thread to sew them up. I was upstairs in the bedroom [mending them] when Reg comes up. And, it was ever so funny, his little brother called up, "Where are you, Reg?" and he said, "In the bedroom with Jackie", and his brother said "I'll tell Mammy!". So Reg shouted down, "Never mind, boyo, it's legal now!". Only little he is, his brother.

Well, we all went out to the club and had a drink and a sing-song. Bit cold to start with, but it got to be good. Some of the girls that I work with came, and relations of his that we couldn't invite to the wedding and with people from the reception there were about eighty of us. We went back to his house at quarter to eleven and got really sozzled – well, his mother had bought in about £30 odd worth of spirits!

Then we had a terrible row, because, at quarter to one, he wanted to go home and I couldn't see why we should go; I wanted to stay at the party. Because, anyway, we had guests at my house so we couldn't have done anything anyway, if you see what I mean. So I told him I'd got the painters in – but he didn't understand! So I said, straight out, I can't sleep with you because it's the wrong time of the month. He was mad!

Anyway, we made it up. We were going to stay up my mother's [which was close to his parents'], but we decided to come down here [to their furnished flat several miles away], but we went by Gower Street [her parents' house] to get some bacon and eggs for breakfast. And when we got here it was getting on for four in the morning! Then when we finally crawled into bed, I felt something; and I said "Oh my God, what's this?". It was a whole box of confetti! I'd gone down there with two friends to make the bed, and one of them must have sneaked back!'

This rather desultory wandering around on the wedding night is not particularly unusual.

The most remarkable joking situation also occurred after a register office wedding, among a very respectable white-collar couple, who, at an earlier point in the interview, had distanced themselves from the bride's rather 'rough', highly fecund mother. Case 47:

After a six-year courtship (including a two-year engagement) they finally married when the bride became pregnant.

(Bride) 'I'd have liked a white wedding, but had a quiet one. Still, I enjoyed myself. Had a really good day . . .

We had a little do up the house [her mother's] – just a few drinks and sandwiches. Only for those who'd come from the church [sic]. Brothers and sisters – but, no, no invitations. Just word of mouth. Then we went out in the afternoon; all went down the pub for a drink – my mother-in-law and her sister and husband and the best man and us. [The groom's father was dead]. Then we came back here [groom's house where they lived after marriage]. Then out to the pub in the night – we all got drunk! We had a great time – went out for a drink and then back here for a little do. Grand time. We had the record player going. All his friends came and my mother-in-law organized a party. His mother and sister did the food. Great. Went on till four in the morning! *Our* friends – his mates and their wives – none of his relations stayed . . .

We was going to go on honeymoon, but it takes up such a lot of money and we needed every ha'penny we had with the baby coming.'

(Did anyone play any jokes on you?)

'Well, at work they asked me what I wanted [as a present] and I said "A bath and pram set for the baby". And the manager come in and held the potty up and we were all laughing.'

(Anything else?)

(Hesitantly) 'No. Well, we played one on my husband. My mother-in-law dressed up in my nightdress and got into our bed. He screamed "Get out, get out!". God, how we laughed!'

The aftermath of the wedding: flowers, cake, announcements, and souvenirs

(1) Flowers

Flowers are widely used for presentations to women in British culture and wearing a single flower or a spray (one or more flowers and foliage) pinned to one's clothes is a sign of a formal, happy occasion. Carrying a bouquet marks one out as the centre of attention. Cut flowers are also used for decoration of a house or church generally, but particularly for celebrations (e.g., Easter, someone's birthday, and weddings).

As much care is taken in choosing the bride's and bridesmaids' flowers as with all other details of the wedding. According to bridal magazines they should be matched to the texture of the material and the style of the bride's dress and to the colour of her complexion. In practice ideas are picked up from other people's weddings and the bride is concerned with having a colour to go with the colour of the bridesmaids' dresses and flowers of the kind that she particularly likes. Most brides in the register office have a spray pinned to their coat or carry a small bouquet if they wear white.

The bouquets have to be made by specialist florists for they consist of a maze of tiny wires – some poked through the stems of flowers so that they can be bent to shape to give the bouquet a definite outline: the bride's is usually trailing to a point, the bridesmaids' rounder, and flower girls carry a basket or hanging ball of flowers (page boys do not carry flowers.) In other cases only parts of flowers are used, e.g., hyacinth bells are taken off their rather thick stems and wired to form a delicate spray; or the flowers are manipulated into unfamiliar forms, e.g., tulips have their petals bent inside out to look like orchids. The 'button holes' and sprays attached to the clothes of the main guests are also usually professionally made and wired, though the flowers in this case are less manipulated.

Unlike other floral presentations, these ritual flowers are not intended for domestic decoration and they cannot be kept in water afterwards for they simply rust. Instead they are either given away formally after the wedding, or blooms are pressed and kept as souvenirs, or the whole bouquet is kept until it is dried and brown.

After half the church weddings (especially chapel weddings)[28] the bride's bouquet was put on a grave; and in a few other cases the bride said that this had been intended but that nobody had got around to doing it, or that they would have put the bouquets on a grave but that nobody appropriate was dead, or that the appropriate graves were too far away (Pembroke, Brighton). The graves marked with bouquets were those of the bride's nuclear family (i.e., mother, father, or sibs), the groom's nuclear family, the grandparents on either side, one of the parents' sibs with whom relations had been particularly close, or a particularly close friend, in roughly that order of precedence. Those who died prematurely – e.g., a neighbour's small child killed in a road accident – are remembered more than those who die in old age; the recently dead are remembered more than those long dead; and close and personally known people rather than those strictly genealogically linked e.g., the bride's mother's friend was given one bouquet for her recently dead sister's grave. The bridesmaids' bouquets are also often put on graves, either of the bride's or the bridesmaids' kin and friends.

Case 42:

'My bouquet went on my father's grave on the Tuesday [the day after the wedding], which I'd always intended. I would have ordered the bouquet if I'd had a Guildhall wedding. Funny, I thought all the way to church: "I wonder if he's there." I've got a marvellous step-father, mind. Funny, when you're in church, you think he's there with you. If people don't, there's something wrong with them. I'm not normally sentimental. My bridesmaids' [bouquets] went on my grand-father and grand-mother's graves – my [step]father took them down. The little one [flower girl] and my sister kept theirs as long as they could.'

Case 51:

'Mine went on my mother's grave. My next door neighbour did it for me [the bride and groom being on honeymoon – there was no indication of why her father did not do it]. She [neighbour] came to the wedding. She was going up there anyway as it was Psalm Sunday – everybody puts flowers on graves then – and she took the flowergirls' and my bridesmaids' as well.'

Case 45:

'My bouquet? [laughed] My niece, she's only two, she fancied it. I took an orchid for going away. My mother took the other two and flowers from the house up onto my auntie's grave [mother's sister]; she only died recently [four months before].
My sister-in-law's [groom's sister who was a bridesmaid] went up to the hospital – my husband's mother's friend was ill. She's from the church: they had to have *something* Baptist in the wedding! And my friend's went on her gran's grave.
His mother wanted me to put mine on his gran's grave; but it would have been lop-sided. So my mother stepped in [presumably saying "give it to the little girl"].
No, we didn't put anything on my grandmother's grave. She's been dead a long time.'

As the last quotation suggests, bouquets may be taken to people in hospital or to those who are too old or infirm to attend the wedding (five cases). Other flowers may be used in a similar way, or as tokens to mothers:

Case 4 (groom's mother):

'At the station [when leaving on honeymoon] he took out his buttonhole and gave it to me. White heather it was. Oh, he's a wonderful son, mine. Told me he'd thought of his mother.'

Case 44:

'I kept my bouquet. I cut a rose off for Des's mother and auntie [father's sister] and for my mother, and I pressed a few in a dictionary upstairs. We've still got the bouquets from my sister's wedding in September [the interview was in April]. And Des's mother kept her spray, and my mother did.'

The church is generally decorated with flowers for the wedding – indeed, one of the reasons suggested by the vicar for the popularity of a little Anglican chapel at Clyne was that people could make it into a 'bower of flowers' for their wedding. Some flowers are part of the standard decoration of the church (except in Lent) but, if the couple so wish, they can provide more (or in the biggest churches they can pay the church florist to have some more provided). After the wedding these flowers are left in the church for the Sunday services and then sent to the local hospitals. In one parish the vicar always tells couples not to spend extra money on flowers because there are always plenty in the church because relatives are encouraged to put flowers in the church rather than in the 'Garden of Remembrance'.

Flowers thus make explicit the over-lap between the life-cycle rituals of marriage and death, seen also in the very act of going to church ('only for weddings and funerals'), the cars hired (though the drivers – in their words – wear 'different ties and expressions'), the hymns sung, and the meetings with distant kin. Flowers emphasize that 'In the midst of life we are in death', and give a sense of family continuity through remembrance of the departed and echoes of the past christenings, marriages and funerals.

(2) Wedding cake

Wedding cakes are formal and immediately recognisable: large, rich, fruit cakes with marzipan topping and hard white icing, decorated with icing loops, shells, rosebuds, etc., and with silvered paper or plastic horsehoes, silver slippers, rings, doves, white heather, etc. Their most characteristic feature is that they are multi-tiered. There are typically three cakes of decreasing size placed one above the other, separated by columns, with a large central decoration – frequently models of a bride and groom, or a basket which holds fresh flowers – on the topmost tier. The cakes themselves are usually round or square, though sometimes horseshoe or heart shaped. They are nearly always bought from professional bakers and cost between £5 and £30 in 1969*. Sometimes the fruit cakes are made by women relatives and then professionally iced (which cost about £5), or some friend of a friend (typically a man) is sought whose speciality and hobby is icing cakes. The wedding cake is quite commonly given as a wedding present (and a substantial one) from a grandmother or aunt on the bride's side, or the groom's mother.

All those who had church weddings had 'proper' wedding cakes – occasionally four-tier, usually three-tier, sometimes two-tier, but rarely

* £15–£90 at 1978 prices.

one-tier. Of those who married in the register office, 70 per cent had a cake, but it was much more common to have just one single tier.

The cake stands in a prominent position at the wedding reception and is ceremonially cut by the couple: they are posed 'cutting' it and photographed before the meal, and later the best man announces the formal cutting. All the guests have a small piece of it during the toasts and some eat only a morsel so as to take the rest home in their wedding serviette for those who could not come.

Figure 12 A typical three-tier wedding cake

After the reception, what is left of the cake is taken home by the bride's mother, who divides it up, giving some (e.g., half the bottom tier) to the groom's mother for her relations who did not come to the reception and for her friends and neighbours; and keeping an equal amount for the bride's side, including some women at the bride's work place. (I rarely heard of the groom distributing cake at his work-place, though he may give some to his friends.) Relatives and friends who live far away are sent pieces of cake in special little boxes. Pieces are also given to people who call at the house, especially those who gave presents: I was quite often given some when I called round shortly after a wedding. Unmarried women are given a piece so that they can put it under their pillow and dream of their husband-to-be. (Yet another way of reminding unmarried women of what they should be thinking about.) The wedding cake thereby serves to advertise the wedding, and to include in commensality many who cannot be included in the reception[29].

It is traditional to keep the top tier of the wedding cake for the christening of the first child and at least four of my informants were actually doing this. (Only one was pregnant when she married.) Another was saving it for the christening of her brother's (newly born) son, another for their first wedding anniversary, another for Christmas. Others said that they had wanted to keep the cake for a special event but had felt that the cake would not last well, or that the icing had started to get discoloured and so they had had to eat it. Most commonly, however, 'by the time we'd given it out to all the people we had to, it had all gone.' One bride was more positive: 'As soon as someone said that (keep the top tier for the christening) to me, I put a knife to it!'. (She wanted to carry on work for some years before having children.) Others reacted in much the same way: 'What christening?!'

The cake decorations are carefully collected and preserved by the bride, her mother, the groom's mother and close friends.

Case 16: (Bride)

'I just like to keep them - so sometimes when I go to the cupboard or drawer to get something, I find them, and it brings it all back.'

Case 42:

The bride kept the bride and groom which had been on the top of the cake and which she had bought herself, as well as the shoes, horseshoes, doves, rings and pink roses from around the sides – though she gave her mother and the groom's mother some of these. She planned to keep them for her children: 'They'll think it cute. My daughter might want it on top of *her* cake.'

But, if the bride is not careful and swift, she will find that many decorations 'disappear'. Case 33:

The bride's younger brother (aged 16) had worked as a holiday washer-up at the Surf Club, where many receptions are held. He said that the women who worked there used to grab cake decorations if they got carried through to the kitchen. (Why?) 'Because they're soppy!' (Repeated question) 'They think they're lucky; lucky charms.'

(3) *Announcements in the local paper*

Few of my informants put an announcement of their wedding in the small advertisements section of the local paper(s) – seven were in the *Evening Post* (and three also appeared in the *Herald of Wales*); i.e., 13 per cent as compared to 60 per cent of those who got engaged. All were church weddings, particularly Roman Catholic weddings (two out of the three in the sample). One in ten of the announcements in the Swansea paper at the time were for the children, mainly the sons, of Swansea residents who married in other towns.

Many people did not put in a notice because they hoped the paper would publish a photograph and/or a report of their wedding; but in the end only sixteen weddings were featured in this way (30 per cent) – three of them being those who had also had an announcement printed. One of the reasons for hiring a professional photographer is the belief that this makes one more likely to get one's photograph in the paper. Because the photograph may not appear for a week to a month after the wedding (in the case of the *Herald* up to two months afterwards), by the time people are sure that they are not going to be featured, it is too late to put in an announcement. Further, the wedding is itself such a public event, and the arranging for the announcement one among so many other arrangements, that it is felt to be less important and it is more likely to be overlooked than for an engagement.

According to journalists on the local paper, it is a very hit and miss procedure whether a photograph is included or not. The quality of the print is of some importance, but it is chiefly a question of whether the editor recognises the couple or their parents – e,g., the daughter of a local headmaster or the son of a publican or the captain of a local rugby team would be likely to be included – and whether or not there is a shortage or surplus of news items at the time. Those not used by the *Evening Post* are passed to the *Herald*, which makes a feature of its double spread of wedding photos in each weekly edition.

(4) *Souvenirs and luck*

In the course of this chapter a whole series of articles have been mentioned as kept by those participating in a wedding: the bride's dress and headdress, rings of various kinds, papers with announcements of engagements, single rose petals from confetti, labels from the 'decorations' on the woman's coat when she left work, service sheets from the church, wedding serviettes and place cards from the reception, all the telegrams and cards received, pressed flowers from bouquets, horse-shoes, black cats and rolling pins given outside the church, pieces of cake, and albums of photos, amongst others.

Things used for a particular purpose are kept 'to bring it all back', but other mementoes are deliberately purchased *as* souvenirs. They are used as tangible objects which cause the memory of a valued past to be brought to mind so that it can be relived, and in its commemoration remain part of the present.

Possession of these objects, and particular actions such as cutting the cake, also bring luck – to those directly concerned, but also to outsiders. The bride and the wedding ceremonial carry luck, and people hope that getting hold of, e.g., a plastic horseshoe from the cake means some of this luck will rub off on them. Those involved in organizing the ceremony try to increase the luck by getting all the ritual right and not skimping on any part[30]. This clear and substantial instance of the continuing importance of non-rational thought in Western culture needs to be stressed, for sociologists and philosophers have generally not seen, or not considered important, Western 'traditional' thought. Thus Wilson insists (1973) that belief in magic is 'marginal and attenuated' in advanced societies, which seems unlikely to be true, but which leads to the implicit racism of comparing, not Western traditional (i.e., mystical and religious) thought and Western science, but always *African* traditional and *Western* scientific thinking.

The duality of the forms of getting married

The ceremonial cycle associated with getting married 'properly' in Swansea is thus complex (with many rituals and a variety of personnel involved in the various activities), expensive, and spread out over a considerable period of time. There is a long drawn out whirl of planning, saving, booking, choosing, discussing, worrying, checking details, and endless expense. Case 42 (bride): 'I'd never have believed the amount of work that could go into a wedding for such a short time. All the expense and saving. You end up thinking, "Well, bloody hell, it's gone quick!". My husband would go through it again. I'm not so sure.' Yet it is perfectly possible to have a wedding arranged at short notice which is very simple and inexpensive. So why do people take the trouble?

Almost everybody who married in church in Swansea in the late '60s had 'the full works'. Those who married in the register office might have anything from a scaled down 'proper wedding' to the bare minimum. But in local opinion there was a marked distinction between church weddings and 'civic centre dos', and this duality seems of longstanding. (I have explored it at length in Barker 1978a.)

When civil marriage was (re)introduced it was closely connected with the poor law machinery, and 'was clearly branded as "a lower caste mode of alliance"; it meant a preliminary Guardians inquisition followed by a casual workhouse wedding' (Anderson 1975).

With the amending legislation of 1856,

> 'civil marriage provided all over the country that widely desired but hitherto unobtainable combination [i.e., since Lord Hardwicke's Act of 1753] a way of marriage which was both cheap . . . and entirely free from publicity. In the mid-nineteenth century both these characteristics contributed to keep it a predominantly "lower caste mode of alliance". The respectable often liked to demonstrate their standing by choosing an expensive legal procedure, whereas to save a few shillings might be vital to the poor, and moreover privacy was then much more often wanted by working people than their betters – partly to escape three weeks rowdiness and often cruel teasing, and "disorderly scenes" at the wedding itself, but often also to avoid their employers' disapproval, and sometimes dismissal . . .
> Civil marriage alone . . . offered what [such] couples wanted, and in a form quite untainted by deferential associations or personal contacts. No one had intended this.' (Anderson 1975:65–6, footnote omitted)

In the late '60s in Swansea, civil marriage was still a 'lower caste mode of alliance'. The main reason for the contemporary duality was that two categories of people married in the register office because their identities were spoilt for marrying in church: those where one of the partners at least had had a previous marriage dissolved, and those where there was premarital pregnancy. Given that both these characteristics were seen as discreditable, they were not always mentioned in interviews as reasons for choosing the register office; but Swansea mores were very firm and in my sample of twenty register office weddings, in seven cases the bride was pregnant[31] and five of the men and four of the women had been married before. In these respects then, only seven out of the twenty couples were 'eligible' to marry in church. The stigma of pregnancy and divorce is seen clearly in the reduced scale of such weddings (see *Figure 13*).

A third factor which might cause a couple to choose a register office wedding was if their parents (specifically the bride's parents, for it is they who traditionally pay most) were not able or willing to meet the costs of the wedding. The couple were then faced with either waiting and saving for a long time to meet the costs of the wedding and their new home; or having a proper wedding and making do with a furnished flat and the

Figure 13 Scale of weddings and the effects of pregnancy and divorce

| | church weddings | register office weddings | | | |
	all 1st weddings*	all	1st weddings not pregnant	1st weddings pregnant	2nd weddings**
	%	%	%	%	%
preceded by engagement	94	37	72	29	0
bride in 'white'	100 (all long)	30 (all short)	52	14	0
groom in morning suit	50	0	—	—	—
hired car with white streamers	100	33	43	29	17
professional photographer	85	32	29	43	17
outside reception	97	30	29	29	33
went on honeymoon or left Swansea immediately after the wedding	66	25	29	14	17
			—	—	—
N	34	20	7	7	6

* No subdivision into pregnant and non-pregnant is possible (see Appendix) as only one bride marrying in church in my sample was pregnant

** One couple had already had a child. None were pegnant at the time of the wedding.

Note: Number of guests at church weddings: 25–116; at register office weddings: 4–50.

wife working for several years till they saved up for a home; or skipping the big wedding. The bride's parents might refuse to pay for a big wedding if the bride was pregnant, or they might be unwilling to pay if their relations with her were strained, or they might be unable to pay if they were poorly off[32] – especially if the father was out of work or ill, or if they had several young children. In any of these situations the young woman might be unwilling to have the spotlight of a big wedding turned on her family of origin anyway. (This was the case with three or four of the seven couples 'eligible' to marry in church in my sample)[33].

Civil weddings were also favoured if the couple wanted to get married quickly – after an 'off-and-on' courtship, or a short acquaintance. But this again was a disfavoured action, the adage being 'marry in haste, repent at leisure'. (This accounts for the remaining couples in my sample.) Finally, the register office might be chosen by atheists and those with a 'contempt for ritual' – and these were perceived as the most deviant group of all[34].

The only acceptable reason for wanting to marry in the register office and not the church is a dislike of 'too much fuss'. This rejection of a white wedding as being 'ostentatious or officious activity; bustle or commotion out of proportion to the occasion' (SOED 1956) carries anti-ritual tones, but its expression was acceptable because it combined this with a stress that it was a personal – not a prescriptive – choice. The individuals explaining their choice in this way emphasized their personal wish not to be thrusting or pushing, not to put themselves in the leading role in the drama, their embarrassment at the ordeal of being in the spotlight, and their not being able to cope with such a situation. Case 1:

> 'I don't like much fuss and it's too dear. Too much fuss. I was never one that wanted . . . oh, the going out of church . . . the "look this way! Look that! Hold hands!" No, not for me. All you have is the worry that something is going to go wrong. I know it sounds soft now [after the wedding] but all I wanted to do was to get it over with.'

In sum, in the 1960s in Swansea people who married in the register office were seen as those who did not have much money, or were 'tight' about spending it, who were foolish enough to have got themselves pregnant, had already had one marriage which had failed, were marrying in indecent haste, had had bad relations with their families – possibly including parental opposition to the marriage, or who were just generally lacking in respect for the important things in life.

Those who married in church, on the other hand, were proper, for this was the way decent, worthy, respectable people married. Further, church weddings were seen as the only way of getting married which really counted, for they could do what register office weddings could not do: make a really lasting, mystical, binding union. They took place in a sacred place with a sacred person conducting the ceremony. They allowed people to express fully in actions and words important sets of social values.

Getting engaged, starting a bottom drawer, being given presents, joking at work and at hen parties, the bride and groom's elaborate costumes, the speeches at the reception, the period of seclusion on honeymoon, the commensality of relatives and friends at the reception and of the wider group in the cake, the use of the silver horseshoes and black cats, and the bride wearing 'something old, something new, something borrowed and something blue' for luck, all contribute 'statements' on the nature of the process of getting married and familial relationships. In addition the scale and publicity of the whole ceremonial cycle is a 'speech' on the importance of the passage rite as a whole (cf. Fortes 1962).

Case 49:

> (Bride) 'I don't think it seems right in the registry office – just in and out. It don't seem real.'
> (Groom) 'Just like getting married in the front room it is, in the registry office.'
> (Bride) 'I believe in God. That's got a bit to do with it.'
> (Groom) 'I shall feel nervous but I think that's good. Otherwise it would just be like meeting Pat from work. If you go to church there's everyone saying "All the best" and "good luck" and so on. Really, you know you've done something special.'

Not only does holding the central element of the cycle in church set it apart from everyday life – make it sacred – and ensure that the service is performed by a 'holy man'; it also allows the bride to dress in a long white dress and the groom in morning suit (and thus express sex and class divisions), for instance, which would seem incongruous in the present register office. Lots of people can attend and show the standing of the couple and their families. One can publicize a church wedding widely by sending out invitations and putting a photograph in the local paper, but a register office wedding is, as one informant said, 'like a glorified form of getting a new dog licence' which is less of a cause for shouting, and which stresses the change of status less[35].

Most important is the fact that the religious service is seen as 'personal'. Given that there are over 200 churches where weddings can take place in this town, as against one register office, a couple stand a high chance of being the only ones married in a particular building on 'their big day'. Even on popular Saturdays at popular churches the weddings will be booked at wide intervals so that two parties are unlikely to overlap. In the register office weddings can take place at fifteen minute intervals, and if the guests arrive early, or the bride for the previous wedding arrives late, one party may have to wait in the waiting room with the guests of the wedding ahead of theirs[36]. The registrar is obviously not concentrating all his attention on any one couple, and the whole ceremony is felt to be hurried, leading to analogies with conveyor belts or battery farming: 'Just like a sausage machine. About twenty people waiting to be done. In one side and out the other, with the registrar calling out "Next please".' A vicar, minister or priest, by contrast, will know at least a little about the couple and may 'say a few words' to or about them directly during the service.

Related to this, the church or chapel is likely to be close to the home of at least one member of the couple so that there is a feeling of 'community' and continuity, especially where the church is eponymous with the district[37]. The particular church is chosen (Case 24 – bride), 'For tradition. Every bride has a certain amount of tradition in her. My parents were married in St Thomas and I was christened and confirmed there. They expected and hoped that if I did marry, I'd marry there.'

The duality of church and civil weddings was certainly not restricted to Swansea in the 1960s, though it may have been less marked in other parts of the country (e.g., the conurbations and the south-east) and among some sections of the middle class. The media stressed the division[38], and the GRO's annual and quinqennial statistics also made the division between 'religious' and 'civil' marriages, although historically and administratively the distinction is between Anglican weddings and the rest.

However, there has been a steady rise in the proportion of civil weddings since their (re)introduction in 1836, and a concomitant decline in the numbers conducted by the Anglican Church (see *Figure 14*). But these national average figures cover great regional variation, and there used to be even greater variation than exists today (see Anderson's study of Victorian England and Wales, 1975). In South Wales more than a third of all weddings have been civil since the 1860s, reaching a peak (nearly a half) in the early years of the century, with a subsequent decline and rise (see *Figure 15*). For a century, despite the religious revivals, civil weddings were more common in Glamorgan than anywhere in England, but the situation is now reversed, with more 'religious' weddings in the whole of Wales, north west England and rural counties, than in the English conurbations and the south east[39], which must make us wary of simple explanations.

I have suggested that the scale and solemnity of a contemporary 'proper' wedding and the choice of location show that marriage is a major and mystical status change. It needs to be conducted in a sacred place, with due time and attention to the individual couple, in the solemn presence of many relatives, neighbours and friends, as part of the families' continuing membership of the local community and wider society. Those who are improvident, on bad terms with the bride's parents, pregnant, or divorced, can and should marry, but their second-class status is affirmed by their second-class wedding.

How then can one explain the recent acceleration in the national trend towards register office weddings? I certainly do not think that it is due to any great change in the nature of marriage as a labour relationship or to changes in the nature of the status change getting married involves, though there may have been changes in the ideology of marriage – from a complementary partnership to companionship – with a playing down of sexual divisions in the sphere of values, if not in behaviour. This may produce a lesser concern for a ceremony where the difference between the man and the woman is so marked. Nor am I convinced that the trend to civil weddings reflects much of a decline in folk religion or in belief in luck, etc., though if this occurs it would have some affect on the Church's perceived capacity to make more binding marriages. Rather, the move to the register office seems mainly due to the decline in institutionalized religion and regular attendance at church, chapel, and especially, Sunday school. People are consequently unfamiliar with the church buildings and the clergy, and attach less importance to them. They are likely to feel as uncertain of the correct behaviour in church as many now are about the right way to behave in the 'wedding room' of the town hall. The church or chapel is no longer (particularly in urban areas) the symbol of the community and nation which it used to be.

Further, if the stigma of divorce and premarital pregnancy is declining, as seems to be the case, so will the 'unrespectability' of marrying in the town hall; hence the duality of the types of wedding will be reduced. As more unstigmatized people marry in the register office, so the dichotomy will decline still further.

The distinction is also being reduced because of improvements in the facilities provided by the local authority. Where the register office is spacious (so that many relatives and friends can attend) and architecturally awe-inspiring, with separate facilities so that one wedding party does not get mixed up with another, so arranged that the bride can make a formal entrance, and so on; and where there are sufficient staff for each wedding to be conducted at a measured pace, one can expect to have more 'white' or 'proper' weddings in civic surroundings[40]. My impression is that this is happening: civil weddings are getting grander.

The account of wedding ceremonial which has been given in the last two chapters has aimed to show how it expresses important ideas about family life, some of which are 'difficult to think' or not expressed directly verbally. Specifically, it has presented rituals as symbolic expressions of the opposed situation of the sexes (and to a lesser extent of the generations) and of the labour relationship of husband and wife: i.e., as showing

Figure 14 Marriages by manner of solemnization, 1844-1972, England and Wales

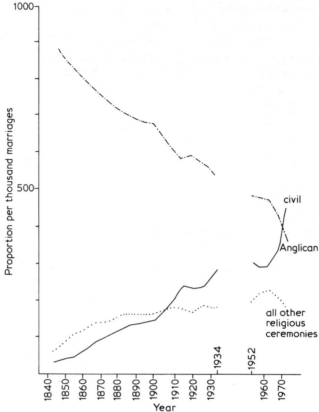

Source: Figures from R.G. 1974, Vol. II, Appendix D.7

that there are not only loving relationships between spouses (and parents and children), but also hierarchies, power relationships, calculation, and exploitation within the family. The husband acquires his wife's unpaid domestic work, sexuality and child-bearing, whilst protecting her and contributing to her upkeep.

This is a very different approach to passage rite rituals from the one current in social science, which seeks solely to explain why people have 'religious' ceremonies for christenings, weddings, and funerals in a 'secular' society (Wilson 1969; Bocock 1974; Pickering 1974). The latter is at best a partially phrased question: it may be what is relevant to the Church, but it tends to ignore the less institutionalized forms of religious belief, and it certainly does not advance our understanding of the family as an institution. Those who get married are generally concerned to effect the status passage properly, which currently involves going to church; but we do

Figure 15 Marriages by manner of solemnization, 1844–1972, Glamorgan

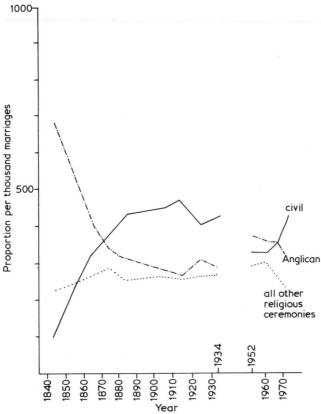

Source: R.G. Statistics[41]

not advance our understanding of their motivations far if we argue about their choice of ceremonial exclusively in terms of their belief in an imminent deity or with regard to rises or falls in their general church-going.

At worst this focus has led to a wholesale neglect of the meanings of the actual words and actions in European rituals. For example, when Pickering decided that the gothic church and the bride's white dress were not chosen for 'religious' reasons, he dismissed them as 'well nigh meaningless' (1974:75). In part this may be due to a belittlement and contempt for ritual and religion which is marked among intellectuals (Douglas 1966, 1973) and which they often assume to be typical of British society as a whole. But arguably in relation to weddings it shows (as did the quotation from Mary Stott with which this book began) an unwillingness to recognize what these rituals are saying about the nature of marriage as an institution, and hence about the author's own most personal relationships.

Notes.

1. The theme of the bride or groom left in the lurch on their wedding day is played on by popular song writers ('There was I, waiting at the church'; 'Get me to the church on time') and novelists (*The Idiot*, *Lorna Doone*, *Far from the Madding Crowd* etc).

2. It is not usual to send out invitations to attend the service only, though it was done for one of the biggest weddings in my period of fieldwork. This caused considerable bad feeling. Some of my neighbours who were sent such invitations spoke of them as 'tickets to go and spectate', and indignantly asserted that one did not have to have a 'ticket' to go to church (*their* church).

3. One firm charged £6 10s to hire 'the big grey Humber' and £3 10s for smaller car(s); another charged £5 for a Daimler or Austin Princess and £4 for the smaller one(s).

   A taxi-driver I spoke to who worked 'on his own' (with his wife taking 'phone calls and another driver) had no bridal limousine of his own and hired it from a firm in town. He had two 'best cars': 'But we've been working very hard over Christmas to save money to buy [a limousine] of our own. I'd like to specialize in weddings. Several firms do nothing *but* weddings and funerals and do very well out of it.'

   The same cars are, in fact, used for weddings as for the mourners at a funeral, and since most weddings are on Saturdays, and funerals during the week, it works in well for the small businessman.

4. *Figure 16* Procession in St Thomas

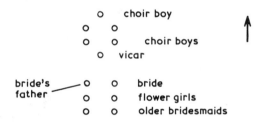

5. Of all the medieval services, a twentieth century worshipper would find Matrimony the most familiar. (See Legge 1905; Brightman 1921; Lacey 1947; Cuming 1969; and Barker 1977, Appendix 5:1.)

6. This may include an account of the Church's mythical charter for marriage:
   – that it was 'instituted of God in the time of man's innocency' in the Garden of Eden;
   – that many Old Testament couples serve as exemplars of married life (Adam and Eve, Abraham and Sarah, Isaac and Rebecca, etc.);
   – that marriage was dignified by Christ's presence and first miracle at Cana;
   – that it is 'commended in Holy Writ' by St Paul;
   – and that it parallels the mystical union between Christ and his Church.

7. God's help and blessing will be needed in preserving the couple from temptation, making their love last, giving them children, preserving them from danger, etc. This blessing by God is sought in the fashion of the particular

denomination – via a mass, the vicar's reciting the liturgy with the congregation, or extempore prayer combined with reading from the bible.

8. The Anglican Church was disestablished in Wales in 1902 and hence it did not need Parliament's permission to establish a standing liturgical commission (1951), nor to institute various revised services (cf. The Church of England). The experimental wedding service was used from 1961–71 and then re-revised (see Barker 1977:539–40).
   The changes in the service aimed:
   (a) to decrease the differential treatment of the bride and groom.
   E.g. the prayer:
   'that this man may love his wife . . . as Christ did love the Church . . . loving and cherishing it even as his own flesh, *and that this woman may be loving*, amiable, *faithful* and obedient *to her husband* and in all quietness, sobriety and peace be a follower of holy and godly matrons'
   has been amended so that only the phrases italicized remain. However, the bride is still given away by her father, whereas the groom is merely supported by his peer; and although it is now possible to exchange wedding rings, the bride is still required to have one and the groom is not. While the bride's promise to obey her husband has become optional, the groom never promises to obey *her*. If, as the Church's Liturgical Commission claims (1975), the service now treats the couple as 'equal partners', one remains more equal than the other;
   (b) to dispense with the more archaic and awe-inpsiring phrases; and
   (c) 'to express a more positive Christian acceptance and enjoyment of sexuality'. Thus, e.g., the phrase 'to satisfy men's carnal lusts and appetites, like brute beasts that have no understanding' has completely disappeared.

9. The cassock is a long black coat with a high collar, reaching to the feet. It thus covers the ordinary clothes of the wearer completely and signifies his separation from the world (Walker 1868) and that the wearer is exercizing his authority in the parish: he wears it in church and maybe also to go visiting his parishioners in their homes, but not to go visiting outside his parish. 'It shows one is "on parade", or to emphasize that it is "the office not the man" . . . anyway the parishioners like it!'
   A surplice is worn over the cassock in church. This is made of white linen, shorter and fuller than the cassock and without a front opening. All those who are in the chancel (priests, choir, and servers) – being directly engaged in the service of God, and in the part of the church symbolic of Heaven – wear 'fine linen', representing the righteousness of the saints, the Church Triumphant, the Bride of Christ.
   When conducting a wedding almost all Anglican clergy also wear a stole, which is strictly speaking a vestment worn for the Eucharist by a priest. It is a long, narrow strip of silk passed round the neck and hanging in front to below the waist and embroidered with three crosses. The stole represents the 'yoke of Christ' which fell from him onto his apostles and their successors, and (with the girdle and maniple worn for the Eucharist) the cords and fetters with which Jesus was bound. It is a symbol of priestly authority: of a man fulfilling

a sacramental ministry. Hence its wearing implies that marriage is a sacrament. Clergy who hold that the only sacraments are 'Baptism and the Supper of the Lord' wear an academic hood in place of a stole.

In addition the cleric may, if the Church owns one, put on a cope – a large semi-circular cloak of silk embroidered down the front and round the hem and at the back of the neck (see this chapter, *Figure 3*). This is part of the 'outdoor' dress of the Church and is worn in processions. In the one church (St Thomas) where the vicar regularly wore a cope for weddings, he also processed. Other vicars may wear it for effect: 'You wear it for the better parishioners!'

10. Some 'read' more than others: some know it off by heart. This introduces anomalies as those who have been doing it longest continue to use old forms (*BCP* or 1928 Prayer Book) – though I am sure I was the only one in the congregation to notice.

11. The promise to obey has been contentious for some years. It was left out in the 1928 prayerbook but was present in the Church in Wales *Experimental Service*. Some vicars would leave it out if the bride objected, others definitely would not. Vicar:

    'She's not promising to obey in every little thing – like cleaning his shoes or when to have sex. But if there came a choice between their parting or one climbing down – then the wife will obey. For example, if the husband gets a job outside Swansea and his wife doesn't want to go.'

    The promise to obey is in fact optional in the new (1971) version of the Church in Wales' marriage service.

12. Some couples who wish to exchange wedding rings ask clergy to allow them to do so as part of the wedding ceremony. Some clergy will do this, modifying the blessing to cover both rings, since they feel the exchange fits with their perception of Christian marriage; and they stress that 'it is an experimental service anyway.' But the bride says nothing as she puts the ring on the groom's finger, so that the bride's ring and groom's putting it on remains the important action.

    Other clergy compromise by blessing the groom's ring separately at another point in the service and it is put on in the vestry when the register is being signed. But they may voice disapproval. Vicar:

    'I'm very much against the exchange of rings in weddings – it's an Eastern Orthodox custom. If they really want it, I will bless the groom's ring at the end of the service. The whole idea of a ring is that it is a *link* between two people. I try to tell them that the ring is *their* ring, not hers: the outward and visible sign [of their marriage].'

13. There is no rubric specifying this action but it was performed at all the weddings I attended, and Legge (1905) suggests it is of very ancient origin. It was certainly approved by the congregation, albeit they understood it only in part, not knowing the significance of the stole for the Church as symbolic of authority (the yoke of Christ) and binding (the cords and fetters of Christ). See note 9.

14. There is little legislation about the use of surnames in Britain. Most other countries are much stricter about requiring or allowing changes. Women usually take their husband's name on marriage, giving up their previous

surname altogether, but there is no obligation to do so. It is also customary for children of the marriage to take their father's name, though again there is no legal requirement that they should (Coussins 1978).

If the couple are leaving the country for their honeymoon they will be given their new passport (if the wife is on her husband's passport – it cannot be the other way round), or the wife is given her own new passport in her married name, by the vicar after the signing of the register.

15. There are specific variations in the service should it be a 'mixed' marriage or the woman a widow.

16. Cf. the Methodists, who have a *Book of Offices* which, while it is for guidance only and not mandatory, is generally followed.

   The services of the early dissenting bodies derive from Luther, Calvin, Knox and the Westminster Directory (see Maxwell 1949). From the mid-nineteenth century onwards, a number of service books were compiled, and all the Nonconformist church unions now publish one or more. For the 'occasional services', all the ministers I interviewed used a manual and kept close to the text. Each man had his own favourite – not necessarily produced by his own denomination – often handed down to him by an older minister he had known.

17. He is attached to the Guildhall as a night watchman and shows people round on Sundays. He was a trick cyclist at the old Empire music hall and thereby was known to quite a number of the parental generation. Some gave him a tip, others a cigarette, for having put them at their ease.

18. No religious service is permitted in the register office. Some superintendent registrars have made efforts to 'improve' the ceremony; e.g., the Brighton registrar was eventually given permission by the Registrar General to play music after trying for three years, but his sale of souvenir wedding brochures was stopped as detracting from the dignity of the occasion (*The Guardian*, 30 October and 3 November, 1971).

19. The other concern is with getting one's wedding photograph in the local paper, see on.

20. A similar tale occurs in the readers' letters page of women's and bridal magazines about other churches in other towns.

21. If no wine is served there may be a wine waiter from whom the guests may order (and whom they pay for) wine or beer, or they may get up and get drinks from the bar in the room.

22. Nicod's analysis of the structure and social meaning of working-class food in England stresses that food is arranged in a structured series through the meal, the day, the week, the year, and the life-cycle. Among the working class, bread and potatoes are the 'staples' and their regular appearance determines the identity of the meal. The main meal of the day has a main course of potato with meat and one or more additional 'items' (vegetables or sauces), followed by wet cereal (pudding) and dry cereal (cake and biscuits). The minor meal is based on bread, followed by cereal (cake and biscuits); and 'tertiary meals' are also based on cereal (biscuits or cake). The main meal is attended by the whole family and may be shared with close friends; the bread event is offered more widely, to all friends and relatives; and cake and biscuits (with a cup of tea or

coffee) may be offered to even casual visitors.

'Special meals' contain one or more extra items (e.g., an extra vegetable, another sauce) in the main course, or an extra course. Expanding or replicating the formula is used to ascend the scale of *formality* (Nicod 1974:97). Within each aspect of the chain of the meal's structure there is a *choice* of which items to serve with the staple.

Roast meat and chicken or turkey are preferred in formal meals as the centre piece because they are structurally whole initially, and also because they allow the separation of items on the plate. (Note here the structural wholeness of the wedding cake.)

Within each meal there is always internal structure between the courses: they get colder, sweeter, and drier. But each step can be modified by adding a sauce of opposing type (e.g. hot custard over an apple pie). Nicod suggests that more intimate meals (in terms of who is sharing the meal) are wetter (note the addition of an extra wet course – the soup – to the wedding reception; and it is very 'wet' cake, often so described as a term of approval, and specifically having alcohol added to it).

23. Nicod's analysis would suggest that the structure of a buffet signifies that it is a less formal meal than even Sunday dinner and that it is shared by a group who are not necessarily particularly intimate. It is entirely bread (not potato) based, cold and dry (much of it can be eaten with the fingers). It omits the two major contrasts (hot-cold, wet-dry) of formal meals – although its informality and lack of intimacy is partly counteracted by having a very large number of different items and several sorts of drink, and a progression from savoury to sweet to cake.

    No similar work has been done on the structure of middle-class meals, but experience suggests buffets are less informal for them. Certainly most middle-class weddings in south east England and the midlands that I have attended have had buffets provided by outside caterers.

24. As when other special cakes (notably birthday cakes) are cut, the bride/couple may make a silent wish as they make the cut, and the luck attached to the cake will make the wish come true.

25. The poems quoted in *Figure 11* were taken from a wedding outside my sample as I wanted to quote them without altering the place names and occupations which are incorporated.

    All cards and telegrams are kept afterwards (e.g., in a paper bag) and the exact number is often known off-hand.

26. This book (Jeffrey 1966) includes advice on:
    (i) 'presenting your speech' – being brief, not reading the speech, practising before the mirror, starting with a joke, etc.;
    (ii) specimen speeches;
    (iii) useful quotations; and
    (iv) suitable comic stories

    Sections on speech-making are found in all wedding etiquette books.

27. It is also socio-economic class related: most grooms in categories I and II left Swansea at once, equal numbers in category III left and stayed, and more of IV and V stayed.

28. My information here is not complete since I only became aware of the custom sometime after the start of my fieldwork. The bride's bouquet was put on a grave after 6/15 Anglican, 4/5 Nonconformist, and 2/17 register office weddings. Of the other register office weddings, 1 bouquet was given to a sick grandmother, 3 to the bride's mother, 1 was pressed by the bride, 2 wanted to put it on a grave but it was too far away, and 3 brides had no spray or bouquet.

29. 'Finally, within a circle anchored to the cake event, we were able to elicit another set of social relationships – a set that includes as well as friends and relatives, a number of casual visitors and acquaintances whose food-sharing extends no further than beyond the cake-and-biscuits stage' (Nicod 1974:72).

30. The concern with getting all the details of a ritual 'right' is very commonly seen in ceremonies in other cultures (see, for example, Malinowski, 1935) and it has often been suggested that one effect is that of catharsis and succour – it gives the actors in a stressful situation help in purging their emotions and also something to do which they believe will bring about their desired ends. And, of course, because they devote so much time and thought and act jointly to achieve an end, it can be argued that ritual makes them more likely to achieve the result anyway.

31. It is difficult to compare this with the number of pregnant brides who marry in church. I had only one case (out of 34 church weddings), but, as was said in chapter 2, this is a specific and important bias due to my sampling technique. None of the couples in my sample marrying in church (inc. chapel) were divorced or widowed.

My findings confirm previous research which has shown that civil and 'quiet' weddings are most common where the bride is young and/or pregnant, and where one partner (especially when this is the bride) has been married before.

> (a) Hollingshead (1952) reports from New Haven, USA, that the greatest ceremonial in weddings occurs where it is the first marriage for both, markedly less where it is the second marriage for the woman, least where it is the second marriage for both.
>
> (b) The PIC national marriage survey of England and Wales in 1959–60 included questions on the manner of getting married, but unfortunately much of their information has not been published. They have reported, however, that brides in their early twenties (i.e., at the normative age for marriage) were more likely to have the full paraphernalia than were either 'older' (over 25) brides (they suggest because these couples had to pay the cost of the wedding themselves and preferred to save), or 'teenage' (16–19) brides (they suggest because of pregnancy) (Rowntree 1962; Pierce 1963).

32. Since white weddings cost more money and confer status it is not surprising that the choice of such a passage rite is associated with socio-economic standing. Half or more of those who had civil weddings were in semi- or unskilled manual jobs and/or came from families where the father was (or had been) in such a job. (See Barker 1977, Figure 6:4 and Pierce 1963.)

33. In 5/33 church weddings and in 10/19 register office weddings the bride's parents were unenthusiastic or hostile to the match. Of course, in the longer run-up to a church wedding, parents had had more time to accept the

situation and they were less likely to feel worried that their daughter was rushing into marriage.

In five church weddings the bride and groom paid much of the costs, and in another two they made a substantial contribution (7/34; 21%). In five register office weddings the couple paid for all the costs – though of course these were much less (5/20; 25%).

34. Anticlericism, atheism, and humanism are deviant attitudes in Swansea and very few people outrightly reject a religious label or generalized support for religion and the Church (see Rosser and Harris 1965). I myself was described to my neighbour as 'amoral' after saying in the hairdressers that I saw nothing wrong with register office weddings.

35. It should, however, be noted that some of the quietest weddings take place in church or chapel. Calvinistic Methodist Minister:

'I had a wedding once – of a friend who was once a minister. He's in his 30s or 40s. It took place at 8 in the morning, "before the streets were aired". He was marrying a divorced woman – the innocent party. I don't know why all the secrecy – people knew they were friendly. He didn't ask me until 3 days before the wedding, and in fact I didn't know whether to agree. But he was a personal friend and there was no minister in the chapel where he was a member. He had everything arranged before he came to see me. He'd seen the deacons . . . It was like a private funeral. Other weddings have been *quiet*, not private.'

36. I spent Whit Saturday morning in the register office and recorded the number of weddings (and the number of people attending each).

wedding at 8.45 am – 4 people (including the bride and groom)
               9.00 am – 4
               9.15 am – 5 (+ 3 who arrived too late)
               9.30 am – 5

(9.45 I had tea with the Superintendent Registrar who confirmed that small parties tend to be in the early morning)

               9.45 am – 15 adults and 6 children
               10.00 am – 10
               10.15 am – 20 + 1 child
               10.30 am – 8
               10.45 am – 18 + 1 child
               11.00 am – 27
               11.15 am – 14
               11.30 am – 4 adults + 1 boy

Office closed at 12.00

Whit Saturday was an unusually busy day, but there was certainly a feeling of tight scheduling. If a bride was ten minutes late – as they tended to be in the middle of the morning, not having allowed enough time for the Saturday morning traffic in the town centre – one party of guests overlapped with the next in the very small waiting room. Some got very agitated and tried to go with the wrong group. (In good weather the staff ask one party to wait outside until the one before has gone on.) As the Superintendent Registrar commented:

> 'It's not like a church: we can't say "We're sorry, we're too busy to marry you that day". After all, you can be married between 8 am and 6 pm (except Saturday, when the hours are 8 till 12) and you can pack a fair number into that time. I've never yet had to refuse to marry someone on a particular day. It should be better now that ruling on tax has ended.* Bristol had 120 weddings one March Saturday! Who wants to marry in March anyway, with the cold winds?'

37. The register office may be many miles away – for example, people living in Gower or in Neath have to come into Swansea to the West Glamorgan register office.

38. *Brides* (1969) carried an article on 'Your Kind of Wedding' which contrasted three church weddings and a 'minimum fuss' (i.e., register office) wedding, and in 1973 the same magazine ran an article called 'Take 3 Girls' where a 'Grand Traditional' and a 'Romantic' wedding were counterposed to a 'Wedding That's Part of Everyday Life'.

39. Today there are more civil weddings in the conurbations (Tyneside, W. Yorks., W. Midlands, and S. Wales) and in south east England, reaching a peak in Greater London (42% in 1967; 53% in 1972); and least in rural areas and small towns (26% in N.W. England in 1967; 37% in N. and Central Wales in 1972) (RG for 1967, Appendix C2, and for 1972, Appendix D2).

40. The Swansea Marriage Room was, I was assured, 'a palace' compared with some register offices provided by local authorities. (Registrars are employed by the GRO, but local rates pay for the register office facilities.)

   The Superintendent Registrar of Swansea said, however, that at one time the possibility of buying a disused chapel across the road from the Guildhall for use as the register office marriage room had been broached. The local council (which includes many supporters of church and chapel – see Brennan, Cooney, and Pollins 1954) opposed this use of rate payers' money. If people wanted big weddings, they should go to a *real* church.

*Until 1968, if couples married in March, the man was able to get the married man's tax allowance for the whole of that financial year.

Figure 17 Marriages by manner of solemnization, 1844-1972, Glamorgan (per 1,000 total marriages)

Year	all marriages	civil marriages	Anglican	marriages with religious ceremonies								
				Total	RC	Meth	Cong	B	CM	other	Quaker	Jews
1844	1,000	95	678	227	5			222				—	—
1854	Not available for Glamorgan – only S. Wales as a whole											
1864	1,000	328	406	267	66			199			1	1
1874	1,000	374	335	291	44			246			—	1
1884	1,000	432	314	253	45			207			—	1
1894	Not available for Glamorgan – only S. Wales as a whole											
1904	1,000	450	285	265	41			221			—	1
1914	1,000	472*	274	253	43			209			—	1
1924	1,000	413	319	268	52	31	68	69	37	9	0	2
1934	1,000	442	288	270	64	29	63	65	31	16	0	1
1952	1,000	322	389	289	73	36	64	71	43		—	1
1957	1,000	329	370	301	78	32	60	73	57		0	2
1962	1,000	336	363	300	92	33	63	71	9	30	0	2
1967	1,000	362	364	274	88	32	51	62	13	27	—	1
1972	1,000	433	333	234	75	36	40**	53	11	26	0	2

* Highest in S. Wales.
   Source: Calculated from R.G. 1846, 1856, 1866, 1876, 1886, 1895, 1914–16; and for 1924, 1934, 1952, 1962, 1967 and 1972.
** On 5th October 1972 the greater part of the Congregational Church of E & W and the whole of the Presbyterian Church of England joined to form the United Reform Church.

7 Starting married life

In this last descriptive chapter I shall look at the setting up of a new household in Swansea, particularly by those marrying for the first time; at the couples' arrangements and future plans on work and money; and at the effects of premarital pregnancy on the couple's postmarital situation. I shall also give further consideration to marriage as a labour relationship and to intergenerational relations, and try to show throughout how easily my informants settle into married life.

Setting up a new household

(1) Housing

Nine couples left Swansea immediately after their wedding and went to live in other parts of South Wales, England, or where the husband was stationed with the army or navy. In all instances this departure followed a church wedding – probably because those already living away would not have felt it worth coming back for a register office wedding; because when children were leaving everybody wanted them to have 'a good send-off'; and because those in the higher socio-economic categories, who were likely to be geographically mobile, were also more likely to have church weddings.

The grooms who left were mainly in professional and managerial occupations (a doctor, a graduate trainee manager, and teachers) or in the armed forces. The only semi-skilled worker was a miner who took his bride to his home town to the north west of Swansea. Their brides were also mainly in 'middle-class' jobs (a nurse, two teachers, secretaries, and a nursery nurse). Most couples were going to live in rented flats (six cases) because they anticipated further geographical mobility. Only one couple, both teachers, had bought their own house (in Cardiff) and seemed settled. The miner was going to live in his parents' old house (both were dead, but his widowed brother and the brother's teenage son also lived there) and he hoped to buy his own house after a year or so. An officer in the Merchant Navy and his wife (who married after a very short courtship) were going to 'look around for something' when they got back from a six-month trip to Africa.

The remaining forty-five couples stayed in Swansea. Here their choice of housing lay between buying their own house, renting a flat (there are few available flats for sale or houses for rent), or moving in with their parent(s) or other kin.

In the late 60s this town was not experiencing the problems associated with a rapidly increasing population found in some cities, and there was relatively little (officially defined) overcrowding – though about 10 per cent of the residents lived in very cramped conditions. Nonetheless, demand for houses was increasing because the rate of household formation was rising. Not only did couples want to establish new households when they married, but the elderly, widowed, and single were less often living with families as relatives and lodgers. That is to say, people were splitting up into smaller households, producing a particular demand for dwellings for one and two people. In addition, much of the stock of housing was substandard: in 1965 a third of all dwellings in the town lacked basic amenities such as piped hot and cold water, a fixed bath, and an inside toilet[1]. Thus finding a satisfactory place to live proved quite difficult for most young couples.

The town has an above average proportion of owner-occupiers: half of all houses are owned by those who live in them[2], and 42 per cent of my informants who settled in the town bought their own house when they married. The fieldwork was conducted before the sharp rise in property prices of 1970 and at a time when it was relatively easy to get a mortgage. Five of my informant couples bought small 'two-up-two-down' houses in the north of the town and in the river valley (Morriston, Hafod, Llangyfelach) for £1,000–£1,250, needing in one case only a 50 per cent mortgage. (This house had no bathroom, but they planned to put one in 'in a year or so', and in the meantime were using her mother's, three doors down the road. It was her mother, indeed, who had dissuaded them from renting this same house for £4 a week, arguing that it gave one security to own one's house and it cost no more.) A sixth couple were given such a house by the groom's grandmother (see p. 223, Case 16) Three couples bought large, 3-bedroomed terraced houses in central areas of the town (Sketty, Uplands, Mt Pleasant) for about £3,000; and nine bought new estate houes in the west (West Cross, Treboeth), costing £4,500, but on which building societies were willing to give 90 per cent mortgages. One bought a caravan (locally called a 'trailer') which probably cost £1,500.

Only 14 per cent of Swansea houses were in the hands of private landlords, and these were predominantly large, multi-occupied houses. Over a third of all houses were owned by the corporation – substantially above the national average. Indeed, the Council 'is well on the way to becoming a monopoly landlord, especially since its houses and flats comprise the vast majority of *modern* houses available to rent' (Fabians 1969:2). Council rents for newer properties are high – so high that in some areas it was actually cheaper to buy an old house and pay mortgage and rates than to rent a local authority one. But the problem for young couples is not so much the *cost* of council housing as its *availability*: local authority housing was simply not obtainable when they first married. Applications to the local authority are filed and dealt with in the date order in which they are made, and Rosser and Harris found that newly married couples might have to wait up to ten years for a house. (The precise length of the queue depends on the area, type of house, and cost of the housing being sought – some areas of the town and some types of houses and price ranges being more popular than others.) Certainly those few of my informants who had put themselves on the council list felt discouraged:

Case 51:

(Living with their baby in the groom's parents' three-bedroomed council house)
'We went down the Council for a flat but they were about as helpful as a duck in a thunderstorm! Really, they like you to have two children of different sex. They said we'd have to wait ages.'

Case 5:

(Bride) 'I don't want to own my own house. I don't believe in spending the best years of my life with a mortgage round my neck. We've been on the list thirteen months [i.e., since five months before they got married]. But they've more or less told us we don't have hope unless we've got two children. I don't think it's right – you pay enough in rates.'

Couples can only get housed out of turn in the queue if they have particular bad housing or overcrowding, or for medical reasons. As Ineichen points out, this means that the workings of the housing market provide an incentive to the youngest and poorest couples to have a second child and to accept poor rented housing, or to live in cramped conditions with relatives, so as to increase their chances of a council house.

'Housing department policies effectively cancel out the aims of another local authority service, family planning; and probably increase the burden on a third, social services (because of family breakdown, the need for temporary accommodation, baby battering) . . .

Decisions on the provision of public housing are based on crude estimates of need. Little consideration is given to the situation of young couples, who are customers of the system, and to the effects of housing market rules, on the decisions these youngsters make. The council system has never resolved its schizophrenic split between providing mass housing for the working class, and a rescue service for social casualties. At present, when demand far outstrips supply, it encourages more and more of those intending to qualify for the first system into becoming clients of the second.' (Ineichen 1975:303)

Since local authority housing is not available, young couples who want to rent somewhere to live must look to the limited privately rented sphere, which is expensive (a flat cost £3 a week and an old house £5–6 in 1968*), poor quality, and often 'furnished' – with little security of tenure. On the council list one has to accept one of the first three 'reasonable' houses or flats offered or lose one's place in the queue (which Rosser and Harris showed results in the scattering of kin). In the private sphere there is not the same limitation on choice of location, but instead there are the limitations deriving from the problem of finding the house/flat in the first place and then persuading the landlord that one is a desirable tenant. Young couples seem relatively favoured by landlords: they are both earning, likely to be out at work all day, and have no children. Also they decorate their new-found home with consummate care and often help the landlord with external repairs. The new housewife keeps the place very clean. They are thus to be preferred to both students (dirty, untidy, and with irregular hours) and couples with children (noisy and producing heavy wear and tear on the house). Further, they require fewer rooms, so that more flats can be got out of one old house.

Well placed as they are, young couples find it hard to find flats and still operate the bush telegraph service mentioned by Rosser and Harris (1965:63) and Young and Willmott (1962) – though Mum is not so influential as in Bethnal Green, her place being taken by sibs and workmates.

Case 44:

'We didn't want to live with parents; we wanted a place of our own. We tried for a few in the paper, but no luck. The owner of this flat [where they were living] works with my [groom's] brother. He mentioned we were looking for somewhere and that we'd looked at a few we didn't

---

* £9 and £15–18 at 1979 prices.

like. So he said, "Why not let them look at the one I've got – if they don't like it, no hard feelings, like". It's unfurnished. We got it five weeks before we got married.'

Case 37:

'Friends of ours, also in the [police] force, used to have it.'

Case 36:

'Ed's brother [groom's brother] used to live here before. He asked the landlord if we could have it when he moved.'

Within the privately rented sphere preference was for a self-contained, unfurnished house – as against a situation where one shares entrance and even bathroom and lavatory with others (sometimes the landlord), or furnished accommodation, or flats. Couples in rented flats often said they were trying to move up the ladder within this sphere, and also to move to parts of the town which they favoured. Only one couple (Case 5 quoted above) were definite that they did not want a mortgage and preferred to rent; most of the others seemed to have drifted into renting because, while they wanted to 'get somewhere of our own', they had no commitment to owning their own home, and renting 'seemed easier'.

Rosser and Harris make the important point (1965:250) that with improved housing there is now more room for people to take in relatives should they so desire, either briefly for holidays, or for lengthier periods to provide them with a home[3]. However, couples always lived with their parents, never with other relatives, if they made their home with kin after marriage. In other words, the relatives people took in for extended periods were exclusively sons and daughters.

This ability to offer a home was especially important *immediately* after mariage, when as many couples lived with one or other set of parents as in flats or houses of their own (see *Figure 1*). But this was a temporary situation. Of those who started off living with parents, five were there because builders had not kept their promises as to completion dates on new houses which the couple had bought (i.e., paid a deposit on) some nine months before the date of the wedding. Some of these luckless couples were still living with in-laws five months after the wedding, but they are better classified with the other home-owners.

Of the other fourteen (all first marriages), four had already moved before the interview after the wedding (three had gone to other kin following disputes, and one had found a flat); and five said they wanted to get a place of their own and had already put in to the council or planned to buy a house in a year or two. Only four were firm that they were going to stay with the parent(s). In all cases they were with an elderly widowed parent in his or her council house, being the only child or the last child to

Figure 1 Where couples were living immediately after their marriage (and return from honeymoon)

	living in Swansea				
	all %	1st marriage	2nd marriage	left Swansea and district	total %
living with parents	19 (42)	15	4	0	35
in own house	13 (29)	12*	1	1	26
in rented flat	11 (24)	10	1**	6	31
other (inc. with kin other than parents)	2 (4)	2	–	2	7
total	45 (99)	39	6	9	99

*   incs. one caravan.
**   a house, not a flat.

marry[4]. They would be able to occupy the council house after the old person's death. Thus the tenancy of the house was an insurance for the parent of care in old age.

Of those who started off by renting a flat, some had also moved before the interview after the wedding: one couple rented a flat for three weeks because of builder's delay with their own new bungalow, and two stopped living in flats because of the expense and discomfort and returned to living with kin till they found better rented accommodation and to save for furniture (paying over a very small sum to the groom's mother in both cases). Both were still with kin but moving out 'next week' when seen; decorating their new flat/house before moving.

No-one in rented accommodation planned to stay in what they had for a long period of time, though in only two cases was renting chosen because of the likelihood of future geographical mobility (cf. those who left Swansea).

The two categorized as 'other' in *Figure 1* also moved in the six months following the wedding, but none of those who bought their own homes did so.

Once the newly married couples had settled (i.e., after the immediately post-wedding shuffling), four out of ten of those living in Swansea had bought their own homes, three out of ten were living with parents, and

Figure 2 Where young couples settled to live shortly after their marriage

	living in Swansea			left Swansea and district	total %
	all %	1st marriage	2nd marriage		
living with parents	13 (29)	9	4	0	24
in own house	19 (42)	18	1	1	37
in rented flat/house	11 (24)	11	0	6	31
other/no information	2 (4)	1	1	2	7
total	45 (99)	39	6	9	99

two out of ten were in rented accommodation (see *Figure 2*)[5].

There was a slight bias towards living with the wife's parents especially in the working class. *In toto* the couples passed through the houses of fourteen bride's parents and eleven groom's; and among those who settled to live with parents, seven lived with her parents (16 per cent) and six with his (13 per cent). This is not as great as the disparity between the two sides found in the earlier study of Swansea and surveys made in London[6]. It may be that these previous studies collected information on the short term contingency living arrangements rather than on the 'first settled home'; or (I think more probable) that the matrilocality they reported was partly an after-effect of the war. (A sizeable minority of the parents of my informants had met and married when the father came to Swansea to work; for example, in an aircraft factory. His kin were else-where and when he married shortly before going on active service he and his wife stayed with *her* parents.) Among my informants, in contrast, it was often argued that while the young husband is working long, irregular or 'unsociable' hours to save up money, there is much to be said for staying close to his work-place – which is likely to be close to his old home; and the tensions between mother and daughter-in-law, made much of by Young and Willmott, seem to build up only when the young wife stops work and is at home all day with small children – by which time most of my informants hoped to have homes (owned or rented) of their own.

Those who bought new houses were the group who had started plan-ning their housing furthest ahead. Generally they had looked at show houses and plans and paid a retainer (£50) some 6–9 months before the wedding. Those who bought older houses had them 1–6 months beforehand and worked on them hard – 'redecorating, rewiring and reflooring'. Case 26:

> When I finally located the couple (after calling at the bride's home I was sent by her sister to their newly-purchased old cottage, three doors down from the groom's parents), the bride, groom, groom's father, a friend of the groom's from work, and the bride's parents were all hard at work laying a floor and decorating. The bride and I sat on the floor in the empty upstairs room to talk, and afterwards she was accused of 'having taken a nice evening off'.

Those who rented flats got them 2–12 weeks before the wedding and they also worked on them. Case 44 (groom): 'She's (bride's mother) been down to see it – but not since the kitchen's been papered and painted. Just brightening it up. Kitchen and bathroom both redone.' In this case the decorating had been done by the groom and his (male) friend (the husband of the couple for whom my informants were babysitting when interviewed), but working on their future home together also provides a place to be alone to court (as does babysitting).

In all except one case (where the couple had bought their own trailer), couples where the bride was pregnant lived with kin after they married. Four started off with his parents (one later left to go to her sister's) and three started off with her parents (two subsequently moved to live with his parents). In the final (ninth) case – students – they stayed with both sets of parents in the vacation immediately after they were married (outside Swansea) and then lived with an aunt in Swansea till the end of the academic year.

(2) Furnishing the home: wedding presents

The furnishings for the new home come from the 'bits and pieces' given as engagement presents and from the 'bottom drawer' collected by the bride (see chapter 5) – towels, coffee tables, saucepans, blankets, dusters, teatowels, pyrex dishes, toasters, irons and ironing boards, water sets (jug and glasses), mixing bowls, cutlery, table cloths and napkins, vases, etc. – and from wedding presents. While engagement presents are 'Just to wish you all the best', wedding presents are more expensive gifts intended to help to get the couple's house furnished. Because donors are spending more, and because the couple have already got some of the articles they need, people usually ask what the couple (or bride) want(s); and it is quite common for her to have a written list of things they/she would like, which she shows them. People tick items or tell her what they are going to give in advance (see Figure 3). Comprehensive suggested lists of wedding presents are given in pull-out sections in the bridal magazines[7].

Figure 3 Wedding present list

Case 35. Typed list sent out by the bride: 'That's if they ask. Everyone has so far.'
A tick indicated someone had promised this gift (facsimile).

```
ironing board ✓
iron ✓
bedding (no p. cases)
standard lamp
table lamp ✓
bed side lamp
clothes horse ✓
saucepan set ✓
electric kettle ✓
kitchen scales ✓
mirror for lounge
kitchen stool (blue) ✓
white fur top bedroom stool
casseroles ✓
plastic kitchen mat (blue kitchen)
step ladder
coffee table ✓
electric fire

electric toaster
prestige egg whisk
coal bunker
coffee perculator ✓
canteen of cutlery
tray
flower vase
vegetable rack ✓
small ewbank ✓
pressure cooker
terylene filled pillows
sweeping brush
mop
dinner service ✓
salad bowl ✓
fruit bowl
spiked stainless steel meat dish ✓
teapot
cushions
wine glasses
```

A substantial minority of my informants saw this list as a new innovation and one they did not like – it seemed to be 'money-grubbing';

'I don't like the idea of a list. Just give how much they can afford.'

'People ask and you just think in your head. To have it written down seems . . . like you're insisting they buy you something. And all the small things go first . . . ' (So those who ask later have to buy bigger presents than they'd intended.)

Those who had lists emphasized that they help people to get ideas of what to give, which donors welcomed. One can include lots of 'small' things (£2–£3), and it avoids duplication: 'the threat of 14 toast racks.' Case 48 (bride): 'I'd say about 80 per cent asked [me] for a wedding list. And the rest asked if "such and such" is suitable. They're spending quite a lot of money and [they'd] rather not take the risk.'

Those who left Swansea when they married generally moved into furnished flats and 'only took bits and pieces'; 'the big presents are waiting (i.e., have been promised but people are not giving them) until we get somewhere unfurnished.' But even those going into furnished accommodation in Swansea added to what was provided[8], since there was often just a bare minimum of furniture – sufficient to make the accommodation fall within the legal definition of 'furnished' (which ensures that the tenant does not get security of tenure). They added personal possessions to make it more comfortable and 'homely'.

The majority of those who rented in Swansea had managed to get unfurnished flats and many of them 'saved hard for furniture'. For example, one couple where the husband was a policeman and therefore liable to be moved around 'had bought furniture as we can't buy a house'. Both they and those with homes of their own may use second-hand furniture from a known source – things inherited when the bride's mother died, things passed on by one or other set of parents who have bought themselves a new one of its kind, furniture bought from people across the road who are emigrating – but only one couple (students) mentioned going round junk-shops. The preference is for new furniture and the order of priorities is: a three-piece suite for the sitting room, a cooking stove, a kitchen set of tables and chairs, a carpet for the front room, and a double bed ('the bedroom suite can come later'). Sometimes all the new furniture is bought in one fell swoop, on hire purchase. Case 26:

'Little things – I bought some every week, and from my bottom drawer and engagement presents. The big things – we bought the lot last Saturday [two weeks before the wedding]. A three piece suite, dining-room suite, stove, sink unit, carpet, and the bed – not the suite yet, we can manage without.'

In addition to the indirect help they give in not taking much (or any) money for board from the young people in the months before the wedding and help in kind with curtain making, carpentry or decorating, parents will also give direct financial aid with housing and furnishing (if they can afford to). Sometimes this help is substantial. For example, giving each child £300 for a deposit on a house; a builder letting his daughter and son-in-law have a flat in one of his properties rent-free; or (see Case 18, p. 118), acting as guarantor on a mortgage. In one case a grandmother came to the rescue. Case 16:

> The groom worked for his parents in their business and the couple could have married earlier if the bride had been willing to move into the [large] flat over one of their shops. She said she 'couldn't bear this'. He had to live near the shop as he started work early and could not drive. Nor could they move into a flat nearby 'because everyone would have been horrified if we'd [done that] with a big empty house over there'.

> Then the groom's grandmother's brother, who had been living in a nearby house belonging to the grandmother, died. The house stood empty for nearly a year and then the grandmother suggested that the couple should have it, since she intended to leave it to her grandson anyway. It was in a terrible state, according to the bride, and they must have spent several thousand pounds having it done up – the downstairs rooms knocked into one, central heating, split level cooker in the kitchen etc. But the situation was saved. 'You have to think a lot about families; whether you're offending them or not.'

Help from parents with furnishings may also amount to several hundred pounds.

Case 24:

> 'We had the carpet and three-piece suite from [her] parents, and her mother also gave the sitting-room curtains [which cost £30]. The bedroom suite was from his parents and the stove from his mother.'

Case 28:

> 'The deposit [on the house] is a wedding present from us [the bride's parents] and her mother bought her a new bedroom suite a year ago and she's taking it with her.'

Parents may help further by storing furniture. For example, one couple whose new house was not ready because of the usual builder's delays, talked to me in the front room of her parents' house. We barely had room to move because of the presence of *two* three-piece suites and boxes of presents. Other parents had carpet rolls on the stairs, etc.

Indeed, it can be argued that most of the wedding presents are indirect help from the couple's parents, since they are a return on the parents' 'investments'. The majority of presents, and certainly the most substantial ones, come from the parents' generation: the parents' sibs, neighbours, etc. The maintenance of such relationships depends on the parents' (especially the mothers') energies, and the presents given to the couple will be paralleled by gifts by the couple's parents to the children of their sibs or neighbours when *they* marry.

This is made more obvious if the sending out of invitations to the wedding and the giving out of cake is compared to the 'bidding' of nineteenth century South Wales, when debts to the bride and groom's parents were formally called in. According to Owen's account (1959), guests used to be invited to the wedding ceremony and feast either by a written notice (bidding letter) or by engaging a bidder to call at houses of friends and acquaintances. The phrasing of the proclamation followed a more or less set pattern, delicately balanced between reminders of the hospitality being offered (e.g., a list of the food at the reception – good beef and cabbage, mutton and turnips, port and potatoes, roast goose, a quart of drink for 4d, a cake for 1d, clean chairs to sit down on, clean pipes and tobacco, and promises of 'attendance of the best', and a good song) and a polite request for return of donations due to the bride and groom's parents, grandparents, aunts, brothers, and sisters (a waggon or a cart, a horse, a heifer, pigs, cocks, hens, geese, a saddle and bridle, a child's cradle, a waggon full of potatoes, a hundred cheeses, a cask of butter, a sack of flour, jugs, basins, saucepans, £5, tea-kettles, plates and dishes, knives and forks, etc.) An account book was kept of all the gifts, and those that were not repayments of debts, the couple would in their turn repay[9].

In contemporary urban Wales the pleasures of the wedding reception are not spelt out on the invitation, and there is a division between those invited to the meal and those given cake afterwards. The 'debt' calling in is also implicit, and more restricted in that it is only 'debts' to the bride and groom themselves and to their parents (and possibly also their grandparents) – not to their aunts and uncles and sibs – that are collected, or established to be repaid in the future. Further these 'debts' are seen as freely given gifts to the young couple, albeit with a feeling of obligation to reciprocity: 'she gave to my daughter so I *should* give to hers.' Anyone actually invited to the wedding feels under a strong obligation to give a present[10], but a great many presents also come from people who do not attend the reception (though they are given cake). Most presents will be reciprocated in due course, but there is no precise equivalence or formal exchange. And, of course, it is important to note that those who do not marry never get a repayment of *their* gifts (or their parents' gifts).

Most presents are given shortly before the wedding, though some relatives coming from a distance will bring theirs with them when they arrive for the wedding, and a few are given 'late' (up to several weeks after the event). They are given to the couple in the person of the bride, kept and displayed at her house, and it is she who is responsible for making sure that people are thanked for their gifts.

The presents are on show in the bride's house (in the front room or a bedroom) for 2–7 days over the wedding (see *Figure* 4). Each has a card showing who it is from. Gifts of money are marked by a card in which it is noted that the person has given 'a cheque' or 'a sum of money' – the amount is not mentioned. Neighbours come in and look at the display during the week and relatives look over after the reception. (According to my waitress informant – see p. 35 – the 'upper class' take their presents to the hotel where their reception is held and have them on show in an adjoining room.)

When the couple move into their new household they are, as it were, surrounded by their kin, in that they have all around them objects which they identify as given by a particular person. (Though, in contrast, more distant kin are identified by what they gave – see the comment quoted on p. 34: at the reception 'I identified [his kin] as "you're Nina, you gave me so-and-so"!'. Thus one informant sat in her sitting room (furnished flat)

Figure 4 Display of wedding presents

and looked around and said (Case 5): 'The companion set was an engagement present from his gran, the lamp was a wedding present from my auntie, the [coffee] table was an engagement present from my mother . . . ' and another bride and groom showed me over their flat identifying their furniture. Case 37:

'Bedroom – old carpet his mother gave.

Bedroom suite and dining room suite – a wedding present from his father.

We bought the 3-piece suite. The carpet and cooker are on H.P. We bought, or rather we're buying them and the carpet over nine months. The TV's rented – 6s a week.

The picture's from a prisoner who became a prison officer, as a wedding present.

Curtains are a wedding present from [groom's] mother (cost £37 10s).

We bought our bed – first thing we bought! 5 foot by 6 foot 6 and I can't buy sheets to fit!

Bedroom suite came separately as part of a deal, for £75; most of that was wedding presents.

Pouffe was a wedding present from the girls at [bride's] work.

Table was a wedding present from [groom's] auntie – I don't like her, and I don't like it!

[Groom's mo. mo.] bought standard lamp and mirror (£10);

[Bride's mo. mo.] bought wedding dress and cake.

Secondhand washing machine from [groom's] mother – she got a new automatic.

Clock from bridesmaid's mother.

Companion set – my cousin (bride's mo. sis. da.).

[Groom's other] gran gave an iron.

[Groom's father's sister] gave an ironing board.

Kettle from the best man – automatic, switches itself off.

Saucepans – [bride's] sister, including a chip pan.

Alibaba basket [for dirty clothes] – friend of [groom's] mother;

[Groom's] mother – dinner service, coffee set. The tea service was an engagement present.

Nigel [a friend] bought us that ornament [£10].

Cut glass sherry glasses off my cousins [bride's mo. sister's da.].

[Bride's] brother gave us £10 with which we bought a camera.

Blankets – [bride's] sister's mo.-in-law – she came to the wedding [lives with bride's sis].

Lot of Pyrex stuff of [bride's] sister's friend: a girl I work with.

And towels! Think we got a hundred towels.

We was fortunate.'

Those who start off with parents obviously need relatively little furniture.

Case 57:

> The bride intended to go on living with her widowed father in his
> council house. (She had dissuaded the groom from his idea of buying a
> small old house from a relative in the town centre on the grounds that if
> they were going to have children they would need three bedrooms.)
> She said that they would need to renew some of the furniture and get a
> new washing machine, but that was about all, and they would do that
> after they were married. Not surprisingly, despite a two-year court-
> ship (including a seven-month engagement) they had not 'stayed in to
> save' at any stage.

Others planning to live with parents had redecorated what were to be
'their rooms' and bought their own bed. They used saucepans, lamps,
crockery, and linen given as presents.

The need to save and to have adequate resources behind one when one
gets married is the most commonly cited reason for 'delay' once one has
met the person one wishes to marry[11]. In many cases it is a question of
completing training – e.g., apprentices, students – so as to be earning
enough to 'keep one's wife in the manner to which she is accustomed'; or,
more importantly, to have been earning enough for some time to have got
substantial savings. In the few cases where the groom worked for his
parents (a builder, on a fairground, in a shop) only when in their twenties
did they stop getting only 'keep and more or less pocket money'.

Evidence of one's ability to get a house and furniture together seemed
sometimes to be part of the bargaining process with parents: a more
acceptable pressure to bring to bear than pregnancy. Case 31: 'Well to be
frank, since this is confidential, they didn't really like him. They kept
hoping it would fall through. But once we'd got somewhere nice and
livable in there wasn't anything they could really say. They could see we
were serious.'

Intergenerational relations

Three-quarters of the couples had their first settled home after marriage
within five miles of their parents (see *Figure 5*). (This includes the one in
six who lived *with* their parents.)

Because of the exigencies of the housing market (at this stage in their
life-cycle the couples could not get council housing and so did not have to
move to the large estates in the west of the town, but rather had to look for
their own houses in the new estates being built to infill between the old

Figure 5 Distance of the couples' 'first settled home' from their parents' home

Distance of the couple from parents	parents of groom		parents of bride	
	N	%	N	%
living with parents	6	(13) ⎫	7	(15) ⎫
within ½ mile	9	(19) ⎬ (77)	7	(15) ⎬ (74)
within 2 miles	9	(19) ⎪	11	(24) ⎪
2–5 miles	13	(27) ⎭	9	(20) ⎭
5–10 miles	3	(6)	4	(9)
10–50 miles	2	(4)	3	(7)
50–200 miles	4	(8)	4	(9)
over 200 miles	2	(4)	1	(2)
N	48		46	

scattered districts, or in the older districts themselves; or for rented flats, again in the older areas) and because of the convenience of living centrally for young men working long irregular hours and for working wives, my informants' new households did not show the westward drift characteristic of the population as a whole in the previous generation (cf. Rosser and Harris 1965:52ff). They did, however, move to a considerable extent between the older central districts; in part, it seemed, deliberately to put a short distance between themselves and their parents.

In the interview I included questions as to how far away from relatives my informants would like to live ideally (and to their parents as to how far away from them young people should live); but the replies need cautious interpretation. Many immediately replied 'A *long* way away!', but then always qualified this to: 'Well, not too far. Not so far that one can't visit easily, but not so near that one is in and out of each other's houses all the time' or 'under each other's feet and noses'. This was then further qualified to 'What we have is just about right' – whether they lived down the road or four miles away. This I interpret as a clear norm that the new household should be separate and independent to establish new statuses (and to avoid conflicts in the meanwhile), but not so far as to cut certain links with the previous family situation. But this norm is differentially interpreted and the links which people seek (and are able) to maintain vary. Differences of interpretation affect what people look for, and what they are able to find in turn affects what is seen to be sought. Tensions occur only when a clear choice is thwarted (e.g. a couple who chose to live with the bride's parents might be content; but a couple who had decided on a house of their own but who had to live with parents even for a short time because of builders' delays could be very miserable). If people had something close to what they'wanted', they were content.

Similarly, while I have information on frequency of contact with kin after marriage, this is also difficult to interpret. The couples were differentially situated as to the length of time since they were married (it varied from less than a week to eight months), so some had a more settled pattern of visiting than others; some were still in temporary accommodation while others were settled; and some brides were working full-time outside the home while others had stopped paid employment because of pregnancy, and a few already had a baby. The sample is too small to control for these variables – not to mention the variables of distance and ease of transport between their house and those of their parents.

In all cases, however, close contact was maintained with parents, and usually also with sibs, especially unmarried sibs of the same sex. Where the couple left Swansea, the parents paid a visit a few months later, often staying for several days, and the young people were expected to return to Swansea for holidays. Letters and/or telephone calls were exchanged about once a week. When the couple returned from honeymoon to a house or flat actually in Swansea, they often called in on their parents on their way home to pick up groceries, etc., which it had been arranged should be bought for them, and 'To say Hullo'. Shortly afterwards the parents were invited over for a meal. This could be a formidable occasion for a new wife who was an inexperienced cook and who had to produce a three-course Sunday lunch for her parents-in-law and her husband.

When the couple have a house close to either set of parents they might see them everyday, and when living 2–5 miles away they would probably see them once or twice a week even when the bride was working full-time: e.g., the bride went to her parents once a week straight from work and her husband picked her up later when he drove home from work, and they both went over on a Sunday. A son might call in for lunch with his mother every day when out driving a delivery van, or occasionally for a cup of coffee, or when he came off shift at mid-day and his wife was at work. A son might see his father every day at work, or once a week in their drinking club or pub, and a daughter-in-law might go to see her parents-in-law every Friday evening. Where regular contact was not possible it was usually regretted Case 40 (bride): 'Pressure of work means we don't see them much. We both start early and finish late. [Her parents lived four miles in one direction, his three miles in the other] I miss my mother! I get awful homesick!'

Visiting is more restricted when the couple are living with 'one side', since the other side will rarely if ever come to see their son or daughter in the in-laws' house and all visiting will have to be by the couple (together or singly). Sibs are not so inhibited – one informant's sister dropped in to see her every Saturday when she came into the town to shop. (The bride was living with her husband's mother close to the town centre.)

When the bride stops paid employment, she may spend several afternoons a week with her mother – though the groom or his side may disapprove. Thus in Case 36, where the bride was off work convalescing after a spell in hospital following an accident, she became quite indignant when described by her husband as 'being down her mother's *every* afternoon'; and retorted 'You're always on at me about it. It's *not true*. I only go down about twice a week.' In another case (no. 12), the reported reason for the row which had led the groom's mother to 'put out' her son and his wife and baby was that the bride had gone out too often (the bride said 'three times a week') with the baby to spend time at her sisters' houses – her mother being dead.

The change of situation at marriage for parents and 'children' is abrupt. There is rarely pre-socialization to the child's living away from home (cf. the middle classes described in North London by Firth, Hubert, and Forge 1970, and in the US by Sussman 1953b, 1954; and Deutscher 1962); and not at all to the idea of the child having left home. This may account for the frequent tendency for the parents to see the young person (and themselves?) as 'not ready' or 'too young' for marriage. However, the departure of the children is seen as inevitable, and parental interference (especially by mothers – see the folk-lore on mothers-in-law) as illegitimate, and so the situation must be accepted. The 'early' marriage is adjusted to by stressing the 'suitability' of the spouses and their 'rightness' for each other; and by continuing frequent contact.

But since women in particular rely on kin for their companions (see chapter 4), mother and daughter may feel very lonely or homesick, especially when the couple leave the district. Case 9:

> When I called round after the wedding to collect the lists the bride had left for me, her mother talked for a long time about how very upset she was by the bride's going to the north of England. She knew off-hand the exact number of weeks and days since the wedding. She only cheered up when we discussed the chances of the couple moving back to Swansea; 'But it won't be for at least two years'.

Even when the couple live with the bride's mother she still finds the situation changes. Case 1:

> (Bride's mother) 'I miss her now she's married, even though she's living here. I used to say "Let's go down to [bride's sister's] tonight, or

out to so and so''. Especially when they were engaged. Raymond was working away – he's a scaffolding erector and they used to send the unmarried ones to far away jobs. The last one was in Somerset. Now he's married he's home.'

The adage that 'A son is a son till he takes a wife. A daughter's a daughter the whole of her life', holds in so far as the links between mothers and daughters after marriage are more important sources of companionship and physical assistance than those between mother or father and son, but a daughter's attachment and interaction with her family of origin is limited by her marital commitment.

Employment after marriage and the division of labour and income within the new household

(1) Employment

Almost all brides (91 per cent) were in paid employment at the time of their first or second marriage (see chapter 3) and, with only a couple of exceptions, they worked full-time. (Those who did not go out to work or who worked part-time either cared for elderly parents or young children.) Almost all intended to continue in their jobs for a year or two full-time after marriage and then to get pregnant and stop working a few months before the birth. They planned to stay at home as full-time wives and mothers while their children were 'young', and then to return to some type of (probably part-time) paid employment. In only one case did a wife say she did not want to have children[12]. No men expressed this view.

The exceptions to this general pattern of 'full-time job – stop for children – part-time job' were women marrying for a second time, those who were pregnant at the time when they got married, and some of those who left Swansea after their marriage. Women entering a second marriage, who had children from their first marriage, did not intend to have any further offspring (in contrast to the situation where the man was entering his second marriage but the woman her first). Otherwise their plans were like those of the rest of the sample – going back to part-time work as soon as their children were in school. Those who had no children from their first marriage intended waiting a short time and then having some.

Of the eight brides who were pregnant when they married, two carried on work after the baby was born (one was a student and the other worked in the family business). Of the others, four stopped as soon as they were married (i.e., when 3–5 months pregnant). (It tends to be assumed that if a woman leaves a job as soon as she marries it is because she wants to avoid the embarrassment of it being revealed that she 'had to get married'.) Two worked till they were 6–7 months pregnant and then stopped.

Couples who left Swansea after their marriage did so because the husband's job was elsewhere. Most wives so relocated had to look for new jobs[13]. Four of them were clerks, teachers, and nurses and they did not imagine they would have difficulty finding work – though one nurse was thinking of giving up nursing (possibly to act as a research assistant on a survey of nurses) since her odd hours never seemed to coincide with her junior hospital doctor husband's irregular hours. The two whose husbands were in the armed services could not easily find new jobs though they would have liked to – one because she was in Germany and spoke no German, the other because she and her husband were going to move several times within the year.

The actual intentions of those who proposed to 'work – stop – work' were themselves not as uniform as appears at first sight. Two started working part-time immediately after marriage. One was a woman who married in her forties a man in his late thirties who already had a fully-furnished home of his own. She said that since she worked shop opening hours and he was in a factory, if she worked full-time there was 'an empty house when he's home off shift' and 'men like their home comforts [presumably supplied by having a wife around]; that's what they get married for.' The second was a younger woman who had worked part-time before marriage and cared for her father. She and her husband continued to live in her father's council house and she looked after him in addition to her husband. She changed to a part-time job with even shorter hours, and she hoped to have a baby 'before the year is out'.

Among other younger couples the wife's earnings were badly needed to establish the new household, and, as will be seen, the difference in standard of living which could be attained with an initial period with two incomes was very marked. Most mentioned two years as the period they wanted to wait before having a child (which was in fact close to the national average gap between marriage and the first child), though some suggested 3–5 years, or 'till (one or other spouse) finishes training', or 'when we get a home of our own', or 'as soon as we can afford to'. A small minority wanted to wait a year at most: 'start towards the end of this year'; 'don't want to wait for kids.' Where the bride and groom disagreed about how long the woman would work before they 'started a family' it was almost invariably the woman who suggested the longer period. Case 6:

(Bride) '3–5 years.'
(Groom) '3!'

and the bride who stressed that she could not afford to stop and the groom who asserted that she could if she/they really wanted her to (i.e., she stressed the importance of her earnings; he stressed his bread-winning capacity). This is counter to the folk-myth that it is women who persuade their husbands to let them have children. (Though of course things and perceptions may change some time into the marriage.)

All were firm that the woman would 'stop [work] altogether when the children are young' – with four notable exceptions: the woman with her own hairdressing business, two who had family shops, and a nursery nurse who could take her child to her work-place. That is to say, those who *could* continue to earn money while looking after their child(ren), wished to do so.

After children, intentions were varied. A small minority did not intend to go back to a job ever. Most would 'devote [themselves] to husband and kids' till the children were 'in school', or 'about 10', or 'in secondary school', or 'grown up'. Again, when the bride and groom disagreed, the groom said her return to work would be later than the bride was proposing. Case 6:

(Bride) 'When the youngest child's 5.'
(Groom) '12!'

For many, the future beyond child-bearing was vague: 'it'll depend', 'see how things stand', 'don't know after; it all depends', 'depends on his position', 'maybe part-time, I'll see how I feel – work is just a chore at the moment'. Most saw themselves as going back to the same sort of work (and work situation) as they were in at the time of their marriage. (However, as has been stressed, this would not be likely if they went back part-time.) Only one bank clerk, the daughter of a professional man marrying a university graduate, had plans to undertake further training (to teach) when the children were older.

Men's future work plans were also little thought out. All saw themselves as continuous members of the labour force: none planned to drop out of paid employment (except for one student couple who wanted to 'go on the road' for a few years once they had finished their degrees). A few men were thinking of changing their occupations – e.g., a welder was thinking of joining the police – but most seemed to feel that the responsibility which they had taken on at marriage (of supporting a wife and possible children) precluded major changes; though quite a number spoke of looking for better paid jobs in the same line, or of hopes of setting up in business themselves as subcontractors. Two mentioned the possibility of emigration.

Men are seen as full-time paid workers who earn the family's main income. Paid employment for wives is seen as something the woman may *choose* to undertake to earn the family a little extra (not essential) money and to give her 'some money of her own', and so as to give her company and a change from domestic work when she is not needed full-time at home. Case 24:

(Bride) 'I expect I'll go back eventually – I'll probably get fed up with housework.'
(Groom) 'I won't stand in her way if she wants to, but I hope it won't be necessary moneywise.'

It is therefore seen as her responsibility to organize her domestic duties around her outside work if *she wishes* to do it. Her husband *may help* with some of the domestic chores if she goes out to work, but he is under no obligation to do so – unless they need the money (i.e., unless he is an inadequate breadwinner).

(2) The division of labour within the home

Much has been made in recent writings on the family of changes towards 'companionship', 'equality', 'symmetricality', etc. in the relationship of husband and wife; of dual careers (with the middle class as vanguard), less sharp domestic division of labour, joint decision making, growth of a financial partnership, greater equality, and desire to spend leisure time together (see especially Rapoport and Rapoport 1971, 1975; and Young and Willmott 1973). According to Gorer, '(husband) responds to (wife) as (wife) responds to (husband), the difference of temperament, of function, of skills are all minimised' (1971; 62). I certainly did not find this to be the case in Swansea in regard to either women and men's employment (as I have shown) or the division of labour within the home.

Young husbands in Swansea 'help' their wives with the housework, notably with the washing up, and most accept that they are competent to do most forms of housework *if necessary*; but they do not *actually do* much cooking, cleaning,washing, or tidying. In contemporary Britain house-work is done by women (see Oakley 1974 a and b; Davidoff 1976). There may have been a blurring of the line between male and female tasks, but there has not been a revolution in the division of labour. The respon-sibilities remain that the husband is to 'win the bread', and the wife is to care for the home, children and kin, though she has lost some of her managerial autonomy within the home[14]. The wife's earnings are played down, though they are often an important addition to family resources (Land 1975; Hamill 1976).

Even at this first stage in marriage, when both partners are out at work all day and keeping house is still a novelty, most housework is done by the wife. But it is perceived as 'shared'; decisions are often made jointly; and husbands do tasks they enjoy or are good at (see Mainardi 1970, Oakley 1972).

Case 17:

> (Bride) 'We'll share it. I suppose I'll do it mostly. But he cooks rather well. He'll help. Probably I'll suggest and he'll do it.'

Case 54:

> When I arrived the wife was not yet home from work and the husband was sitting watching television. He wasn't interested in being interviewed but his wife was, provided I didn't mind if she did the cooking in the meantime. She peeled potatoes and apples, and cooked chops, mashed potatoes and peas and stewed apples and custard, and made coffee, while talking to me. Her husband continued to watch the television. Later he joined in the interview and said, in answer to the question 'How do you divide up domestic work between you?';
>
> 'She's adamant that she does most – but really we share it. I cook *if she's not here.*' (My emphasis)

Relatively rarely is there such declared double thinking. More often it is accepted that there *should* be a division of labour: that the husband will help his wife with what is basically her responsibility. 'He's pretty domesticated. He helps me with what I'm doing.' Often the groom's lesser participation is explained by his longer hours of work or need to study:

Case 45:

> (How do you divide up domestic jobs between you?)
> 'He's fantastic. Tremendous. Fair does. Mind, he's only been married for three months. I'm waiting for the novelty to wear off! In the evening he does the veg and I prepare the meal. I do most of the washing up – he's swotting again now.'

Case 26:

> (Bride) 'I do most of the housework. He works [as a welder] all week till 6.00 – gets almost no time off and I get Thursday and Saturday afternoons [as shop assistant].'

Case 52:

> 'There's not much to do. I do all the cleaning in the evening he goes to tech. He does odd jobs, but not cleaning. I did quite a lot at home. I like it.'

It was suggested occasionally that the extent of husbandly involvement was temporary. The wife of a management trainee said (Case 9): 'While I'm working he'll help. But once I stop he won't do anything – he believes it's women's work.'

One thing which I found perhaps surprising was the extent to which the bride's mother (and the groom's mother and the two fathers to a limited extent) work gratis for the couple. She (they) may offer occasional help and advice (Case 9):

> The bride had been at work at her new job in the north of England only a week when her parents went to see the couple. Her mother said 'She was a bit tired by it – on top of the housework. But she was coping. Told me it was nice to have me there to cook a meal for her when she got back [in the evening]. I advised her to make a plan to do certain things each evening so that they didn't all pile up at the weekends.'

Or she may give loans of money if her daughter runs out before the end of the week. Often she (or they) help(s) with babysitting. In one instance the baby slept at its grandmother's every Saturday and Sunday evening so that its parents could go out. In another, the groom's parents looked after the baby entirely during term time while the young couple finished their teacher-training course (which involved the groom's mother giving up her job as a waitress). In a third, the baby, which was conceived accidently on the first night of the honeymoon, was going to be looked after during the day by the bride's mother so that the bride could go on working for a year or so. In addition, where possible, mothers may do a great deal of day to day housework for their married children Case 53:

> 'My mother comes in [lives down the street] and does a lot while I'm at work. Cooking and so on, dusting, and part of my washing.' The groom in this couple had his lunch each day with [i.e., cooked by] his mother because he finished work (as a van driver) at 1.00 pm. He did no housework at all.

When the couple live with parents, the mother (especially if it is the bride's mother) will do most of the cleaning and maintenance, though the bride usually shops and cooks an evening meal for her husband and herself. Only when they live with a widowed parent, or when the bride stops work with a baby, do they 'live through and through'. Case 4:

> The groom's widowed mother did all the housework, including the shopping and cooking. Her daughter-in-law made up a shopping list and gave it, and the money, to her each week. In return the couple paid part of the rent on the (mother's) council house and paid for all the food. This woman also did much of the washing and cleaning in her daughter's house, a few doors up the road. This daughter had just recently returned to work as a primary school teacher.

When the parent with whom they lived was a widower, the young wife cared for him as for her husband. One bride who had already been living with her husband for some years (since their child was born – until his divorce) did all the housework for her mother (in whose council house they lived) while her mother went out to work. This domestic work done by the mother (and also occasional handiwork – carpentry, decorating, car maintenance – done by the father) is seen as done 'for love', just as it was when the young adult was living at home. The question 'have you had any help from your parents?' brought answers in terms of financial aid or gifts of furniture, not direct labour or advice. The latter could be taken for granted and was perceived as different in kind.

Only one new wife – a school teacher – had paid domestic help, and this was presented as help from the husband's parents (though it was not clear who actually paid) (Case 16):

> (Bride) 'I do all the housework – except Colin helps with the washing up occasionally. He works in the evenings. I've a woman who comes in once a week to do the floors. She does for my mother-in-law [who worked full-time in one of the family's shops] and she pops across to me for an hour.'

(3) Distribution of income

I collected regrettably little information on the handling of money by the couple, and there is a dearth of systematic consideration of this topic against which I might consider my findings. Both the main secondary analyses (Young 1952; Oren 1974) and the study by Grey in Edinburgh (1974) consider only working-class couples with children, and pay little if any heed to women's earnings.

Grey suggests, on the basis of her own fieldwork and a survey of the community study and family sociology literature from Britain, that it is helpful in understanding most household budgets to have in mind a flow diagram (see *Figure 6*).

She suggests that there are three main types of budget:

(a) *whole wage/pocket money system* – where the husband gives his wife his entire wage and is given a fixed amount of pocket money back, or where he keeps pocket money and gives her the rest. He then pays for only a few minor (or no) collective expenses – and where there is little 'third level' readjustment: if the wife runs out of housekeeping or has particular expenses her husband is unlikely to help her out with money from his 'pocket money'; and conversely, the wife is not likely to buy things for her husband (e.g., cigarettes) out of her 'housekeeping'.

(b) *allowance system* – where the husband gives his wife a housekeeping allowance (which is always expected to cover food and cleaning materials), but he keeps a quite large retention because he pays for at least one,

Figure 6 Distribution of income within the family (with children; husband only working)

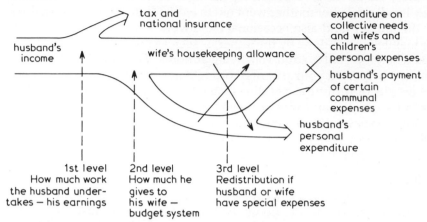

1st level
How much work the husband under-takes – his earnings

2nd level
How much he gives to his wife – budget system

3rd level
Redistribution if husband or wife have special expenses

Source: modified from Grey (1974)

and often several, or most, major household expenses (mortgage or rent, savings, consumer durables such as furniture and linen, fuel, holidays, wife and children's clothes, etc.).

(c) *pooling* – where both put into and both draw from a common pool (e.g. bank account). This would require a modification of the flow diagram in *Figure 6*, but Grey does not develop this.

The 'allowance system' accounted for half of her working class informants in Edinburgh and the 'pocket money system' for a further 30 per cent. She suggests that the 'whole wage/pocket money system' is more common among families with very low incomes (including pensioners and those on social security and with large families), and that pooling is more common (though it is never very common)[15] where both partners are earning. She cites an as yet unpublished study of family life-styles by Tom Burns as showing the allowance system and the pooling system as each being used by half the Edinburgh middle class.

There are certainly regional variations as to the frequency of various systems. The Government Social Survey study of matrimonial property, for example, found that 5 per cent of wives in England and Wales as a whole were given their husbands' entire pay packet, but that this varied from 15 per cent in the north of England, through 8 per cent in the east midlands, south west and South Wales, to 2 per cent in the south east and London (Todd and Jones 1972). There may also be life-cycle variation: e.g., in Aberdeen a couple may change from the whole wage system to the pocket money system when the wife stops work and the first child is born (Rowntree 1954). Young (1952) and Shaw (1954) and a recent National Consumer Council Survey (1975) all found that the value of housekeeping allowances does not change much within the course of a marriage[16]. (Thus most of the financial, as well as the labour burden of extra children falls on the wife.) There is often a change back to the whole wage system on retirement.

Jephcott and colleagues' work on the Bermondsey biscuit factory workers (1962) found that women going out to work breaks down somewhat the husband/breadwinner, wife/manager role structure, and they suggest that as more married women have gone out to work there has been a change over to husband-wife discussion of financial organization and decision-making, with a more flexible system of housekeeping than in previous generations. Who pays for what varies from week to week depending on fluctuations in male earnings. When the wife is earning the husband can keep more for himself: the pressure of collective needs on his personal expenditure is reduced. The wife's earnings are earmarked for consumer durables and some weeks all her money goes on these and they live on the husband's earnings; but if he earns less than usual, they draw on hers.

Among my newly married informants there was almost universally a distinction between 'his' and 'her' money: the recurring refrain being 'we're trying to live on his and save mine'. When 'his' was not enough to live on (e.g., a refuse collector), some of 'hers' was added to it. But, for the majority, the husband earned 'the bread' (i.e., money for food, rent, fares, entertainment, clothes, and other recurring expenses) and the wife's money was used for furniture (including repayment of loans already incurred) and for other consumer durables, or it was saved, sometimes towards a deposit on a house.

Among those without children and with the wife working, half operated an allowance system with the husband's money[17]:

Case 16:

> 'He gives me – far too much – housekeeping, and I spend it all! He handles the bills. It's the way his father [a shopkeeper] does it.' (The bride's father used to give his wife his whole pay-packet.)

About 20 per cent used the pocket-money arrangement:

Case 40:

> 'He opens his pay-packet and takes his needs. I know how much he gets because the payslip is still inside. I'm well provided for.'

With a further 15 per cent of husbands handing over their whole wage:

Case 50

> 'He gives me his wage packet. He always opens it to check it's right,

but he gives me the lot. I organize things and give him some money; if he's lucky! Really, so far, it's all gone on mortgage and bills.'

Case 25:

Another couple who operated this system said that the husband got back £1 out of his £10 (apprentice) wages.

Only 15 per cent used the pooling system:

Case 54:

'We put our wages together and sort out expenses. The rest goes in the bank [joint account]. [The wife] usually gets the groceries out of hers on the way home – puts in the rest.'

Unfortunately my information is not sufficient to comment on the changes when the wife stops working full-time, nor when there are children, nor by socio-economic category.

Only one wife (Case 36) did not know how much her husband earned (there was no direct question on this, however). He was an industrial painter and (she thought) earned large lump sums. He gave her a regular £12.50 a week. Only one bride (Case 11) mentioned that she kept a quarter of her money as 'pin money' for her own expenses; the rest was used to pay off the furniture. (Again, the proviso must be made that there was no direct question.) Seemingly at this stage in the marriage, as Grey found out at a later stage, the wife's personal expenses come out of her 'house-keeping allowance'; or her clothes, outings, etc., may be paid for by the husband out of his retention. She does not have her own 'pocket money' earmarked. Most couples had not discussed how they were going to organize money before they married, though 'I suppose we ought to'.

Conclusion

A major point, which emerged from looking at the situation of these newly married couples, was that their standard of living was determined not only by the socio-economic situation of the husband-provider, but also by the events of courtship and early married life itself[18]. If we take, for example, cases 27 and 46 and compare them, we see in each a groom in his early twenties (aged twenty-five and twenty-one) and in skilled manual work (an electrician and a fitter). But Brian Benson and his fiancée married, with parental blessing and aid, after a seven-year courtship, which included three and a half years of engagement and steady saving. They had a newly built house of their own and most of the furnishings they felt they needed, and they intended that Marilyn should carry on with her hairdressing business full-time for a couple of years so that they could buy what they lacked and have some savings behind them before they had their first child. Richard and Christine Jones, on the other hand, had married after they had known each other just over a year and against her mother' wishes. They had no money saved – they did not even have the £20–30 needed for an engagement ring at Christmas (they married in March) – and Christine had to stop work almost as soon as they were married because of difficulties in the pregnancy which precipitated the wedding. They were living with Richard's parents (and sister and her two children) in a small terraced house when interviewed, with no prospect of a council house for some years.

In contrast to many members of the spiralist middle class of my acquaintances in and outside Swansea, the local middle class and skilled working class do not marry and then build up a home together; they build up a home and then marry. Their ideal is to start married life in a newly decorated, newly furnished home, watching their newly purchased television – sometimes welcoming visitors because, after the rush of preparations before the wedding, they suddenly feel 'flat' with 'nothing to do'. If babies then arrive smartly, it is not too disastrous. But if children arrive before the home is set up, there is no middle-class safety net of intergenerational aid or steadily-rising income.

It seems likely that these courtship effects are long-lasting for most people. A longitudinal study in Detroit found that differences in income and standard of living related to the timing of family formation (age at marriage, premarital pregnancy, and family spacing) could be detected twenty years afterwards (Freedman and Coombs 1966 a and b; Coombs et al 1969–70; and Pratt 1965). The material problems associated with young marriages are probably one of the major factors that lead so many of them to end in divorce; perhaps rather more than the 'personal immaturity' to which much attention has been directed.

This chapter has also provided empirical material relevant to the main theme of the book: the inter-relations of the sexes and generations. Again it is seen how the maintenance of kin ties depends on the work of the wives. Not only does the wife-mother take the brunt of the labour and cost of the children when young and when as young adults they live at home, but it is mainly she who continues to work for the new couple gratis or to maintain contact via letters or visits when they move to live some distance away. The return on this – the status from being a successful parent (and grandparent) and pleasure from the company of the young people (and grandchildren), together with the assurance of care in old age – accrues to both the husband and wife in the older couple, though perhaps rather more to the wife. (It is certainly more important to her since she has fewer other sources of prestige or companionship, and she is likely to live longer.)

The continuing difference between the social situation of men and women is again clear – in this chapter in regard to their relationship to the labour market after marriage, the domestic labour they are responsible for and which they actually do when both husband and wife are employed, and their rights to 'pocket-money' from the 'joint' income[19]. It is this theme of the difference of social situation of husband and wife which will be developed in the next, concluding chapter.

Notes

1. For further details see Rosser and Harris (1965:52-56) and Swansea Fabian Society (1969).

2. Rosser and Harris's survey (of persons not houses) showed that 48% of household heads in the town were owner-occupiers, 29% council tenants, and 23% other tenants, as compared with Donnison et al's national survey findings, which showed that in towns of over 20,000 inhabitants, 40% were owner-occupiers, 19% council tenants and 40% other tenants (quoted in Rosser and Harris 1965).

3. NB, however, that since large families contribute more people to the marriageable population than do small ones, the majority of people who marry come from families with 3 or more children, and a quarter from families with 5 or more. As might be expected, the last child to marry was more likely to be able to continue to live in the parents' home than was the first to marry, if for no reason other than that more space was available.

4. 22% of brides and grooms who were the last child in the family to marry continued to live in their parents' house after marriage as against 10% of brides and grooms who were the first child to marry.

   Taking all those cases (1st and 2nd marriages) where only one parent was left alive and the 'child' was the last in the family to marry (or an only child):

   – in the 6 cases where the daughter was the last to marry, in 5 cases she stayed (though in one case only for '5 months' till her new house was completed). The one exception was a girl who had kept house for her widowed father for years, all through her time at college. He had remarried, and subsequently separated, so he was technically not a widower but a divorcee.

   – in the 4 cases where the groom was the last to marry, in 2 cases he and his wife lived with his mother, one exception was where the groom was in the MN and they left for a 6 months trip; and in another case the couple simply chose not to live with his father (who did not have a council house) and rented a flat instead.

6. Recalculation of Rosser and Harris's 'Table 7:5' shows that 40% of those married between 1940 and 1960 started married life with the wife's parents, 22% with the husband's parents, 31% on their own, and 7% with other relatives, while in the Bethnal Green 'marriage sample', 33% lived with the wife's parents and 13% with the husband's parents – there is no information on the rest (Young and Willmott 1962:31).

5. *Figure 7 Type of household composition after marriage*

where living	Rosser and Harris Table 7:5 'immediately after marriage'				My sample, excluding those who left the town, when 'settled' after marriage	
	married 1914–39		married 1940–60		married 1968–69	
	MC*	WC*	MC*	WC*	husband's s.e.c. I II IIInm	IIIm IV V
	%	%	%	%	%	%
with husband's parents	11	12	20	22	22	17
with wife's parents	20	28	31	42	11	30
with other relative(s)	2	11	7	7	—	—
in own house or flat	67	49	42	29	67	53
N	119	511	118	502	9	36

* For Rosser and Harris's use of 'middle' and 'working class', which includes a measure of self-perception, see 1965: 99ff.

7. In other parts of Britain I have come across a scheme where the couple choose goods from the various departments in a large store (e.g., John Lewis's or a branch of Habitat) and the shop keeps a list of 'Miss Smith and Mr Brown's wedding presents'. Would-be donors go to the shop, see the list and choose and pay for an item. The shop sends all the presents to the bride, each with a card signed by the gift-giver.

   I picked up a booklet (*Brides Book*) in one large local store suggesting it would do this, but I never came across it being used, nor was there any indication of the service in the store.

8. Those going into married quarters in the forces rent houses furnished 'down to the last tea towel'. However, the husband who was in the army in Germany had to go on a waiting list for accommodation, and the husband in the navy was too young to qualify. Both couples, therefore, had to use privately rented accommodation in the towns near the bases.

9. This general process of giving a feast to accumulate capital (or labour) 'owed' by the guests for a particular purpose – be it building a house, harvesting a crop or mourning a relative – is worldwide. Cf., as examples, Firth 1943; Williams 1956; Bloch 1971.

10. Cf. the middle class of North London, who were clear that anyone who attended the wedding should give a present but were divided as to whether one was under an obligation if one *declined* the invitation (Firth, Hubert, and Forge 1970). In Swansea, however, people whom it was known would not be able or not keen to attend were less likely to be invited.

11. E.g., respondents in the national *New Housewife Survey* (BMRB 1967) gave this as *the* most common reason for delay.

12. She was not certain what she would do in the future, but she was certainly not choosing between children and 'a career', since she was not attached to her job (as a cashier) – rather, she said (defiantly) that she did not like small children.

13. The brides who did not look for new jobs were:
    - the bride who married a miner and moved only a few miles outside Swansea. She continued to work in Morriston;
    - one couple, where both were teachers, who had both managed to get their first jobs after training in the same area of the south west six months before the wedding;
    - the wife of a naval officer. She did not plan to have a permanent job in the near future.

    Burtenshaw (1973) reports on a study of the effects on wives of husbands' 'job relocation' (from London). Many could not find work, or had to accept lower salaries, lower status, and longer journeys to work.

14. Within a society divided by sex, a rigid division of labour can, of course, provide an autonomous sphere and be a form of 'protective legislation' for the weaker group. Consequently women may, rightly, value the cult of 'true womanhood' or 'domesticity'. See, for example, Papanek (1971) on *purdah* and the way in which it allows a full occupational stucture to women (e.g., as women's doctors) and a warm, caring women's community, and the excellent article by Faragher and Stansell (1975) on the overland trail in the US in the mid-nineteenth century.

    The latter offers an interesting parallel to the increasing involvement of married women in paid employment in Swansea. Faragher and Stansell argue that women tried hard to maintain their autonomous feminine sphere in the covered wagon, for it provided them with 'companionship, a sense of self-worth, and most important, (quasi) independence from men in a patriarchal world'. Life on the trail was too hard to allow 'the relegation of women to purely domestic tasks'. Yet the new work women had to do 'was performed in a male arena, and many women saw themselves as draftees rather than partners . . . They refused [or were not able?] to appropriate their new work to their own ends and advantages. In their deepest sense of themselves they remained estranged from their function as "able bodies".' Women in Swansea need to work for the family to have a comfortable standard of living. But their jobs are particularly boring, lacking in status and low paid as compared with those of men. The women 'remain estranged from their function' as wage earners.

15. Only one in five of personal accounts, and one in seven deposit accounts at Barclays are joint (Wilsher 1975).

The GSS survey on matrimonial property found that of couples with current bank accounts (53% of their total sample):

60% of couples had only individual accounts $\left\{\begin{array}{l}\text{36% only husband had account}\\ \text{6% only wife had account}\\ \text{18% husband and wife each had an account}\end{array}\right.$

40% of couples had joint accounts $\left\{\begin{array}{l}\text{33% only joint account(s)}\\ \text{7% joint and individual account(s).}\end{array}\right.$

(Todd and Jones 1972:14)

16. Thus, 'There seemed to be little attempt to adjust the allowances as family expenses increased, though in some cases certain outgoings were taken over by the husband as the children grew older, for example, major items of clothing for school children . . .' (Shaw 1954). The survey of *Women's Own* readers for the NCC found that, on average in 1975, in families with

no children, the wife was given housekeeping of £14.06 a week
1 child, the wife was given housekeeping of £16.70 a week
2 children, the wife was given housekeeping of £17.21 a week.

Thus much of the financial burden (budgetting, or earning herself, or foregoing her own expenditure) for extra children fell on the mother.

17. The way in which people are paid may affect their domestic financial arrangements: e.g. one woman said:
'We haven't got round to saving yet. We live week to week on his money and pay the bills out of mine as I'm paid monthly.'
another (case 44):
'We live off his money. He gives me his pay packet. Mine's all saved – as it's a salary it's paid straight into the bank.'

18. My data and those from other larger-scale studies show that socio-economic class and courtship behaviour are themselves related. Men in manual occupations start courting earlier than those in professional and managerial jobs; the brides of manual workers are more likely to be pregnant, and men in Categories IV and V are less likely to get engaged – though there seems little difference in the actual length of courtship by class. (See Barker 1977 Figures 4:16, 4:23, 5:30, and p. 205; Rowntree 1962; Pierce 1963; and Gorer 1971.)

19. Unfortunately I do not have information on ownership of property – i.e., in whose name the home is owned or the tenancy held. Todd and Jones (1972) found that it was either in the man's name or held jointly. It was very very rarely in the woman's name. Likewise the car.

8 Concluding comments

This book has described a study of marriage and family relations in a provincial town in South Wales at the end of the 1960s, concentrating on the erstwhile neglected life-cycle phases of adult children living at home, courtship, and setting up a new household. It has focused on the material relationships between the sexes and generations, using ceremonials as a 'window' through which to view 'opaque urban social processes.'

Some of the main points which have been stressed are, first, the extent to which courtship dominates young people's lives (especially girls' lives) after, and even before, leaving school, and how short the period as an unmarried and unattached wage earner has become – some three years for young women and four or five years for young men. Second, the importance of moral decorousness in achieving and maintaining status – how one should get engaged and married 'properly' with due deliberation and decorum, and what stigma is attached to premarital pregnancy, divorce, undue haste, poverty, or bad relations with parents, and to the associated 'second class' form of marriage in the register office. Third, the importance of courtship events in determining differences in standard of living attained at marriage, and their possible long-term consequences for prospects and life-styles. And fourth, how complex are the rituals comprising the ceremonial cycle of getting married, and how limited the explanations which the most actors can produce to explain why they are doing what they are doing (in contrast to the accounts given to anthropologists describing comparable activities in so-called undeveloped societies). In Britain there is merely a recourse to the nebulous concepts of 'luck' and 'tradition', and the sense of continuity between the passage rites of birth (christenings), marriage (weddings), and death (funerals).

More generally, what has been described shows strikingly how little the form of weddings varies by class: the weddings of the elite, as featured in *The Tatler*, differ only in detail and scale from the 'proper' weddings of the provincial lower middle and working class; and even the 'lower caste alliances' in the register office are but scaled down, *ad hoc* variants. Very, very few people set out to have a consciously different wedding format or to make an active gesture of alternative values, which suggests that, in regard to marriage at least, Britain is an extremely cohesive society, with shared values and aspirations across the social strata.

Throughout the long period of planning and organizing a wedding, the concern that the ritual be 'got right', and therefore be effective, is associated with a concern by the man and woman involved that the event be personal: each detail of each symbol used is selected with care so that their wedding is different and distinct from all others. Yet this very fact serves to deflect their and our attention from marriage as an institution. That is to say, our stress (as members of the culture and as sociologists) on marriage and divorce as the plurality of individual decisions, events, and couples distracts our attention from uniformities of behaviour; from the powerful external constraints within which the individual interprets his or her role, and how little questioning of, or awareness of alternatives to, the family exist. Yet one can clearly see, if one stands back and looks at the cycle as a whole, that the couple move from individuality of choice in courtship, through a process of generalization: from being John and Mary into being 'the groom' and 'the bride'. The initial stress on the personal characteristics which made them choose each other gets lost, swamped by the general characteristics of husbands and wives. This reaches its apogee in joking (at stag and hen parties, in the cards at the receptions, and in the rough-housing when the couple leave for their honeymoon) and the formal speeches at the reception. This cannot but affect each couple's sense of themselves and of each other.

A further point which emerged from the study was that most lower middle and working class young people live with their parents until they marry (and return on divorce until they remarry), which continues parental control and enables them to keep their children dependent in a variety of ways so that they hold on to the young adults and the new domestic group. This contrasts sharply with the upper middle-class ideal of young people attaining some measure of psychological, economic, and social independence before marriage, and relates to what it is that parents are seeking from their grown-up children and what means of continuing influence are available to them (broadly transfer of property and financial aid, or help in kind which requires that the couple live nearby).

Within the nuclear family household the elders now derive little or no direct economic advantage from the younger generation, except in family businesses or farms. Not only do young people not work for or pay over the bulk of their wages to their parents once they are earning good money, they may not even pay over enough to cover the costs of their keep – and they certainly do not increase their contribution to keep pace with inflation. While parents are relatively better off once their children start work because they do not have to meet the costs of teenage leisure spending and clothes, and because they may get a few pounds contributed to the housekeeping, young people exploit their parents, using the cheap housing, food, and domestic servicing they provide, while themselves doing no domestic work and enjoying a much higher expenditure on holidays, clothes, drink, entertainment, etc. than their parents are able to afford. This bears particularly heavily on the wife/mother.

Couples nowadays have children partly because if they are conceived within marriage it is nearly impossible in our culture to get rid of them (see MacIntyre 1976; Mathieu 1979), but mainly because children are desired as particularly valuable objects of consumption. They give status (including proof of sexual potency), the direct pleasure of their company, and a means of living vicariously. Fathers encourage their sons to realise the ambitions they themselves failed to achieve, while mothers – though in no way acting to prevent their daughters from reproducing their own life pattern of marriage and motherhood – encourage them to 'live a little' in the short period between leaving school and settling down, and they themselves 'live' again through the younger generation.

To continue to benefit from their children, parents try to control the occupations they enter and their courtship and to hold onto them at the time of potential schism when they set up a new household (see the suggestion in chapter 3 as to the importance of spoiling in this connection). They want to have their children's company, and to be near to their grandchildren (who are also sources of status and pleasure) and – though this is perhaps not uppermost in their minds at the time, unless they are already widowed – to ensure their own care and companionship in old age.

The material exchange between parents and children is indirect: between the generations that have gone before and those that come after. The care for the old and the young is provided by the mature (i.e., those from 20–50 years of age); but of course the bulk of the labour of caring for the young and the old is done by women – as wives, mothers, and daughters or (significantly) daughters-in-law. The husband/father/son provides some of the money to buy the raw materials on which his wife works when providing for the young, old, and infirm, but the evidence presented in chapters 3 and 7 suggests that the housekeeping allowance paid to the wife increases very little when the first child is born, and hardly at all with subsequent children; nor does it increase as the children grow up and cost more (indeed, the wife may herself go out to work specifically to meet the increased costs of teenage children – clothes, treats, school trips, etc). (Unfortunately I know of no information on changes, if any, in housekeeping allowances when an elderly person is taken into the household or is being given substantial care and attention.) The benefits from the wife's caring work accrues to her husband as much as to herself and is thus one means by which he appropriates her labour in marriage.

While it seems clear that relations between parents and children have undergone great changes in the past century – parents may now oppress their children in various ways but they rarely exploit their labour – the relationship between husband and wife, although not unchanged, is still essentially the same. In marriage the woman still pledges her labour for life (with limited, though now greater, rights to quit) and she is given/takes responsibility for routine, daily domestic work and the care of children, the sick, and the elderly. She provides sexual services and bears the man's children. In return she gets protection, guaranteed upkeep (though she will be expected to contribute to the household income by doing paid work herself when this is convenient), and nowadays certain rights to the children. It is a total relationship of personal dependency: the man acquires the women's labour, time, and baby, to be applied to whatever he needs, in so far as he can control/persuade her, and within certain legal and customarily defined parameters, in return for support and protection.

Marriage also involves an important shift in customary and legal relations between children and their parents. The next of kin (the one for whom one is responsible and on whom one depends) becomes the spouse. Parental authority is asserted less forcefully, and possession of an independent household allows for retreat and greater self-regulation. The state and its agents also regard having been married as an element in the attainment of adult status (e.g., a widow or widower who marries for a second time under the age of majority does not require parental consent; young women who behave criminally or 'promiscuously' who have been married will be dealt with, but not as 'in need of care and control' (see Smith 1975; Rush 1972)). However, this attainment of adulthood via marriage applies more to women than to men; and within marriage the woman is treated in a variety of ways as dependent on her husband (nowadays more in practice than in the letter of the law) and as under his authority and support.

It should be noted also that the equation of adulthood with marriage affects the evaluation of adolescent experience. Adolescence is see as *essentially* a phase, 'a mere passing moment in an individual's development'.

'The years taken up by adolescence apparently have no intrinsic worth: all that can be hoped for is that they will not inconvenience adults too much, or lead to the adolescent himself having a breakdown' [or doing something which will irrevocably prejudice his or her life-chances as an adult, e.g., failing examinations or getting pregnant].

'This adult emphasis on adolescent change and turmoil may not, however, be entirely accidental. It may subtly ensure that adults continue their very powerful control over the young. For to say, in effect, that adolescence has no real value implies that only the end product of the adolescent's development – adulthood, maturity – matters. The sole purpose of adolescence then becomes early entry into the final perfect state. Thus there is no incentive or opportunity to ask; but is this state so perfect? Sceptical responses to this are therefore muted, or by careful labelling ("irresponsible", "unrealistic", "immature") made unacceptable.' (Davies 1975:714–16)

This applies *a fortiori* to the search for the 'final perfect state' of stable monogamous, heterosexual partnership in marriage. Case 44 (groom): 'Like my brother – he's married; he's got his family; he's alright. My sister she's married; she's got her family; she's alright They [parents] just worried over me.'

The social pressures to marry – to become independent and adult; to be seen as normal, personally competent, attractive, and heterosexual; to be socially able to have sexual intercourse and children; to avoid loneliness and the jokes, advice, and gossip and criticism of the married – perhaps need little stressing. What is much less commented on is the economic pressure on women to marry if they wish to maintain (or improve on) the standard of living of their family of origin, given their disadvantaged labour market position. The values loudly asserted within the society (and within sociology) concerning the 'naturalness', goodness, fundamental importance and inevitably of the family, and of 'sex roles', and the related asertion that the family is now 'symmetrical or 'companionate', are ideological (in the pejorative sense of that word). They serve to distract attention from the economics of the family and to keep any change within domestic groupings and male-female relations 'off the political agenda' (see Bachrach and Baratz 1962, 1963; Lukes 1974). It is only the efforts of the women's and gay liberation movements, and to a lesser extent the radical psychologists and the Freudian Marxists (see Morgan 1975, chs. 4 and 6) which have produced any sort of sustained critical approach to the family and heterosexuality, and which have succeeded in putting in question the structured power within 'private', 'personal', and sexual relations.

For the rest, sociology, whether phenomenological or functionalist, has restricted itself to arguing at the level of the emotional relationship between husband and wife and their adjustment/means of coping with the tensions between 'the home' and 'the world'. In its most extreme form (e.g. Berger and Kellner's paper on 'Marriage and the Construction of Reality' (1964), reprinted at least four times, see Morgan n.d.), the 'spouses' are treated as interchangeable and marriage is seen as having the same 'meaning' for both – as being their principal nomos-creating institution. This totally ignores the work the two sexes do – the different ways in which they make their living – and the consequent disparity, and indeed antagonism, of their life-situations; and it has made it impossible to integrate the study of kinship or the family, or indeed women, children, and the old, into the study of the rest of society (which is taken to be *the whole of* society): the world of adult men.

If we recognise that the basis of marriage is a labour relationship, then the social pressures to marry, the devaluation of adolescent and/or transient courtship involvement, romanticism, and hostility to homosexuality are seen in a very different light – as social pressures towards this labour relationship; and Church and State control of marriage is seen as the judicial apparatus of a particular set of relations of production. The marriage ceremony thus emerges as having parallels with the signing of indentures, or even more with the selling of oneself into personal, domestic slavery when one can see no other way to support oneself adequately (see Derrick 1975). Marriage, however, differs from these other labour relations in being shrouded in talk of love, companionship and sharing, and of 'making a life together', so that the economic aspects of the agreement are more than usually occluded. It is therefore significant that the terms of the marriage contract are never spelled out[1].

To recognise that marriage is a labour relationship also throws new light on courtship and its very different meaning for men and women. Societies vary considerably in regard to who is primarily responsible for making the choice of spouse from within the field of eligibles. It may be held to be a matter for the individuals concerned (as in our present culture), but it is much more common for the responsibility to be vested in the parents or the wider kinship group to which they belong. Although one party makes the final decision, in all marriage systems the interests of the spouses, their families of origin, *and* their wider kin are taken into account to some extent, directly or indirectly, formally or informally. Thus where the (senior male of the) kin group makes the choice, parents are consulted and there is usually some means whereby, if the man or woman concerned finds the match obnoxious, and if all persuasion and threats fail, alternative arrangements can be made. In our society, conversely, where individual, unforced choice is the norm, parents and other kin have (limited) means of action to influence the decision (as outlined in chapter 4).

We often caricature the difference between *our* system of 'mate selection' and that of other cultures as the difference between a love match allowing individual freedom on the one hand, and a heartless exchange between groups on the other. However, like all marriage systems, ours involves bargaining and exchange. Depending on whether the kin group or the individual is making the choice, cultural emphasis will be placed on alliances and property or on the attractiveness of the spouse, but in all cases a whole series of factors (compatibility of social, economic, racial or religious status, kinship status, personal attractiveness, the possession of appropriate skills, norms or values, or the existence of love) will be considered. Contemporary Western society is peculiar in the stress we place on the personal compatibility of the spouses, assessed not by the 'objective' evaluation of others, but in terms of the subjective feelings of the spouses. That is to say, 'love' is the major means of legitimizing the choice of a spouse in our 'open'[2] and 'individual' marriage system; whereas, as Goode points out (1959), anthropologists rarely need to mention the word when discussing the arranging of a marriage – though love may be expected to develop after marriage.

Love is also important, along with romance, as the means by which women in our society resolve the contradiction between being sexually desirous but not sexually experienced. They sublimate their sexual feelings into a 'courtly love' mould (see Willis 1977:45), and thereby also ignore the passive, dominated role they must occupy in heterosexual courtship. And for both sexes, the near inevitability of entry into the labour contract of marriage is obscured by the process being seen as one of choice, attainment, love, sexual excitement, and individual development.

While both men and women in our culture want to be 'in love': to experience the 'violent emotional attachments between persons of opposite [sic] sex . . . [the] psychological abnormality to which our own culture has attached an extraordinary value' (Linton 1936), are jealous of those in that state (see Barker 1972a), and justify their alliances on this basis, almost everybody uses the language of bargaining when talking about everybody *else's* choice of spouse. Thus the rich man of sixty married to a girl of twenty will say they married for love: others will suggest alternative explanations. When a mother and daughter discuss whether a particular man is the 'right' one for a particular girl, the girl may be thinking entirely in terms of romantic love and 'Mr Right'; her mother is more likely to be wondering if he is 'good enough for her'. Even young people 'in love' are aware that for love to last and a marriage to be stable it must be based on (what are seen as) more fundamental compatibilities.

Courtship is thus a structurally important institution in those marriage systems that do not prescribe who one should marry (i.e., are 'open') and that vest much of the right of choice in the individual. Where legitimation in terms of love is also operative, courtship as a process acquires a new dimension, for not only is it a means of negotiation between the parties, it also constitutes the arena within which the necessary subjective feelings can develop (Bolton 1961; Reiss 1960). It is significantly the only period of life when the sexes spend most of their time together in Britain.

Our apparent freedom of choice as to whom we shall (fall in love with and) marry (anyone of the opposite sex who is over sixteen, not already married, and not a close relative) is in fact limited in at least three ways. First, we can only marry people we meet – and who we meet is far from random. Second, the individuals concerned narrow the field of potential mates they meet by eliminating those who do not share the same social situation, values, and attitudes (which generally means those from a different background). (Such limitation is, of course, necessary, since in our society spouses are expected to co-operate intimately and the sharing of common background and associated values, especially those concerned with the family, is a necessary condition of a minimally satisfactory relationship as culturally defined.) Third, although the amount of pressure that parents and kin can exert is limited, they are expected to take an interest in their children's choice of spouse and would be thought to be failing in their duty should they stand idly by and allow their child to make the 'wrong' decision. While their power *at the time when the choice is made* is small, their influence beforehand, in the inculcation of values and expectations, in precept and example, and in choice of neighbourhood, schooling, vetting friends, etc. can be extensive (especially in the upper and upper middle classes). Even when an engagement has been announced, they may threaten, cajole, wheedle, and bribe to persuade the couple to change their minds – though they must tread carefully lest their pressure provoke escape or rebellion.

While the freedom of both men and women to choose a spouse is limited by who they meet, who they consider suitable, and pressures from kin and peers, women's choice of a husband/'employer' is further hamstrung by their enforced passivity: they may not take the initiative in courtship. On the other hand, they need a courting relationship more and at an earlier age than do men – because of the restrictions on their physical mobility when unescorted, the (related) break-up of the girls' peer group once they stop meeting (at school) each day, their lower earnings, and because a stable relationship is the only locus for any sexual activity for girls (otherwise they risk being labelled as 'slags' or 'knockers'). They are therefore impelled to accept courting relationships and even marriage with men to whom they are (initially at least) less than totally attracted (this difference by sex is specifically commented on, though not explained, by Gorer 1955 and Slater and Woodside 1951), and they are inclined to hang on to an existing relationship (which puts them into a disadvantageous bargaining position within it).

The differentiation of power of men and women is located in such courtship and marriage rituals as his being the one to ask for dates (times and places at his convenience); his paying for her; his having the car and seeing her home; her having to be in at set times and not going out 'too often'; his asking her to marry him; his asking her father's permission to marry her; his placing an engagement and wedding ring on her finger as symbolizing *their* relationship; her never removing her wedding ring (except in the event of divorce); her starting (or keeping) the bottom drawer of household goods, and thanking people for gifts given to them as a couple; her wearing a costume indicating a transitional marital status while he wears one indicating his social class (cum transitional marital status – since men do not often wear morning suits); and his being handed the magazine of nude women when going on honeymoon, and being solicited as to his sexual activity on their return.

Since costume and the bride's person is of such significance in the wedding ceremonial itself, it is noteworthy that when I started to make return visits after the wedding I gradually became aware that I often did not at once recognise the young women I had previously interviewed. In particular, many of them cut their long hair and changed its colour (usually blond to darker)[3]. Others wore less makeup, or had put on weight, or changed their style of dress. I saw less of the grooms so I cannot say definitely if they showed a comparable change, but I think not. In any event, whilst people sometimes say of a man that 'he *looks* married' (when he looks content, self-satisfied, or harassed!), the change in women's appearance is remarked more often and more specifically[4]. Other commentators have suggested that it is the strain of child-rearing which has this effect on women's appearance: 'In three years, one can see a prancing stylish 17 year old turn into a pale, sluttish irritable woman who might be ten years older. It is as if all the energy and high spirits (not to mention the elegant clothes) had been drained off for the toddler and the pram baby.' (Loughton 1969:386) But my informants were only 1–5 months married and not 'pale, sluttish and irritable' – just less attractive than before. Whilst many of the changes were doubtless due to having less money which they felt free to spend on themselves (it being seen as a diversion away from *joint* spending) and less time because of the 'dual load' of a job and housework[5], the changes in their appearance are normative as well as due to circumstance. They are no longer nubile and become private not public persons.

At the beginning of the book, two contrasting views were put forward:

- that people do not take the white wedding symbolism seriously and that it is an outdated charade;
- that, as a ritual, weddings reveal the deepest values of the group/ society about marriage.

To a certain extent it could be argued that these two attitudes are not antithetical. The more or less abstract values (kin groupings, community, and family unity; maleness and femaleness; luck, etc.) which wedding arrangements and symbols express may not be upheld by particular individuals, and for them the ceremonial may be empty: a charade. I certainly know of people who have gone through a particular form of marriage to please others, or under pressure so as not to offend their parents; holding themselves aloof and declaring (to another audience) that 'it is all a load of nonsense'. Further, due to their ambiguity, the same symbol can mean different things to different groups, or different things to the same group at different times, so that the bride, the groom, their relatives, and the world at large may produce different interpretations for their decision to conform to 'proper behaviour' at the particular time. (For instance, I suggested that men get engaged for respectability and to have a tag on their woman, while women see engagement as evidence of the man's seriousness and evidence that they can stop looking around for a possible spouse.) But this is not at all the same thing as saying that there is not some general agreement about the meaning of particular rituals and symbols, nor that rituals do not express 'real' societal values or the views of the majority. I suspect that most people would be surprised that Mary Stott protests when 'intelligent women' agree to a ceremony involving virginal white, a wedding ring, and a change of name for the woman, since for them marriage *does* entail submission for the woman. Liberal intellectuals are resorting to wishful thinking on the basis of their own individual rejection of some or all of these values – and the location as dominators or dominated in which they find themselves – if they try to pretend that what the rituals say no longer holds for the majority most of the time, or for themselves some of the time.

They are equally deluded if they are contemptuous of the rituals themselves, in the sense of regarding them as unimportant, for symbols are, literally, effective. Social dramas 'try to effect a transformation in the psyches of the participants, conditioning their attitudes and sentiments, repetitively renewing beliefs, values and norms and thereby creating and recreating the basic categorical imperatives on which the group depends for its existence' (Cohen 1974:132). Participation in rituals and the use of symbols may cause people to feel particular sentiments, to accept norms and concepts, and to objectify and confirm certain social roles. The ceremonial seeks to conjure belief; focusing attention on a symbol causes a value to be accepted, or held more strongly; and acting out a role makes it real and important. People may marry in church because it is the done thing and pressures are put on them to conform, or because it is an opportunity for conspicuous consumption, but in the process of participating in the rituals they will be pushed to accept a view of marriage that is conformist and traditional.

Of course, this should not be taken simplistically: the trip down the aisle is not for a conforming, 'liberated' man or woman the equivalent of the road to Damascus and, for example, a man who holds the view that both sexes should be sexually experienced before marriage is not going to be converted to the dual standard by the sight of a, or even his, bride in white. But, more generally, the realization that one is prepared to go through with the sort of wedding decreed by one's spouse, parents, local community, Church, and State makes one recognize the continuing strength of their authority.

To devote one's energies to the detailed and lengthy preparation needed for a proper wedding is likely to lead to changes in self-evaluation. Once engaged (and even more, once married) the man and woman are treated as a couple (even if they stress they are only doing it to please their parents or for convenience). It is repeatedly stressed that their primary commitment is now to each other rather than to their families. Their sexuality is contained, since a courtship relationship with anyone else is rigidly precluded. And if they were not already, they start to be treated according to the differentiated sex-typed roles of husband and wife: she to care for domestic matters, he to represent the couple and to be their financial support. The very scale of the wedding stresses that they are taking a big step, making a big change, 'taking on the responsibilities of marriage'. They face concerted pressure to build up property (which makes it hard – before and after marriage – to quit) and 'to settle down'. The rituals and assumptions as to behaviour change people, even if the individuals fight against the values expressed in the rituals. Most, of course, do not: the rituals affirm values to which they subscribe.

What, then, are the main societal values which are being expressed – the 'categorical imperatives' of the society as a whole, and the State and the Church specifically, on marriage and parenthood? As institutions in our society these are both treated as inevitable (because 'natural') and good. But, further, they are accorded a transcendental nature, a sacramental element – thus we talk of 'the sanctity of the family' and of marriage. Forming a new family unit, i.e., getting married, is very different from making other forms of contract. A major, mystical union is effected. The experience is dramatized with magic, myth, and religion, rather than rationally considered and effected. Stress is laid on expressive and symbolic actions rather than legally prescribed technical aspects. Indeed, this 'siding with the poets rather than the scientists' (Beattie 1970) is exemplified in the duality of the system of weddings. In the register office one can get a licence, but it is in the church wedding, with its access to the power of God and with the paraphernalia that bring luck, that one can get a binding, life-long, holy union. The building and the officiant are sacred; the Church as a whole is the custodian of established, morally right behaviour; and the ceremony is dramatic, expressive, and impressive.

The second main value expressed is certainly that concerning the relationship between husband and wife. The emancipation of married women has advanced considerably in the last hundred years, but they still do not have the same customary or legal rights as married men. (The *Sex Discrimination Act* 1975, for instance, specifically excludes all family law and social security provisions.) Within individual marriages the wife may contribute considerable personal strength – but no woman is happy to have a husband who is seen to be and spoken of as 'weaker' than she is (Stiehm 1976; Whitehead 1976). It is possible that wives now show less deferential behaviour than in the past – are less inclined to stay silent, to show respect, or to serve and service their husbands – though we have very little *observation-based* information on this, as opposed to replies to questionnaires, or opinions off the top of 'experts' ' heads. Nor do we know if or how husband-wife interaction varies with the wife's degree of dependence; i.e., whether a wife in a well-paid job is, on average , less deferential than one who has been out of the labour market (hence deskilled) for some years and who has several small children.

It is probably true that the general values of the society are less supportive of overt male dominance than in the past (and this is reflected in the wedding ritual – note the changes in the Anglican revised service on p. 215), and that various aspects of the legal system of marriage have been changed to even out the rights of the two spouses. However, to say that the legal, economic, and social position of women has changed is not to say that the sexes are now equal, nor that marital roles are now 'symmetrical', 'joint', 'complementary', or whatever, if this implies equity, let alone similarity. Indeed the ideological stress (generally, and particularly within the sociology of the family) on equality between the sexes *having been attained* is a bromide. Women's position in the labour market has changed little, so marriage remains economically necessary for them. And within marriage, though the division of *tasks* is less rigid (husbands may push a pram or do the washing up), the division of *responsibility* is as before (they do it to help their wives; and wives who go out to work do so because they 'choose to', and they have to make such arrangements as necessary to accomodate to it). A wife, while not a 'human door-mat', *is*

still expected to mould her life round her husband's: to go and live where it suits him, to keep to his timetable and style of life, to care for their children and elderly parents, and to provide him with unpaid sexual and domestic services. The essence of the labour relationship of marriage is unchanged, and the ceremonial associated with courtship and wedding affirms this[6].

Notes

1. 'The marriage contract is unlike most contracts: its provisions are unwritten, its penalties are unspecified, and the terms of the contract are typically unknown to the "contracting" parties. Prospective spouses are neither informed of the terms of the contract nor are they allowed any options about these terms. In fact, one wonders how many men and women would agree to the marriage contract if they were given the opportunity to read it and to consider the rights and obligations to which they were committing themselves'. (Weitzman 1974:1170, footnotes omitted)
   See also Barker 1978b.
2. The wide range of marriage systems described by ethnographers have been seen to lie along a continuum from 'open' – where with the exception of

people held to be closely related any individual may choose any mature, unmarried person of the opposite sex as a spouse – to 'closed' – in which rules couched (usually) in kinship terms specify within which group in the society an individual must seek a partner.

3. Variations in the colour, length, and styling of hair have been used to indicate age, sex and social (including marital) status in a great many cultures (see Leach 1958; Hallpike 1969; Ebling 1969; and Firth 1973). 'Traditionally in the West a woman's long hair has been an ultimate token of her femininity' (Firth 1973:267), her 'crowning glory', and a sexual device by which men are attracted and disarmed (cf. folk tales of sirens, or Rapunzel). Mature women used to put their hair 'up' when they entered society (at 17) and let it down only in the privacy of their own homes (or bedroom). Today the variety of forms of hair treatment and of fashion make social differences less clear cut (between women – though cf. men in military service), but long, loose, especially blond hair continues to have connotations of uncontrolledness and sexuality (e.g., young girls or whores). The fact that they have such choice of colour and style makes my informants' uniformity of decision to cut and darken their hair all the more significant.

4. For example, it was brought up by the secretaries in the University and one (unmarried) woman said:

'Yes, they go from being "mod" and "with it" to being dowdy and plain. One friend in particular, her mother said she'd change now that she's married. Be more sensible. She was mod at the time, but she didn't shorten her skirts, so she got . . . well, more elegant. Not dowdy, but not . . . Her husband's still mod; you'd think he'd expect if of her as well. I was shocked. I hadn't seen her for ages and I thought she would be mod . . . '
(Do you think she doesn't have as much money? Is that why?)
'Oh no, I should think she could afford it. Her husband's got a good job. She has lots *of* clothes.
Another friend with long hair had it cut short because she's married. That's illogical. To my mind it's not a thing that comes over you over night, is it?
They look . . . *responsible* . . . Yes, they actually look older. I suppose it's that they don't want to look frivolous anymore. "Sensible" is the only word.
If you see someone with skirts just above the knee [at a time when skirts barely covered buttocks], it puts you in a different class. You know . . . I asked her why her skirts weren't short, and she said "I can't, I'm married now". She doesn't wear clumpy shoes either – possibly because of the length of her skirt – it would look really horrible then. But she still wears false eyelashes – even now she's got a child! I thought that would be the first thing to go by the board. I wouldn't have time to put them on!'

My neighbour's daughter (aged seventeen) spent hours (literally) in front of the mirror before venturing out of the house, with her mother alternatively exasperated and saying, 'Never mind, in a few years she'll be lucky to have time to drag a comb through her hair!'. Women when married expressed mild regret about their changed appearance. For instance, one young wife discussed with me how much weight she had put on since she married. Case 5:

> 'I used to be 7 stone 10, and now I'm 9 stone!' Her hair was still long but pulled back. 'I've no time now. I used to have new nail varnish on every week; now it's only every other. I've no time to do my hair. My weight worries me – obviously shows married life suits me!'

5. Some of the time which had previously been the women's own was now controlled – e.g., by a husband who would not let his wife wear curlers in bed.

6. This must not be taken to imply that symbols are mere reflections of the socio-political order. Rather that the symbolic system has some autonomy and its own viability, though there is a close, continual, and dialectical relationship between it and other relationships in society.

Appendix : Methodology

This study began with the general aim of looking at marriage as an institution via a study of the passage rite of wedding. The choice is telling. This was a subject which it was suggested, and which I myself felt, would be of interest to me as a recently married woman, and one where it was anticipated I should be able easily to establish rapport with the main performer. Thus the 'main' performer was presumed to be the bride and not the groom or either set of parents, and ease of rapport was thought to lie in being age and sex peers.

An important feature of the choice of topic and approach was that people I spoke to found it acceptable that I should be 'writing a book on weddings', which was how I introduced myself. A man doing such a thing would have been seen as effeminate and odd. Comments were even made spontaneously (usually by men) that they could see why 'they' needed to get a woman to do this job, because a man 'would look pretty silly sitting and asking questions about wedding dresses and looking at photos'. When the groom was present he took an active part in the conversation, and men were as likely as women to say they were enjoying or had enjoyed discussing their courtship and marriage; but while men are interested in their *own* wedding, they are not (culturally defined as) interested in weddings in general; women are.

Informants were often dubious about being interviewed on a subject such as courtship, which is concerned with personal feelings and sexual behaviour. They declared themselves hostile to 'nosey parkers' who asked about the minutiae of everyday (especially family) life. But they seemed to think it reasonable and useful to investigate 'important events' and they were generally happy to describe their own ritual behaviour and their attitudes towards this and what they took to be the attitude of their kin and friends, and to describe and comment on the behaviour of their peers. Overall I think that studying a social drama did indeed prove to be a successful means of observing marriage and the family.

At the level of description it is an advantage to be of the culture one is studying: one has few problems of language and can understand nuances which would be lost on an outsider. One also has a rough outline of some of the likely points of interest in the field of study before starting. On the other hand, analysis is in some ways more difficult than of an alien system, for one must try to note one's implicit assumptions and to describe as to an outsider, while overcoming the depressing conviction that one is stating the obvious. And the obverse of understanding nuances, etc., is that one is aware of – indeed anticipates – embarrassments; and one is not excused, as a foreigner might be, the asking of naive, impertinent, or prying questions. These two constraints can be combined when one is interviewing in people's homes, where one feels that one is, in some ways, a guest.

Whilst not a 'foreigner', I did have 'outsider' status in Swansea: my accent, not to say my eccentric behaviour, at once revealed I was not local. But since I lived in the town and my informants might know and be known to some of my neighbours, and since my informants' names were known to me, I think at times they kept their counsel in case I might gossip (in contrast to the anonymity of street interviews). On the other hand, being able to place me sometimes acted in my favour. Case 45:

> One young woman, who was unenthusiastic when I first called round, saying she 'supposed she could spare me half an hour' the next night, checked out on me (one of the girls in her office was married to a student at the university who knew my husband and knew of me) and she then became very friendly and helpful and not only answered all my questions, but invited me to her hen party and reception.

When planning fieldwork, some sort of balance has to be struck between how many people can be seen and how much information can be collected from each, particularly if one wants to combine people's accounts with observation of what they actually do in various situations. I was certainly not willing to sacrifice the understanding which comes from the researcher conducting his/her own interviews and observation, even had it been financially possible to employ assistants. Interviews are negotiations between the two sides and the virtues and the limitations of this need to be recognised.

A good case can obviously be made for the intensive study of a few cases rather than a survey of a large number in exploratory studies (and the paucity of research in the area of courtship in Britain has been detailed in chapter 1). Elizabeth Bott's study of twenty 'ordinary urban families' is repeatedly produced as validation for such an approach (Bott 1957). However, despite the importance of her *Family and Social Network* for the sociology of the family in Britain, it has drawbacks which I wanted to avoid: in particular I wanted to situate my findings. Too often the actors 'on stage' have been studied while the questions of how the scene was set and the script written and amended, and the theatre as a whole organized, have been ignored. That is to say, families have been treated as givens and as closed systems, or (as in Bott's case) as units interacting with local communities, whereas I wished to explore critically the relationship between the *institution* of the family (which Bott ignores[1]), the local *and* the wider society. To do this requires specification of the particular characteristics of location and period (cf. Bott's informants and their networks which are merely 'in London' at no particular moment in time) and ensuring as far as possible that informants are typical. I was anxious to meet as many couples (and their families) as was commensurate with collecting the amount of information I thought was essential, and to ensure that the sample was drawn as haphazardly as possible.

Relatively few people are prepared to co-operate for the very long periods needed to gather what anthropologists would regard as 'full information' – an average of thirteen home interviews and three clinical interviews in Bott's study, spread over months or even years; an average of eleven hours in the Highgate sample of Firth, Hubert, and Forge (1970)[2]. Who *will* co-operate is not random. Thus Bott's sample of twenty families includes no unskilled manual workers' families, and only two semi-skilled and two skilled manual workers, but five clerical, supervisory, and other higher grade non-manual, two managerial and executive, and three professional and high administrative workers' families. Long, repeated visits, focused on verbal interchange and abstract description, fit the pattern of visiting and form of self-expression of the middle rather than the working classes (cf. Marie Corbin's account of interviewing for the Pahls' *Managers and their Wives* 1972: Appendix 3; and Bernstein 1971).

The compromise I planned to adopt was to contact about fifty couples, in as unbiased a way as possible, and to collect a certain minimum amount of information from each, but looking for the possibility of getting additional information wherever I could. I aimed to interview the couple before they were married so as to get invited to attend the ceremonials, where I could observe and participate, to ask them to keep records (of costs, guests, etc.), and to call round again a few months later to discuss how the wedding went and see their new housing situation. (It also formed a check on pregnancy, though I did not originally think of this.) Extra information and a different perspective could be gained by talks with the bride and groom separately and with both sets of parents. To collect as much basic information as possible in a short time, I planned to use a semi-structured interview based on a schedule.

I knew I would also be living in the town and able to talk about familial values and behaviour with my neighbours and friends. In the event, I lived in Swansea for four years: the first year on a new, barren, rented-housing estate in Killay, and the next three years in a small, owner-occupied terraced house in Brynmill. I became involved in various weddings in this way, just as have other community studiers (Kerr 1958; Young and Willmott 1962) and I was told about quarrels related to courtship and between parents and grown children, as well as observing more everyday amicable relationships, and occasional bickering. In the course of everyday life and when doing interviews, I met and talked to journalists on the local paper, jewellers, photographers, dress shop owners, bakers, car hirers and drivers, caterers, estate agents, and a probation officer – and of course the clergy. I went to the marriage preparation classes held in St Marys.

(1) Getting a sample

I used kinship and friendship networks to find couples for two pilot samples, but since I attached importance to getting a haphazard, representative sample, I planned to get names of couples from Anglican vicars and from the advance notices given to the local superintendent registrar for the main sample. I anticipated no problems, but in fact encountered civil service paternalism run wild, which caused very considerable delay.

From the start I assumed that drawing a sample from those whose engagements and weddings appeared in the local paper would give a very partial sample. Indeed, as I found out (see chapter 5), only those who are getting married for the first time get engaged (so such a sample would exclude all second marriages); only 80 per cent of those getting married for the first time get engaged; and only 60 per cent of those who get engaged put an announcement in the paper (i.e., less than half of my total sample)[3]. In addition, since engagements are very varied in length, if one took all those who put an announcement in the paper on one day, some might be marrying in a few months, some in a few years' time.

In order to understand how I finally drew my sample it is necessary to have an outline of the plethora of documents relating to the registration of marriage in England and Wales: the notices, banns, notice books, registers, indexes, etc. and to be clear that, for historical reasons (see chapter 1), the procedure in the Anglican Church (the Established Church – albeit now disestablished in Wales[4]) differs from that for other churches and the register office.

All marriages in England and Wales must take place either in the register office or in a church (Anglican or an Authorized Place of Worship registered to perform weddings). There is not a universal compulsory civil ceremony followed (in some cases) by a religious ceremony – as in France, nor can weddings take place in, e.g., private houses – as in the USA.

When a couple approach an Anglican clergyman saying they wish to get married in his church, he takes down their particulars in his banns book. If one of the couple lives in another parish, he or she will be told to give notice to the vicar of his or her parish as well. Notice of the forthcoming marriage (banns) is read in the parish church(es) of the couple for three weeks during Sunday morning service. In a few cases (about 5 per cent) banns are not read and instead a licence is obtained from the bishop of the diocese. This allows a marriage to take place more swiftly and with less publicity[5].

Notice of marriages in all other churches – in which term I include Roman Catholic churches, Nonconformist chapels, synagogues, ecclesia, gospel halls, etc. – and in the register office, is given to the superintendent registrar of the district(s) in which the couple live and he writes the details down in his notice book[6]. When the marriage is to be by his certificate, he 'must display the notice or an exact copy of it in a conspicuous place in his office for twenty-one successive days' (*Marriage Act 1949*); usually in a glass-fronted case on the wall of the waiting room. When the marriage is to be by his certificate with licence (39 per cent of all marriages passing through the register office – 13 per cent of those in non-Anglican churches and 50 per cent of those in register office itself [7]), notice need only be given in one district even if the couple live in different districts, the notice is not displayed (though the 'marriage notice book shall be open for inspection free of charge at all reasonable hours'), and the marriage can take place after one clear day.

After the conclusion of the religious or civil ceremony the marriage is registered by the Anglican clergyman, an authorized person from the church or chapel, a registrar, or the secretary of the Society of Friends or synagogue. All such persons are supplied with special Marriage Register Books by the Registrar General and given minute instructions on keeping records and making returns (down to the type of ink to use and the chest to keep the books in) (General Register Office, n.d.). All except the registrars fill in the particulars for each marriage in two separate marriage register books.

Every quarter (January, April, July, and October) those in charge of registering marriages make exact copies of the entries in their register books during the preceding three months (on forms supplied by the R.G.) and they send the copies to the local superintendent registrar. He checks through these certified copies, makes an index of them (names and date) and then sends on the copies to the General Register Office in London, where they are kept 'in such order and such manner as the Registrar General under the direction of the Minister of Health may think fit so that they may be readily seen and examined' (*Marriage Act*, 1949, section 58:2). While the G.R.O. has a complete collection of copies of marriage certificates, the local superintendent registrar has details of only the marriages recorded in the registers of his registrars (and his index) until such time as a pair of marriage register books in a church is full. Then one copy is delivered to the register office[8] and the other copy is kept by the incumbent or authorities of the building.

The *Marriage Act* of 1949 specifies that marriage register books and the indexes at the local and General register offices are open to inspection and that certified copies of entries can be obtained on payment of a set fee.

A few months after starting this research I tried to collect local statistics relating to marriage for background information – e.g., on the numbers of people getting married in various districts and churchs in the town, their age at marriage, their social and economic status and that of their parents, and their places of residence (to get an estimate of locality homogamy). (The Registrar General's annual statistics do not give information for anything below the County Borough level – and rarely for this, generally the figures are e.g., for 'Wales I' or 'Glamorgan' – nor does he give appropriate cross tabulations.) I then discovered that, despite the wording of the *Marriage Act* quoted above, which I had taken to give clear indication that marriage records were public and accessible, I was not automatically going to be allowed to see the marriage registers held by the local superintendent registrar, nor those at the G.R.O., nor to see the superintendent registrar's notice book – nor even to take down information about forthcoming marriages from the 'conspicuously placed' notice case. This last was a major setback since I had relied on using these notices as the source of marriages taking place in the register office and non-Anglican churches.

Between December 1967 and the late summer of 1968 I sought access from the G.R.O. to notices of forthcoming marriages (see Barker 1977, Appendix 1:3); but not until November 1968 were matters finally settled, and then I was allowed limited access only to records of *past* marriages in the registrars' marriage register books, but not to any information on forthcoming marriages.

In any case, by late summer 1968 I had decided I could delay no further and I started fieldwork on the presumption that I would have to restrict myself to weddings in church. I began to contact Anglican vicars and priests and ministers of other denominations. I still had no figures on the frequency of weddings in different churches, (which the G.R.O. had promised me in May), but I thought that four out of the twenty-one Anglican parishes would suffice. On the basis of Rosser and Harris's findings (survey based on a 2 per cent sample of the electoral register of Swansea in 1960), and after talking with a colleague who was an active Anglican, I chose Morriston, St Mary's (town centre), St Thomas's, and Oystermouth parishes as being distinctive on two of the major variables of their study (Rosser and Harris 1965) – i.e., social class and proportion of Welsh speakers (hence active church-goers and Nonconformists), and as having obliging incumbents.

I wrote to the vicars of these parishes and all agreed to see me (after the second letter in one case). In two cases where the churches in the parish were run with considerable autonomy, I also had to contact curates. I called on the vicars and curates in October and November 1968, and they gave me details of the weddings booked in their churches between then and the following summer (in one case after some persuasion). Their general experience was that people booked weddings up to fifteen months ahead, usually 6–12 months ahead, though some were arranged at 1–2 months notice, generally because of pregnancy. To prevent a bias against such weddings, I wrote to the vicars again in January to see if they had had any extra weddings and was sent information concerning eight out of the eleven churches. Whether or not the vicars and curates censored the lists they gave me, I do not know; I think probably not, except once to exclude an elderly couple, both widowed. I also asked the vicars to indicate on a map of Swansea the geographical limits of their parishes[9].

I then drew up a list of other Certified Places of Worship Registered for Marriages located within the four parishes[10]. The list was out of date and addresses were sometimes vague, but there were clearly about sixty different buildings. To reduce this to rather more manageable proportions, knowing that 90 per cent of non-Anglican religious ceremonies in Glamorgan are conducted by Roman Catholics, Baptists, Congregationalists, Methodists, and Presbyterians (R.G. for 1967, Vol. II), I decided to leave 'other denominations' (i.e., Jehovah's Witnesses, Brethren, Spiritualists, Pentecostalists, Jews, et al.) out of my sampling frame. The chances of a wedding occurring in such a church during the following six months was slight[11], and I found I had actually to go and see each priest, minister, etc. to get the information I wanted, which was arduous. I did, however, meet and talk about weddings with religious leaders or members of all these small denominations during the following summer (1969).

I wrote to the priests of the four Roman Catholic and the ministers of the thirty-nine Nonconformist churches located in the Anglican parishes[12] and paid visits to the men (and one woman) responsible for twenty-nine churches between late October and early December 1968[13]. Although these contacts with priests and ministers were originally only the means to the end of getting names of couples who had

Figure 1 Examples of marriage certificates
Source: G.R.O. (n.d.) Appendix E:30–31. Reprinted by permission of H.M.S.O.

EXAMPLES SHOWING HOW MARRIAGES, SOLEMNIZED BY CLERGYMEN OF THE CHURCH OF ENGLAND, SHOULD BE REGISTERED—*continued*

Example 2.—Marriage after banns

1947. MARRIAGE solemnized at *the Parish Church*, in the *Parish of St. Martin, Dorking*, in the *County of Surrey*.

Col.	1.	2.	3.	4.	5.	6.	7.	8.
No.	When Married	Name and Surname	Age	Condition	Rank or Profession	Residence at the time of marriage	Father's Name and Surname	Rank or Profession of Father
32	*Seventeenth January, 1947*	*Henry Harker*	*37 years*	*Widower*	*Bank Clerk*	*6, Epsom Road, Croydon*	*Charles Harker (deceased)*	*Timber Merchant*
		Patricia Dawson	*29 years*	*Widow*	—	*Holmwood, Dorking*	*James Martin*	*Farmer*

Married in the *Parish Church*, according to the Rites and Ceremonies of the *Church of England*, $\overline{\text{by}}$ $\overline{\text{m.}}$ after Banns,

This Marriage was solemnized between us, { *Henry Harker* *Pat. Dawson* } in the Presence of us, { *W. J. Thompson* *Robert Martin* }

by me,
MONTAGU CURTIS Vicar.

APPENDIX E—*continued*

EXAMPLES SHOWING HOW MARRIAGES, SOLEMNIZED BY CLERGYMEN OF THE CHURCH OF ENGLAND, SHOULD BE REGISTERED—*continued*

Example 3.—Marriage on production of superintendent registrar's certificate. [The bridegroom is of illegitimate birth and the name and rank of his father are not given.]

1947.   MARRIAGE solemnized at the *Parish Church*, in the *Parish of St. Nicholas, Liverpool*, in the *County Borough of Liverpool*.

Col.	1.	2.	3.	4.	5.	6.	7.	8.
No.	When Married	Name and Surname	Age	Condition	Rank or Profession	Residence at the time of Marriage	Father's Name and Surname	Rank or Profession of Father
85	*Twelfth February, 1947*	*Richard Wilson*	*28 years*	*Bachelor*	*Ship's Steward*	*32, Clayton Street, Liverpool*	—	—
		Emma Murray	*25 years*	*Spinster*	*Dress Maker*	*96, Vauxhall Road, Liverpool*	*Patrick Murray*	*Railway Guard*

Married in the *St. Nicholas Church*, according to the Rites and Ceremonies of the Church of England, उँ after by me,   *WILLIAM CRANFIELD Curate.* on Superintendent Registrar's Certificate, by

This Marriage was solemnized between us,	{ *Richard Wilson*	in the Presence of us,	{ **X** *The Mark of Edward Jackson*
	Emma Murray		*Caroline Murray*

booked weddings, I became interested in them for themselves. I asked systematically about the relationships of couples with the church in which they married (and this and other material was compared with what the couples gave as their view of the role of the clergy), the minister's role in marriage preparation, whether or not they attended wedding receptions, denominational differences in wedding ceremonies, and their views on marriage. Not all the material collected can be included in the present account.

The yield of forthcoming weddings from all this work was poor and patchy. I did not get to see some ministers until November or even December because all interviews had to be in the mornings (in the afternoons the clergy are involved with visiting, and in the evenings with societies or services). Many seemed to enjoy talking about their work in a way which may rarely be possible for them and so conversations were long and it was seldom possible to fit in more than one a day. I therefore missed some weddings simply because I saw the minister too late; and whilst it was feasible to write to and see the vicars again in January to ask if they had any further weddings booked, with my limited resources it was not possible to contact the clergy of the other denominations. Other losses occurred where the minister did not reply, or, in the case of Catholic priests, where he refused to give me any names because of his 'pastoral responsibility', or he left the room to make a list for me – a list which included only half of the weddings that took place in his church in the following five months. But the most serious shortcoming was that at one particularly important 'Congregational' church (described in note 18 p. 22–3) the minister 'couldn't remember' if he had any weddings booked[14] and certainly did not have details he could/would let me have.

The churches in the four parishes eventually yielded seventy-six weddings in the five months from the time when interviewing was well under way (November 1968) to Easter (end of March 1969). The latter was chosen as the cut-off point as it was the end of a G.R.O. registration period, and because it seemed likely that if I continued after Easter without returning to all the ministers, etc., I would have a final sample significantly biased towards weddings arranged a long time in advance.

The seventy-six weddings were not evenly spread, being clustered around Christmas and before Easter (March). A further difficulty, since I was anxious to attend weddings and receptions, was that almost all weddings were at the same time on Saturdays, usually in the morning. In addition, because all the young people were at work, interviewing had to be done in the evenings, and since they went out quite often, I had to go to their homes at tea-time (c. 6.00 pm) to catch them in and arrange a time to call back. Hence I found I could only average two or three completed couples a week. I therefore put all the couples who were marrying 3-8

Figure 2 Total number of weddings from November 1968 – March 1969 by parish and denomination (and number known to me in advance)

parish	Angli-can	Roman Catholic	Non-conformist	total
Morriston	16 (10)	9 (3)	14 (9)	39 (22)
Town Centre	26 (21)	2·(0)	11+9 (4+0)	48 (25)
St Thomas	18 (14)	1 (0)	2 (0)	21 (14)
Oyster-mouth	14 (12)	1 (1)	4 (2)	19 (15)
total	74 (57)	13 (4)	40 (15)	127 (76)
proportion known of in advance	77%	31%	48%	60%
number known of in advance if churches where the clergy did not reply or refused to give information* are excluded	74 (57) 77%	10 (4) 40%	31 (15) 48%	115 (76) 66%

* not excluding those who did not give further information in January.

weeks ahead into a pool at the beginning of each week, and drew out three couples at random to contact. Other evenings were occupied by interviews with the couple or their parents and, towards the end of the fieldwork, with calling back after the wedding. I went to at least one wedding every Saturday.

The completed sample of church weddings consisted of twenty-four Anglican, three Roman Catholic, and seven Nonconformist couples, whereas in Swansea as a whole in the first quarter of 1968 there were 159 Anglican, forty-three Roman Catholic, and fifty-two Nonconformist weddings (figures eventually supplied by the G.R.O.). My sample therefore under-represents Roman Catholic weddings (I should have had about twice as many) due to the reluctance of priests to tell me about weddings in their churches.

I was later able to get some indication of the biases produced by the sampling method because the G.R.O. finally gave me access to information in the registrar's books and quarterly returns on past marriages and I was then able to discover how many weddings in each church I had 'missed', and to ascertain various details about them, either from the certificate of marriage, or by going back to the minister and talking with him, or from peers in the locality who I interviewed because they were themselves getting married, or on the university student network.

Many of the weddings during the five-month period which I missed hearing about in advance were in no way unusual: I did not hear of them because I saw the minister shortly after they took place (see above), or I saw or heard from him once only, in October or November, and the wedding was then booked for March shortly after my visit. The only actual screening by clergy seems to have been not telling me about weddings of older couples (aged over fifty). These were few and far between (but I was not told about either of the two which took place soon after my visit). The most important shortcoming is its under-representation of brides who married in church when pregnant and whose weddings were arranged at short notice. From information received I estimate that between 1 in 10 and 1 in 5 of the young women who married in the Anglican churches during the period of fieldwork was pregnant, but only one bride of the twenty-four was in my sample. Occasionally quiet church weddings were planned following a death in the family (two cases during fieldwork period).

When the G.R.O. give me access to records of past weddings, I decided to interview a sample of those who had married in the register office during the same period (November 1968–March 1969) as used when sampling church weddings – albeit those married in the register office would be seen once only, after their marriage. In April 1969 I was given details of every fifth wedding which had taken place in the register office during the five months (forty-one cases) and since the figures supplied for Swansea for the first quarter of 1968 by the G.R.O. showed roughly equal numbers of register office (N=155) and Anglican weddings (N=159), I decided to take a one in ten sample (i.e., every other case, N=20) of civil weddings and to replace any non-contacts or refusals with the neighbouring case which had been skipped.

In all cases I went first to the bride's house (i.e., the address given for her to the clergyman or superintendent registrar) and arrived unannounced (i.e., I sent no advance letter). I asked to see the couple together and suggested coming back at a convenient time; but if the only way to get an interview was to see the bride alone (e.g., because I was assured the groom would not be interested, or he was working on evening shift, or was very shy), I accepted this.

The interviews with couples who had married in the register office were much easier, despite the fact that we were discussing their having had a somewhat stigmatized wedding. The address for the bride which I was given was her (supposed) address at the time of her marriage, so I often had to go round to several houses before finally finding the place where she and her husband were living. However, this could be done in the day-time (and the day-light), since quite a number of these women had given up work shortly after they were married (or, when marrying for the second time, were not working because they had children) (see chapter 7). What was important was that the general pressure on the couples' time and nervous energy was much less than shortly before the wedding, and there were not the same constraints on cross-sex inter-action.

a) Summary of achieved interviews

In 33/34 church weddings I saw the couple (N=15) or the bride (N=18) before the wedding. (In the other case, I called two weeks beforehand and, due to a chapter of accidents, we could not fix a time to meet until after the wedding.)

Of all the eighteen cases where the interview was with the bride only, in four cases the groom was not in Swansea before the wedding.

Of the fifteen cases where I saw both members, in five cases the groom only arrived or joined in halfway through.

In 21/34 church weddings and 19/20 civil weddings I saw the couple (N=15 and 8) or the bride (N=6 and 11) after the wedding.

Of the other thirteen church weddings, nine couples left the district after they were married (though in four of these cases I talked to the bride's mother and/or father afterwards); one refused when I went back; one I forgot to ask for her new address and no one was ever in at her old home; two were never in (but in one of these cases I had a three-hour long talk with the groom's mother about the wedding).

In one civil wedding I never met the couple concerned because they left the district before I made contact, but I was given a great deal of information by the new tenant of their council house and two neighbours (see on) and I decided to include them as I did not want to exclude mobile couples.

I formally interviewed ten sets of bride's parents and five sets of groom's. though I talked casually for an hour or more with many others.

Twelve more detailed interviews with brides (N=8) and grooms (N=4) were conducted. In the case of brides, the constraint was time rather than informant's willingness; but it was very difficult to see unmarried working-class young men on their own. The class divide was more evident because of the lack of shared gender. But, in addition, there being no asexual leisure-time contact between young adults of opposite sex in normal situations (see Whitehead 1976 and chapter 4), the suggested interviewing situation appeared uncomfortable and worrying, and excuses were produced to avoid it. Indeed, it was only quite late on that I realized what was happening, so 'natural' was the avoidance of the situation.

I attended twenty-five weddings, nine receptions, and four hen parties among my informants, though I went to many others.

b) Refusals and non contacts

There were so few refusals and non-contacts – only eleven all told (17 per cent) – that although the question of who it is that refuses is of interest (cf. Hubert, Forge, and Firth 1968), it would be ill-advised to generalize. The characteristics on the marriage certificates suggest that those who were not seen were not peculiar in terms of age or occupation. All their weddings which were in church were 'white'. (I attended several and made enquiries about the rest.)

In three of the four cases of non-contact it was simply that I called too close to the wedding and the bride in particular was busy. In the fourth, where I called on a couple who had married in the register office, I found that both had given the bride's aunt's address to the registrar, though they did not appear to have been living there for any length of time, and they had subsequently moved to London. No further information was forthcoming.

In two cases of refusal it was a parent who refused an interview outright and despite my insistence that it was their daughter I wished to see and whose permission I sought. In a third instance, the bride agreed to see me, but when I called back at the agreed time a middle-aged woman told me the bride had changed her mind: 'she's decided it's her own personal business.'

On the other hand, one young woman declined despite her parents' eagerness:

> The Minister had mentioned to the parents that I might come, and when I did they welcomed me and fed me coffee and cakes and we talked for over an hour. The daughter, Jean, remained in another room and only came in when called. The mother and daughter then snapped at each other as to whose idea it had been to have a big wedding. Each claimed it was the other's. It was suggested that since the groom was not there that night, I should 'phone the next night and arrange a time. When I did, the father apologized and said the couple had 'changed their minds. They don't want to do it. They don't see the point of it.'

In a later interview the informant turned out to be this young woman's friend. She broached the subject and said she'd been surprised by the refusal: 'Jean's not usually an antisocial person.' She thought it was probably because Jean had had a previous engagement (when she was seventeen, lasting three years) and when it was broken off in the September, the wedding had already been fixed for the following March. 'It was very painful – lots of arrangements to unmake.' Jean had known her present fiancé less than a year. 'She possibly didn't want to talk about weddings because it was "tempting fate".'

In two other cases (one before the church wedding, and one after the civil wedding) I think the refusal was because of pregnancy; the fiancé/husband was sent to the door to relay the message.

In the single case where, after having talked to the bride (and her mother) beforehand, I was refused a talk after the wedding, I was told by other informants that this refusal (Case 29) was probably because

> 'Oh, everybody said "Poor Jill's wedding". Well, you know, it was the weekend we had that snow. The wedding cars couldn't get through and they had to get to church in a jeep. They had to carry her into church; and a lot of guests couldn't come. On top of that, the week before the wedding, her mother was moving some furniture and dropped a piano on her foot and broke some bones. So she had to go to the wedding in a wheelchair. And you know they were having the reception at home? Well, of course her mother couldn't see to that. It was just a disaster. I don't think she'd want to think about!'

Despite its defects (e.g., too few pregnant brides, no couples from the upper middle class, no unmarried cohabitees), my sample is a considerable advance on those used in other studies of adolescents and young adults, in that mine is a haphazardly drawn sample which includes some of those who are geographically mobile as well as the majority of non-mobile. Many perceptive studies of young people have simply ignored the problem of getting a representative sample altogether and have made contacts along friendship networks, at youth clubs, around coffee-stalls, at weekend parties, in cafés and dance halls, or day release courses at technical colleges (e.g., Jephcott 1942, 1948; Goetschius and Tash 1967; Morse 1965). Other studies, with larger budgets and different aims, have used the electoral registers or address lists to sample households and have interviewed young people living in the households (Schofield 1968; Willmott 1966; Government Social Survey for the Latey Committee 1967) – but this misses those under twenty-one (since 1970 under eighteen) living alone or with age peers, and transitory older individuals; it probably underestimates lodgers; and it often omits altogether those living in institutions (nurses' hostels, army barracks, colleges, merchant vessels, borstals, hostels, etc.), which must seriously influence their findings on, for example, sexual behaviour. This limitation has generally not been commented on by those using this approach.

(2) Information gathered

'It is hard to decide what to study and how to begin in a very complex situation where there is much variation and any particular piece of behaviour is affected by a multitude of factors. It is also easy to prove what one wants to prove, if one is so inclined. When there are many factors one can choose some particular aspects of the situation and remain blind to the others. One is caught in a dilemma between succumbing in confusion and choosing some simple but false explanation. We decided to succumb in confusion in the hope it would be temporary . . . Our task . . . was not to test hypotheses but to develop them, and to be sure that they were appropriate to the field material.' (Bott 1957:8–9)

When I started this research I was concerned to provide a description of a particular phase in the development cycle of the domestic group, and I was especially interested in showing what the associated ceremonial was saying about structures and implicit values. Only later, after the experience of fieldwork, did I come to analyse the material in terms of inter-sex and inter-generational relations in a particular socio-historical context. The collection of material was catholic and eclectic.

The combination of as rigorous sampling as possible and living in the town allowed me to combine a stranger role (arriving at the bride's door and announcing myself as someone from the university who was doing research on weddings) with participant observation (where I was in a set social position – that of married woman with young children[15] – and friendly with the mothers of brides, rather than with unmarried women).

As previously mentioned, the restricted (basic) amount of time with informants meant that the conversation needed to be semi-structured around an interviewing schedule so as to collect as much information as possible. This also fitted in with my informants' expectations of how social research is done. I used two pilot studies to make the schedule as conversational in form as possible (passing through the informants' backgrounds, meeting, courtship, wedding, and setting up house, plans for the future, effects of pregnancy, and the experiences of friends), and I shortened it so that it took about two hours to complete, since after this length of time concentration waned. (See Barker 1977, pp. 488–511 for the interviewing schedules.)

I took notes during the interview. Since I write quickly I could take down almost verbatim what was said at the time and I also read through and added in details immediately afterwards. People seemed to like to see something being noted when they spoke, but I regret not having taped the conversations as well. The problems of transcription of so much material (in all cases, but particularly given my limited resources) were put to me very forcefully; but I do not think that tapes need to be transcribed if full notes are made, and they do preserve nuances and modes of expression which are lost in writing and which one may want later to check back on. For example (see chapter 4), I became aware of the absence of a term for 'dating', but could not go back to see how people had got around it.

Since the interviews took place in people's homes, quite a lot could be seen of my informant's background while drinking tea with everyone in the 'living room' after the interview in the 'front room' (e.g., relations in public with parents, type of house and furnishings, participation within the domestic group of kin and neighbours, etc.). In some cases the interview itself was built into the family's ongoing evening's entertainment: it was sometimes quite impossible to see the couple on their own – the bride's mother sat by the fire, cousins dropped in, demands were made to 'ask *me* about *that*', there was joking, banter, and discussion as to 'the right answer' or when exactly something had happened. On visits after the wedding I would be shown over the new house or flat, and the wedding presents would be pointed out and the donors identified. Thus to a certain extent I was a participant observer in people's houses as well as at hen parties, wedding receptions (when I might be introduced as 'our sociologist'), and seeing couples off on honeymoon. I was also myself subject to a good deal of comment on my unsatisfactory role performance – 'Fancy wearing a miniskirt when you're pregnant'; or (repeatedly) 'How *do* you manage (to combine a job and children)!?'.

Two topics specifically not covered in the interview were sexual behaviour, and 'money' and social class.

(a) sexual behaviour

South Wales is generally prudish about sexual matters (see chapters 2 and 4) and while it might have been possible to get as good a response rate as Schofield achieved (1968)[16] had sexual matters been introduced as an important area within the interview, I doubt this. In the pilot interviews I found that general questions about sexuality (i.e., not about the informants' personal behaviour) might cause a chill to descend when only one person of the same sex as myself was present. When both members of the courting couple were present, even hints in that direction (e.g., 'what do you think about a bride wearing white when she isn't a virgin?') severely reduced rapport, especially in interviews before the wedding had taken place. While people in other situations may use an unknown interviewer cathartically or to gossip about sexual matters, especially if they are assured of total anonymity (cf. Kinsey *et al*. 1948, 1953), those about to get married, in Swansea, being interviewed by name in their own homes, clearly regard information on their sexual behaviour as private and somewhat embarrassing as a topic of conversation. Comments made generally about my research ('What's it about then – family planning?!') persuaded me to make it quite clear when I introduced myself that I would not ask about sex, for fear of a high rate of refusal.

However, information was sometimes proffered or gleaned during informal chats, sometimes lasting several hours, after the formal schedule had been completed and when the interviewee had satisfied her curiosity about me and was prepared *to exchange* information. And of course I heard tales from my neighbours, some of which I have quoted.

(b) social class and income

These comprise two other very sensitive areas and ones which, while important, were not my central concern. On the advice that partial information on income is worse than useless (Gittus 1968)[17], I did not ask (what my pilot interviews showed were seen as) 'personal questions' about money[18]. To put other prices in this account into perspective, however, it should be noted that the average UK adult male full-time manual worker's wage in 1969 was £24.82, and the average female full-time manual worker's wage was £12.11 (Department of Employment 1974:61, Table 36). The cost of living index has roughly trebled since 1969.

I used the Registrar General's five-point Classification of Occupations as my measure of socio-economic category or 'standing in the community' of my informants and their fathers (hence their families of origin), following Willmott and Young (1960) and Rosser and Harris (1965) in dividing Category III into manual and non-manual occupations:

Category I	professions and higher managerial
Category II	intermediate professional and managerial (and farmers)
Category III	non-manual: clerical and shopworkers manual: skilled manual
Category IV	partly skilled manual
Category V	unskilled manual

Students were classified in Category II and apprentices and trainees in the occupation for which they were preparing. In a few cases the job history showed a series of changes in the first years after leaving school or completing an apprenticeship. In such cases I used my discretion as to which was the main/continuing occupation.

One of the chief reasons for using the R.G.'s classification, which is not a very refined instrument and which is notably bad for rating women's socio-economic standing, was that with relatively small numbers an eight or sixteen fold division (e.g. Hall-Jones) was impossible and nothing better on women exists; but I did not want to follow a simple manual/non-manual divide – which seems dubious when applied to urban men's occupations and hopeless when applied to urban women's jobs.

The other reason was that it makes my findings easy to compare with other studies – the R.G.'s classification is a national scale and widely used, and it is generally recommended that when other scales, specific to particular studies, are needed, they should be 'collapsible' to the R.G.'s scale (Bechoffer 1968). One of the major drawbacks of the R.G.'s classification – the lack of discrimination within Categories I and II (divided into 1–4 on the Hall-Jones index) – was not particularly important since so few of my informants or their fathers had professional or managerial jobs, and none were upper middle class (e.g. senior civil service or top management of large companies).

I did not include any questions about self-rated class, since without some control for the various 'images of society' held by my informants, one does not seem to be comparing like with like (cf. however, Rosser and Harris 1965; Ch. 3).

The cases have been numbered chronologically (i.e., Nos. I and 2 married in October 1968, 3–7 in November, etc.). I have given informants local names but in no case does this relate to his or her actual name. I have also disguised occupations as far as possible.

Notes

1. 'The research families were studied as examples of urban families, not as a random or representative sample. We have made a comparative study of the relations between several factors for the twenty families, considering each family as a social system' (Bott 1957:9)
2. Jane Hubert has provided a most illuminating account of the problems encountered in the LSE study of kinship in North London (Hubert, Forge, and Firth 1968).
3. Only 23 couples out of my final sample of 54 had any announcement of their forthcoming wedding in the local paper (43% of the total sample).
   Even fewer couples have their weddings in the papers (13% of my sample), and the majority of small advertisement announcements of marriages (i.e. as opposed to photos and reports) are of weddings which take place elsewhere. (Mainly those of Swansea men marrying young women from other towns.)

4. On disestablishment of the Church in Wales see Williams (1961).
5. A third alternative, getting the Archbishop of Canterbury's Special Licence, is used in only 0.4% of Anglican weddings. (Figures are for 1972, R.G. for 1972, Vol. II, Appendix D3.)
6. Whatever the additional practice of the denominations may be; eg, the Roman Catholic searches described in Ch.1
7. Figures are for 1972, R.G. for 1972, Vol. II, Appendix D3.
8. How long it takes to fill a Marriage Register Book depends on how many pages it has (they are not all of the same thickness) and how many marriages the holder registers per year. Thus registrars' books are filled rapidly, while those in some churches last years. A register from a country church had just come in to the West Glamorgan register office when I was there (Autumn 1967) which had been started in 1830.
9. The diocesan records were destroyed by fire so the only source for the extent of the parishes is the vicars' working practice.
10. From *The Offical List*, 1965. See Barker 1977:61–2, Table 1:12.
11. There were in fact only two 'other denomination' weddings in churches in the four parishes during the 5/6 month fieldwork period.
12. I tried to find out the names of the priests and ministers and their home addresses from the Yearbooks of the various denominations and a card index which I eventually discovered in the town reference library. I wrote individual letters to each. Where there was no minister I wrote to the secretary at his home; failing this I wrote to 'The Minister' at the church. If no reply was received I wrote a second letter. Notwithstanding this the response was disappointing – particularly from the town centre churches.
    For details of the churches see Barker 1977, Figure A1:6.
13. In 5 cases all the necessary information – which was, e.g., that there had been no weddings in that church for two years and none were booked – was sent in a letter.
14. This at first sight rather unlikely tale may in fact be genuine. The register office staff told me that 'He does often 'phone, or he calls in [his church is close to their office] to ask "what have I got booked for next weekend?".'
15. I was married with a six-month old child when we moved to the town, a second was born in the middle of the field work, and a third six months before we left.
16. Schofield (1968) had a sample of 1873 unmarried 15–19 year olds in urban England, and a refusal rate of 15%.
17. A great many questions must be asked systematically: about basic average wage or salary, other benefits, perks, profits from investments, etc., etc.
18. When rapport was good some information was given spontaneously, e.g., about how much they had had to pay for an item – a three piece suite, a house, or the wedding photos – which they felt to be ludicrously overpriced; and when discussing with one couple the cost of some houses on the new estate which we had lived in when we first moved to the district, I commented that the rents were £6 a week, and the bride commented 'Well that would be my week's wages gone for a start' (aged 20, a clerk in an office). Where details were asked for directly, as in the lists about who had given them what for their

wedding presents, it was recorded that 'Auntie May' had given 'a cheque', or even more obliquely, 'a sum of money'; and they would go to some length and uncomfortable sentence construction to avoid saying how much they handed over to their parents each week (see Ch. 3).

Bibliography

Abrams M. (1961) *Teenage Consumer Spending in 1959 (II) : Middle Class and Working Class Boys and Girls*, London Press Exchange.

Allcorn D.H. (1955) *The Social Development of Young Men in an English Industrial Suburb.* Unpublished PhD., University of Manchester.

Allen A. (1968) *People on Honeymoon*, Sunday Mirror Publications.

Allen S. (1968) Some Theoretical Problems in the Study of Youth, *Sociological Review* **16** (3):319–31.

Allport G. (1955) *The Nature of Prejudice*, Cambridge, Mass: Addison-Wesley.

Anderson E.W., Kenna J.C., and Hamilton M.W. (1960) A study of Extra-Marital Conception in Adolescence, *Psychiatria and Neurologia* **139** :313–62.

Anderson M. (1971) *Family Structure in Nineteenth Century Lancashire.* London : Cambridge University Press.

Anderson O. (1975) The Incidence of Civil Marriage in Victorian England and Wales. *Past and Present* (69) November: 50–87.

Atteridge Y. (1965) *Courting Couples in the Youth Club and the Effects of Courtship on Friendship Patterns.* Unpublished dissertation, Dept. of Education, University College Swansea.

Aubrey M. (1968) *Education for Parenthood.* Unpublished dissertation, Dept. of Education, U.C. Swansea.

Bachrach P. and Baratz M.S. (1962) The Two Faces of Power. *American Political Science Review* **56**: 947–52.

—— (1963) Decisions and Nondecisions: An Analytical Framework *American Political Science Review* **57**: 641-51.

Baker M. (1974) *The Folklore and Customs of Love and Marriage.* Aylesbury: Shire.

Banks J.A. (1954) *Prosperity and Parenthood: A Study of Family Planning*

Among the Victorian Middle Classes. London: Routledge and Kegan Paul.

Barker D. (1972a) The Confetti Ritual. *New Society*, June 22: 514–17.

—— 1972b Young People and their Homes: Spoiling and "Keeping Close" in a South Wales Town. *Sociological Review* **20** (4): 569-90.

Barker D. Leonard (1977) *Sex and Generation: A Study of the Process and Ritual of Courtship and Wedding in a South Wales Town*. Ph.D. thesis, University of Wales.

—— (1978a) A Proper Wedding. In M. Corbin (ed), *The Couple*. Harmondsworth: Penguin.

—— (1978b) The Regulation of Marriage: Repressive Benevolence. In B. Smart *et al.* (eds.): *Power and the State*. London: Croom Helm.

Barker D.L. and Allen S. (eds.) (1976a) *Sexual Divisions and Society: Process and Change*. London: Tavistock.

Barker D.L. and Allen S. (eds.) (1976b) *Dependence and Exploitation in Work and Marriage*. Harlow: Longman.

Barker D. and Thompson P. (1973) The Comparative Study of Courtship and Marriage in Twentieth Century Britain. Paper presented to 13th seminar of ISA Family Research Committee.

Baron R. and Norris G. (1976) Sexual Divisions and the Dual Labour Market. In Barker and Allen (eds.) (1976b).

Bates A. (1942) Parental Roles in Courtship. *Social Forces* **20**.

Beattie J. (1966) Ritual and Social Change. *Man* **1**: 60–74.

—— (1970) On understanding ritual. In B. Wilson (ed.): *Rationality*. Oxford: Blackwells.

Bechoffer F. (1968) Occupations. In M. Stacey (ed.), *Comparability of Data Collection and Presentation with Special Reference to Locality Studies*. BSA publication, mimeo.

Beechey V. (1978) Women and Production: A Critical Analysis of Some Sociological Theories of Women's Work. In A. Kohn and A.M. Wolpe (eds.): *Feminism and Materialism*. London: Routledge and Kegan Paul.

Bell C.R. (1968) *Middle Class Families: Social and Geographical Mobility*. London: Routledge and Kegan Paul.

Bell C. (1972) Marriage. In P. Barker (ed.), *A Sociological Portrait*. Harmondsworth: Penguin.

Bell C. and Newby H. (1976) Husbands and Wives: The Dynamics of the Deferential Dialectic. In D.L. Barker and S. Allen (eds.) (1976b).

Bengis I. (1973) *Combat in the Erogenous Zone*. London: Wildwood House.

Berent J. (1954) Social Mobility and Marriage: A Study of Trends in England and Wales. In D.V. Glass (ed.): *Social Mobility in Britain*. London: Routledge and Kegan Paul.

Berger P. and Kellner H. (1964) Marriage and the Construction of Reality. *Diogenes, Summer*, **46**: 1–24.

Bernard J. (1972) *The Future of Marriage: His and Hers*, Souvenir Press.

Berne E. (1964) *Games People Play*. Harmondsworth: Penguin.

Bernstein B. (1971) *Class, Codes and Control*, Vol 1. London: Routledge and Kegan Paul.

Bingham M. (1969) *Your Wedding Guide*. London: Corgi Mini-Book.

Blau P. (1964) *Exchange and Power in Social Life*. New York: Wiley.

Bloch M. (1975) *Political Language and Oratory in Traditional Society*. London: Academic Press.

Blood R.O. and Wolfe D.M. 1960 *Husbands and Wives*, Free Press, Glencoe.

Bocock R. (1974) *Ritual in Industrial Society: A Sociological Analysis of Ritualism in Modern England*. London: Allen and Unwin.

Bolton C.D. (1961) Mate Selection as the Development of a Relationship. *Marriage and Family Living*, August.

Book of Common Prayer and Administration of the Sacraments, and other Rites and Ceremonies of the Church, according to the Use of the Church of England, 1662. London: Oxford University Press.

Bossard J.H.S. and Boll E.S. (1956) *The Large Family System*. Philadelphia: University of Pennsylvania Press.

Bott E. (1957) *Family and Social Network*. London: Tavistock.

Brennan T., Cooney E.W., and Pollins H. (1954) *Social Change in South-West Wales*. London: Watts.

Brides (1969) Your Kind of Wedding. Autumn Preview.

Brides (1973) Take 3 Girls. Autumn Preview.

Brides Book (n.d.), Produced by Roger Hughes Marketing for the Independent Stores Association.

Brightman F.E. (1921) *The English Rite: Being a Synopsis of the Sources and Revisions of the Book of Common Prayer*, Vol. II. London: Rivingtons.

British Market Research Bureau (1967) *The New Housewife Survey*, 3 vols. London: J. Walter Thompson.

Bromley P.M. (1966) *Family Law*. 2nd edn. London: Butterworths.

Brown Roger L. (1973) *Clandestine Marriage in London, especially within the Fleet Prison and their effects on Hardwicke's Act 1753*. Unpublished M.A. Thesis, U.C. London.

Brownmiller S. (1975) *Against our Will: Men, Women and Rape*. London: Secker and Warburg.

Burchinal L.G. (1964) The Premarital Dyad and Love Involvement. In H.T. Christensen (ed.), *Handbook of Marriage and the Family*. New York: Rand McNally.

Burtenshaw D. (1973) Relocated Wives. *New Society*, 21 June: 688.

Busfield J. (1972) 'Age at Marriage and Family Size: Social Causation and Social Selection Hypotheses', *J. Biosocial Science*, 4, pp. 117–134.

Busfield J. (1974) Ideologies and Reproduction. In M. Richards (ed.), *The*

Integration of the Child into the Social World London: Cambridge University Press.

Butler R.M. (1956) Mothers' Attitudes Towards the Social Development of Their Adolescents. *Social Casework*, 2 parts: 219–225, 280–87.

Cahill L. (1969) *The Development of Drinking Patterns from Early to Late Adolescence in Some Industrialised Areas* (Swansea, Luton and Liverpool). Unpublished dissertation, Dept. of Education, UC Swansea.

Cardiff Archdiocesan Year Book 1967, Archbishop of Cardiff and Hoxton and Walsh, London.

Carter M. (1966) *Into Work*. Harmondsworth: Penguin.

Chapman J. (1968) *Girls During Courtship: Are They Isolated?*. Unpublished dissertation, Dept. of Education, UC Swansea.

Church of England Liturgical Commission (1975) *Report on the Solemnisation of Matrimony*. London: S.P.C.K.

Civil Judicial Statistics. London: HMSO.

Cohen A. (1974) *Two-Dimensional Man*. London: Routledge and Kegan Paul.

Cohen E.C. (1973) *Recruitment to the Professional Class*. Ph.D. thesis, University of Surrey.

Coleman D. (1973) A Geography of Marriage. *New Society* March 22: 634–36.

Comer L. (1974) *Wedlocked Women*. Leeds: Feminist Books.

Coombs L.C., Freedman R., Fiedman J., and Pratt W.F. (1969–70) Premarital Pregnancy and Status Before and After Marriage. *American Journal of Sociology* **75**: 800–820.

Coussins J. (1978) *What's in a Name?* London: National Council for Civil Liberties.

Cox P.R. 1970a 'Sex Differences in Age at Marriage', *J. Biosocial Science*, September, Supplement 2, 73.

—— 1970b 'International Variations in the Relative Ages of Brides and Grooms', *J. Biosocial Science*, 2, pp. 111-121.

Crichton A., James E., and Wakeford J. (1962) Youth and Leisure in Cardiff. *Sociological Review* **10** (2): 203–220.

Criminal Statistics, England and Wales (Home Office). London: HMSO.

Crockford's Clerical Directory. Oxford: Oxford University Press.

Cuming G.T. (1969) *A History of Anglican Liturgy*. London: Macmillan.

Cunnington C.W. (1952) *English Women's Clothing in the Present Century*. London: Faber and Faber.

Cunnington P.E. and Lucas C. (1972) *Costumes for Births, Marriages and Deaths*, Edinburgh: A & C Black.

Davidoff L. (1974) Mastered for Life: Servant and Wife in Victorian and Edwardian England. *Journal of Social History*.

—— (1976) The Rationalization of Housework. In D.L. Barker and S. Allen (eds.) (1976b).

Davidoff L., L'Esperance J., and Newby H. (1976) Landscape with Figures: Home and Community in English Society. In J. Mitchell and A. Oakley (eds.) *The Rights and Wrongs of Women*. Harmondsworth: Penguin.

Davies B. (1975) The Life of Adolescence. *New Society*, March 20: 714-16.

Davies E.T. 1965 *Religion in the Industrial Revolution in S. Wales*, University of Wales Press

Day G. and Fitton A.M.H. (1975) Religion and Social Status in Rural Wales: 'Buchedd' and its Lessons for Concepts of Stratification in Community Studies. *Sociological Review*, November:867–92.

Delphy C. (1970) L'ennemi principal. In *Partisans*, No 54–55.

—— (1976) Continuities and Discontinuities in Marriage and Divorce. In D.L. Barker and S. Allen (eds.) (1976a).

Delphy C. and Barker D.L. (in progress) *Women and the Family*. London: Tavistock.

Dept. of Employment (1974) *Women and Work: A Statistical Survey*. Manpower Paper No.9. London: HMSO.

Derrick J. (1975) *Africa's Slaves Today*. London: Allen and Unwin.

Deutscher I. (1962) Socialisation for Postparental Life. In A.M. Rose (ed.), *Human Behaviour and Social Processes*. London: Routledge and Kegan Paul.

Douglas M. (1966) The Contempt of Ritual. *New Society*, March 31: 23–4.

—— (1968) The Social Control of Cognition: Some Factors in Joke Perception. *Man*: 361–76.

—— (1973) *Natural Symbols*. Harmondsworth: Penguin.

Douglas M. and Nicod M. (1974) Taking the Biscuit: The Structure of British Meals. *New Society*, December 19: 744–47.

Ebling J. (1969) Crowning Glory. *New Society*, February 27.

Edwards C. (1961) *Swansea: A study in Urban Geography*. Unpublished B.Sc. thesis, U.C. Swansea.

Eekelaar John 1971 *Family Security and Family Breakdown*, Penguin, with an Introduction by O. Kahn-Freund and K.W. Wedderburn.

Eisenstadt S.N. (1956) *From Generation to Generation: Age Groups and Social Structure*. Chicago: Free Press.

Emmett I. (1971) *Youth and Leisure in an Urban Sprawl*. Manchester: Manchester U.P.

European Market Research Bureau (1970a) *Engagement and Marriage Customs*. An International Study conducted by EMRB Limited for De Beers Consolidated Mines Limited. Presented by Miss Frances Freedman, mimeo.

European Market Research Bureau (1970b) *Engagement in the United Kingdom. A Depth Investigation Among Recently Married Women*. March 1970.

EMRB/PB/30263, mimeo.

European Market Research Bureau (1970c) *Engagement in the U.K. A Depth Study Among Young Unmarried Women*. September 1970. EMRB/PB/30300, mimeo.

Eversley D.E.C. (1965) Population, Economy and Society. In D.V. Glass and D.E.C. Eversley (eds.)

Fabians (1969) *Swansea Fabian Society: Housing Study Group, 1st Report*. Mimeo pamphlet.

Faragher J. and Stansell C. (1975) Women and their Families on the Overland Trail, 1842-1867. *Feminist Studies* 2, November.

Firestone S. (1970) *The Dialectics of Sex*. London: Paladin.

Firth Rosemary (1943) *Housekeeping among Malay Peasants*. London: Athlone Press.

Firth Raymond (1973) *Symbols: Public and Private*. London: Paladin.

Firth R., Hubert J., and Forge A. (1970) *Families and Their Relatives: Kinship in a Middle-Class Sector of London*. London: Routledge and Kegan Paul.

Fletcher R. 1966 *The Family and Marriage in Britain*, Penguin.

Fogelman K. (1976) *Britains Sixteen Year Olds*. London: National Children's Bureau.

Forder C.R. (1959) *The Parish Priest at Work*. London: SPCK.

Forster P.G. 1972 'Secularization in the English Context: Some Conceptual and Empirical Problems', *Sociological Review*, Vol. 2, No. 2, pp. 153–168.

Fortes M. (1962) Ritual and Office in Tribal Society. In M. Gluckman (ed.) *Essays on the Ritual of Social Relations*. Manchester: Manchester U.P.

Frankenberg R. (1966a) British Community Studies: Problems of Syntheses. In M. Banton (ed.), *The Social Anthropology of Complex Societies*, London: Tavistock.

—— (1966b) *Communities in Britain*. Harmondsworth: Penguin.

—— (1976) In the Production of Their Lives, Men (?) . . . Reflections on Sex and Gender in British Community Studies. In Barker and Allen (eds.) (1976a).

Freedman R., and Coombs L. (1966a) Childspacing and Family Economic Position. *American Sociological Review* **31**.

—— (1966b) Economic Considerations in Family Growth Decisions. *Population Studies* **20** (2) November: 197–222.

Gavron H. (1968) *The Captive Wife: Conflicts of Housebound Mothers*. Harmondsworth: Penguin.

General Register Office (1965) *Official List*. Part III. *List of Certified Places of Worship*. London: HMSO.

—— (n.d.) *Suggestions for the Guidance of the Clergy with Reference to the Marriage and Registration Acts*. London: HMSO.

Gillis J.R. (1974) *Youth and History: Tradition and Change in European Age*

Relations 1770–to present. New York: Academic Press.

Girard A. (1964) *Le Choix du Conjoint: Une enquête psycho-sociologique en France.* Paris: PUF.

Gittins Report (1968) Department of Education and Science, Central Advisory Council for Education (Wales). *Primary Education in Wales.* London: HMSO.

Gittus E. (1968) Income. In M. Stacey (ed.), *Comparability of Data Collection and Presentation.* BSA publication, mimeo.

Glaser B.G. and Strauss A.L. (1971) *Status Passage.* Chicago: Aldine.

Glass D.V. and Eversley D.E.C. (1965) *Population in History: Essays in Historical Demography.* London: Arnold.

Gluckman M. (1956) *Custom and Conflict in Africa.* Oxford: Blackwell.

Goetschius G. and Tash M.J. (1967) *Working with Unattached Youth.* London: Routledge and Kegan Paul.

Goffman E. (1968) *Stigma.* Harmondsworth: Penguin.

—— (1969) *The Presentation of Self in Everyday Life.* London: Allen Lane.

Goode W.J. (1959) The Theoretical Importance of Love. *American Sociological Review* **24** February: 38–47.

Goody J. (ed.) (1966) *The Development Cycle in Domestic Groups.* London: Cambridge University Press.

Gorer G. (1948) *The Americans.* London: Cresset.

—— (1955) *Exploring English Character.* London: Cresset.

—— (1971) *Sex and Marriage in England Today.* London: Nelson.

Grebenik E. and Rowntree G. (1963) Factors Associated with Age at Marriage in Britain. *Proc. of the Royal Society*, Series B, 159, part 974: 178–98.

Grey A. (1974) *The Working Class Family as an Economic Unit.* Unpublished Ph.D. thesis, University of Edinburgh.

Hadow Report (1926) *The Education of the Adolescent.* London: HMSO.

Hajnal J. (1965) European Marriage Patterns in Perspective. In D.V. Glass and D.E.C. Eversley (eds.).

Hall J.C. (1966) *Sources of Family Law.* London: Cambridge University Press.

—— (1971) *Supplement* to *Sources of Family Law.* London: Cambridge University Press.

Hallpike C.R. (1969) Social Hair. *Man* **4**: 256-64.

Hamill L. (1976) Wives as Sole and Joint Breadwinners. Dept of Health and Social Security, mimeo.

Hammond E. (1968) *An Analysis of Regional Economic and Social Statistics.* University of Durham.

Hamner J. (1964) *Girls at Leisure.* A study for the London Union of Youth Clubs.

Hareven T. (1977) 'Family Time and Individual Time. In A. Rossi., J

Kagan and T. Hareven: *The Family*. New York: Norton.

Harris C.C. (1963) Church, Chapels and the Welsh. *New Society*, February 21: 18-19.

—— (1966) Family and Kinship. Unpublished survey for the SSRC, mimeo.

—— (1970) *The Family*. London: Allen and Unwin.

—— (1974) *Growing Old in Swansea: A Contribution to the Sociology of Aging*. Unpublished Ph.D. thesis, University of Wales.

Hart N. (1976) *When Marriage Ends*. London: Tavistock.

Heaton V. (1966) *Best Man's Duties*. RightWay Books.

Helmholz R.H. (1975) *Marriage Litigation in Medieval England*. London: Cambridge University Press.

Henryon C., and Lambrechts E. (1968) *Le Mariage en Belgique: Étude Sociologique*. Brussels: Editions vie ouvriere.

Henson T. Knicely (1976). *The Wedding Complex: The Social Organization of a Rite of Passage*. Omaha: Park Bromwell.

Hilton K.J. (ed.) (1967) *The Lower Swansea Valley Project*. Harlow: Longmans.

Hoggart R. (1957) *The Uses of Literacy*. London: Chatto and Windus.

Hollingshead A.B. (1949) *Elmtown's Youth*. New York: Wiley.

—— (1950) Cultural Factors in Selection of Marriage Mates. *American Sociological Review* **15**: 619–27.

—— (1952) Marital Status and Wedding Behaviour. *Marriage and Family Living*: 308–11.

Holmes T. (1971) In *Medical News Tribune*. Quoted in *The Guardian*, September 3.

Holt J. (1974) *Escape from Childhood*. Harmondsworth: Penguin.

Hopwood E.L. (1963) *A Study of a Group of Non-Apprenticed Boys in Industry*. Unpublished dissertation, Dept. of Education. UC Swansea.

Horton R. (1970) African Traditional Thought and Western Science. In B. Wilson (ed.), *Rationality*. Oxford: Blackwell.

Hubert J. (1965) Kinship and Geographical Mobility in a Sample from a London Middle-Class Area. *International Journal of Comparative Sociology* **VI**: 61–80.

Hubert J., Forge A., and Firth R. (1968) *Methods of Study of Middle-Class Kinship in North London: A Working Paper on the History of an Anthropological Project*, 1960-65. Occasional Paper of the Department of Anthropology, LSE, mimeo.

Hunt A. (1968) *A Survey of Women's Employment*, 2 vols London: HMSO.

Hutchinson D. (1968) How We Saved £500 in One Year. *(Woman) Bride and Home*, Spring 1968: 143.

IPC (International Publishing Company) (1969) *Young Magazines Research Services Survey*. IPC Magazines Ltd., London, mimeo.

Ineichen B. (n.d.) *A Place of Our Own*. London: Housing Research Foundation.

—— (1975) Teenage Brides. *New Society*, August 7.

Jacobsohn P. and Matheny A.P. (1962) Mate Selection in Open Marriage Systems. *International Journal of Comparative Sociology* **3**: 98–123.

Jeffrey B. (1966) *Wedding Speeches and Toasts*. London: Foulsham.

Jephcott P. (1942) *Girls Growing Up*. London: Faber and Faber.

—— (1948) *Rising Twenty*. London: Faber and Faber.

—— (1967) *Time of One's Own: Leisure and Young People*. London: Oliver and Boyd.

Jephcott P., Seear N., and Smith J.h. (1962) *Married Women Working*. London: Allen and Unwin.

Jones V. (ed.) (1970) *The Church in a Mobile Society*. Swansea: Christopher Davies.

Josling J.F. (n.d.) *Change of Name*. Oyez Practice Note. London: Oyez Publishing.

Joyce G.H. (1948) *Christian Marriage: An Historical and Doctrinal Study*. Second edition. London: Sheed and Ward.

Keil T., Riddell D., and Green B.S.R. (1966) Youth and Work: Problems and Perspectives. *Sociological Review* **14** (2).

Kerckhoff A.C. 1963-4 'Patterns of Homogamy and the Field of Eligibles', *Social Forces*, 42, pp. 289–97.

Kerr M. (1958) *The People of Ship Street*. London: Routledge and Kegan Paul.

Kinsey A.C., Pomeroy W.B., and Martin C.E. (1948) *Sexual Behaviour in the Human Male*. Philadelphia: Saunders.

Kinsey A.C., Pomeroy W.B., Martin C.E.., and Gebhard P.H. (1953) *Sexual Behaviour in the Human Female*. Philadelphia: Saunders.

Klein J. (1965) *Samples from English Cultures*. London: Routledge and Kegan Paul.

Klein V. (1965) *Britain's Married Women Workers*. London: Routledge and Kegan Paul.

Lacey T.A. (revised Mortimer) (1947) *Marriage in Church and State*. London: SPCK.

Land H. (1975) The Myth of the Male Breadwinner. *New Society*, October 9: 71–3.

—— (1978) Who Cares for the Family? *Journal of Social Policy*.

Laslett P. (1973) The Family Cycle and the Process of Socialisation; Characteristics of the Western Pattern considered over Time. Paper presented to the 13th ISA Family Research Committee, Paris.

Latey Report (1967) *Report on the Committee on the Age of Majority*. Cmnd 3343. London: HMSO.

Law Commission (1969) *Report on Breach of Promise of Marriage*. London: HMSO.

—— (1970) *Report on Nullity of Marriage*, HMSO.

—— (1973) *Report on Solemnisation of Marriage in England and Wales*, HMSO.

Leach E.R. (1958) Magical Hair. *Journal of the Royal Anthropological Institute* **88**: 147–64.

Legge J. Wickham (1905) Notes on the Marriage Service in the Book of Common Prayer of 1549. In his *Ecclesiological Essays*. London: De La Mare Press.

Leigh J. (1971) *Young People and Leisure*. London: Routledge and Kegan Paul.

Lewis E. (1958) *Prayerbook Revision in the Church in Wales*, Church in Wales Provincial Council for Education, Cardiff.

Linton R. (1936) *The Study of Man*. New York: Appleton-Century Crofts.

Loudon J.B. (1961) Kinship and Crisis in South Wales. *British Journal of Sociology* **12**, (iv).

—— (1970) Teasing and Socialization in Tristan de Cunha. In P. Mayer (ed), *Socialization: The Approach from Social Anthropology*. London: Tavistock.

Loughton M. (1969) The Young Mothers. *New Society*, September 11: 386.

Lukes S. (1974) *Power*. London: Macmillan.

MacIntyre S. (1976) Who Wants Babies? The Social Construction of 'Instincts'. In D.L. Barker and S. Allen (eds.) (1976a).

Maher V. (1976) Kin, Clients, and Accomplices: Relationships among Women in Morocco. In Barker and Allen (eds.) (1976a).

Mainardi P. (1970) The Politics of Housework. In R. Morgan (ed.), *Sisterhood is Powerful*. New York: Vintage Books.

Malinowski B. (1935) *Coral Gardens and Their Magic*. Vols I and II. London: Allen and Unwin.

Marceau J. (1976) Marriage, Role Division and Social Cohesion: the Case of Some French Upper-Middle Class Families. In D.L. Barker and S. Allen (eds.) (1976b).

Marriage Act (1949). 12 and 13 Geo. Ch. 76. London: HMSO.

Marris P. (1968) *Widows and their Families*. London: Routledge and Kegan Paul.

Martin D. (1967) *A Sociology of English Religion*. Heinemann, London

Matthieu N.C. (1978) Man – Culture and Woman – Nature? *Women's Studies International Quarterly* **1** (1).

—— (1979) Social Maternity and Biological Fraternity. In C.C. Harris (ed.), *The Sociology of the Family*. Sociological Review Monograph.

Mauss M. (1954) *The Gift: Forms and Functions of Exchange in Archaic Societies* (trans I. Cunnison). London: Cohen and West.

Maxwell W.D. (1949) *The Book of Common Prayer and the Worship of the Non-Anglican Churches*. London: Oxford University Press.

May I. (1968) *An Inquiry into the Leisure Time Activities and Social Relationships of the 17–20 year olds*. Unpublished dissertation, Dept. of Education, U.C. Swansea.

Mayer J.E. 1967 'The Invisibility of Married Life', *New Society*, 23 February, pp. 272–3.

Meillassoux C. (1972) From Reproduction to Production: A Marxist Approach to Economic Anthropology. *Economy and Society* **1** (1): 93–105.

Michel A. (1965) Mate Selection in Various Ethnic Groups in France. *Acta Sociologica* **8** (1–2): 163–76. Reprinted in C.C. Harris (ed.) (1970), *Readings in Kinship in Urban Society*. Oxford: Pergamon.

Milgram S. (1976) The Image Freezing Machine. *New Society*, June 3: 519–522.

Millward N. (1968) Family Status and Behaviour at Work. *Sociological Review* **16** (2): 149–64.

Monger G. (1971) A Note on Wedding Customs in Industry Today. *Folklore* **83**: 314–16.

—— (1974-5) Further Notes on Wedding Customs in Industry. *Folklore*: 50–61.

Monsarrat A. (1973) *And the Bride Wore . . . The Story of the White Wedding*. London: Gentry Books.

Moore M. (1970) *The Wedding*. Unpublished masters dissertation, University of Kent at Canterbury.

Morgan D.A.J. (1969) *Theoretical and Conceptual Problems in the Study of Social Relationships at Work: An Analysis of the Differing Definitions of Women's Roles in a Northern Factory*. Unpublished Ph.D. Thesis, University of Manchester.

—— (1975) *Social Theory and the Family*. London: Routledge and Kegan Paul.

—— (n.d.) Berger and Kellner's Construction of Marriage: An Assessment. Typescript.

Morse M. (1965) *The Unattached*. Harmondsworth: Penguin.

Morton J. (1976) Who'll House the Single?. *New Society*, March 25.

Morton Commission (1956) Report of the Royal Commission on Marriage and Divorce. London: HMSO.

Moss P. (1976) The Current Situation. In N. Fonda and P. Moss (eds.) *Mothers in Employment*. London: Brunel University Management Programme and Thomas Coram Research Unit.

National Consumer Council (1975) *For Richer, For Poorer: Some Problems of Low Income Consumers*. Pamphlet of the report to the consumer congress, Manchester. September. London: HMSO.

Nicod M. (1974) *A Method of Eliciting the Social Meaning of Food*. Unpublished M. Phil. thesis, University of London.

Oakley A. (1972) Are Husbands Good Housewives?. *New Society*, February 17.

—— (1974a) *Housewife*. London: Allen Lane.

—— (1974b) *The Sociology of Housework*. London: Martin Robertson.

O'Neill Peter T. 1974 *An Analysis of the Development of the Legal Relationship of Husband and Wife*. Ph.D. thesis, University of London.

Oren L. (1974) The Welfare of Women in Labouring Families, 1850–1950. *Feminist Studies*.

Owen M. (1968) At First Sight. *Observer Colour Supplement*, May 5.

Owen T.M. (1959) *Welsh Folk Customs*. St Fagans: National Museum of Wales.

Pahl J.I. and Pahl R.E. (1972) *Managers and their Wives*. Harmondsworth: Penguin.

Papanek H. (1971) Purdah: Separate Worlds and Symbolic Shelter. *Comparative Studies in Society and History* **15** (3) June.

Parkin F. (1971) *Class Inequality and Political Order*. London: MacGibbon and Kee.

Parnham J. (1966) *A Study of the Influence of Youth Club Climate on Boy-Girl Behaviour*. Unpublished dissertation, Dept. of Education, UC Swansea.

Parsons T. (1943) The Kinship System of the Contemporary United States. *American Anthropolgist* **XLV**: 22–38.

—— (1962) Youth in the Context of American Society. *Daedalus* **XCI**: 97–123.

Perry I.J. (1969) Working Class Isolation and Mobility in Rural Dorset, 1837–1936, A Study of Marriage Distances. *Transactions of the Institute of British Geography* **49** (7): 121–40.

Peters E.L. (1972) Aspects of the Control of Moral Ambiguities: A Comparative Analysis of Two Culturally Disparate Modes of Social Control. In M. Gluckman (ed.), *The Allocation of Responsibility*. Manchester: Manchester U.P.

Pickering W.S.F. (1974) The Persistence of Rites of Passage; Towards an Explanation. *British Journal of Sociology*: 63–78.

Pierce R. (1963) Marriage in the Fifties. *Sociological Review* **11**.

Pitts J. (1960) The Family and Peer Groups. In N.W. Bell and E.F. Vogel (eds.), *A Modern Introduction to the Family*. Glencoe: Free Press.

Poggi D. and Coornaert N. (1974) The City: Off Limits to Women. *Liberation*, July/August.

Pratt W.F. (1965) *A Study of Marriages Involving Premarital Pregnancy*. Ph.D. thesis, University of Michigan.

Preston B. 1974 'The Surplus of Women', *New Society*, 28 March, pp. 761–63.

Radcliffe-Brown A.R. (1940) On Joking Relationships. In *Structure and Function in Primitive Society*. London: Cohen and West (1952).

—— (1949) A Further Note on Joking Relationships. In Radcliffe-Brown (1952).

Rapoport Rh. (n.d.) *Transition to Marriage*. Unpublished manuscript.

—— (1963) Normal Crises, Family Structure and Mental Health. *Family Process* **2** (1).

—— (1964) The Transition from Engagement to Marriage. *Acta Sociologica* **8**: 36–55.

—— (1968) Family Transitions in Contemporary Society. *Journal of Psychosomatic Research* **12**: 29–38.

Rapoport Rh. and Rapoport R. (1964) New Light on the Honeymoon. *Human Relations* **17** (1).

—— (1971) *Dual Career Families*. Harmondsworth: Penguin.

—— (1975) *Leisure and the Family Life Cycle*. London: Routledge and Kegan Paul.

Registrar-General (1846) *Registrar-General's 7th Annual Report 1844*, P.P. 1846 (727), xix.

—— (1856) *Registrar-General's 17th Annual Report 1854*, P.P. 1856 (2092), xviii.

—— (1866) *Registrar-General's 27th Annual Report 1864*, P.P. 1866 (3712), xix.

—— (1876) *Registrar-General's 37th Annual Report 1874*, P.P. 1876 (C.1581), xviii.

—— (1886) *Registrar-General's 47th Annual Report 1884*, P.P. 1886.

—— *Registrar-General's 57th Annual Report 1894*, P.P. 1895 (C.7768), xxiii, part II.

—— (1905) *Registrar-General's 67th Annual Report 1904*, P.P. 1905 (Cd. 2617), xvii.

—— (1914-16) *Registrar-General's 76th Annual Report 1913*, P.P. 1014–16 (Cd. 7780), ix.

—— (1895) *Registrar-General's Statistical Review of England and Wales* for 1924, 1934, 1952, 1957, 1962, 1967, 1972, Vol. II, Population. For 1964, Vol. III, Commentary.

Reiss I.R. (1960) Toward a Sociology of the Heterosexual Love Relationship. *Marriage and Family Living* **22**: 139–145.

—— (1969) Premarital Sexual Standards. In C. Broderick and J. Bernard (eds.), *The Individual, Sex and Society*. Baltimore: John Hopkins Press.

Rodman H. (1966) *Marriage, Family and Society*. New York: Random Press.

Rosser and Harris C.C. (1965) *The Family and Social Change: A Study of*

Family and Kinship in a South Wales Town. London: Routledge and Kegan Paul.

Rowntree G. (1954) The Finances of Founding a Family. *Scottish Journal of Political Economy* **1** (3): 201–232.

—— (1962) New Facts on Teenage Marriage. *New Society*, October 14.

Rush F. (1972) The Myth of Sexual Delinquency. Paper to a Woman's Conference on Prostitution (1971), published in *Rough Times* **2** (7) and reprinted in *The Florence Rush Reader* by KNOW, Pittsburgh (n.d.).

Scanzoni J. (1972) *Sexual Bargaining: Power Politics in the American Marriage*. Prentice Hall.

Schochet G.J. (1975) *Patriarchalism in Political Thought: The Authoritarian Family and Political Speculation and Attitudes Especially in Seventeenth Century England*. London: Oxford University Press.

Schofield M. (1968) *The Sexual Behaviour of Young People*. Harmondsworth: Penguin.

—— (1973) *The Sexual Behaviour of Young Adults*. London: Allen Lane.

Sedgwick F. (1975) Bachelor Gay? *Sunday Times*, September 21.

Seligman M. (1974) *The Eternal Bliss Machine: The American Way of Wedding*. London: Hutchinson.

Sharman A. (1968) Joking in Padhola: Categorical Relationships, Choice and Social Control. *Man*: 103–117.

Shaw L.A. (1954) Impressions of Family Life in a London Suburb. *Sociological Review* **1** (4): 179–193.

Shorter Oxford English Dictionary (1956) Oxford: Clarendon.

Shurmer P. (1972) Popping the Question. *New Society*, February 24: 386–88.

Sirjamaki J. (1948) Culture Configurations in the American Family. *American Journal of Sociology* **53**.

Slater R. and Woodside M. (1951) *Patterns of Marriage: A Study of Marriage Relationships in the Urban Working Class*. London: Cassell.

Smith C. (1966) *Young People at Leisure: A Report on Bury*. Manchester: Dept of Youth Work, University of Manchester.

Smith L. Shacklady (1975) Female Delinquency and Social Reaction. Unpublished paper presented at University of Essex, Women and Deviancy Conference, Spring.

Speed B. (1968) *A Study of Two Groups of Adolescents*. Unpublished dissertation, Dept. of Education, UC Swansea.

Spencer G. (1947) *Catholic Life in Swansea: The Centenary of St David's Church, Swansea, 1847–1947*, pamphlet.

Stead P. (1972) 'Welshness and Welsh Nationalism'. *New Community*, Autumn **1** (5).

Stiehm J. (1976) Invidious Intimacy. *Social Policy* March/April.

Stott M. (1971) Getting Uptight About White. *Guardian*, August 26: 11.

Sussman M. (1951) *Family Continuity: A Study of Factors which Affect Relationships Between Families at Generation Levels*. Unpublished PhD. thesis, Yale University.

—— (1953a) Parental Participation in Mate Selection and its Effects upon Family Continuity. *Social Forces* 32: 76–81.

—— (1953b) The Help Pattern in the Middle Class Family. *American Sociological Review* 18 (1): 22–8.

—— (1954) Family Continuity: Selective Factors Which Affect Relationships Between Families at the Generational Level. *Marriage and Family Living* **16**.

—— (1960) Intergenerational Family Relationships and Social Role Changes in Middle Age. *Journal of Gerontology* **15** (1): 71–5.

Sussman M., Coates J.N. and Smith D.T. (1970) *The Family and Inheritance*. New York: Russell Sage.

Terray E. (1975) Classes and Class Consciousness in the Abron Kingdom of Gyaman. In M. Bloch (ed.) *Marxist Analyses and Social Anthropology*. London: Malaby.

Thomsell G. (1969) *An Enquiry into Adolescent Drinking*. Unpublished dissertation, Dept. of Education, UC Swansea.

Thompson D. (1975) Courtship and Marriage in Preston Between the Wars. *Oral History*, Family History issue, **3** (2) Autumn.

Tilly L.A., Scott J.W., and Cohen M. (1973) Women's Work and European Fertility Patterns. Unpublished paper.

Tindall G. 1968 'Housewives-to-be', *New Society*, 30 May, pp. 794–5.

Todd J.E. and Jones L.M. (1972) *Matrimonial Property*. London: HMSO.

Townsend P. (1957) *The Family Life of Old People*. London: Routledge and Kegan Paul.

van Gennep A. (1960) *The Rites of Passage*. London: Routledge and Kegan Paul.

Veness T. (1962) *School Leavers: Their Aspirations and Expectations*. London: Methuen.

Walker D. 1967 (a) *A Short History of the Parish Church in Swansea*, Clergy of Parish of St Mary's Swansea, 3rd edn.

—— 1967 (b) *The First Hundred Years. St James Church, Swansea, 1867–1967*, Clergy of Parish of St. Mary's Swansea.

Walker C. (1868) *The Ritual Reason Why*. J.T. Hayes.

Waller W. (1937) The Rating and Dating Complex. *American Sociological Review* **2**: 727-34

Wallace C. (1956) *The Pocket Book of Etiquette*. London: Evans Bros.

Ward J. (1974) Adolescent Girls: Same or Different?. Paper presented to the British Sociological Association Conference, Aberdeen.

Watson W. (1964) Social Mobility and Social Class in Industrial Communities. In M. Gluckman and E. Devons (eds.). *Closed Systems and Open Minds*, Edinburgh: Oliver and Boyd.

Weitzman, Leonore J. (1974) Legal Regulation of Marriage: Tradition and Change. *California Law Review* **62** (4) July–Sept.

Whitehead A. (1971) *Social Fields and Social Networks in an English Rural Area*. Unpublished PH.D. thesis, University of Wales.

—— (1976) Sex Antagonism in Herefordshire. In Barker and Allen (eds.) (1976b).

Williams D. (1961) *A Short History of Modern Wales; 1485 to the Present Day*. London: John Murray.

Williams W.M. (1956) *The Sociology of an English Village: Gosforth*. London: Routledge and Kegan Paul.

—— 1963 *Ashworthy: Family, Kinship and Land*. R & KP, London.

Willis P. (1977) *Learning to Labour*. Farnborough: Saxon House.

Willmott P. (1966) *Adolescent Boys of East London*. London: Routledge and Kegan Paul.

Willmott P. and Young M. (1960) *Family and Class in a London Suburb*. London: Routledge and Kegan Paul.

Wilsher P. (1975) Two Hands on the Purse Strings. *Sunday Times Colour Supplement*, November 2: 39–43.

Wilson M. (1954) Nyakyusa Ritual and Symbolism. *American Anthropologist*, **56** (2).

Wilson B. (1969) *Religion in Secular Society*. Harmondsworth: Penguin.

—— (1973) *Magic and the Millenium*. London: Heinemann.

Woman (1973) Why Do We Do It?. January 6.

Woodman M. (n.d.) *Wedding Etiquette Under All Denominations*. London: Foulsham.

Wynn M. (1972) *Family Policy*. Harmondsworth: Penguin.

Young M. (1952) The Distribution of Income Within the Family. *British Journal of Sociology* **III**: 305–21.

Young M. and Willmott P. (1962) *Family and Kinship in East London*. Harmondsworth: Penguin.

—— (1973) *The Symmetrical Family*. London: Routledge and Kegan Paul.

Name index

Subject index